Chinese Language Learning Sciences

This book series investigates several critical issues embedded in fundamental, technical, and applied research in the field of Chinese as second language (CSL) learning and teaching, including learning mechanism in the brain, technology application for teaching, learning and assessment. The book series discusses these issues from the perspectives of science (evidence-based approach) and technology. The studies in the book series uses the methods from the fields of linguistics (such as corpus linguistics and computational linguistics), psychological and behavioural sciences (such as experimental design and statistical analyses), informational technology (such as information retrieval and natural language processing) and brain sciences (such as neuroimaging and neurolinguistics). The book series generally covers three main interdisciplinary themes: (1) fundamental investigation of Chinese as a first or second language acquisition, (2) development in Chinese language learning technology, and (3) applied research on Chinese language education.

More specifically, the book series involves seven research topics:

- Language transfer mechanism in Chinese as a second language
- Factors of Chinese as a second language acquisition in childhood
- Cultural influence on Chinese acquisition
- Information technology, corpus
- Teaching material design
- Teaching strategies and teacher training
- Learning models
- Assessment methods

More information about this series at http://www.springer.com/series/13176

Dongbo Zhang · Chin-Hsi Lin
Editors

Chinese as a Second Language Assessment

 Springer

Editors
Dongbo Zhang
Department of Teacher Education
Michigan State University
East Lansing, MI
USA

Chin-Hsi Lin
Department of Counseling Educational
 Psychology, and Special Education
Michigan State University
East Lansing, MI
USA

ISSN 2520-1719   ISSN 2520-1727 (electronic)
Chinese Language Learning Sciences
ISBN 978-981-10-4087-0   ISBN 978-981-10-4089-4 (eBook)
DOI 10.1007/978-981-10-4089-4

Library of Congress Control Number: 2017934214

Printed on acid-free paper

This Springer imprint is published by Springer Nature
The registered company is Springer Nature Singapore Pte Ltd.
The registered company address is: 152 Beach Road, #21-01/04 Gateway East, Singapore 189721, Singapore

Acknowledgements

This book would not have been possible without the generous support of various people. First, our deepest thanks go to the authors of the chapters, all of whom were enthusiastic about being invited to contribute their research and highly professional during the process of uniting their work into this volume. We are also indebted to the reviewers, both those who reviewed manuscripts at our request and the external reviewers commissioned by Springer. We deeply appreciate their timely completion of the reviews and the valuable comments they provided, which improved the quality of every chapter and of the book as a whole. In particular, we would like to thank Li-ping Chang, Yunjeong Choi, Wenhao Diao, Yufen Hsieh, Sihui Ke, Jiahang Li, Shuai Li, Zhi Li, Ya Mo, Zhaomin Shu, Yanjiang Teng, Miao-Fen Tseng, Hong Wang, Sue-Mei Wu, and Binbin Zheng.

This book would not have been conceptualized, let alone published, without the inspiration and support we have received from many friends, colleagues, and mentors during our engagement with language education and research over many years. Dongbo Zhang would like to extend his special thanks to Keiko Koda, Susan Polansky, G. Richard Tucker, Sue-Mei Wu, and Yueming Yu; all were wonderful mentors at Carnegie Mellon University where he learned how to teach Chinese and to conduct research on the acquisition and teaching of that language. He is also grateful for the friendship and collegiality of the former Chinese Language Research Team in the Centre for Research in Pedagogy and Practice at Nanyang Technological University in Singapore, and particularly, Goh Hock Huan, Yongbing Liu, and Shouhui Zhao. Chin-Hsi Lin would like to thank Mark Warschauer, Greg Duncan, and Penelope Collins at the University of California, Irvine and Shih-Chang Hsin at National Taiwan Normal University for their generous mentoring over the past few years.

The preparation of this book was partly supported by a start-up grant awarded to Dongbo Zhang by Michigan State University (MSU)'s College of Education, and by the Delia Koo Endowment Fund administered by MSU's Asian Studies Center. We are deeply grateful for this support.

Last but not least, we would like to thank Springer editors Ang Lay Peng and Lawrence Liu for the wonderful support they gave us at all stages of the preparation of this book.

Dongbo Zhang
Chin-Hsi Lin

Contents

Part III   Assessing Language Skills

Part IV   Assessment, Teaching, and Learning

Acronyms

AAPPL	ACTFL Assessment of Performance toward Proficiency in Languages
ACTFL	American Council on the Teaching of Foreign Languages
AES	Automated Essay Scoring
AP	Advanced Placement
AWE	Automated Writing Evaluation
BCT	Business Chinese Test
CAT	Computerized Adaptive Test
CCCC	Children's Chinese Competency Certification
CEFR	Common European Framework of References for Languages
CFL	Chinese as a Foreign Language
CL	Chinese Language
CLPS	Chinese Language Proficiency Scales for Speakers of Other Languages
COPI	Computerized Oral Proficiency Instrument
CPT	Chinese Proficiency Test
CSL	Chinese as a Second Language
HSK	Hanyu Shuiping Kaoshi (Chinese Proficiency Test)
HSKK	Hanyu Shuiping Kouyu Kaoshi (Chinese Speaking Proficiency Test)
MHK	Minzu Hanyu Shuiping Kaoshi (Test of Chinese Proficiency for Minorities)
OPI	Oral Proficiency Interview
OPIc	Oral Proficiency Interview-computerized
SAT	Scholastic Aptitude Test
SCT	Spoken Chinese Test
SC-TOP	The Steering Committee for the Test of Proficiency
SOPI	Simulated Oral Proficiency Interview
TCFL	Teaching Chinese as a Foreign Language

TCSL	Teaching Chinese as a Second Language
TCSOL	Teaching Chinese to Speakers of Other Languages
TOCFL	Test of Chinese as a Foreign Language
TOP	Test of Proficiency
WAT	Word Associates Test
WPT	Writing Proficiency Test
YCT	Youth Chinese Test

Introduction

There has been unprecedented growth in the global popularity of Chinese language and culture over the past two decades. Hanban (2014), also known as the Chinese National Office for Teaching Chinese as a Foreign Language, estimated that there were more than 100 million learners of Chinese around the world in 2014, twice as many as in 2004. This rapid growth has arguably been facilitated by the Chinese government's efforts to project the country's "soft power" through establishing nonprofit, government-affiliated educational organizations including Confucius Institutes and Confucius Classrooms (Hartig 2012; Yang 2010). In particular, the establishment of Confucius Classrooms in non-tertiary institutions, such as K-12 schools, has led to the rapid growth of the population of young learners of Chinese (Li and Tucker 2013). The global agenda of the Chinese government also runs parallel to an increased recognition of the social and economic value of learning and knowing the Chinese language in the non-Chinese-speaking world. A case in point was the Obama administration's 2015 announcement of the "1 Million Strong" initiative, which aims to increase the total number of learners of Chinese in the USA to 1 million by the year 2020 (The US-China Strong Foundation 2015). England's National Curriculum mandates that Mandarin Chinese be one of the foreign languages taught in Key Stages 2 and 3 (ages 7–14); and a recently launched multi-million-pound "Mandarin excellence programme" involving hundreds of secondary schools in England has students learn Mandarin for eight hours a week over four years, with the aim of having "at least 5000 " young people "on track toward fluency in Mandarin Chinese by 2020" (Department for Education in the United Kingdom 2016).

The global expansion of Chinese programs has also gone hand in hand with other governmental agendas that involve the promulgation of various "national" Chinese proficiency tests, notably China's *Hanyu Shuiping Kaoshi* (HSK; Teng, this volume) and Taiwan's Test of Chinese for Speakers of Other Languages (TOCFL; Chang, this volume). Along with the development, validation, and promotion of such tests, increased attention has been directed to testing and assessment research by scholars of Chinese as a Second/Foreign Language (hereafter, CSL). Yet, as various chapters of this volume make clear, many issues surrounding CSL testing and assessment have remained unexplored; and what we do know is still very limited—whether about the policy and social contexts of testing, or the mechanics of testing specific aspects of knowledge and skills in Chinese, or the differences between large-scale testing and classroom-based assessments.

As noted by Zhang (this volume), little research literature on Chinese-language assessment is accessible to the international community, as a significant proportion of it has been conducted by test developers in China and Taiwan and written largely in Chinese. Existing monographs and edited volumes focused on CSL and published in English rarely include studies that touch directly on Chinese testing and assessment issues (e.g., Chen et al. 2010; Everson and Shen 2010; Jiang 2014; Han 2014; Ruan et al. 2016; Tsung and Cruickshank 2011). Ke and Li's (2011) review of CSL research in the USA only included two studies that were specifically focused on assessment. While the number of assessment-focused studies has necessarily increased in the six years since Ke and Li wrote, it is evident from the reviews included here (e.g., Liu, this volume; Zhang, this volume) that overall, the research literature on CSL assessment remains limited in both scope and depth.

Another notable characteristic of the existing research is that it tends to focus primarily on testing, and particularly large-scale testing, of Chinese proficiency, with little attention to alternative, classroom-based assessments (Zhang this volume). Tests are a form of assessment, but not all assessment practices involve the use of tests (Brown and Abeywickrama 2010), and educational-assessment scholars differentiate between assessment *of* learning, assessment *for* learning, and assessment *as* learning (Black et al. 2003; Dann 2002; Rea-Dickins 2008). While tests can provide summative information about student learning and performance (i.e., assessment *of* learning), their influence or backwash effect on classroom instruction and learning is often very limited. It is argued by Sun et al. (this volume) that classroom-based formative assessments should have the primary goal of attending to learners' progression, with teachers using ongoing assessments to diagnose students' learning needs and provide them with differentiated support (see also Heritage 2007); and Wang (this volume) further argues that students' involvement in the process of such assessments can promote metacognition and self-regulated learning (see also Dann 2002). Yet, despite their widely acknowledged importance (e.g., Stiggins 2005), little attention has been paid to these assessment practices in the CSL literature.

The aforementioned knowledge gaps, in addition to many others that are alluded to in various chapters that follow (e.g., assessing grammatical knowledge and diagnostic assessment), motivated us to produce this volume, which brings together original research from scholars on the frontline of teaching, assessing, and researching CSL learners. More specifically, this book closely examines CSL assessment in a global context: covering research and practices not only in Chinese-speaking societies (e.g., Mainland China, Taiwan, Hong Kong, and Singapore) but also in contexts where Chinese is not a societal language (e.g., the USA). It also covers a broad but balanced range of issues, including policies for and contexts of assessments and assessment practices; large-scale testing and classroom-based assessments; assessment of younger and older learners;

development and validation of new tests and closer examination of existing tests; and assessment's role in classroom instruction, among others.

Each chapter in this volume brings a unique perspective and contribution to the literature, and collectively, they enlighten us about many issues that deserve continued attention in the future. Some chapters report original research studies on issues that have rarely been explored in the CSL literature, such as depth of vocabulary knowledge (Zhang, Yang, Lin, and Gu) and self- and peer-assessment (Wang), while others carefully survey the literature and provide well-articulated directions for future research (Chang; Liu; Teng; Zhang). Three chapters bridge Second Language Acquisition (SLA) research and assessment in Chinese (Li; Loh, Tam, Lau, and Leung; Zhang et al.), and two focus primarily on the classroom context and the implications of assessment for instruction and student learning (Sun et al.; Wang). Still others address issues related to assessment of language performance (Hsieh, Hiew, and Tay; Shang and Zhao; Zhu, Fung, Tse, and Hsieh) and diagnostic assessment (Li and Wang), which have recently attracted increasing attention in the international language-assessment community (e.g., Lee 2015; Sandrock 2014), albeit seldom in Chinese contexts.

The volume is divided into four parts: (I) Overview of Tests and Research, (II) Assessing Orthography, Vocabulary, and Grammar, (III) Assessing Language Skills, and (IV) Assessment, Teaching, and Learning.

Part I Overview of Tests and Research

Part I's four chapters provide overviews of some major tests of Chinese and of research on Chinese testing and assessment. In Chap. 1, Yanjiang Teng provides an account of the historical development of the HSK and critically examines its challenges and future prospects. Despite its general familiarity to learners and teachers of Chinese and administrators of Chinese programs worldwide, the HSK's format and function have both undergone many changes over the past two decades. Teng divides these changes into three major periods and highlights the strong political agenda behind the Chinese government's global promotion of Chinese. The author also questions the legitimacy of Hanban's assertion that the HSK provides valuable guides for classroom teaching, given the diversity of Chinese-language curricula, teaching styles, and learners' needs around the world. The tension between the monolithic linguistic standard embodied in the HSK and the promotion of the test in an international context where diverse varieties of Chinese are used also seems to warrant particular attention in the future (see also Shang and Zhao this volume).

The HSK is not the sole case that reveals governmental efforts to promote national tests of Chinese beyond national borders. In Chap. 2, Li-ping Chang traces the historical development of Taiwan's TOCFL, the successor of the Chinese Proficiency Test (CPT) and the Test of Proficiency-Huayu (TOP), the development of which started in the 1990s. Having been closely involved in the development and validation of the TOCFL, Chang provides an insider's perspective on the many challenges that the test development team faced and how they were resolved. Her discussion of the mapping of the TOCFL and its predecessors onto the Common European Framework of Reference for Languages (CEFR) is particularly informative; and the validation process has strong implications for standards-based test development in other contexts. Like Teng (this volume) and Shang and Zhao (this volume), Chang alludes to contextual variations in the use of Chinese and their implications for test development, with particular reference to the different scripts (i.e., simplified versus traditional characters) and lexical usages between Mainland China and Taiwan. Chang's discussion suggests that this "standards" issue, in addition to being subject to sociopolitical contestation (Shang and Zhao this volume), could have strong impacts on the psychometric properties of large-scale tests like the TOCFL, which deserve attention from CSL test developers and researchers in the future.

In Chap. 3, Yan Liu reviews the major tests of Chinese used in the USA, including the Oral Proficiency Interview (OPI) developed by the American Council on the Teaching of Foreign Languages (ACTFL); the ACTFL's Writing Proficiency Test (WPT); the Advanced Placement (AP) Chinese Language and Culture Test; and the SAT II Chinese Subject Test, among others. The review indicates that such tests usually are tailored to specific local needs or educational agendas. For example, the AP Chinese Language and Culture Test, developed and administered by the College Board, aims to provide evidence of high school graduates' Chinese proficiency to aid decision-making on their eligibility to claim university course credits. In addition to an informative introduction to these tests, Liu reviews the small body of research that has aimed to validate them or use them as instruments for various research purposes. The review reveals a number of issues that warrant attention in the future: for example, a fundamental mismatch between the rise of computer-based testing of writing proficiency and the strong curricular objective that students learn to handwrite Chinese characters with accuracy and fluency. In addition, existing testing practices and prior research seem equally to have ignored the diverse linguistic backgrounds of Chinese learners in the USA, an issue that is also brought up elsewhere in this volume (e.g., by Teng).

While Chaps. 1–3 survey major tests of Chinese proficiency, Dongbo Zhang's Chap. 4 reviews empirical research on CSL testing and assessment over the past two decades, with the objective of making its findings—which have mostly been published in Chinese—accessible to the international language-assessment community. Zhang focuses his review on two types of language knowledge (vocabulary and grammatical knowledge) and four language skills (listening, speaking, reading, and writing) and critically delineates issues that warrant future research for all six of them. The review suggests that there has been an imbalance in the research attention devoted to various issues within as well as across the six areas. For example, though considerable attention has been paid to tests of speaking ability and to automated essay scoring, little research has been conducted on the assessment of grammatical knowledge or reading. In addition, many issues that specifically pertain to Chinese (e.g., orthography, computer input of characters and its implications for assessment of writing) failed to receive the attention they warranted. Taken as a whole, Zhang's findings echo many of the recommendations made by the earlier chapters in this volume, and provide strong justification for the research reported on in Parts II, III, and IV.

Part II Assessing Orthography, Vocabulary, and Grammar

Parts II and III bring together seven original studies of the assessment of various aspects of Chinese-language knowledge and skills. The three chapters in Part II focus on orthography, vocabulary, and grammar, respectively. All three situate their explorations in broader contexts of second-language (L2) learning and address the interface between SLA research and assessment, with a focus on CSL learners.

In Chap. 5, Elizabeth Loh and her colleagues report on their development of a battery of tests that assess various aspects of knowledge in the structure of Chinese characters among ethnic minority (EM) adolescents in Hong Kong and Macau. Unlike their Chinese-speaking peers, these students—whether born in Hong Kong/Macau or new immigrants—had no exposure to Chinese before they learned to read in the language. To understand the orthographic knowledge of the identified group, the authors adopted three tests: of (1) the learners' ability to separate various orthographic components from their host character; (2) their ability to utilize the components commonly used in their curricular materials in the construction of Chinese characters; and (3) their awareness of common spatial configurations of Chinese characters. The assessment results revealed that the participants, who had never received systematic or formal training in Chinese-character components or their spatial configurations, not only had a limited level of knowledge about these matters, but that their generally poor performance on all three tests was not significantly affected by their age of arrival in Hong Kong/Macau or by the amount of time they spent in studying Chinese outside of class. The authors therefore recommend that the development of orthographic knowledge should be a primary function of explicit classroom instruction on character structures, rather than presumed to grow organically as a function of a person's length of residence in a particular territory or his/her dedication to individual study.

Chapter 6 investigates CSL learners' knowledge about word meanings, or to be more exact, the interrelationships between such meanings. As Dongbo Zhang and his colleagues note at the beginning of the chapter, *depth* is an important dimension of vocabulary knowledge that has attracted considerable attention in research on vocabulary learning and assessment; and a common way of assessing vocabulary depth is the Word Associates Test (WAT) (for English learners). Yet, vocabulary depth has received little attention in the CLS literature, and there are also important unresolved issues about the WAT as a measurement of depth. The authors were thus motivated to develop and validate a Chinese WAT (WAT-C) for intermediate and advanced learners of Chinese. In this chapter, they first provide details of the test development process and then report on a validation study that involved a group of adult CSL learners studying abroad in China, and three different scoring methods. The study reveals that, as intended, the WAT-C could effectively measure an aspect of vocabulary knowledge distinct from vocabulary size (i.e., depth), and the best scoring method was also identified. At the end of the chapter, the authors discuss the limitations of and future directions for assessing Chinese vocabulary depth using WAT-based instruments.

Chapter 7 focuses on grammatical knowledge: an aspect of linguistic knowledge that, as revealed in Zhang's review (this volume), has received very limited attention in the CSL assessment literature. In this chapter, based on recent SLA research, Liu Li differentiates between implicit and explicit knowledge of grammar. The timed version of her grammaticality judgment test (GJT) and oral repetition test are used as measures of implicit grammatical knowledge, while the untimed form of GJT coupled with an error-correction test is used for measuring explicit grammatical knowledge. The chapter reports on the administration of this battery of grammatical-knowledge tests, together with a general proficiency test, to a group of English-speaking Chinese learners in American universities, with the aim of determining the relationships among the participants' general Chinese proficiency and the implicit and explicit aspects of their grammatical knowledge. Implicit knowledge did not correlate significantly with general proficiency or any of its subcomponents (i.e., listening comprehension, reading comprehension, and writing), whereas general proficiency's correlations with explicit knowledge were all significant. Overall, the findings suggest that grammar is indeed important in the development of language proficiency among CSL learners. Yet, the lack of a significant relationship between implicit knowledge and general proficiency runs counter to the findings of prior research on learners of L2 English. The author explains this from the perspective of cultural context, learning stages, and differences in how general proficiency has been measured.

Part III Assessing Language Skills

Part III focuses on the assessment of three major skills in Chinese, namely speaking, reading, and writing. From a linguistic and sociolinguistic perspective, Chap. 8 discusses the assessment of speaking in light of various language-standards issues. Chapter 9 draws upon a standardized Chinese proficiency test to examine the significance of diagnostic assessment. Chaps. 10 and 11 both examine writing, but differ significantly in focus: with the former focusing on raters of writing and the latter on learners' perceptions of computer-mediated assessment of writing.

In language assessment, especially of speaking performance, raters/teachers are often provided with descriptors of competence to aid or shape their judgments of whether the language forms produced by learners are acceptable. Yet, as Chap. 8 contends, this deceptively easy process is problematic due to the lack of a single language standard in international contexts where many varieties of Chinese are used. To unravel the complexities of this issue, Guowen Shang and Shouhui Zhao critically examine the impact and implications in Singapore of that country's absence of any officially endorsed standard for Chinese-language education and assessment. In doing so, they draw upon the challenges they encountered during a project aimed at developing Chinese proficiency descriptors there. The authors highlight some major differences in pronunciation, vocabulary, and grammar between Putonghua (Mandarin Chinese in China) and Singapore Huayu ("a new variety of Modern Chinese developed in Singapore's particular pluralinguistic environment"). Given that no language standard is endorsed by Singapore's government, the authors sought to ensure that they did not impose one in cases where a descriptor seemed to require a standard-oriented expression. Based on the Singapore case, the authors argue that the development of language tests be situated in broader sociolinguistic and sociopolitical contexts, with indigenized varieties recognized, and tests focused on communicative adequacy rather than linguistic accuracy.

In Chap. 9, Shuai Li and Jing Wang explore the feasibility of applying the Rule Space Method (RSM) to diagnosis of the strengths and weaknesses of Chinese learners' reading ability, drawing upon the reading-comprehension part of the C. Test, a standardized Chinese proficiency test developed in China for CSL learners. As the authors point out, there has been an increasing demand that language tests provide diagnostic results regarding learners' mastery or non-mastery of knowledge and skills that can guide subsequent teaching and learning. Yet, this cannot be achieved by traditional language tests that report only total test scores. In their application of the RSM, the authors first used experts' reports to identify eight key attributes of reading comprehension among CSL learners and then created a hierarchical structure of those attributes as assessed by the reading-comprehension part of the C. Test. This led to the identification of 50 pre-specified knowledge states, and a high classification rate was achieved: with more than 90% of those who took the test classified into 39 of the 50 states. Level of mastery, meanwhile, was found to vary considerably across the eight attributes. Li and Wang's results make it possible to provide individualized diagnostic reports for successfully classified test-takers. The authors highlight two interesting scenarios that have strong implications for teaching and learning. One is that test-takers classified into the same knowledge state, despite their varied levels of ability, would benefit from the same type of instruction for developing non-mastery attributes. The other is that test-takers with the same overall ability level could demonstrate different mastery and non-mastery patterns, and would thus require differentiated instruction. Both scenarios clearly attest to the inappropriateness of using a single score to indicate a test-taker's ability level, and to the advantages of diagnostic assessment for refined teaching and learning objectives.

The psychometric properties of a performance-based language assessment such as essay writing depend not only on the assessment task and the scoring rubric, but also on raters. In Chap. 10, Yu Zhu and his colleagues report on a preliminary study of the possible relationships between raters' personality traits and their severity of rating, in the case of essays written by CSL learners. The authors asked a group of master's students in China who were studying Teaching of Chinese as a Foreign Language to rate a total of 154 essays written in Chinese by intermediate foreign learners of the language. The raters' personality traits were measured using the Chinese version of a personality inventory based on the Five-Factor Model of personality, whose 240 items cover five domains (i.e., neuroticism, extraversion, openness, agreeableness, and conscientiousness) with each domain including six facets. Age, gender, educational background, and rating experience—all factors that might affect raters' severity in essay rating—were carefully controlled. After training, the raters were divided into three groups that independently rated three different batches of the essays collected, and rater severity was then estimated using Many-Facet Rasch Modeling. Regression analysis revealed that at the facet level, straightforwardness and positive emotions were significant predictors of severity, and at the domain level, extraversion significantly predicted severity. Based on these findings, the authors highlight the limitations of uniform rater training, which is pervasive in current practice, and argue that raters should receive individualized training based on assessments of their personalities.

Teachers of writing strive to provide prompt and effective feedback for learners, who often tend to have mixed levels of proficiency and thus different needs for feedback. With this challenge in mind, Yufen Hsieh and her colleagues developed a prototype automated essay-marking system for primary-school Chinese learners in Singapore, allowing learners to receive instant feedback on errors pertaining to linguistic features such as Chinese characters, collocations, and grammar, and to use it to correct such errors before submitting their final essays to the teacher. Chapter 11 introduces that marking system's architecture and major features, and reports on an evaluation study that sought students' perceptions of the system after their preliminary use of it. The feedback the authors collected was quite positive: with a majority of the students saying that they perceived the system to be an effective tool; enjoyed using it to improve their writing; believed that it could help them notice errors in their writing; and found it convenient, fast, and easy to use. On the other hand, the study reveals a number of issues that deserve attention in the future development and implementation of essay-marking systems for Chinese learners or L2 learners in general. For example, learners' perceptions of the effectiveness of the system appeared partially to depend on their typing skills; and metalinguistic feedback (i.e., explanations of grammatical rules in Chinese) were found to be incomprehensible among some students with lower general proficiency.

Part IV Assessment, Teaching, and Learning

While the chapters in Parts I, II, and III occasionally touch on issues of assessment and teaching, all take assessment itself as their primary focus. The two chapters in

Part IV, in contrast, specifically examine assessment's relationships to classroom instruction and learning.

As noted by Xiaoxi Sun and her colleagues in Chap. 12, the home-language shift from Chinese to English over the past few decades in Singapore Chinese communities has greatly changed the linguistic landscape of schools in the country. Notably, an increasing number of ethnic Chinese students are learning Chinese as an L2 in school. The differential levels of oral competence that students bring to Chinese-language classes in Singapore have created an urgent need to empower teachers with effective tools and strategies to diagnose students' learning needs and provide them with contingent and differentiated instructional support. To this end, commissioned by the Singapore Ministry of Education, the authors developed an assessment and instruction package, the Oral Proficiency Diagnostic Tool (OPDT), for use by Primary 1 Chinese-language teachers in Singapore. The chapter provides details of the authors' involvement in multiple cycles of developing, refining, and validating the OPDT's diagnostic rubrics, which include qualitative descriptors as well as quantifiers for both linguistic competence (vocabulary, grammar and sentence structure, and pronunciation and intonation) and communicative competence (interaction and expression). It also gives specific examples of activities that could support the OPDT's objective of helping teachers to engage students in using Chinese, such that adequate student output would be available for teachers' diagnoses. Lastly, the authors offer a detailed account of how OPDT could be used by teachers to differentiate their instructional support on the basis of their diagnosis results. A subsequent intervention study confirmed that the OPDT was a useful and effective tool for Chinese-language teachers in Singapore, in that students from the classes where OPTD was used demonstrated significantly better performance on linguistic as well as communicative competencies in Chinese than those from regular classes that did not use the package. Echoing a point noted by Li and Wang on diagnostic assessment of reading (this volume), the OPDT project provides convincing evidence that effective classroom assessments can and should be conducted by teachers.

Formative assessment can involve engaging learners themselves in the assessment process, with the aim of promoting their reflection on language competence and thus facilitating learning (i.e., assessment *as* learning). For this reason, self- and peer-assessment have been strongly advocated for L2 classrooms (Brown and Hudson, 1998). In Chap. 13, Dan Wang explores how these two forms of alternative assessment could be used to facilitate the development of CSL learners' oral-presentation skills. Focusing on advanced learners at an American university, the study reported on in the chapter involved multiple stages, through which (1) the instructor and students collaboratively designed an assessment rubric for oral presentations; (2) students were trained to use the rubric; (3) the rubric was used for self- and peer-assessment; and (4) feedback from students was collected. The author found that stage 2, the training session, significantly improved the accuracy of students' self- and peer-assessment (as compared to assessment by the instructor), highlighting the critical importance of learner training for improving the reliability of self- and/or peer-assessment. In addition, a large majority of the students provided very positive feedback on the process, indicating, for example, that it increased their ability to identify their strengths and weaknesses and to establish goals for their subsequent learning. Chapter 13 thus provides further evidence in favor of the closer integration of assessment, instruction, and learning in language classrooms.

Conclusion

It is our hope that this volume, which to our knowledge is the first to be published in English on Chinese-language assessment, could facilitate conversations between scholars of Chinese assessment and those in the international language-assessment community who are studying other languages. While we have striven to provide a broad coverage of CSL assessment issues in a global context, the scope and depth of this volume are necessarily limited, and a number of important issues that are not covered or are merely touched upon in the pages that follow deserve to be addressed in the future. Nevertheless, we hope that this modest effort achieves its aims of attracting more attention to testing and assessment issues in the CSL community, and inspiring researchers to contribute to the advancement of scholarship on language testing and assessment, in general, and Chinese-language testing and assessment in particular.

References

Black, P., Harrison, C., Lee, C., Marshall, B., & Wiliam, D. (2004). Working inside the black box: Assessment for learning in the classroom. *Phi Delta Kappan, 86*(1), 8–21.

Brown, H. D., & Abeywickrama, P. (2010). *Language assessment: Principles and practices* (2nd ed.). White Plains, NY: Pearson.

Brown, J. D., & Hudson, T. (1998). The alternatives in language assessment. *TESOL Quarterly, 32,* 653–675.

Chen, J., Wang, C., & Cai, J. (Eds.). (2010). *Teaching and learning Chinese: Issues and perspectives.* Charlotte, NC: Information Age.

Dann, R. (2002). *Promoting assessment as learning: Improving the learning process.* London: Routledge Falmer.

Department for Education in the United Kingdom. (2016). Pupils across England start intensive lessons in Mandarin. Retrieved from https://www.gov.uk/government/news/pupils-across-england-start-intensive-lessons-in-mandarin

Everson, M. E., & Shen, H. H. (Eds.). (2010). *Research among learners of Chinese as a foreign language* (Chinese Language Teachers Association Monograph Series: Vol. 4). Honolulu: University of Hawaii, National Foreign Language Resource Center.

Han, Z.-H. (Ed.). (2014). *Studies in second language acquisition of Chinese.* Clevedon: Multilingual Matters.

Hanban. (2014). *More than 100 million learners of Chinese.* Retrieved from http://www.hanban.edu.cn/article/2014-09/01/content_549303.htm

Hartig, F. (2012). Confucius Institutes and the rise of China. *Journal of Chinese Political Science, 17*, 53–76.

Heritage, M. (2007). Formative assessment: What do teachers need to know and do? *Phi Delta Kappan, 89*(2), 140–145.

Jiang, N. (Ed.). (2014). *Advances in Chinese as a second language: Acquisition and processing.* Newcastle-upon-Tyne: Cambridge Scholars.

Ke, C., & Li, A. (2011). Chinese as a foreign language in the U.S. *Journal of Chinese Linguistics, 39*, 177–238.

Lee, Y.-W. (2015). Diagnosing diagnostic language assessment. *Language Testing, 32*, 299–316.

Li, S., & Tucker, G. R. (2013). A survey of the U.S. Confucius Institutes: Opportunities and challenges in promoting Chinese language and culture education. *Journal of the Chinese Language Teachers Association, 48*, 29–53.

Rea-Dickins, P. (2008). Classroom-based language assessment. In E. Shohamy & N. H. Hornberger (Eds.), *Encyclopedia of language and education: Language testing and assessment* (2nd ed., Vol. 7, pp. 257–271). Heidelberg, Germany: Springer.

Ruan, J., Zhang, J., & Leung, C. B. (Eds.). (2016). *Chinese language education in the United States.* Berlin: Springer.

Sandrock, P. (2014). *The keys to assessing language performance.* Yonkers, NY: ACTFL.

Stiggins, R. (2005). From formative assessment to assessment for learning: A path to success in standards-based schools. *Phi Delta Kappan, 87*(4), 324–328.

The US-China Strong Foundation. (2015). 1 million strong: Growing US Mandarin language learners to 1 million by 2020. Retrieved from http://100kstrong.org/2015/09/25/obama-announces-new-program-to-dramatically-expand-u-s-manadarin-learning/

Tsung, L., & Cruickshank, K. (Eds.). (2011). *Teaching and learning Chinese in global contexts.* London: Continuum.

Yang, R. (2010). Soft power and higher education: An examination of China's Confucius Institutes. *Globalisation, Societies and Education, 8*, 235–245.

Part I
Overview of Tests and Research

Chapter 1
Hanyu Shuiping Kaoshi (HSK): Past, Present, and Future

Yanjiang Teng

Abstract Hanyu Shuiping Kaoshi (HSK, 汉语水平考试) is China's national standardized test designed to assess the Chinese language proficiency of non-native speakers such as foreign students and overseas Chinese. This chapter opens with a brief account of the history and development of HSK over the past thirty years (1984–the present): How it came into being, the aim of the test, the levels of the test, and the outline of the test. For the convenience of discussion, this chapter divides the development of HSK into three stages: Old HSK, HSK (Revised), and New HSK. The review indicates that HSK has developed from a domestic test to an influential international proficient test; it has expanded from a test with a focus on assessment of linguistic knowledge to a test of all four language skills (i.e., listening, reading, writing, and speaking); its exam outline has also undergone huge revisions to better meet the demands of the examinees and the society. Based on the history and development of HSK, the last section discusses its future prospects with challenges identified and suggestions proposed.

Keywords HSK · New HSK · Chinese as a foreign language

Introduction

Since the inception of the Open-Door Policy in the late 1970s and early 1980s, the People's Republic of China has witnessed the deepening of communication with the outside world in a variety of fields, including education. In the past few decades, there has been a steady increase in the influx of students from foreign countries coming to study in China (Meyer 2014; Wang 2016), and Chinese programs outside

Y. Teng (✉)
Michigan State University, East Lansing, USA
e-mail: tengy@msu.edu

© Springer Nature Singapore Pte Ltd. 2017
D. Zhang and C.-H. Lin (eds.), *Chinese as a Second Language Assessment*,
Chinese Language Learning Sciences, DOI 10.1007/978-981-10-4089-4_1

of China have also seen fast growth (Zhang 2015; Zhao and Huang 2010). The increasing interest in studying Chinese language and culture has led to a lot of discussions not only in how Chinese language curriculum and pedagogy could best serve the learning needs of learners of Chinese as a second language (CSL) or foreign language (CFL) but also in how learners could be assessed appropriately for diverse academic as well as professional purposes. Within the context of this changing landscape of CSL/CFL education, HSK (acronym of Hanyu Shuiping Kaoshi or the pinyin of 汉语水平考试; literally translated as Chinese Proficiency Test) was developed in China and later became the country's national standardized test of Chinese language proficiency for non-native speakers.

HSK was first developed in 1984 by the HSK Testing Center of Beijing Language Institute (now Beijing Language and Culture University, which is often referred to as Beiyu [北语], the short form of the university's Chinese name). It is the predecessor of New HSK (新汉语水平考试), which is currently administered and promulgated both within and outside of China by Hanban (汉办, the colloquial abbreviation for 中国国家汉语国际推广领导小组办公室 [Zhongguo Guojia Hanyu Guoji Tuiguang Lingdao Xiaozu Bangongshi], the Chinese name of the Chinese Language Council), a non-government organization affiliated with the Ministry of Education (MOE) of China. Hanban is also the executive headquarters of the Confucius Institutes (CI) (Li and Tucker 2013; Zhao and Huang 2010) and is committed to making Chinese language teaching resources and services available to the world. Over the past thirty years, HSK has developed from a domestic test for assessing foreign students preparing to study or studying in China to an influential international test of Chinese language proficiency that serves assessment needs and purposes in diverse contexts. It has expanded from testing only listening and reading skills at one level in its earlier form to all language skills across a wide range of language skills and performance and proficiency levels. The testing outlines and guidelines of HSK have also undergone substantial revisions to better meet the demands of examinees and society.

This chapter aims to provide a historical review of HSK and its reforms and discusses its challenges and future directions as an international test of Chinese language proficiency. It opens with a brief account of the history and development of HSK over the past thirty years (1984–the present): How it came into being and its aims, levels, and testing outlines at different historical periods. For the convenience of discussion, this chapter divides the development of HSK into three stages, namely Old HSK (1980s–2000s), HSK Revised (2007–2011), and New HSK (2009 onward) and discusses each stage in one of the three sections that follow. Based on this historical review, the last section of this chapter discusses the future prospects of HSK with challenges identified and suggestions proposed. It is hoped that the review in this chapter with a focus on HSK has broader significance to theory and practice of CSL/CFL assessment and language assessment in general.

Old HSK[1] (1980s–2000s): Emergence and Growth

The development of HSK was first initiated in 1984 by a team of experts in the field of CSL teaching and assessment in the HSK Testing Center at Beiyu, which, according to the university profile, is "the only university of its kind in China that offers Chinese language and culture courses to foreign students" and "has the longest history, the largest size and the most well qualified academic faculty" in the area of teaching Chinese and promoting Chinese culture to non-native speakers of Chinese.[2] Given the university's unique identity, it did not seem a surprise that Beiyu undertook the earliest mission of developing a Chinese proficiency test for foreign students in China. This section addresses the historical development of HSK in its pioneer stage in terms of key events, test format, achievements, and limitations.

The first or earliest form of HSK came into being in 1985 for Chinese proficiency testing at only one level, that is, HSK (Basic), which targeted test-takers with Chinese proficiency at the elementary and intermediate levels. In 1988, the first public HSK test was held at Beiyu, and three years later, it was launched at National University of Singapore as its first attempt at overseas promotion of HSK. In 1992, HSK was officially made a national standardized test of Chinese for non-native speakers of Chinese, with the release of the document entitled Chinese language proficiency test (HSK) guidelines (中国汉语水平考试 [HSK] 办法, Zhongguo Hanyu Shuiping Kaoshi [HSK] Banfa) by the then State Education Commission (now the Ministry of Education). After a few years' development and testing practice, with the consideration of more diverse needs of foreign Chinese learners, the HSK Testing Center started to develop an HSK test for test-takers with an advanced level of Chinese proficiency, that is, HSK (Advanced), which was first introduced in 1993. Later, the original HSK (Basic) was renamed HSK (Elementary and Intermediate). In 1997, the HSK Testing Center also launched the HSK (Beginning) in order to meet the needs of beginning learners on the lower level of Chinese proficiency. By this time, HSK has established itself as a three-level comprehensive test system from the beginning to the advanced level, namely HSK (Beginning), HSK (Elementary–Intermediate), and HSK (Advanced).

These three levels of the HSK test were further divided into eleven grades benchmarked on the teaching of foreign students at Beiyu and Peking University with each level generally subdivided into three grades (Liu et al. 1988). As shown in Table 1.1, within each level, A was the lowest whereas C was the highest in proficiency except that there was an overlap between Basic A and Elementary C, which means these two levels were viewed as similar in proficiency. According to Liu (1999), this arrangement was due to the big transition from the Basic level to

---

[1]"Old" is added by the author to refer to the early stage of HSK development and make a differentiation from the versions of reformed HSK at the two latter stages. In other words, Old HSK is by no means the official title of HSK testing in its earliest stage.

[2]Sources: http://english.blcu.edu.cn/col/col9242/index.html.

Table 1.1 HSK test levels, certification levels, and grade components

Test levels	HSK (beginning)			HSK (elementary and intermediate)						HSK (advanced)		
Level	Basic			Elementary			Intermediate			Advanced		
Certificate	C	B	A	C	B	A	C	B	A	C	B	A
Grade	1	2	3		4	5	6	7	8	9	10	11

Note Grade refers to the qualified score scope based on HSK test scores. It corresponds to the specifications in the document entitled *Chinese Language Proficiency Grade Standards and Grade Outline* (Hanyu Shuiping Dengji Biaozhun he Dengji Dagang, 汉语水平等级标准和等级大纲). For details, see Liu et al. (1988)

the Advanced level. Although there were only three levels in the test, it had four levels of certification: Basic, Elementary, Intermediate, and Advanced. Test-takers were issued a certificate in correspondence to the level tested as long as they met the minimum level of proficiency required within that level of testing (e.g., Basic C, Elementary B, Intermediate C, or Advanced A).

In its initial stage, HSK was primarily a multiple-choice-based written test that paid much attention to assessing test-takers' language proficiency with a focus on vocabulary and grammar through the format of testing listening and reading (Xie 2011). For example, at the Beginning level (i.e., HSK [Beginning]), only listening comprehension, reading comprehension, and grammatical structure were tested in the form of multiple-choice questions; in HSK (Elementary and Intermediate), an integrated cloze, an assessment consisting of a portion of text with certain words removed where test-takers were asked to restore the missing words based on the context of a reading passage, was added as the fourth section. At the Advanced level (i.e., HSK [Advanced]), in addition to listening comprehension, reading comprehension, and integrated cloze, the fourth section, which carried the name of Comprehensive Expression, asked test-takers to rearrange the order of sentences provided in the test to make a coherently structured paragraph. Another distinctive feature of HSK (Advanced) is that it was the only level of HSK where a writing section and an oral test were included (Jing 2004).

The teaching of Chinese language to international students in China in the late 1980s and early 1990s was largely non-degree bearing and oriented toward proficiency enhancement. The primary aim of Chinese classes then was to ensure international students could become proficient in Chinese so much so that they could attend college science or liberal arts classes for regular native Chinese-speaking students with Chinese as the medium of instruction. At that time, HSK was not a high-stakes test in that a demonstrated level of proficiency through certification was not required, and a certificate of (a certain level of) HSK was not necessarily recognized across universities and colleges in China. This began to change in 1995 when the State Education Commission (now the Ministry of Education) mandated that international students should possess a test certificate that shows their Chinese language proficiency before they could be enrolled in higher institutions across the country. Ever since then, HSK test scores and certificates were acknowledged by more and more educational institutions and business organizations as well, in China, which promoted the popularity and increased the high-stakes status of HSK.

The creation and establishment of the HSK test system were great breakthroughs in the field of teaching Chinese as a second language (TCSL) in China. Before the birth of HSK, there was no systemic, objective, or standardized testing for evaluating international students' Chinese proficiency. According to Sun (2007), an inherent motivation for developing the HSK was to provide a benchmark by which foreign students' learning achievement could be assessed for varying decision-making purposes. In other words, to some extent, a consciousness of standards (to guide Chinese teaching in addition to testing) was the impetus or underlying factor for the creation of the HSK testing system. There is no denying that HSK has exerted a great impact on the development of TCSL in China. As Sun (2007) pointed out, there would be no standardization of TCSL without the creation of the HSK.

Throughout the early years of its development from the mid-1980s to late 1990s, HSK has proved itself as a standardized Chinese proficiency test with high reliability and validity, and its item designing, test administration, and grading have all been scientific (Sun 2007). Despite its significance and the great influence on TCSL in China then, HSK, as it was initially designed and structured, also raised a lot of concerns and bore some inevitable limitations. To begin with, the rationale of early HSK testing was a reflection of CSL teaching at that time in China. Liu (1983) held that there was a connection between the ways foreign languages were tested with the ways they were taught. For example, the teaching of Chinese to international students then had a primary focus on the training in linguistic knowledge with little emphasis on the communicative use of the language in real life. Under such an influence, HSK, at its initial stage, placed an emphasis on testing linguistic accuracy rather than language use or language performance (Wang 2014), despite the knowledge now shared by second language acquisition scholars, language testers, as well as teachers that linguistic accuracy does not translate into socially and culturally appropriate use of the target language and thus could not properly measure test-takers' actual language proficiency (Meyer 2014; Xie 2011). Take HSK (Elementary and Intermediate) as an example; it consisted of four sections of test questions, namely listening comprehension, grammatical structure, reading comprehension, and integrated cloze. Except the integrated cloze questions, which accounted only 10% of the test score, the rest of test questions were all multiple choice (around 90%), and there was no testing at all for language performance, such as writing and speaking, at this level.

No Chinese language proficiency standards were available for international students to guide the development of HSK at its early stage. Thus, interestingly, as noted earlier, HSK developers hoped to use the test and its benchmark levels to guide TCSL practice instead of standards-based language teaching and assessment practice. Consequently, HSK developers chose to refer to the teaching syllabi of a few universities for foreign students and dictionaries for native Chinese-speaking users for the selection of grammatical structures and vocabulary to be considered for constructing test questions. The graded wordlists and grammatical structures in HSK exam outlines or guidelines then had to be revised and adjusted in accordance with how a few universities required their foreign students to learn at different levels. As a result, scholars questioned the criteria of such choices and asserted that the choice of wordlists and grammatical structures could be too prescriptive and narrow in scope (Liu 1999; Wang 2014). Due to these limitations, HSK developers began to undertake significant reforms on the test in the past decade. The forthcoming sections focus on what changes have been made to the Old HSK via two different lines of efforts and why such changes have taken place.

HSK Revised (2007–2011): Beiyu's Effort to Reform HSK

After nearly twenty years' practice, at the beginning of the twenty-first century, HSK has become one of the most influential and authoritative Chinese proficiency tests in the world. A large increase in test-takers was witnessed both domestically and internationally. It was estimated that about a million people took the test from 1990 to 2005 (Sun 2009). Along with the increasing popularity of the HSK, complaints about the drawbacks of the test also emerged from both test-takers and CSL practitioners, two major ones being its difficulty level and an orientation toward linguistic knowledge rather than skills for real communication (Meyer 2014).

Based on the feedback from all stakeholders, efforts were made to reform the (Old) HSK test to meet the increasingly diverse needs of examinees both in China and abroad. Two separate efforts were taken by two different agencies to reform the Old HSK. One was from the HSK Testing Center of Beiyu, the original developer of the HSK; the other was from Hanban. These two agencies took two different approaches to revising the HSK to better meet the needs of targeted test-takers in and outside of China in the first decade of the twenty-first century. For a better discussion on the innovation of these two approaches, this section focuses on the effort Beiyu made in revising the Old HSK, which resulted in HSK (Revised), and then, the next section will specifically address Hanban's reform effort, which led to the New HSK.

As discussed in the previous section, the Old HSK had three levels (i.e., Beginning, Elementary and Intermediate, and Advanced) with 11 grades; its unique structure was not aligned with other established proficiency standards or standardized language tests, which affected its wider promotion and recognition in the world. As Meyer (2014) pointed out, the (Old) HSK score and the level system were not easy to understand, which made it difficult for stakeholders to interpret the meaning of HSK scores, particularly when the scores needed to be compared with those of other international language proficiency tests. Since 2007, the HSK Testing Center at Beiyu has begun to revise the Old HSK. The improved or revised version of the HSK (hereafter, HSK [Revised]) consisted of three levels: HSK (Revised, Elementary), HSK (Revised, Intermediate), and HSK (Revised, Advanced).

According to HSK Testing Center (2007), the test structure of the HSK (Revised), compared to the Old HSK, is more reasonable in testing item design and better reflects the principles of language teaching and acquisition (Spolsky 1995).

To begin with, the HSK (Revised) began to pay more attention to testing examinees' real communicative competence in addition to linguistic knowledge. For example, the HSK (Revised) added into the elementary and intermediate levels (i.e., HSK [Revised, Elementary] and HSK [Revised, Intermediate]) a component that tests speaking, which used to be tested only at the Advanced level (i.e., HSK [Advanced]). With this change, test-takers at all levels now have a choice of testing their speaking in Chinese in correspondence to their actual language proficiency. Such an improvement also indicated a shift from a more vocabulary and grammar oriented paradigm to a more usage or performance based paradigm in the designing of the test (Meyer 2014). In addition to the test format changes, HSK (Revised), compared to its predecessor or the Old HSK, includes more diverse items for testing Chinese speaking and writing. Grammatical structures, based on test-takers' feedback, were no longer a stand-alone section and tested in a decontextualized way; rather, they are integrated into the test of reading, speaking, and writing. In the HSK (Revised), the integrated cloze section, which required Chinese character writing, was totally removed due to its duplication with a separate writing section.

Another revision in the HSK (Revised) is that multiple-choice test items are reduced, and the test is characterized by more integrated testing of language skills and performance. For example, writing after listening and speaking after listening are added on top of multiple-choice questions to test examinees' comprehensive language skills. As for testing reading comprehension, HSK (Revised, Intermediate) includes questions that ask test-takers to identify errors from one sentence as well as traditional multiple-choice questions; at the Advanced level (i.e., HSK [Revised, Advanced]), reading comprehension questions consist of error identification from one sentence, reordering of scrambled sentences, and questions that test fast reading skills.

New HSK (2009 Onward): Hanban's HSK Reform

This section turns to the line of effort that Hanban has taken to reform the (Old) HSK. The outcome of the reform is the New HSK, which was officially launched in 2009 by Hanban. As indicated at the beginning of this chapter, Hanban is the executive body of Chinese Language Council International and also headquarters of the Confucius Institute (CI). It is a non-profit organization affiliated with the Chinese Ministry of Education committed to the global promotion of Chinese language and culture.[3] Ever since the first CI was established in South Korea in 2004, Hanban has established over 480 CIs and many more Confucius Classrooms

---

[3]Source: http://www.hanban.ca/hanban.php?lang=en.

around the world with overseas partners in the next 10 years.[4] This global promotion of Chinese language and culture programs has arguably brought about a lot of assessment demands. Among the many missions that CIs have for advancing China's soft power (Zhang 2015; Zhao and Huang 2010), there is the important one of establishing local facilities for promoting the HSK among learners outsides of China.[4] With this mission in mind, Hanban's efforts to upgrade the HSK took a different approach than Beiyu did. An important initiative of Hanban's reforming effort was to lower the test-taking threshold to cater to the needs of test-takers with a more diverse range of learning experience and proficiency in Chinese so that more learners around the globe could be attracted to take the test.

An important note to make here before a detailed discussion on the New HSK is the debate among HSK developers on who owns the HSK along with the promotion and reforms of the test: HSK Testing Center at Beiyu, which is the early developer of the HSK, or Hanban, which was established with support from the Chinese government for global promotion of Chinese. While it is beyond the scope of this paper to offer a detailed account of the debate (interested readers may refer to this Chinese news report for details[5]), it is clear that the separate reforms by the two agencies (and hence, two different versions of reformed HSK) have hampered the Chinese government's effort to regulate and standardize its initiative to advance the country's soft power. In 2010, an agreement on the intellectual property of HSK was made between Hanban and Beiyu, with Hanban becoming the only property owner of HSK. The HSK (Revised) tests conducted by Beiyu came to a complete stop in 2011, and Beiyu agreed to collaborate with Hanban and support Hanban's development and promotion of the New HSK. In other words, any HSK test after 2011 refers to the New HSK administered by Hanban (Ji 2012); and the New HSK is the second-generation HSK that is promulgated as China's national Chinese proficiency test for non-native speakers both in and outside of the country. The following subsections first discuss why the Old HSK was reformed into the New HSK and then introduce the structure, format, and major features of the New HSK.

Why New HSK?

The original or Old HSK had met many challenges in its early promotion around the world, a major one being the difficulty of the test to meet the needs of test-takers with a very wide range of Chinese learning experience and proficiency levels and to serve diverse testing purposes. Specifically, the Old HSK was targeted at students who study Chinese in China and coincided with four-year university classroom teaching there. In other words, the Old HSK was largely developed based on

---

[4]Source: http://confuciusinstitute.unl.edu/institutes.shtml.

[5]Source: http://edu.sina.com.cn/zgks/2011-01-20/0804283115.shtml.

four-year Chinese programs for international students at universities in China with little, if any, consideration of those who learn Chinese overseas. Along with the fast increase in the number of overseas Chinese learners in recent years, there is also a very wide range of needs among the learners, which has made potential HSK test-takers more diverse in regards to their learning experience, motivation, and interests in taking the test. For example, people of different ages or educational levels (young learners in K-12 educational settings vs. adult learners in higher institutions), learning Chinese through different ways (informal learning vs. formal learning through classroom instruction), and with different professions may all be interested in taking the HSK for diverse purposes, such as studying in China, career preparation or advancement, or simply taking the test to know the level of their Chinese proficiency.

Under such circumstances, many test-takers outside of China complained that the Old HSK was too hard to reach the level requirement for them to receive a certificate that matches their actual level of proficiency. As Meyer (2014) argued, "many Western learners did not consider Old HSK 'scores' a valid measure of their Chinese language competence" (p. 14). For example, after two or more years of formal Chinese learning, lots of learners still had difficulty in passing the Elementary and Intermediate level test (i.e., HSK [Elementary and Intermediate]). As a result, some learners might have felt fearful toward Chinese language and could have easily given up their Chinese learning. In addition to complaints from students themselves on the Old HSK, teachers also thought that the bar of each level of the test was too high to reach for their students. Take the Elementary and Intermediate level in the Old HSK, for example, the vocabulary requirement of the level is up to 3000 words, which could be a big challenge to test-takers. The poor performance on the Old HSK often led to teachers' resistance to asking their students to take the test. It was argued that the HSK should act as a springboard instead of a stumbling block on the way of learning Chinese (Hanban 2014), or the test should have a positive washback effect on students' committed interest in learning the language rather than eliminating that interest (Xie 2011). Based on the feedback, like the aforementioned ones, from overseas test-takers and teachers, test developers from Hanban decided that the Old HSK should be reformed.

A major change from the Old HSK to the New HSK is the way in which different languages skills should be tested. According to Meyer (2014), the Old HSK resembled the format of a discrete point test, in which language knowledge was tested through a number of independent elements: grammar, vocabulary, spelling, and pronunciation. These are usually tested by multiple-choice questions and true or false recognition tasks, which are meant to measure test-takers' language proficiency separately without a comprehensive assessment of their communicative competence. Thus, discrete point tests have been criticized for testing only recognition knowledge and facilitating guessing and cheating, "answering individual items, regardless of their actual function in communication" (Farhady 1979, p. 348). More recently, most scholars favor integrated testing for language performance (e.g., Adair-Hauck et al. 2006), which requires test-takers to coordinate many kinds of knowledge and tap the total communicative abilities in one linguistic event in a format of papers and projects focusing more on comprehension tasks, cloze tasks, and speaking and listening tasks. HSK test reformers have made efforts to change the HSK from a discrete point test to an integrative test.

Another major consideration during the reform of the HSK was the relationship between testing and teaching. In the Old HSK, testing was considered separate from teaching, even though interestingly, the test was originally developed on the basis of the curriculum and instruction for international students in a few universities in China. On the contrary, the New HSK takes the opposite direction: advocating for the principle of integration between teaching and testing in that it aims to "promote training through testing" and "promote learning through testing" (Hanban 2014). It sets clear test objectives to enable test-takers to improve their Chinese language abilities in a systematic and efficient way. While it emphasizes objectivity and accuracy, as is true of any traditional large-scale standardized test, the New HSK, more importantly, focuses on developing and testing examinees' ability to apply Chinese in practical, real-life situations (Hanban 2010). Overall, there is a clear effort in the development of the New HSK to better serve the learning needs of Chinese language learners through testing.

New HSK: Structure, Levels, and Format of Questions

As a large-scale international standardized test, the New HSK combines the advantages of the original HSK while taking into consideration the recent trends in Chinese language teaching and international language testing. The levels of the New HSK correspond to those of the Chinese Language Proficiency Scales for Speakers of Other Languages (CLPS 4) developed by Hanban,[6] and there was also an effort to align the levels with those of the Common European Framework of Reference for Languages (CEFR) (Council of Europe 2002).

The New HSK consists of two independent parts: a written test (by default, the New HSK refers to the written test) and an oral test (HSKK; acronym of Hanyu Shuiping Kouyu Kaoshi 汉语水平口语考试 or HSK Speaking Test). There are six levels to the written test and three levels to the speaking test. For the written test, it consists of six bands (levels), namely HSK (Level I), HSK (Level II), HSK (Level III), HSK (Level IV), HSK (Level V), and HSK (Level VI). It is apparent that

---

[6]Chinese Language Proficiency Scales for Speakers of Other Languages (CLPS) is a guideline document developed by Hanban for teaching Chinese to speakers of other languages. It provided detailed descriptions for five proficiency benchmarks in six areas, including communicative ability in spoken Chinese, communicative ability in written Chinese, listening comprehension, oral presentation, reading comprehension, and written expression. The document serves as an important reference for developing Chinese language syllabi, compiling Chinese textbooks, and assessing the language proficiency of learners of Chinese (Source: http://chinese.fltrp.com/book/410).

Table 1.2 Comparison of new HSK, CLPS, and CEFR

Written HSK (level)	Vocabulary	CLPS	CEFR	HSKK
HSK (level VI)	Over 5000	Level V	C2	HSKK (advanced)
HSK (level V)	2500		C1	
HSK (level IV)	1200	Level IV	B2	HSKK (intermediate)
HSK (level III)	600	Level III	B1	
HSK (level II)	300	Level II	A2	HSKK (beginning)
HSK (level I)	150	Level I	A1	

compared with its predecessor, the New HSK has more refined test levels; in particular, the HSKK also has three levels (i.e., Beginning, Intermediate, and Advanced in correspondence to CEFR Levels A, B, and C), thus making more level choices available to learners who want to have their oral proficiency in Chinese tested. Table 1.2 shows the correspondence between the levels of the New HSK (including HSKK), the levels of the CLPS, and the CEFR.

It is beyond the scope of this chapter to provide details about the format of all test sections/questions at each level of the New HSK. Interested readers can refer to the Web site of Hanban.[7] For a quick overview here, the New HSK (with HSKK included) attaches great importance to all four language skills and reflects a balanced proportion between receptive skills and productive skills, even though it tests primarily listening and reading comprehension at the lower levels (Levels 1 and 2). Pictures are widely used in the lower levels to provide some clues for students' listening or reading comprehension. Across the six levels, the listening section consists of different types of questions that test listening abilities from as simple as making a true or false judgment on whether a given picture matches a word heard to such complex skills as long conversation and short passage comprehension. The reading section also consists of different types of questions that test different levels and types of Chinese reading; from as simple as matching a printed word (with pinyin at Levels 1 and 2) with a picture to as complex as cloze, sentence reordering, and passage comprehension. Writing is only tested from Level 3, which consists of two parts that ask test-takers to write a complete sentence either rearranging character orders or filling in the missing character in a sentence with pictures given. More complex writing skills, such as keywords and picture-based sentence or essay writing, are tested at Levels 4 and 5. The writing at Level 6 tests the ability to condense a passage from 1000 words to 400 words without personal views added.

HSKK, as the HSK speaking test, is comprised of three levels, all of which have the first part that asks test-takers to repeat or retell what is presented to them—repeating sentences heard at the Beginning and Intermediate levels and retelling a passage presented in print at the Advanced level. The Beginning level also involves answering a number of questions either briefly after the recording of the questions is played or with a minimum of five sentences for each question presented in pinyin.

---

[7]Source: http://english.hanban.org.

The Intermediate level, in addition to sentence repetition, involves describing two pictures and answering two questions presented in pinyin. At the Advanced level, test-takers, in addition to retelling three passages, are asked to read aloud a passage and answer two questions. All passages and questions are presented in print to the test-takers at the Advanced level.

New HSK: Concluding Remarks

Since it was first launched in 2009, the popularity of the New HSK is fast growing and it has become widely promoted and accepted both in and outside of China. According to Hanban (2014), by the end of 2013, 56 HSK test centers had been established in 31 cities in mainland China, and internationally, there were over 800 overseas test centers in 108 countries and regions and over 370,000 international test-takers took the New HSK in 2013 (Hanban 2014). According to Zhang (2015), by the end of 2014, there had been 475 Confucius Institutes with more than 1.1 million registered students learning Chinese in 126 countries and regions around the globe. It is reasonably anticipated that the increasing number of students in CI should also promote the popularity of the New HSK in the years to come.

The New HSK, on the one hand, retains the former HSK's orientation as a general Chinese language proficiency test; on the other hand, it has expanded the scope of its predecessor, in particular, the application of its scores for diverse decision making in a globalized world (Wang 2014). The result of the test could not only be used for assessing students' proficiency and evaluating their learning progress but also be extended to use as a reference: (1) of an educational institution or program for student admission or placement and differentiation in teaching; (2) for employers' decision making concerning staff recruitment, training, and promotion; and (3) for Chinese program evaluation purposes (e.g., how effective a program is in training Chinese learners) (Hanban 2014).

Despite its increasing popularity and expanded use of test scores, the New HSK is not free of critiques and concerns (Wang 2014). As an example, as indicated earlier (see Table 1.2), there was an effort during the reform of the New HSK to align it with the levels of the CEFR and the CLPS. However, the CEFR does not give specific considerations to Chinese characters, and CLPS also does not seem to pay adequate attention to character competence or competence of Chinese orthography, which is very different from alphabetic languages but an essential part of Chinese language competence. In the New HSK, there is no written test (character writing) at Levels 1 and 2, which does not seem to be aligned with the typical Chinese learning experience of test-takers. Such an arrangement might have resulted from a consideration of the challenge of character writing, particularly among beginning learners/test-takers with an alphabetic language background, despite the fact that these learners/test-takers do typically learn how to write characters as an integral component of their Chinese learning process. A related concern rests on test reformers' effort to accommodate the testing needs of beginning learners by lowering its difficulty level so that the New HSK could be of interest to test-takers with minimal learning experience and a very limited foundation in Chinese words and grammar. For example, New HSK (Level 1) could be taken by those who have learned 150 words and New HSK (Level 2) by those with 300 words, according to the test outline of the New HSK (Hanban 2010). While these low requirements could make the New HSK more widely appealing internationally, it seems questionable if the effort behind this reform to attract more test-takers, along with Hanban's global mission to promote Chinese language and culture, would be desirable. In other words, while the number of HSK test-takers might increase as a result of this change, in the long run, this practice could have some negative effects on the promotion of Chinese language internationally (Wang 2014). That is, the easy access to an HSK certificate at such a low standard might weaken the authority of the test itself.

Looking Ahead at the HSK: Challenges and Future Directions

As the historical overview above shows, HSK has undergone major changes and made great advancements in the past thirty years in line with new trends in international language testing and the changing landscape of Chinese teaching and learning around the world. However, HSK has also encountered many challenges despite the recent reforms. In what follows, some challenges the HSK has encountered are discussed, and at the same time, some suggestions are made on the future directions of its development.

First, the test needs to be consistent across levels in light of difficulty and learner diversity in how Chinese is taught and learned in the global context. Meyer (2014) argued that consistency or the lack thereof was a big issue in HSK in that the transition from one level to another is not necessarily similar in the level of difficulty. Take the New HSK vocabulary requirements, for example, for Levels 1, 2, and 3, the required vocabulary is 150, 300, and 600 words, respectively; whereas for Levels 4, 5 and 6, the required vocabulary is 1200, 2500 and 5000 words, respectively. Such a big jump from low to high levels suggests that the beginning level (i.e., Level 1) might be too easy (150 words) (as I also indicated earlier), while the Advanced levels (Levels 5 and 6) may be too hard for test-takers. There are also concerns about some drawbacks in the choices of overall vocabulary (e.g., away from the teaching context of learners outside of China) and the distributions of vocabulary across different levels (Zhang et al. 2010).

Second, as I discussed, the New HSK advocates a close relationship between testing and teaching, arguing that New HSK testing could offer valuable guidelines for teaching practice (Hanban 2014). In reality, such an idea seems more of an expectation or a point to help promote the New HSK than possibly effective in practice in an international context, given, as we all know, that the teaching of

Chinese around the world is so diverse in regards to curriculum, teaching force, learners' needs, and textbooks. Take the textbook in the market, for example, it was estimated that there are over 3300 different kinds of Chinese textbooks on the international market (Pan 2014). There are huge variations in these textbooks in terms of target learners/programs, the principle of material selection, and unit organization, and so on. Many of them were not necessarily published in China with support from Hanban and in alignment with CLPS guidelines, which serve as the basis on which the New HSK was developed. While Hanban has strived to make a lot of curricular materials produced in China available to overseas learners through Confucius Institutes and Confucius Classrooms, it is not uncommon that these materials are not used at all in K-12 as well as university-based Chinese programs. In the USA, for example, K-12 Chinese programs usually do not mandate the use of a textbook series, and university Chinese programs tend to adopt locally produced textbooks, such as Integrated Chinese (Yao and Liu 2009) and Chinese Link (Wu et al. 2010), which are developed on the basis of the National Foreign Language Standards (ACTFL 1995). Consequently, the various levels of the New HSK and the test as a whole could not easily match the curriculum and the development trajectory of overseas students, which effectively makes it challenging for HSK testing results to be used by teachers to guide their teaching and learners to guide their learning practice.

Third, test items need to be updated, and modern technology should be integrated into the test. Scholars have pointed out that there is an urgent need to update the item bank of the HSK, and test items should reflect the development of society in a globalized world, and the gap between HSK test items and social demands should be bridged (Ren 2004). Moreover, despite the current trend of Internet-based, computerized adaptive testing (Suvorov and Hegelheimer 2013), such as TOEFL iBT and Business Chinese Test (BCT; another test administered by Hanban), New HSK is still a largely paper-based, non-adaptive test. Over the past few years, Internet-based New HSK testing has been conducted in some places of the world. However, the test is largely a Web-based version of the paper test with the possibility for test-takers to input Chinese characters through a computer-based input program, as opposed to handwriting, for writing, in addition to enhanced efficiency in test administration and test-taking. Web-based, self-adaptive testing is certainly the direction for HSK's future development (Sun 2007). Another technology-related issue is computer-assisted scoring of written Chinese. Over the past years of HSK development, there has been some effort to study automated scoring of HSK essays and L2 Chinese essays in general (see Zhang et al. 2016, for a review), such as exploring distinguishing features (e.g., token and type frequency of characters) that predict essay scores (e.g., Huang et al. 2014). However, HSK essay scoring has by far relied on human raters, and at the time of writing this chapter, automated essay scoring (AES) is yet to be applied in HSK testing.

Fourth, there is a need to enlarge the scope of spoken Chinese tested in the HSKK. As I indicated earlier, the current format of the HSKK focuses largely on testing presentational skills, such as repeating sentences or answering questions heard, picture-prompted narration, and reading aloud or retelling. Test-takers' oral productions are recorded for later scoring. However, there is no testing of test-takers' interactive use of Chinese, such as with a certified tester as in the case of ACTFL's Oral Proficiency Interview (OPI) (Liskin-Gasparro 2003; see also Liu, this volume) or between test-takers themselves. The lack of direct testing of spoken interaction seems to constrain the space of the HSKK to meet the needs of test-takers and any washback effect that the test could have on communication-oriented Chinese language teaching and learning.

Finally, what standards to follow is also a big issue that the New HSK needs to deal with while being promoted in an international context. Two types of standards seem particularly relevant. The first concerns the standards for Chinese (or foreign language in general) learning or proficiency development, which was indicated in the first point made above. To recap, a lack of alignment between the standards/proficiency guidelines on which the New HSK is based and those diverse ones on which Chinese curricula are set up around the world would limit the washback effect that HSK developers claim to have on Chinese teaching and learning. The second issue concerns the standard of language. As discussed earlier, Chinese language learners and test-takers are becoming more diverse than ever before. They include not only those non-native speakers who learn Chinese as a Foreign Language, but also descendants of Chinese immigrants in diaspora communities who learn Chinese as a heritage language. These diverse learners tend to speak different varieties of Chinese and have different demands and expectations for Chinese learning and use in their life. What standard or standards of language should a globally promoted test like the New HSK follow? Is Putonghua, the standard variety of Chinese in China and on which the New HSK is based, the sole legitimate standard for international testing of Chinese, or should the New HSK as an international test consider diverse varieties of the language in the Chinese-speaking world? In view of the global spread of Chinese, some scholars recently proposed Global Huayu (literally, language of the Chinese) to capture the evolving nature of Chinese as a lingua franca and discussed its implications for Chinese language teaching and testing (Lu 2015; Seng and Lai 2010; Wang 2009; See also Shang and Zhao, this volume). According to Lu (2015), a preeminent scholar of Chinese linguistics and Chinese as a second language who previously served as the president of the International Society for Chinese Language Teaching (世界汉语教学学会), Global Huayu Putonghua could not and should not be adhered to as the norm in Chinese language teaching, whether it is pronunciation, vocabulary, or grammar. In this regard, the discussion on World Englishes in language testing (Elder and Davies 2006) should be pertinent to HSK and international testing of Chinese in general. However, the HSK testing community has been barely responsive to such an issue.

Conclusion

This chapter provided a historical review on the HSK. Over the past 30 years, HSK has witnessed fast development and established itself as a well-known international test of Chinese proficiency, along with the growth of the discipline of TCFL in China and Chinese government's global promotion of Chinese language and culture (Sun 2007). Through ongoing reforms, HSK has been updated to meet the diverse needs of test-takers internationally. Despite the progresses highlighted in this historical account, there are also a lot of issues and challenges that have emerged and are yet to be addressed with Hanban's effort to promulgate the New HSK in an international context. As Meyer (2014) noted, Chinese proficiency testing, be it Old HSK or New HSK, "is strongly affected by the field of language testing, which is mostly dominated by Anglo-Saxon countries, particularly the United States and England" (p. 15). While the effort to align with proficiency guidelines or frameworks like the CEFR is arguably helpful to internationalize the New HSK, there are also issues to be resolved in the development of the test with "Chinese" characteristics. It is hoped that the challenges discussed earlier on Chinese program, curricula, teaching, and learner diversities, among others, will shed light on the future development of the HSK and research on the test and large-scale testing of Chinese proficiency in general.

Acknowledgements I would like to extend my gratitude to Dr. Dongbo Zhang for his trust and encouragement in including this chapter in the book and his writing and resource support in the writing process. Special thanks also go to the reviewers' feedback and comments on the early draft of the manuscript.

References

Adair-Hauck, B., Glisan, E. W., Koda, K., Swender, E. B., & Sandrock, P. (2006). The integrated performance assessment (IPA): Connecting assessment to instruction and learning. *Foreign Language Annals, 39*(3), 359–382.

American Council on the Teaching of Foreign Languages (ACTFL). (1995). *ACTFL program standards for the preparation of foreign language teachers.* Yonkers, NY: Author.

Council of Europe. (2002). *Common European framework of reference for languages: Learning, teaching, assessment.* Cambridge: Cambridge University Press.

Elder, C., & Davies, A. (2006). Assessing English as a lingua franca. *Annual Review of Applied Linguistics, 26*, 282–304.

Farhady, H. (1979). The disjunctive fallacy between discrete-point and integrative tests. *TESOL Quarterly, 13*, 347–357.

Hanban. (2010). *New Chinese proficiency test outline (level 1-6).* Beijing: The Commercial Press.

Hanban. (2014). www.hanban.org. Retrieved from http://english.hanban.org/node_8002.htm

HSK Testing Center. (2007). Scheme for a revised version of the Chinese proficiency test (HSK). *Chinese Teaching in the World, 2*, 126–135.

Huang, Z., Xie, J., & Xun, E. (2014). Study of feature selection in HSK automated essay scoring. *Computer Engineering and Applications, 6*, 118–122+126.

Ji, Y. (2012). Comments on new Chinese proficiency test. *Journal of North China University of Technology, 24*(2), 52–57.

Jing, C. (2004). Rethinking Chinese proficiency test HSK. *Journal of Chinese College in Jinan University, 1*, 22–32.

Li, S., & Tucker, G. R. (2013). A survey of the US Confucius Institutes: Opportunities and challenges in promoting Chinese language and culture education. *Journal of Chinese Language Teachers' Association, 48*(1), 29–53.

Liskin-Gasparro, J. E. (2003). The ACTFL proficiency guidelines and the oral proficiency interview: A brief history and analysis of their survival. *Foreign Language Annals, 36*(4), 483–490.

Liu, L. (1999). The grading system of Chinese proficiency test HSK. *Chinese Teaching in the World, 3*, 17–23.

Liu, X. (1983). A discussion on the Chinese proficiency test. *Language Teaching and Researching, 4*, 57–67.

Liu, Y., Guo, S., & Wang, Z. (1988). On the nature and characteristic of HSK. *Chinese Teaching in the World, 2*, 110–120.

Lu, J. (2015). The concept of Dahuayu meets the demands of Chinese integration into the World. *Global Chinese, 1*, 245–254.

Meyer, F. K. (2014). *Language proficiency testing for Chinese as a foreign language: An argument-based approach for validating the Hanyu Shuiping Kaoshi (HSK)*. Bern: Peter Lang.

Pan, X. (2014). Nationality and country-specific of international Chinese textbooks. *International Chinese Language Education, 2*, 154–159.

Ren, C. (2004). Exploratory research on objective scoring of HSK composition. *Chinese Language Learning, 6*, 58–67.

Seng, G. Y., & Lai, L. S. (2010). Global Mandarin. In V. Vaish (Ed.), *Globalization of language and culture in Asia: The impact of globalization processes on language.* London: Continuum.

Spolsky, B. (1995). *Measured words: The development of objective language testing.* Oxford: Oxford University Press.

Sun, D. (2007). On the scientific nature of HSK. *Chinese Teaching in the World, 4*, 129–138.

Sun, D. (2009). A brief discussion on the development of the Chinese proficient test. *China Examinations, 6*, 18–22.

Suvorov, R., & Hegelheimer, V. (2013). Computer-assisted language testing. In A. J. Kunnan (Ed.), *Companion to language assessment* (pp. 593–613). Malden, MA: Wiley-Blackwell.

Wang, H. (2009). On the cornerstone of Huayu test. *Journal of College of Chinese Language and Culture of Jinan University, 1*, 83–88.

Wang, R. (2014). Review of the study on the assessment of Chinese as a second language proficiency. *Language Science, 13*(1), 42–48.

Wang, Z. (2016). A survey on acculturation of international students in universities of Beijing. *China Higher Education Research, 1*, 91–96.

Wu, S., Yu, Y., Zhang, Y., & Tian, W. (2010). *Chinese link.* Upper Saddle River, NJ: Prentice Hall.

Xie, X. (2011). Why Hanban developed the new Chinese proficiency test (HSK)? *China Examinations, 3*, 10–13.

Yao, T., & Liu, Y. (2009). *Integrated Chinese.* Boston, MA: Cheng & Tsui Company.

Zhang, D., Li, L., & Zhao, S. (2016). Testing writing in Chinese as a second language: An overview of research. In V. Aryadoust & J. Fox (Eds.), *Current trends in language testing in the Pacific Rim and the Middle East: Policies, analysis, and diagnosis.* Cambridge: Cambridge Scholars Publishing.

Zhang, J. (2015). Overseas development and prospect of Confucius Institute. *Journal of Hebei University of Economics and Business, 4*, 122–125.

Zhang, J., Xie, N., Wang, S., Li, Y., & Zhang, T. (2010). The new Chinese proficiency test (HSK) report. *China Examination, 9*, 38–43.

Zhao, H., & Huang, J. (2010). China's policy of Chinese as a foreign language and the use of overseas Confucius Institutes. *Educational Research for Policy and Practice, 9*(2), 127–142.

Chapter 2
The Development of the Test of Chinese as a Foreign Language (TOCFL)

Li-ping Chang

Abstract This chapter describes the development of the Test of Chinese as a Foreign Language (TOCFL), which is a proficiency assessment tool for Chinese learners. It is divided into four major sections. First, a brief background of Teaching Chinese as a Second Language in Taiwan is provided together with the historical development of the Chinese Proficiency Test (CPT) and the Test of Proficiency-Huayu (TOP), which were the predecessors of the TOCFL. The second section discusses issues that the TOCFL research team faced in its effort to map the test to the Common European Framework of Reference (CEFR). The third section then discusses four challenging issues that the TOCFL research team has faced over the years in its effort to develop and maintain a standardized CSL/CFL test. The final section presents some washback effects of the TOCFL and work in progress.

Keywords Proficiency test · Chinese as a second/foreign language · CSL/CFL testing · TOCFL · CEFR

Introduction

Teaching Chinese as a Second Language (TCSL) began in the 1950s in Taiwan as a branch of the Yale University system of teaching Mandarin Chinese. At that time, most Mandarin Chinese centers used textbooks from the Yale University series, for example, Tewksbury's *Speak Chinese* (1948), and offered small-group classes of two to three people for two hours per day, five days per week. In response to the global increase in the study of Chinese language, in 1995, National Taiwan Normal University (NTNU) founded the first graduate institute to offer an MA program in the field of TCSL. As TCSL slowly but steadily became an important academic discipline, a test designed for Chinese as a Second Language was necessary. In 2001, some professionals and scholars from the Mandarin Training Center (MTC),

L. Chang (✉)
National Taiwan Normal University, Taipei, Taiwan
e-mail: lchang@ntnu.edu.tw

© Springer Nature Singapore Pte Ltd. 2017
D. Zhang and C.-H. Lin (eds.), *Chinese as a Second Language Assessment*,
Chinese Language Learning Sciences, DOI 10.1007/978-981-10-4089-4_2

the NTNU Graduate Institute of TCSL, and the NTNU Research Center for Psychological and Educational Testing (RCPET) formed a research team that started to construct a Chinese Proficiency Test referred to as the CPT (華語文能力 測驗), which later became what is now the Test of Chinese as a Foreign Language (TOCFL).

This chapter focuses primarily on the early development of the TOCFL from 2001 to 2011, the 10-year period that witnessed the test's advancement from the embryonic stage to the forming stage. It is divided into four sections. First, a brief overview is provided on the historical development of the Chinese Proficiency Test (CPT) and the Test of Proficiency-Huayu (TOP), which were the predecessors of the TOCFL. The second section discusses issues that the TOCFL research team faced in its effort to map the test to the Common European Framework of Reference for Languages: Learning, Teaching, Assessment (CEFR). The third section then discusses four challenging issues that the research team has faced over the years in developing and maintaining a standardized test of Chinese as a Second/Foreign Language (CSL/CFL). The fourth section presents some washback effects of TOCFL and work in progress. We believe that the issues discussed in this chapter will be useful to others who are interested in either the TOCFL or CSL/CFL test development and research in general.

Overview of Historical Development

Literature Review

To develop and deliver a high-quality proficiency test, the CPT research team started by searching for previous literature on testing Chinese as a Second/Foreign Language. We found that the body of research in this area was very limited. In Taiwan, Ko and her team pioneered in research in this area. For example, Ko and Chang (1996) and Ko et al. (1995, 1997) conducted some experiments with a few test item types and task types to develop a Test of Chinese as a Second Language. However, there were several limitations with those studies in that (a) only one level of the test was developed, (b) some test tasks seemed to be too difficult for foreign language learners, and (c) most pilot samples were Chinese native speakers studying in local elementary schools rather than adult foreign language learners. Therefore, other than gathering some ideas about test item types and task types, the CPT research team was not able to follow the line of research conducted by Ko and her team.

In addition to searching the literature, the CPT research team also investigated existing Chinese proficiency tests created in other countries (Chang 2002), such as the *Hànyǔ Shuǐpíng Kǎoshì* (HSK; 漢語水平考試) in mainland China (HSK Test Center) (Liu 1997; Teng, this volume), the *Zhōngguóyǔ Jiǎndìng Shìyàn* (中國語 檢定試驗) in Japan (The Society for Testing Chinese Proficiency), the Scholastic Aptitude Test—Chinese (SAT II—Chinese) (The College Board; Liu, this volume), the Chinese Proficiency Test (CPT) and the Preliminary Chinese Proficiency Test (Pre-CPT) developed by the Center for Applied Linguistics (CAL) in the USA. The investigation revealed the following 5 points:

1. Most proficiency tests set the target examinees at above 18 years of age.
2. Except for the HSK's cloze section of the basic/intermediate level, which included 16 items that required examinees to write Chinese characters, and the test administrated in Japan, which included a translation task and a sentence writing task, most proficiency tests used multiple-choice questions in reading and listening tests.
3. All proficiency tests investigated emphasized grammar structures either by testing grammar as one separate part such as the grammar section of SAT II—Chinese or by including grammar items in the reading section such as the reading section of CAL's CPT.
4. With the exception of the HSK, which used only Chinese in the test booklet, the tests developed in Japan and the USA used Japanese and English (the test takers' native languages), respectively, for test instructions, multiple-choice options, and some test questions.
5. It seems that each test defines the notion of proficiency differently, making it hard for the research team to interpret the tests' results in relation to one another. That means, for example, level one of one test is not equal to that level of another test.

The First Version of Chinese Proficiency Test: Listening and Reading Tests

After the review of literature, the research team created the first version of the CPT. To meet learners' demands and in consideration of the limited human and financial resources available at that time, the research team focused solely on designing tests of listening and reading comprehension targeting learners who had studied Chinese for more than 360 h (approximately 9 months) in Taiwan. To help with the creation of different test levels, the research team decided to use the Chinese proficiency guidelines developed by the American Council on the Teaching of Foreign Languages (ACTFL 1987). The ACTFL guidelines were used because they were the only international framework for Chinese teaching and testing available in Taiwan at that time, and more importantly, ACTFL's five major levels of proficiency—novice, intermediate, advanced, superior, and distinguished—were readily accepted by local teaching specialists.[1] The advantages of the ACTFL guidelines

---

[1]The distinguished level did not exist in speaking and writing guidelines until 2012. For detailed information, please visit the Website: http://www.actfl.org/publications/guidelines-and-manuals/actfl-proficiency-guidelines-2012.

were that they spelled out linguistic characteristics for each level of four language skills: listening, speaking, reading, and writing. For example, a description of the intermediate-high level of listening proficiency stated that the candidate at this level can "understand major syntactic constructions, e.g., *Shì-de* (是…的)-focus, *bǎ* (把)-disposal, and *bèi* (被)-passive" but may still make mistakes with "more complex patterns, e.g., *jiào/ràng* (叫/讓)-passive, *lián* (連)-emphasis/contrast, *chúle* (除了)-exclusion/inclusion" (ACTFL 1987, p. 477). Although these structures are mainly defined by the authority of scholars rather than empirically validated (De Jong 1990; Liskin-Gasparro 2003), the concrete descriptions were helpful in setting the levels for the tests.

Based on the ACTFL scales, the research team created different forms of listening and reading tests covering three levels: basic, intermediate, and advanced, which were designed to reflect the novice-high, intermediate-high, and advanced-low to superior levels of the ACTFL scales. The structure of the three levels of CPT is provided in Table 2.1. As Table 2.1 shows, all levels of CPT included three sections: listening, vocabulary/grammar, and reading. The time allocation for each section was equal across proficiency levels, and the task types were almost the same except for the reading section. These task types reflected the influence of other Chinese proficiency tests investigated by the CPT research team, as reported earlier. In addition to the time allocation and test content, Table 2.1 also includes short descriptions that were shown to prospective test takers indicating the hours of Chinese instruction that they should have received as well as the amount of vocabulary that they should have learned prior to attempting the test.

The Pilot Tests

The pilot tests of the CPT took place during 2002–2003 with a total of 2160 listening and reading test items. Approximately 1000 foreign learners of Chinese in language centers across Taiwan took the pilot tests and completed questionnaires. The aim was to test the suitability of task types and item difficulty. After two years of pilot testing, the research team gathered sufficient evidence to support the division of the test into three proficiency levels (basic, intermediate, and advanced) and the use of the task types listed in Table 2.1. Subsequently, the listening and reading tests, which were comprised of multiple-choice items in a paper-based format, were administered semiannually in Taiwan starting in December 2003. This transformed the CSL situation since prior to 2003 students of CSL in Taiwan had no common tool to measure their proficiency; instead, they had to rely on grades from the various language training centers and documentation of the time spent studying the language.

Table 2.1 Content breakdown of the CPT listening and reading tests

Levels/format	Test of basic	Test of intermediate	Test of advanced
Listening	Sentence (20) Conversation (20) Paragraph (10)	Sentence (15) Conversation (20) Paragraph (15)	Sentence (15) Conversation (20) Paragraph (15)
Vocabulary and grammar	Vocabulary (20) Grammar (20)	Vocabulary (10) Grammar (20)	Vocabulary (20) Grammar (10)
Reading	Sentence (10) Authentic material (20)	Sentence (10) Authentic material (10) Passage (20)	Sentence (10) Passage (20)
Suggested learning hours	360–480 h	480–960 h	Over 960 h
Vocabulary base	1500 words	5000 words	8000 words
Others	1. There are 120 test items in each level. All items are multiple-choice questions 2. The approximate test time is 110 min, with 40 min for the listening test and 70 min for the reading test		

Note The Arabic numerals in parentheses indicate the number of test items. The suggested learning hours have to be doubled for test takers from overseas (i.e., not studying in Taiwan)

The Steering Committee for the Test of Proficiency—Huayu

In 2005, the Taiwan Ministry of Education (MOE) entrusted NTNU with a mission to organize a testing center that promotes an effective CSL assessment system. As a result, the CPT project was funded by the MOE. While its Chinese name remains the same (i.e., 華語文能力測驗), the CPT's English name was changed to Test of Proficiency-Huayu (TOP).[2] The Steering Committee for the Test of Proficiency—Huayu (SC-TOP) (國家華語測驗推動工作委員會) was created to oversee test development and validation.

In 2007, the Taiwan Ministry of Education mandated that the SC-TOP evaluates the possibilities of mapping TOP test results to the CEFR proficiency scale (Council of Europe 2001) (See the next section). The research team began to reexamine and modify the test format and content of the original three levels of the test to meet this challenge. In this revision of the tests, the basic, intermediate, and advanced tests were renamed into Level 3, Level 4, and Level 5, and corresponded to CEFR levels B1, B2, and C1, respectively. TOP was subsequently renamed TOCFL (in 2011) after this revision. In the meantime, the writing and speaking tests were launched. And furthermore, all TOP/TOCFL tests administered in Taiwan since then became computer-based instead of paper-based. Since 2011, the (new) TOCFL test is delivered via the Internet with automatic scoring so that test takers can get their test

---

[2]"Huayu" is a Taiwanese reference to Chinese as a Second/Foreign Language. For more information, please visit the Website: http://www.sc-top.org.tw.

results right away. In addition, all levels corresponding to CEFR (six levels) were finished in 2013. Participants who pass the test are given a certificate indicating their level of Chinese proficiency, which is used when applying for Taiwanese scholarships and university enrollment.

Mapping the (Old) TOP to the CEFR Can-Do Statements

This section discusses the effort of the SC-TOP on mapping the TOP/TOCFL with the CEFR, and some issues the research team faced during the mapping process. According to Council of Europe (2001), the CEFR is a common framework created to provide an extensive and transparent reference for language users and for teaching and testing specialists to communicate what kind and what degree of language knowledge is certified through a particular examination result, diploma, or certificate. The CEFR adopts the *can-do* statements that describe in general terms what language learners can typically do with a language at different levels of ability. It also raises key issues for the user to consider what language learners have to learn to do in order to use a language for communication. The CEFR levels are presented in three broad categories, A, B and C, with six levels: A1 and A2 for "basic" users; B1 and B2 for "independent" users; and C1 and C2 for "proficient" users. These levels are related to the three meta-categories: communicative activities, strategies employed in performing communicative activities, and aspects of linguistic, pragmatic, and sociolinguistic competence (Council of Europe 2001).

The Steps of Mapping

The first step that the research team took to explore the possibility of mapping the TOP results to CEFR was to follow the draft manual on relating examinations to the CEFR (Council of Europe 2003; Figueras et al. 2005). The research team followed the first three steps suggested in the draft manual: familiarization, specification of examination content, and standardization of judgments (Figueras et al. 2005). First, a basic-level TOP test paper was selected (refer to Table 2.1 for the components of the test). Next, five research team members divided all test items (i.e., 120 items) into 14 communication themes in the CEFR framework (Council of Europe 2001). Then, the team members discussed what communication activity each test item involves (e.g., whether a listening item involves listening to public announcements or listening to media or listening as a member of a live audience). Finally, the team members judged which CEFR level a test taker would need to have in order to answer each item correctly. Results showed that the TOP basic-level test items mostly belong to the CEFR B1 level (86.67%), with less items from the A2 level (12.5%) and B2 level (0.83%) (Gao et al. 2007).

The Difficulty of Mapping

Despite the high percentage of items belonging to the B1 level, the research team members found that judging which level is needed to complete an item was not straightforward. For example, two items may be identified as involving the personal domain, such as travel or daily life, which is mentioned by both the CEFR A2 and B1 overall listening comprehension scales. The A2 descriptor states the following: "Can understand phrases and expressions related to areas of most immediate priority (e.g., very basic personal and family information, shopping, local geography, employment) provided speech is clearly and slowly articulated." The B1 descriptor states the following: "Can understand the main points of clear standard speech on familiar matters regularly encountered in work, school, leisure, etc., including short narratives" (Council of Europe 2001, p. 66). However, a listening test item that talks about negotiating apartment rental fees with the landlord or interviewing for a job would be harder to understand than another listening test item that simply talks about making a hotel reservation. Therefore, the research team had to create its own criterion and specify that the ability to handle short-term learning or traveling experience would belong to the A2 level and the ability to handle long-term learning or traveling experience (e.g., living abroad) would belong to the B1 level. The draft manual expects test developers to decide by themselves what contextual parameters are appropriate at different levels on the CEFR scales (Weir 2005). This dependence on subjective judgment is a two-edged sword. The negative side is that it poses some difficulty when a test item is borderline between two CEFR levels, but the positive side is that it requires the research team to be very explicit in its distinction of the levels of ability that are required by the test items. This requirement for a clear distinction is useful for future item development.

In addition to the problem judging test items' CEFR levels, another problem that the research team faced in its attempt to link the TOP to the CEFR is related to the difficulty levels of the can-do statements. In order to solve the issue, in 2008, the research team created a self-assessment questionnaire of can-do descriptors based on the European Language Portfolio (ELP) (Council of Europe 2004) for 1500 students learning Mandarin Chinese at MTC, NTNU (SC-TOP 2009a). These statements included five communicative activities covered by the CEFR: listening, reading, spoken interaction, spoken production, and written production.[3] The first purpose of the study was to better understand the relationship between the test takers' language learning backgrounds (e.g., learning hours, teaching materials) and their CEFR levels including listening, reading, speaking, and writing skills. The second purpose was that we wanted to familiarize CSL teachers and learners in Taiwan with the CEFR can-do statements. The questionnaire was translated into 12 languages to ensure that all students would be able to read the statements easily. The students were divided into four groups according to the Mandarin courses they

---

[3]The speaking and writing tests had not yet been completed, but they were in the stage of pretest at that time.

were studying (i.e., their proficiency[4]). The first group received a Level 1 questionnaire that was composed of 68 statements targeting CEFR A1 and A2 levels. The second group received a Level 2 questionnaire that was composed of 97 statements targeting CEFR A2 and B1 levels. The third group received a Level 3 questionnaire that was composed of 72 statements targeting CEFR B1 and B2 levels. Finally, the fourth group received a Level 4 questionnaire that was composed of 40 statements targeting CEFR B2 and C1 levels. Statements that targeted the same CEFR level sometimes appeared in two questionnaires (e.g., the A2 statements in Level 1 and Level 2 questionnaires) so that they would serve as anchor items to be analyzed by the Item Response Theory (IRT) method.

IRT analysis showed that item difficulty levels of some statements did not necessarily follow the expectation in the ELP (Chang 2010). For example, the statement "I can say what I like and dislike" (Council of Europe 2004, p. 60), which was labeled in the ELP as belonging to the A2 level of spoken interaction, turned out to be much easier (difficulty value = −5.736) than a statement such as "I can indicate time by such phrases as 'next week', 'last Friday', 'in November', 'three o'clock'" (Council of Europe 2004, p. 76), which was labeled in the ELP as belonging to the A1 level (difficulty value = −2.012). Chang (2010) speculated that this result was caused by the large discrepancy between time expressions in Chinese and European languages. To express the specific time, Chinese uses prepositions like *zài* (在) "in" or determiners such as *shàng* (上) "last" and *xià* (下) "next," or localizers like *yǐqián* (以前) "before" or *yǐhòu* (以後) "after"—a complicated list of options for CSL learners. On the other hand, it is easier for learners to express "like" or "dislike" in Chinese by simply using these two verbs without worrying about tense and subject-verb agreement. The results of this questionnaire study were very useful in creating CSL course objectives. More importantly, we learned from this experience that the difficulty level of the ELP can-do statements would need to be empirically tested with CSL learners in Taiwan before they could be used for TOP item development.

The Results of Mapping: The Modified Version of TOP

The experience of mapping each TOP test item to the CEFR scale made the research team realize that the old version of TOP needed to change. The old version of TOP/CPT included many context-free vocabulary and grammar items. The sentence tasks in the reading and listening sections were context-free as shown in Table 2.1. These context-free items posed a difficulty when the research members tried to identify the communication activity that each item involved—a necessary

---

[4]If we had not divided the students into four groups, every student would have to answer all the statements, the number of which was huge. Our expert knowledge helped us predict which statements would be out of the range of the proficiency of a student; on this ground, grouping was made possbile.

Table 2.2 Content breakdown of the modified TOP listening and reading tests

Levels/format	Test of level 3 (B1)	Test of level 4 (B2)	Test of level 5 (C1)
Listening	Short conversation: Single-round (20) and multiple-round (15) Paragraph (15)	Short conversation (20) Long conversation (15) Paragraph (15)	Short conversation (10) Long conversation (20) Paragraph (20)
Reading	Cloze (20) Authentic material (15) Short essay (15)	Cloze (15) Authentic material (10) Short essay (25)	Cloze (15) Short essay (35)
Other	1. There are 100 test items in each level. All items are multiple-choice questions 2. The approximate test time is 110 min, with 50 min for the listening test and 60 min for the reading test		

Note The Arabic numerals in parentheses indicate the number of test items

step in mapping a test item to the CEFR (Council of Europe 2003; Figueras et al. 2005). It was decided that a new version of TOP would no longer have the vocabulary/grammar section. Instead, grammar, vocabulary, and reading are tested in the context of a cloze test, which is part of the new reading section. A communication theme can first be identified before a cloze passage is written to test grammar and vocabulary. Hung (2009) has studied the design of cloze tests for Chinese reading and suggested that the blanks can be designed based on Bachman's (1985) categorization: (1) within clause, (2) across clause within sentence, (3) across sentences within text, and (4) extratextual. Hung also suggested that the new TOP that corresponds to the CEFR B1 level would include items from categories (1) and (2), the B2 level would include items from categories (2) and (3), and the C1 level would include items from category (3). Her further study has verified the above suggestion (Hung 2013).

The single-sentence task is also removed from the new TOP listening section. The conversation task is expanded to include three item types: one-turn conversation, two-turn conversation, and longer conversation. These three item types provide more contexts to assist with the identification of CEFR communication activity. The content of the modified version (TOP) is presented in Table 2.2. The major difference between Tables 2.1 and 2.2 is the test items designed within broader language contexts instead of in a single sentence in the listening and reading tests.

Empirical Studies

After modifying the test, the research team began to conduct empirical studies to validate this modified version (i.e., new TOP). Chang's (2009) study is one of the first efforts. In her study, 55 CSL students at the Mandarin Training Center at NTNU took the listening section of the new TOP that was designed to correspond to the B1 level; and 56 students took the new B1 reading section. Simultaneously, 127 CSL students took the new B2 listening section and 126 students took the new

B2 reading section. The students who took the listening and reading sections at the same level were mostly the same people, but some students took only one section due to absence. These students' ability levels were also evaluated by 45 CSL teachers. The Spearman's rank correlation of the teachers' ratings and the students' performance on the B1 listening test was moderate (0.553). On the other hand, the correlation of the teachers' ratings and the students' performance on the B1 reading test was relatively low (0.296). The correlations of the teachers' ratings and the students' performance on the B2 listening and reading tests were also moderate and low, respectively (0.389 and 0.262). Thus, from the results of this study, it seemed that the B1 and B2 listening tests functioned a bit better than the reading tests, but both tests still required revision.

The results of K.C. Chang's study also informed the team that there are limitations when teachers' ratings are used to compare test results as teachers may not be able to evaluate the same constructs being tested by the new tests. In other words, unless classroom activities include the same tasks that are on the listening and reading tests, teachers may not be the best judge of the extent to which students can perform these tasks. In fact, in another study by a SC-TOP researcher that compared students' self-assessment with teachers' evaluation, Li (2009) found that students and teachers had many disagreements. For example, more than 40% disagreement was found in two descriptors: "Can understand the best part of a narrative passage or a well-structured contemporary literary text with a dictionary if need be" and "Can understand mail I receive well enough to be able to correspond regularly." Li speculated that this discrepancy resulted from the fact that some descriptors are hard for teachers to observe in class activities. Thus, although self-assessment and teachers' assessment are important data sources for a test validation project, they also have limitations. More training is needed for teachers to assess their students in terms of the CEFR.

Summary

To sum up, due to the need to map the test to the CEFR, we analyzed the TOP items using the CEFR framework and encountered several issues. In the process, we also realized that new test formats are needed to facilitate mapping. However, perhaps the most valuable gain for the research team in this whole experience is the chance to become familiar with the CEFR. Some scholars may question the idea of mapping the TOP to the CEFR because, after all, Chinese is not a European language and Taiwan is not a European country. A simple answer might be that a test development project funded by the government is part of a nation's language policy, which needs to be considered by test developers. On top of any consideration of that kind, the research team, however, also recognized the inherent importance of the work of mapping TOP to the CEFR, as we believed that it is important to have a common scale for CSL teaching and learning, and that it is useful for test users to be able to interpret different test results using the same scale.

On the other hand, we would like to argue that any effort to map tests to the CEFR will not be useful unless language teachers are well-informed about the CEFR itself. Without adequate knowledge of the CEFR, CSL teachers will not fully understand the test results or be able to use them in their teaching. The research team has conducted several workshops for CSL teachers familiarizing them with the CEFR, and over the years, it is clear to us that teachers appreciate the clarity of the ELP can-do statements and the CEFR domains of language use (Chou and Chang 2007). However, more efforts must be made to help teachers apply the CEFR and the test scores in their teaching.

Issues Related to the Listening and Reading Tests

Apart from the aforementioned issues of aligning the TOP test to the CEFR, over the years some other issues have been challenging to the development of the new TOP/TOCFL (thereafter, TOCFL). They include the training of test item writers, the research of word/grammar lists to help design the test items, the suggestion of learning hours for test takers, and the discrepancy in the use of Mandarin Chinese between mainland China and Taiwan. This section of the chapter will discuss each of these four issues.

Issue 1: Training of Test Item Writers

An important issue relating to the development of TOCFL involves the training of test item writers. In Taiwan, there are two types of Mandarin teachers: those who had training in CSL (referred to as "the L2 teachers") and those who were trained to teach Mandarin Chinese to native Chinese speakers at elementary, junior high, and senior high schools (referred to as "the L1 teachers"). At the beginning of the CPT project, it was thought that any Chinese teachers can be trained to write standardized proficiency test items. However, our experience showed that L1 teachers were not the best item writers for a CSL test due to their limited experience teaching Chinese to non-native speakers. The main problem was that they had less sense of how to create useful distracters in a multiple-choice item. Take a vocabulary question as an example:

他右手 _____ 著手錶。

Tā yòushǒu _____ *zhe shǒubiǎo.*

He right hand   wear   ASP watch.

"He wore a watch on his right hand."

Four possible options written by an experienced item writer would be (A) *dài* (帶) "bring," (B) *dài* (戴) "wear," (C) *chuān* (穿) "wear," and (D) *dài* (袋) "bag."

The correct answer is option (B), with options (A) and (D) serving as phonological distractions and option (C) serving as a semantic distraction (the word *chuān* (穿) "to wear" is used in Chinese when talking about clothes and shoes but the word *dài* (戴) "to wear" is used in Chinese when talking about hats and wristwatches). Native speakers of English might choose option (C), which would be an error caused by direct English-Chinese translation. This direct translation problem is well-known by CSL teachers, who could use this type of item as a diagnostic test. L1 teachers, on the other hand, were less intuitive about creating these distracters. This is why the research team decided to invite only CSL (L2) teachers to write items.

To qualify as a TOCFL item writer, a CSL teacher has to have at least two years of CSL teaching experience, be currently teaching CSL, and pass the item writing training. The first stage of training is a six-hour training course that familiarizes the CSL teachers with the test specifications. The teachers are then asked to write 10 items of a specific task type per week. These items are reviewed by the research team and an outside panel of experts. After a few weeks, qualified item writers are selected. To improve their item writing skills, after their items are used in a trial, the writers have meetings to discuss item qualities such as difficulty values, discrimination values, and distracter analysis results. The item writers then must revise their items for another round of trials.

While there are more things that we can do to improve item writers' training, we realize that the most challenging problem is not the training of item writers but how to keep a well-trained item writer to work for us on a long-term basis. The TOCFL project does not have adequate funding to hire full-time item writers. Our item writers are full-time CSL teachers who have their own teaching responsibilities while helping us part-time. Given the workload that the teachers face, the turn-around rate of our item writers is very high and we have to constantly train a new group of item writers. This is a real-world problem that the TOCFL project cannot avoid because of funding issues.

Issue 2: Word/Grammar List Used to Help Design the Items

The second issue also relates to item writing. To enable the TOCFL test item writers to distinguish different levels of test items, it is necessary to rank the difficulty levels of lexical and syntactic patterns in Mandarin. From August 2003 to July 2005, I conducted a two-year research project funded by Taiwan's National Science Council (NSC-92-2411-H-003-04; NSC-93-2411-H-003-066) to rank both the vocabulary and syntactic patterns of the Chinese language. The vocabulary pool was obtained from various sources, including the Academia Sinica Corpus (Chinese Knowledge and Information Processing Group [CKIP] 1998) that contains five million words, CSL textbooks often used by Taiwanese language centers and American colleges, and a vocabulary list constructed by the HSK office (Liu and Song 1992). The research team used the frequency information from the

CKIP (1998) and the weighting method to rank each word. Each word was tagged with its frequency and source (i.e., the corpus, the textbooks, or the HSK). If a word was listed in all three sources, it received greater weight. Chang and Chen (2006) reported the details of the procedures involved. Based on the frequency and the weight of the information, 1500 words with the highest weights were set for the basic level, an additional 3500 words were set for the intermediate level, and another 3000 words were set for the advanced learners (Chang and Chen 2006). These numbers are also listed in Table 2.1. The decisions on these numbers (1500; 5000; and 8000) were based on our surveys of the students' learning hours and teaching materials (Chang 2002). Cheng (1998) also suggested that knowledge of approximately 8000 words is needed to function in a Chinese academic setting.

With the development of the TOCFL, we need to reexamine this issue of the number of words needed to pass each test. Recently, Hanban (2010) suggested 600 words for a CEFR B1 proficiency level and 1200 words for a CEFR B2 level (see also Teng, this volume). On the other hand, the Fachverband Chinesisch e.V. (Association of Chinese Teachers in German Speaking Countries) (2010) has proposed a 2500-word threshold for the CEFR B1 proficiency level and a 5000-word threshold for the CEFR B2 level. The latest research was done by Chang (2012). It is a corpus-based study, and the results suggest the vocabulary size for A2 level is 1000; B1 level is 2300–3000; B2 level is 4500–5000; C level is 8000–10000.

Further research is needed to investigate whether the current setting of words will be adequate for students to pass the TOCFL tests that are linked to the CEFR.[5] One option is to recruit students who have completed the learning hours specified by the TOCFL. Those students' test performance as well as a survey of their learning hours and instruction materials will provide important information not only about the required number of words but also about the required minimum number of learning hours.

Issue 3: Suggestion of Learning Hours for Test Takers

The issue of a minimum number of learning hours required to pass each level of the TOCFL is an important one for test takers. From 2003 until the present, the number of test takers has increased gradually to more than 10,000 annually. So far, the test results can be used for various purposes. Foreign students wishing to study at Taiwanese universities can use the test results to apply for academic programs at Taiwanese universities either through the "Taiwan Scholarship (台灣獎學金)," a scholarship given by the Taiwanese government, or through their own funding

---

[5]The current setting of words is that A1 level is 500; A2 level is 1000; B1 level is 2500; B2 level is 5000; C1 level is 8000. The word lists can be retrieved freely from http://www.sc-top.org.tw/english/download.php (8000 Chinese words).

sources. Overseas students of the Chinese language can use the test results for University Entrance Committee for Overseas Chinese Students (海外聯招). The TOCFL certificates can also be used as a proof of Chinese language proficiency for employment.

As more students have the need to take the test, more and more language centers and teachers are aware of this test and are willing to use it to measure their students' abilities. To help students pass the TOCFL, some language centers have adjusted their curriculum design. When this occurs, CSL learners gradually become familiar with the relationship between performance on the TOCFL and their learning hours and learning materials. Chang and Chen (2008) analyzed the relationship between the results of the TOCFL and the learning hours that the students had taken at the Mandarin Training Center. They found that higher numbers of hours completed correlated positively with higher TOCFL scores. The students with around 360 h of learning can correctly answer 80% of the items in the TOCFL B1 level test; students with around 610 h can correctly answer 67% items in the B2 level test.

To check the relationship between the suggested learning hours and the pass rate, a chi-square test of association was conducted with survey data collected from TOCFL test takers during 2008–2009. Table 2.3 reports chi-square results of test takers from various Mandarin centers in Taiwan ($N = 3505$), and Table 2.4 reports the chi-square results of overseas test takers ($N = 1229$). Both showed that for all three levels, the pass rates of test takers whose learning hours were more than the hours suggested in Table 2.1 were significantly higher than for those whose learning hours were less than suggested. Table 2.3 shows that 47.4% of CSL learners in Taiwan who completed 360 learning hours passed the basic-level test while only 39.4% of learners who had not yet completed those hours passed the basic-level test. The percentages were 46.2% versus 38.8% at the intermediate level, and 67.9% versus 55.5% at the advanced level. For Chinese learners from overseas, the SC-TOP suggests that the minimum learning hours are doubled. Table 2.4 shows that 44.6% Chinese learners from overseas who had completed 720 learning hours passed the basic-level test while only 24.3% of learners who had not yet completed those hours passed the basic-level test. The percentages were 51.8% versus 37.1% at the intermediate level, and 84% versus 64.4% at the

Table 2.3 Learning hours versus pass rates for Chinese as a second language (2008–2009)

Suggested hours = 360, 480, 960	Basic (B1 level)		Intermediate (B2 level)		Advanced (C1 level)	
	N = 1321		N = 1492		N = 692	
	Failure	Pass	Failure	Pass	Failure	Pass
Less than suggested hours	341 (60.6%)	222 (39.4%)	296 (61.2%)	188 (38.8%)	133 (44.5%)	166 (55.5%)
More than suggested hours	399 (52.6%)	359 (47.4%)	542 (53.8%)	466 (46.2%)	126 (32.1%)	267 (67.9%)
χ^2	8.245**		7.248**		11.186**	

**p < 0.01

Table 2.4 Learning hours versus pass rates for Chinese as a foreign language (2008–2009)

Suggested hours = 720, 960, 1920	Basic (B1 level)		Intermediate (B2 level)		Advanced (C1 level)	
	N = 664		N = 274		N = 291	
	Failure	Pass	Failure	Pass	Failure	Pass
Less than suggested hours	321 (75.7%)	103 (24.3%)	78 (62.9%)	46 (37.1%)	99 (35.6%)	179 (64.4%)
More than suggested hours	448 (55.4%)	361 (44.6%)	289 (48.2%)	311 (51.8%)	77 (16.0%)	403 (84.0%)
χ^2	48.993**		8.928**		37.818**	

**$p < 0.01$

advanced level. These results provide supporting evidence for the suggested minimum learning hours presented in Table 2.1.

Despite the significant chi-square test results in Tables 2.3 and 2.4, a close look at the percentages indicates that less than 50% of the test takers who completed 360 h in Taiwan passed the TOP basic level, and less than 50% of the test takers who completed 480 h in Taiwan passed the TOP intermediate level. Similarly, less than 50% of the test takers from overseas who completed 720 h passed the TOP basic level. Chang (2011) further examined the suggested learning hours for learners of different L1s, including Japanese, Korean, and English. She found only the data of Japanese learners showed significance. Additionally, in Guder and Kupfer's (2005) report, the Association of Chinese Teachers in German Speaking Countries estimated that between 1200 and 1600 h of instruction (plus private study time) are required to attain oral and written proficiency in Chinese, which is comparable to CEFR level B2. Taken together, these findings suggest that the issue of suggested learning hours for test takers could be complex, and depends on individual differences, especially learners' native language background.

Issue 4: Mainland China Versus Taiwan's Use of Chinese

Another issue that the tests have to deal with is the discrepancy in the use of Mandarin Chinese between mainland China and Taiwan, which occurred due to the political separation in 1949. This discrepancy in language use has created several problems for language learning and testing alike (also see Shang and Zhao, this volume). The first problem is the fact that some high-frequency words have a variety of forms across the straits. For example, a taxicab is called *jìchéngchē* (計程車) (literal translation "mileage counting car") in Taiwan but *chūzūchē* (出租車) (literal translation "rental car") in China. A taxi driver is referred to as *sījī xiānshēng* (司機先生) (literal translation "Mr. Driver") in Taiwan but *shīfù* (師傅) (literal translation "master") in China. Computer software and hardware are called *ruǎntǐ/yìngtǐ* (軟體/硬體) (literal translation "soft/hard body") in Taiwan but they are called *ruǎnjiàn/yìngjiàn* (軟件/硬件) (literal translation "soft/hard device") in China. The list goes on. While this discrepancy may not cause problems for test takers who are above the intermediate proficiency level, who can guess the meaning of a word from its context, or for CSL learners in Taiwan, it often causes difficulties for basic-level overseas learners of Chinese because they may use textbooks published by mainland Chinese publishers. In most cases, the TOCFL uses words that are common in Taiwan. However, we also do our best to avoid idiosyncratic words that are used only in Taiwan. For example, we do not use the word *jiéyùn* (捷運) to refer to subway train even though this word is commonly used in Taiwan. Instead, we use the word *dìtiě* (地鐵), which is more commonly used in the Chinese-speaking world outside of Taiwan.

Another difference between mainland China and Taiwan lies in the use of Chinese characters. These days, learners may be exposed to either simplified characters used in mainland China or traditional characters used in Taiwan. The current strategy employed by SC-TOP is that when administering the TOCFL outside of Taiwan, test takers are allowed to choose either the simplified or traditional version of the test. However, this strategy is a post hoc method to deal with this practical issue and not a part of the initial test development plan. Therefore, it is essential to the SC-TOP to ensure that the different character versions are similar in difficulty. Using IRT, the team analyzed the difficulty of all items in the same advanced level for traditional and simplified character versions of the test that had been taken by more than 200 candidates and found a similar level of difficulty (see Fig. 2.1) (SC-TOP 2009b).

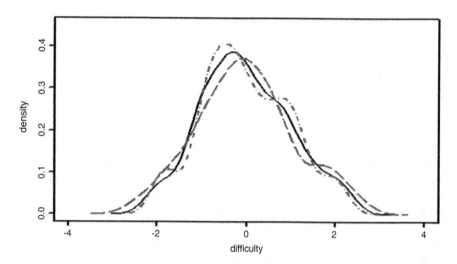

Fig. 2.1 Distribution of item difficulty in the reading section (67 items). *Note* ———— indicates the difficulty for all the testees, – - – indicates the difficulty of the traditional version for the testees, —— indicates the difficulty of the simplified version for the testees

To sum up, all the issues raised in this section are related to the development of a standardized CSL/CFL test that the research team has faced over the years. Further studies are needed to explore issues such as the analysis of item difficulty for traditional and simplified character versions in each TOCFL level, the suggested learning hours for test takers of different L1 backgrounds, and the training and maintaining of item writers.

Concluding Remarks

The previous sections of this chapter described the motivation for creating the listening and reading tests of the then Chinese Proficiency Test (CPT) in 2001 and provided a brief overview of the historical development of the TOCFL and its predecessors (i.e., CPT and TOP). They also discussed SC-TOP's alignment of the TOP/TOCFL to the CEFR and some issues that the team faced in that effort. A few research studies conducted by SC-TOP researchers were also reviewed. In addition, these sections also highlighted four issues that the research team had faced over the years in its effort to develop and maintain a standardized test of CSL/CFL. In what follows, I present a brief account of the most recent development of the test. It is beyond the scope of this chapter to provide details of validity and reliability evidence of the four components of the TOCFL (i.e., listening, reading, speaking, and writing). Interested readers can refer to SC-TOP's technical reports (2014a, b, c, d).

From 2011 to Present

Since 2011, the SC-TOP has paid much attention to research on test validity and reliability, mainly including setting the passing grade for the new test and standard setting research of TOCFL in corresponding relationship with CEFR and ACTFL proficiency guidelines. The new version of TOCFL became available in 2013. In terms of task types, the old TOCFL and the new one are similar; the only difference is the scoring method. The new TOCFL results are presented in the form of scale scores instead of raw scores (the number of test items answered correctly). The scale score is more objective since it is not affected with the different item difficulties of each test. The new TOCFL has three proficiency bands: Band A, Band B, and Band C. Each of the bands has two levels. Therefore, there are a total of six levels: Levels 1–6. Test takers do not choose from the six levels, but only one of the three bands. In other words, two proficiency levels are distinguished in each band test to be taken by a test taker. The advantage of the new version is not only to simplify the administration of the test but also to save the quantity of test items in the item bank. Before 2013, each level of listening and reading test used 100 test items. After 2013, two levels use the same number of items. Furthermore, the SC-TOP is developing the computerized adaptive test (CAT), which can significantly enhance test efficiency and accuracy by automatically adapting item difficulty to examinees' ability levels. In the near future, the test will require fewer test items to arrive at equally accurate scores; and test takers also need not choose which level of test they should take. Lastly, to provide more useful information to test takers and widen the scope of the use of the test, SC-TOP also did a series of standard setting research during 2012–2014 in order to let test takers or school administrators know the relationship of a TOCFL proficiency level with that of CEFR and ACTFL (e.g., TOCFL level 3 equivalent to CEFR B1 and ACTFL intermediate-high level). More information about the research can be found on the SC-TOP Website (http://www.sc-top.org.tw/english/LS/test4.php).

Washback Effects of TOCFL and Future Directions

With the increasing number of test takers, positive impact on teaching and learning has been observed. Firstly, in order to help students pass the levels of the TOCFL, some language centers have adjusted their curriculum design and paid attention to learners' language performance, including abilities in practical writing. Second, the SC-TOP team has spent a lot of time conducting trial tests in language centers across Taiwan and overseas. During the process, learners gradually know how many hours they should take their Chinese lessons and what they can do with the Chinese language after they finish their formal study. A clear sense of learning and professional targets could make learners' CSL teaching and learning better targeted and more effective. Lastly, a lot of undergraduate and graduate programs in Taiwan adopt the TOCFL certificate as the evaluation of an applicant's Chinese proficiency and a requirement for admission.

Unlike its predecessors, the current TOCFL targets both CSL and CFL learners in a global context. To address the diverse backgrounds of learners in different places of the worlds, the TOCFL team has been cooperating with oversea universities and colleges, providing free tests to their students in order to collect and analyze the Chinese proficiency information of global learners and better support these learners in the future. Additionally, to accommodate the downward extension of CFL curriculums to young learners, a test named Children's Chinese Competency Certification (CCCC) for 7–12-year-old children was also developed by the SC-TOP and launched in 2009. How to best meet the needs of test takers from different backgrounds or with different purposes of taking a test is certainly a challenging task that the SC-TOP needs to address continuously in the future. It is hoped that this chapter has achieved its purpose of informing the international language testing community on the development of the TOCFL and that the issues discussed in this chapter that have challenged the SC-TOP can shed light on CSL/CFL test development and research.

Acknowledgements Some research studies described in this chapter were funded by the Ministry of Education, Taiwan. The author would like to express sincere thanks to the colleagues who worked in the SC-TOP, especially Ling-ying Lin and Pei-jun Lan. The author is also greatly indebted to Dr. Shou-hsin Teng, who has guided her in this field over the years, and Dr. Viphavee Vongpumivitch, who assisted her in the writing of this article. The author would also like to thank anonymous reviewers who gave valuable suggestions that have helped to improve the quality of the manuscript. Of course, all remaining errors are my responsibility.

References

American Council on the Teaching of Foreign Languages [ACTFL]. (1987). ACTFL Chinese proficiency guidelines. *Foreign Language Annals, 20*(5), 471–487.

Bachman, L. F. (1985). Performance on cloze tests with fixed-ratio and rational deletions. *TESOL Quarterly, 19*(3), 535–556.

Chang, K. C. (2009, November). *Xīnbǎn huáyǔwén nénglì cèyàn xiàobiāo guānlián xiàodù yánjiù* [*The research of criterion-related validity of updated test of proficiency-Huayu*]. Paper presented in American Council on the Teaching of Foreign Languages (ACTFL) Annual Meeting, San Diego, CA.

Chang, L. P. (2002). *Huáyǔwén nénglì cèyàn lǐlùn yǔ shíwù* [*Theoretical and practical relevance of Chinese proficiency test*]. Taipei: Lucky Bookstore.

Chang, L. P. (2010, December). *Huáyǔwén nénglì zhǐbiāo nándù fēnxī* [*Scaling descriptors of Chinese proficiency*]. Paper presented in Annual Conference of the Association of Teaching Chinese as a Second Language, Fu-Jen Catholic University, Taiwan.

Chang, L. P. (2011, January). *Duìyìng yú Ouzhou gòngtóng jiàgòu de duì wài hànyǔ xuéshí jiànyì* [*Suggested CSL learning hours based on the CEFR scale*]. Paper presented at the First East Asian Forum for Graduate Students of Teaching Chinese as a Second Language. Taipei: National Taiwan Normal University.

Chang, L. P. (2012). Duìyìng yú Ouzhou gòngtóng jiàgòu de huáyǔ cíhuìliàng [The study of the vocabulary size at the CEFR levels for CFL/CSL learners]. *Journal of Chinese Language Learning, 9*(2), 77–96.

Chang, L. P., & Chen, F. Y. (2006). Huáyǔ cíhuì fēnjí chūtàn [*A preliminary approach to grading vocabulary of Chinese as a second language*]. In X. Su & H. Wang (Eds.), *Proceeding of 6th Chinese Lexical Semantics Workshop (CLSW-6)* (pp. 250–260). Singapore: COLIPS publications.

Chang, L. P., & Chen, F. Y. (2008, November). *Nénglì kǎoshì yǔ xuéxí zhījiān de guānxì* [*Relationship between proficiency test and learning*]. Paper presented in American Council on the Teaching of Foreign Languages (ACTFL) Annual Meeting, Florida.

Cheng, C. C. (1998). Cóng jìliáng lǐjiě yǔyán rènzhī [*Quantification for understanding language cognition*]. In B. K. T'sou, T. B. Y. Lai, S. W. K. Chan, & W. S.-Y. Wang (Eds.), *Quantitative and computational studies on the Chinese language* (pp. 15–30). Hong Kong: City University of Hong Kong.

Chinese Knowledge and Information Processing Group [CKIP]. (1998). *Accumulated word frequency in CKIP Corpus* (Tech. Rep. No. 98-01). Taipei: The Association for Computation Linguistics and Chinese Language Processing.

Chou, C. T., & Chang, L. P. (2007, October). *Huáyǔwén nénglì fēnjí zhǐbiāo zhī jiànlì* [*Proposal of a framework of Chinese language competence scale*]. Paper presented in the Forum for Educational Evaluation in East Asia: Emerging Issues and Challenges. NTNU, Taipei.

Council of Europe. (2001). *Common European framework of reference for languages: Learning, teaching, assessment.* Cambridge: Cambridge University Press.

Council of Europe. (2003). *Relating language examinations to the common European framework of reference for languages: Learning, teaching, assessment (CEF). Manual: Preliminary pilot version.* DGIV/EDU/LANG 2003, 5. Strasbourg: Language Policy Division.

Council of Europe. (2004). *A bank of descriptors for self-assessment in European language portfolios.* Strasbourg: Language Policy Division. Retrieved August 1, 2010 from http://www.coe.int/T/DG4/Portfolio/documents/descripteurs.doc

De Jong, H. A. L. (1990). Response to masters: Linguistic theory and psychometric models. In H. A. L. De Jong & D. K. Stevenson (Eds.), *Individualising the assessment of language abilities* (pp. 71–82). Cleveland: Multilingual Matters.

Fachverband Chinesisch e. V. (2010). *Statement of the Fachverband Chinesisch e. V. (Association of Chinese teachers in German speaking countries) on the new HSK Chinese proficiency test.* Retrieved August 1, 2010, from http://www.fachverband-chinesisch.de/fachverbandchinesischev/thesenpapiereundresolutionen/FaCh2010_ErklaerungHSK.pdf

Figueras, N., North, B., Takala, S., Verhest, N., & Avermaet, P. V. (2005). Relating examinations to the common European framework: A manual. *Language Testing, 22*(3), 261–279.

Gao, S. H., Chen, L. P., & Lan, P. J. (2007). *TOP yǔ CEFR chūbù duìyìng jiéguǒ* [*The preliminary study of relating TOP to CEFR*]. Unpublished manuscript. Taipei: SC-TOP.

Guder, A., & Kupfer, P. (2005). *Empfehlungen des Fachverbands Chinesisch e.V. zur Stellung der Fremdsprache Chinesisch in chinawissenschaftlichen Studiengängen* [*Suggestion of TCFL in Germany University from the Fachverbands Chinesisch e.V.*]. Retrieved August 1, 2010 from http://www.fachverband-chinesisch.de/fachverbandchinesischev/thesenpapiereundresolutionen/resolution%20erlangen%20zweisprachig.pdf

Hanban (Confucius Institute Headquarters). (2010). *HSK.* Retrieved March 15, 2010, from http://english.hanban.org/node_8002.htm#nod

Hung, X. W. (2009, November). *Duì wài hànyǔ cèyàn kèlòuzì (wánxíng cèyàn) wénběn fēnxī chūtàn* [*A study of cloze design for the TOP reading test*]. Paper presented in American Council on the Teaching of Foreign Languages (ACTFL) Annual Meeting, San Diego, CA.

Hung, X. W. (2013, March). *Yǐngxiǎng duì wài hànyǔ yuèdú cèyàn nándù de yīnsù* [*The factors of item difficulty in TOCFL reading test*]. Paper presented in CLTAC Spring Conference, Stanford University, CA.

Ko, H. W., & Chang, Y. W. (1996). *Huáyǔwén nénglì cèyàn biānzhì yánjiù II* [*Research of Chinese Proficiency Testing II*]. National Science Council Research Report (NSC85-2413-H194-005).

Ko, H. W., Li, J. R., & Chang, Y. W. (1995). *Huáyǔwén nénglì cèyàn biānzhì: yǔfǎ shìtí nándù cèshì* [*Research of Chinese proficiency testing: Difficulty of grammatical items*]. National Science Council Research Report (NSC83-0301-H194-050).

Ko, H. W., Li, J. R., & Chang, Y. W. (1997). Huáyǔwén nénglì cèshìtí de biānzhì yánjiù [Research of Chinese proficiency testing]. *World Chinese Language, 85,* 7–13.

Li, C. C. (2009, December). *Cóng yuèdú píngliáng tàntǎo duì wài huáyǔ kèchéng guīhuà* [*An investigation of learners' self-assessment in reading Chinese as a second language*]. Paper presented in Annual Conference of the Association of Teaching Chinese as a Second Language, Miaoli, Taiwan.

Liskin-Gasparro, J. E. (2003). The ACTFL proficiency guidelines and the oral proficiency interview: A brief history and analysis of their survival. *Foreign Language Annals, 36*(4), 483–490.

Liu, L.-L. (Ed.). (1997). *Hànyǔ shuǐpíng cèshì yánjiù* [*The research of Chinese proficiency test*]. Beijing: Beijing Language Institute Press.

Liu, Y. L., & Song, S. Z. (1992). Lùn hànyǔ jiāoxué zìcí de tǒngjì yǔ fēnjí [Calculating and ranking of Chinese Characters and words]. In The Office of Chinese Language Council (Ed.), *Hanyu Shuiping Cihui yu Hanzi Dengji Dagang* (pp. 1–25). Beijing: Beijing Language College Press.

Steering Committee for the Test of Proficiency—Huayu [SC-TOP]. (2009a, January). *2008 TOP Annual Report.* Taipei: SC-TOP.

SC-TOP. (2009b, October). *Monthly meeting handout.* Taipei: SC-TOP.

SC-TOP. (2014a). *Technical Report of TOCFL 2012 (1): Reliability and Validity of the Listening Test*. Linkou: SC-TOP.

SC-TOP. (2014b). *Technical Report of TOCFL 2012 (2): Reliability and Validity of the Reading Test*. Linkou: SC-TOP.

SC-TOP. (2014c). *Technical Report of TOCFL 2012 (3): Reliability and Validity of the Speaking Test*. Linkou: SC-TOP.

SC-TOP. (2014d). *Technical Report of TOCFL 2012 (4): Reliability and Validity of the Writing Test*. Linkou: SC-TOP.

Tewksbury, M. G. (1948). *Speak Chinese*. New Haven, CT: Far Eastern Publications, Yale University.

The College Board. (n.d.). *Scholastic Aptitude Test-Chinese*. Retrieved September 30, 2009, from http://www.collegeboard.com/student/testing/sat/lc_two/chinese/chinese.html?chinese

The Society for Testing Chinese Proficiency, Japan. (n.d.). *Zhōngguóyǔ Jiǎndìng Shìyàn* [*Chinese Proficiency Test*]. Retrieved September 30, 2009, from http://www.chuken.gr.jp/

Weir, C. J. (2005). Limitations of the Common European framework for developing comparable examinations and tests. *Language Testing, 22*(3), 281–300.

Chapter 3
Assessing Chinese in the USA: An Overview of Major Tests

Yan Liu

Abstract The past few decades have witnessed a rapid expansion of Chinese language and culture programs in higher education institutions as well as PreK-12 schools in the USA. The fast growth of Chinese education has naturally boosted assessment demands. To satisfy the demands, many tests and assessment tools have been developed in the country. Contextualized in the recent history of foreign language education in the USA, this chapter provides an overview of Chinese assessments in the country. Major tests reviewed include the ACTFL Oral Proficiency Interview (OPI) and its computerized version (OPIc), the Simulated Oral Proficiency Interview (SOPI), the Computerized Oral Proficiency Instrument (COPI), the ACTFL Writing Proficiency Test (WPT), the Advanced Placement (AP) Chinese Language and Culture Test, the ACTFL Assessment of Performance toward Proficiency in Languages (AAPPL), the SAT II Chinese Subject Test, and the Chinese Proficiency Test (CPT). In addition, this chapter also reviews a small number of studies that either aimed to validate these tests or used them as instruments for various research purposes.

Keywords Chinese · Proficiency test · Performance test · Standardized test

Introduction

The education of Chinese as a foreign language (CFL) has been growing rapidly in the USA since the early twenty-first century (Wang & Ruan 2016). According to the most recent survey on college enrollments in languages other than English, Chinese enrollments in American institutions of higher education were 61,055 students in 2013. This number has more than tripled compared with 19,427 in 1990 (Goldberg et al. 2015). In addition to colleges, Chinese was also offered at 3% of

Y. Liu (✉)
Duke University, Durham, NC, USA
e-mail: yan.l@duke.edu

© Springer Nature Singapore Pte Ltd. 2017   43
D. Zhang and C.-H. Lin (eds.), *Chinese as a Second Language Assessment,*
Chinese Language Learning Sciences, DOI 10.1007/978-981-10-4089-4_3

elementary schools and 4% of secondary schools (both public and private) in 2008, which rose from 0.3 and 1%, respectively, in 1997 (Center for Applied Linguistics 2008). The growing popularity of Chinese education in the USA has greatly increased the demands for assessments. While the (new) HSK, a standardized Chinese proficiency test developed by China's Hanban or Office of Chinese Language Council International, has been actively promoted in the USA (see Teng, this volume), many tests and assessment tools have also been developed in the country.

This chapter provides an overview of the development of Chinese language assessment in the USA by first reviewing some major tests and then a small number of studies that aimed to validate these tests or used these tests for different research purposes. Due to space constraints, only a selected number of major or well-known tests are reviewed. Interested readers are referred to the Foreign Language Assessment Directory (http://webapp.cal.org/FLAD/) developed by the Center for Applied Linguistics (CAL) for a detailed list of tests that assess foreign languages—many include Chinese—in the USA. In what follows, we first review some proficiency tests developed on the basis of ACTFL (American Council on the Teaching of Foreign Languages) Proficiency Guidelines (ACTFL 2012a), such as the Oral Proficiency Interview (OPI), the Oral Proficiency Interview-Computer (OPIc), the Simulated Oral Proficiency Interview (SOPI), the Computerized Oral Proficiency Instrument (COPI), and the Writing Proficiency Test (WPI). We then review two additional tests developed on the basis of the World-Readiness Standards for Learning Languages (National Standards Collaborative Board 2015) or its predecessor the National Standards for Foreign Language Learning in the 21st Century (National Standards in Foreign Language Education Project [henceforth National Standards] 1996, 1999, 2006). They include Advanced Placement (AP) Chinese Language and Culture Test and ACTFL Assessment of Performance toward Proficiency in Languages (AAPPL). For each test, its background is introduced first followed by assessment criteria, test structure and content, test administration, and rating scheme. Finally, two standardized tests are also reviewed, including the SAT II Chinese with Listening Subject Test and the Chinese Proficiency Test (CPT).

An Overview of Major Tests in Chinese

Foreign language education in the USA has experienced many curricular changes in history due to economic and political pressures (Kramsch 1989). For example, the 1979 President's Commission on Foreign Language and International Studies Report first recorded the lack of foreign language proficiency among Americans and called for a reform in foreign language education (Perkins 1979). The concept of language proficiency has been expanded to include not only linguistic but also functional, cultural, and esthetic competences (Kramsch 1989). Moreover, teaching methodologies moved from the audio-lingual method toward a communicative approach during the 1970s and 1980s. In this approach, competence in a foreign language is defined as the learner's ability to communicate in the target language in real situations (Canale & Swain 1980; Savignon 1972). As a result, foreign language curriculum started to focus on learners' communicative proficiency in a language.

Along with this curricular change, language standards and guidelines were also introduced to guide classroom instruction and assessment practices, such as the ACTFL Proficiency Guidelines (ACTFL 1986, 1999, 2012a), the National Standards for Foreign Language Learning in the 21st Century (National Standards 1996, 1999, 2006), World-Readiness Standards for Learning Languages (National Standards Collaborative Board 2015), and the ACTFL Performance Descriptors for Language Learner (ACTFL 2012b). Based on these guidelines and standards, a number of tests have been developed to assess proficiency in a variety of languages, including Mandarin Chinese.

Proficiency Tests Developed on the Basis of ACTFL Proficiency Guidelines

Driven by the aforementioned proficiency movement that stressed real-world communication in foreign language education in the 1970s and 1980s, ACTFL developed proficiency guidelines in listening, speaking, reading, and writing. The ACTFL Proficiency Guidelines (hereafter, The Guidelines) were first published in 1986, and subsequent revisions were made in 1999 and 2012. Language-specific guidelines were also developed in a variety of less commonly taught languages, including Mandarin Chinese (ACTFL 1987).

The guidelines (ACTFL 2012a) describe what individuals can do with a language in terms of speaking, writing, listening, and reading in a spontaneous context. Proficiency is presented as a hierarchical continuum that consists of four or five ranges of proficiency levels (novice, intermediate, advanced, and superior in speaking and writing, but one more level of distinguished in reading and listening) and each higher level subsumes all lower levels. The major levels of advanced, intermediate, and novice are further divided into three sublevels: high, mid, and low.[1] Since they were first released in the 1980s, the guidelines have been widely used in the field of foreign language education in the USA not only for assessment development but also for teacher training, curriculum development, and instructional planning (Liskin-Gasparro 2003). In terms of assessment development, the guidelines have been used as the theoretical backdrop for a number of widely known and used tests, such as the ACTFL Oral Proficiency Interview (OPI), the

---

[1]Descriptions of each level and sublevel for each skill are available with samples in both simplified and traditional Chinese characters on ACTFL's website (http://www.actfl.org/publications/guidelines-and-manuals/actfl-proficiency-guidelines-2012/chinese).

ACTFL Oral Proficiency Interview Computer Test (OPIc), the Stimulated Oral Proficiency Interview (SOPI), the Computerized Oral Instrument (COPI), and the ACTFL Writing Proficiency Test (WPT).

The ACTFL Oral Proficiency Interview (OPI)

Since it was first developed in the late 1980s, the OPI has been widely used to assess a learner's oral proficiency in foreign language education in the USA. In the context of the OPI, proficiency is defined as the ability "to use language to communicate meaningful information in a spontaneous interaction, and in a manner acceptable and appropriate to native speakers of the language" (Swender & Vicars 2012, p. 1). There are four assessment criteria that underlie the OPI (ACTFL 2012a): the function performed in the language (i.e., what a speaker can do with the language, such as asking and answering questions, describing and narrating, supporting opinions); the contexts and content areas in which the language can be used (i.e., circumstances in which tasks are performed and topics that relate to these contexts); the accuracy/comprehensibility of the speaker's language performance in the tasks relevant to the contexts and content areas assessed; and the text types (i.e., discrete words, sentences, paragraphs, or extended discourses) that the speaker produced.

The OPI is a face-to-face interview or a phone interview between a certified tester and an examinee. It lasts for 10–30 min depending on the examinee's oral proficiency. The interview consists of four phases: warm-up, level checks, probes, and wind-down. During the interview, the tester formulates questions based on the examinee's previous responses, which is like a spontaneous conversation in real life. In addition, the tester adapts the difficulty to the examinee's proficiency level and considers the examinee's interests or experiences when formulating questions.

In the phase of warm-up, the tester asks some general questions about the examinee to establish rapport with the examinee and has a preliminary evaluation of his/her oral proficiency level. Then in the phase of level checks, the tester elicits the examinee's responses with more questions to determine whether the examinee can function at a given ACTFL oral proficiency level. In the phase of probes, the tester needs to find out whether the examinee performs sustainably well to meet the requirements of the next higher proficiency level. A role-play may also be used to elicit the examinee's oral performance outside of the context of an interview. When the tester is confident that she or he has enough oral responses to determine the examinee's proficiency level, she or he will conclude the interview with a wind-down to ease the examinee out of the test by returning to a level of conversation that the examinee is comfortable to handle. After the test, the tester and another certified tester will rate the speech sample produced by the examinee based on the ACTFL Proficiency Guidelines-Speaking (ACTFL 2012a). Once the two raters' ratings agree exactly, an official OPI rating will be awarded to the examinee.

The OPI aims to assess an examinee's oral proficiency through a natural conversation with the tester. However, the quality of the interview heavily depends on the tester's skills in formulating level-appropriate questions and quick but accurate judgments about the examinee's oral proficiency during the interview. Even though each OPI will be double rated by two certified raters, there is still criticism about inter-rater reliability and the test's consistency across raters (Malone 2003). Thus, ACTFL has a lot of requirements for OPI tester certification.[2]

The ACTFL Oral Proficiency Interview-Computer (OPIc)

In response to the demand of large-scale oral proficiency testing, ACTFL also developed a computer-delivered version of the OPI or the Oral Proficiency Interview-computer (OPIc) in 2007. Currently the OPIc is available in Mandarin Chinese and 12 other languages.

The OPIc starts with a background survey and a self-assessment. From the background survey, a pool of topics will be determined and then the computer will randomly select topics and generate different types of questions. The self-assessment provides an examinee with six different descriptions of oral proficiency levels and asks the examinee to select which description best describes how he/she can speak a language. The answer then determines which of the four OPIc test forms will be used. Each test form targets a certain range of proficiency levels. For example, Form 1 targets proficiency levels of novice low through novice high. In this way, each examinee can have an adaptive and unique test.

When the OPIc begins, a female avatar figure appears on the screen and delivers questions to the examinee. Like the OPI, the OPIc also includes four components: warm-up, level checks, probes, and wind-down. After the interview is done, the examinee's speech sample will be automatically saved and uploaded to a place online where certified OPIc raters can access it anytime and anywhere. Then, two certified raters will rate the speech sample following the same rating procedure and rating standards to those of OPI.

Compared with the OPI, the OPIc is more flexible in terms of test time and location. Test-takers can take it whenever and wherever there is a computer with a Web browser connected to the Internet. Their responses can be automatically saved on the computer, and test raters can access them at anytime and anywhere. However, as an Internet-delivered test, OPIc has some limitations, such as the technical requirement of fast and stable Internet connection. If a test-taker takes this test in a place where the Internet connection is neither stable nor fast, he/she will likely experience difficulties in logging into the test system or opening a web page. He/she may even need to start the test all over again if a web page freezes and the test cannot proceed to the next question. In this case, the test-taker is likely to feel

---

[2]Detailed information about tester certification can be found on ACTFL's website (http://www. actfl.org/professional-development/training-certification/how-become-certified-tester).

frustrated and his/her test performances will possibly be affected. The author proctors OPIc to a number of students each year, and there were a few cases in which students needed to retake the test because of technical difficulties. For example, one student was so frustrated that she quit the test halfway as a result of unstable Internet connection; another student retook the test because his voice was low and his answers could not be recorded appropriately on the computer. In addition, even though talking to a computer may be less intimidating to a test-taker, it is not as natural as talking to a person as in the case of the OPI. Thus, a test-taker's performance in the OPIc may not reflect his/her competence in real-life communications.

Which test do students prefer, the OPI or the OPIc? Thompson et al.'s (2016) study showed that the majority of their Spanish learning informants (about 71%) preferred the OPI to the OPIc for the following major reasons. Firstly, speaking with a live person in the OPI made them feel more natural than speaking with a computer as in the case of the OPIc. Secondly, the students felt comfortable and beneficial because they could get immediate feedback from the interviewer in the OPI. Thirdly, some students thought that the topics provided by the OPI were more interesting than those by the OPIc. Finally, the students felt that the human interviewer allowed them to finish their responses instead of cutting off their responses. On the other hand, about 21% of the students expressed their preference for the OPIc because they were less anxious when speaking with a computer than talking to a real person. Another reason was that they could let the computer repeat the questions as many times as they wanted without worrying about being judged. Lastly, these students felt that the OPIc gave them more freedom to express themselves. The reason for the test preference difference, according to the authors, is the setting in which the students acquired their second language. Many of the participants in this study had 18–24 months of study abroad experience in a foreign country or extensive immersion experiences in the USA. Consequently, a large majority of them felt more comfortable speaking with a live person. Thompson et al. (2016) also compared the students' OPI and OPIc performances in Spanish and found that more than half of the students (about 54.5%) received the same ratings on both tests, but 31.8% of students had higher ratings on the OPIc and 13.6% of students scored higher on the OPI. It can be seen that the majority of students tended to receive the same or higher ratings on the OPIc even though they preferred the OPI.

No similar studies have been conducted on Chinese OPI and OPIc, so it is not yet known which one test-takers of Chinese would prefer and whether they would be rated similar or higher on the OPIc. However, a speculation based on the author's own experiences of administering the OPI and personal communications with other certified OPI testers is that OPI and OPIc in Chinese may have some negative wash-back effect on speaking instruction, especially with respect to the instruction of pronunciation at the novice and the intermediate levels. One reason for this concern is that test-taker's speech samples are evaluated by the standard whether they are understandable to sympathetic interlocutors "who are accustomed to dealing with non-native learners of the language" based on the descriptions for those levels in the ACTFL Speaking Proficiency Guidelines (ACTFL 2012a, p. 7). As a result, students may not pay much attention to their pronunciation accuracy, such as tones. This would be a problem for learners of Chinese, especially beginning-level English-speaking learners in the USA, because Chinese is a tonal language and the accuracy of tones is very important in Chinese oral communication. This issue certainly warrants attention from Chinese OPI/OPIc raters and research in the future.

The Stimulated Oral Proficiency Interview (SOPI)

As introduced above, a successful OPI requires skilled and well-trained interviewers. Due to the limited resources (especially trained interviewers) available, it is hard to do a face-to-face OPI in less-commonly taught languages (Malabonga et al. 2005). Therefore, the Center for Applied Linguistics (CAL) followed the general structure of the ACTFL OPI and developed the first Simulated Oral Proficiency Interview (SOPI) for Mandarin Chinese (Clark & Li 1986).

The SOPI has the same four phases of the OPI: warm-up, level checks, probes, and wind-down. However, instead of a live interviewer, the SOPI uses a test tape of recorded instructions and a test booklet of tasks to elicit speech samples. In addition, each test-taker has a response tape to record his or her responses. Each task has English instructions with information about the context and the situation of the task, the person the examinee is talking to, the purpose of the task, and other relevant information. Before performing the task, the examinee will also hear a prompt (a statement or a question). A typical full length of the SOPI has 15 tasks and lasts about 45 min, while a typical short form has 7 tasks and lasts about 25 min. For each task, an examinee has 15–45 s to think and 1 min and 45 s to respond. The amount of time given depends on the complexity of the task.

Different from the OPI that must be administered individually to an examinee by a trained interviewer, a SOPI can be administered by anyone to a group in a language laboratory or to an examinee individually with a two-tape recorder. A master tape plays the instructions of tasks and a blank tape records the examinee's responses. Another difference is that the SOPI is not as personalized as the OPI because the former treats all test-takers equally and cannot adapt the difficulty level as the latter does. The conversation topics in the OPI are based on the examinee's experience while the SOPI has set topics for all examinees. Moreover, the SOPI sets a time limit for test-takers to think and respond to each task, but the OPI does not. There are also differences between the OPI and the SOPI in test rating (Kuo & Jiang 1997). To be specific, an OPI tester constantly evaluates an examinee's proficiency throughout the whole interview and then gives a final rating. A SOPI rater assigns a rating for an examinee's response to each task independently and then determines a final rating based on all the individual ratings. All these differences will surely give test-takers different test experiences and will need to be considered when a decision is made on which test is to be used (Kuo & Jiang 1997).

The Computerized Oral Proficiency Instrument (COPI)

With the advancement of computer technology, researchers at CAL also investigated the feasibility of delivering the SOPI test via computer. The computerized format, the Computerized Oral Proficiency Instrument (COPI), is now available in Mandarin Chinese and a few other languages. It has a pool of 100 tasks adapted from those used in the SOPIs. The whole test lasts about 30–50 min, depending on the level of tasks a test-taker chooses.

A COPI test begins with a welcome message and a brief introduction of the test. Then, test-takers need to input their personal information and self-evaluate their oral proficiencies. Based on the self-assessment, the computer will suggest a starting level and give a sample task at that level for test-takers to practice. The appropriate response to the sample task is also available for test-takers to check. If they think that the suggested starting level is not appropriate, they may choose one more sample task at either one level higher or one level lower to practice. Then the actual test begins and test-takers need to respond to the given tasks at the level they chose. After completing all the tasks, test-takers will see some feedback on the levels of tasks they chose and then they can choose to end the test.

Compared with the SOPI, the COPI has a larger pool of tasks, which gives examinees more task selection choices. In addition, the COPI has no time limits for examinees to think about or respond to a task, which gives them more control of the test. It also has a self-assessment to help examinees select tasks at appropriate difficult levels. According to Malabonga et al. (2005), the majority of examinees (92%) were able to do so. Lastly, the COPI is also more convenient than the SOPI in terms of rating. In a SOPI test, responses are recorded in a tape and raters need to rewind or fast-forward to find the segment they would like to listen to. Speech samples of the COPI, such as the OPIc, however, can be saved in a designated place online, which enables the raters to access them anytime and anywhere. Raters can listen to the task responses in any order, in part or as a whole. They may also listen to any segment of the responses for as many times as they want.

Kenyon and Malabonga (2001) compared examinees' attitudes toward the COPI, the SOPI, as well as the OPI. Among the 55 participants, 16 students participated in the Chinese study, 15 in the Arabic study, and 24 in the Spanish study. All the participants took both SOPI and COPI, but the participants in the Spanish study also took a face-to-face OPI. After taking each test, the participants were given two questionnaires about their attitudes toward each test. Results showed that the students had positive attitudes toward both the SOPI and the COPI in general. However, when they were asked to compare which test was better, most students chose the COPI because they thought it was less difficult, had fairer questions and situations, had clearer instructions, made them feel less nervous, and could better reflect their strengths, weakness, and abilities in speaking the target language. Another interesting finding was that the Spanish students rated the SOPI, the COPI, and the OPI similarly, but considered the OPI as a better measurement of real-life speaking skills. This finding echoed Thompson et al. (2016), in which students indicated a preference of the OPI to the OPIc. As Norris (2001) noted, even though computerized oral proficiency assessments offer a lot of advantages, it is worth-while to investigate whether these assessments can capture the important features and the complexity of individual or interactive speaking performances that enable us to know learners' knowledge and abilities.

The ACTFL Writing Proficiency Test (WPT)

The ACTFL WPT assesses how well a person can write without help. This test is available in both a paper-and-pencil format and a computerized format, and both formats are available in Chinese. Rated on the ACTFL Proficiency Guidelines 2012 —Writing (ACTFL 2012a), the WPT begins with an introduction of the test fol-lowed by a warm-up activity at the novice level (about 10 min). After the warm-up, there are four separate prompts for a variety of writing tasks (about 80 min in total). The prompts elicit responses dealing with practical, social, and professional topics that are encountered in informal and formal contexts. Each prompt requires multiple writing tasks, such as descriptive, informative, narrative, and persuasive writing. Each prompt provides the writer with information about the audience, the context, and the purpose of the prompt. Through these prompts, WPT raters can obtain enough writing responses to assess the writer's writing proficiency levels across different contexts and content areas. Each prompt also suggests the length of the response and a time allotment for completing the response. Tasks and prompts are written in English but the responses need to be written in the target language.

The paper-pencil WPT requires test-takers to handwrite their responses. In the Chinese case, they may choose to write in either simplified or traditional Chinese characters. However, a mixture of the two forms is not acceptable. The comput-erized WPT requires test-takers to complete a background survey and a self-assessment at the beginning with the same aims as those in the OPIc. In addition, there is a warm-up grid for test-takers to familiarize themselves with the keyboard options: virtual keypad, language-specific virtual keyboard, and local computer keyboard. After a test-taker finishes the warm-up, the actual test starts and he/she cannot change the selected keyboard. The rating procedure is the same as that of the OPIc.

Two issues need to be attended to for the WPT or any other writing tests in Chinese due to its unique writing system. Unlike English, Chinese uses characters instead of the alphabet in writing. Each character is made up of strokes, which are the smallest building materials for written Chinese. The average stroke number of 2000 commonly used characters is 9.0 for their simplified forms and 11.2 for traditional forms (Chan 1982). In the USA, depending on the Chinese program, a student learns either the simplified or the traditional form. The first issue, which concerns the paper-pencil formatted WPT, is that test-takers are required to hand write their responses to the four prompts for a variety of tasks within 80 min. Therefore, how fast and how well one can write characters, which may be impacted by the form of Chinese characters she or he uses, may affect her or his ratings in the WPT.

Discarding the paper format and adopting only the computerized format does not seem to resolve the issue, as character writing is an important part of Chinese learning. ACTFL Proficiency Guidelines-Writing (ACTFL 2012a) actually include character writing as a criterion to describe writers at the novice level [i.e., "They can transcribe familiar words or phrases, copy letters of the alphabet or syllables of a syllabary, or reproduce basic characters with some accuracy" (p. 14)]. Thus, the second issue is that it would be hard to accurately assess writers' writing proficiency based on typed responses in the case of the computerized format; and computer-based assessment of writing may also result in a belief among students that handwriting is unimportant (i.e., negative wash-back effect). In addition, due to the large number of homophones in Chinese, test-takers, if using Pinyin- or Zhuyin Fuhao-based input methods, need to discriminate the orthographic forms of multiple characters and select the ones they need, which leads to a concern about low writing efficiency.

Proficiency Tests Developed on the Basis of National Standards

Foreign language assessment, including the assessment of the Chinese language, in the USA has also been influenced by the Standards for Foreign Language Learning: Preparing for the 21st Century (National Standards 1996, 1999, 2006) (hereafter, the Foreign Language Standards) and its successor, the World-Readiness Standards for Learning Languages (hereafter, the World-Readiness Standards) (National Standards Collaborative Board 2015). Based on these standards, two tests of Chinese were developed, including the Advanced Placement (AP) Chinese Language and Culture Test (hereafter, the AP Chinese Test) and the ACTFL Assessment of Performance toward Proficiency in Languages (AAPPL).

The Foreign Language Standards (National Standards 1996) were first developed for K-12 grades and described five goal areas that K-12 students should develop in a foreign language: Communication, Cultures, Connections, Comparisons, and Communities. These five goal areas were further divided into eleven standards.[3] For example, Communication is further divided into Interpersonal Communication, Interpretive Communication, and Presentational Communication. In alignment with these standards, communication skills thus are assessed in three modes: Interpersonal, Interpretive, and Presentational. The World-Readiness Standards (National Standards Collaborative Board 2015) retained the five goal areas and the eleven standards, but revised their descriptions and the performance indicators for learners at different proficiency levels.

---

[3]Detailed information about the five goal areas and the eleven standards can be found on ACTFL'S Website   (http://www.actfl.org/sites/default/files/pdfs/World-ReadinessStandardsforLearning Languages.pdf).

The AP Chinese Language and Culture Test (the AP Chinese Test)

AP courses are college-level courses offered by the Boards AP Program for high school students. After finishing an AP course, students need to take a test in May of each year. Such tests are called AP tests, which assess whether high school students can be placed into an advanced-level course in the given subject when they go to college. The grade scale for AP tests is 1–5 (from no recommendation to extremely well-qualified). If a student receives a grade of 5 (extremely well-qualified and equivalent to a grade of A in a college course), 4 (well-qualified and equivalent to grades of A−, B+, and B), or 3 (qualified and equivalent to grades of B−, C+, and C), he/she may get credit for lower level courses or be permitted to take an advanced course at college. Each higher education institution makes the decision based on its own criteria or policies, but many require a score of 4 or 5.

The current AP Chinese Test lasts for about 2 h and 15 min. It tests Chinese culture knowledge and three modes of communication skills (Interpersonal, Interpretive, and Presentational) in Mandarin Chinese. The examination is totally administered on computer. There are two sections in the examination, and each section has two parts. The first section consists of 70 multiple-choice questions that assess Interpersonal Listening and Interpretive Reading. The reading texts can be displayed in either traditional or simplified characters. The second section also has two parts: The first part tests Presentational Writing skills by asking examinees to narrate a story based on a series of pictures and Interpersonal Writing skills by a task that requires examinees to read and answer an email message. When typing responses in Chinese, examinees can choose the Microsoft *Pinyin* IME that is based on Hanyu Pinyin to type in either traditional or simplified characters. They can also choose the Microsoft *New Phonetic* IME that is based on Zhuyin Fuhao (Bopomofo) to type in traditional characters. The second part assesses Interpersonal Speaking by asking examinees to respond to a series of thematically linked questions as part of a simulated conversation. It also assesses Presentational Speaking skills by requiring examinees to make a presentation on a given aspect of Chinese culture. The results of the computer-scored multiple-choice questions will be combined with those of reader-scored free-response questions. Each of the four parts, listening, reading, writing, and speaking, equally contributes 25% of the final AP examination score. The weighted raw scores are summed into a composite score. Then, the composite score is converted to a score on AP's 5-point scale.

The first AP Chinese test was administered during the 2006–2007 academic year. Since then, this test has attracted an increasing number of high school students. Chen (2011) analyzed the number, demographics, and scores of AP Chinese test-takers from 2007 to 2010. Results showed that the total number of test-takers had increased by 96%, and the number of test-takers without any Chinese-speaking family background had grown 218% from 2007 to 2010. About 96.5% of the test-takers scored above 3 in 2010. More recently, according to the 10th annual AP report on score distribution of AP examinations (College Board 2014), there were 5684 examinees for the AP Chinese test and 94.6% of the test-takers scored above 3 in 2013. The number of test-takers rose from 1992 in 2008 to 5684 in 2013 and

90.8% of them were Asian/Asian American/Pacific Islander. No direct information was available about the detailed composition of high school students enrolled in AP Chinese courses. However, according to the table of 2015 AP examination score distributions,[4] 83% of AP Chinese students learned Chinese at home or abroad and only 17% of them learned it primarily in class, which seems to suggest that the majority of AP Chinese test-takers have Chinese family backgrounds.

The AP Chinese Test provides useful information about a test-taker's Chinese proficiency. Nevertheless, college and university instructors may still need to give a placement test of their own so as to place a student into an appropriate Chinese course. The listening and reading parts are assessed only with multiple-choice questions, which may enable students to get right answers by guessing. In addition, the writing part requires students to type instead of writing by hand, which leads to a similar concern, as in the case of the WPT, that it is hard to know how many characters a student can write and how well he/she can write by hand. To the author's knowledge, most Chinese programs in post-secondary institutions in the USA require students to write by hand for assignments and/or tests. A student's ability of writing characters by hand, therefore, is often an important consideration for deciding which level of course the student should be placed into. Another concern pertains to the student's ability in using Chinese to communicate in real-life situations. The speaking part of the AP Chinese test only requires test-takers to make a presentation on a given aspect of Chinese culture (i.e., presentational speaking skill), which does not provide much evidence on how well they can use Chinese to carry out real-life interactions (i.e., Interpersonal speaking skill).

The ACTFL Assessment of Performance Toward Proficiency in Languages (AAPPL)

The AAPPL, which is available in Mandarin Chinese and 7 other languages, is a new online performance-based assessment developed on the basis of the World-Readiness Standards (National Standards Collaborative Board 2015) and the ACTFL Performance Descriptors for Language Learners (hereafter, the Performance Descriptors) (ACTFL 2012b). The Performance Descriptors, which were first developed for K-12 language learners in 2008 and then expanded to K-16 learners in 2012, aim to reflect how well students can perform after receiving explicit language instruction at school, online, in hybrid environments, or through independent projects. They are organized according to three ranges of performances (novice, intermediate, and advanced), three modes of communication (Interpersonal, Interpretive, and Presentational) defined by the World Readiness Standards (National Standards Collaborative Board 2015), and three domains of

---

[4]Available at http://www.totalregistration.net/AP-Exam-Registration-Service/2015-AP-Exam-Score-Distributions.php.

performance (Function, Contexts and Content, and Text Type) defined in the ACTFL Proficiency Guidelines (ACTFL 2012a).

Developed mainly for students in 5th through 12th grades, the AAPPL uses a video to provide a setting that simulates a classroom, in which a teacher will guide students through their day by doing various tasks such as participating in a video chat with a native speaker, creating posters or wikis, emailing native speakers, and using apps to demonstrate their language ability. It assesses three modes of communication: Interpersonal, Interpretive, and Presentational. To be specific, it assesses Interpersonal Listening and Speaking (ILS), Interpretive Reading (IR), Interpretive Listening (IL), and Presentational Writing (PW). These four components can be tested together or separately.

Different from previously introduced assessments, the AAPPL measures students' language performance in a classroom setting that they are familiar with. The test has two forms: Form A and Form B. Form A includes six tasks targeting novice to intermediate levels in each mode of communication (3 for novice level and 3 for intermediate level), while Form B has six tasks assessing proficiency of intermediate to advance levels in each mode of communication (3 for intermediate and 3 for advanced level). Within the novice level, there are four sub-levels from N-1 to N-4, corresponding to novice low through novice high described in the ACTFL Proficiency Guidelines (ACTFL 2012a). Within the Intermediate level, there are five sub-levels from I-1 to I-5, corresponding to intermediate low through intermediate high. There is no sub-level for the advanced level.

For each component tested in the AAPPL, there is a separate score. In addition to a score, the AAPPL provides a detailed score description, which helps students understand what they can do and cannot do in terms of each task. Together with the score, the report also provides some suggestions that students can use to improve their performances in different modes of communication. For example, a student with a score of N-1 in interpersonal listening and speaking will get a score description like "Your AAPPL Interpersonal Listening/Speaking score of N-1 means that you can say a few things about yourself. You can list, name, and identify common things with single words. You can answer one or two of the basic kinds of questions that you have learned and practiced in class. You can do this in a way that your teachers and others who are used to language learners can understand some of what you are saying." The strategies that he/she gets are "when you answer questions, try to use more than one word and even a phrase. Practice asking questions and keep learning new words" (ACTFL 2015, p. 1). For more examples of score descriptions or more information about the AAPPL, please refer to the AAPPL Website (http://aappl.actfl.org).

Compared with the tests reviewed earlier, the AAPPL has several distinctive features. Firstly, it is specifically designed for learners in Grades 5–12. Secondly, it measures how well learners perform in a classroom setting that they are familiar with. Learners, especially young learners, will be put at ease. Meanwhile, the AAPPL Website provides an overview of the tasks and topics addressed in the test. This overview can help teachers plan their curriculum. Therefore, the AAPPL is likely to have positive wash-back effects on instruction due to its close connection between instruction and assessment. Thirdly, the four components of the test can be tested together, separately, or in any combinations. This gives learners great flexibility in test ordering. Finally, it provides a detailed score explanation that helps students understand what their scores mean in terms of what they can do with Chinese. It also provides students with suggestions about how to improve their performances in the future.

Nevertheless, as a newly developed test, the AAPPL needs to be validated. It should also be noted that learners' language proficiencies are assessed through role-plays in a simulated classroom setting, which may not accurately reflect what they can do in real-life situations. Another potential problem lies in test ordering. According to the introduction on the AAPPL's Website, students need to enter their grade levels, based on which they will be automatically assigned a test. To be more specific, students in Grade 6 or below will be assigned Form A (N-1 to I-4) while those in Grade 7 or above will be assigned Form B (N-4 to A). As a result, the automatically assigned AAPPL test may not be appropriate for those students who are in Grade 6 or lower grades but their proficiencies are higher than the criteria for I-4 or those students who are in Grade 7 or higher grades but their proficiencies are lower than the criteria for N-4. Lastly, as an Internet-delivered test, the AAPPL also has the same limitations that were discussed earlier on the OPIc and the COPI, such as the demand of a stable and high-speed Internet.

Standardized Proficiency Tests in Chinese

In addition to the assessments reviewed above, which are primarily performance-based, there are also some Chinese standardized tests in the USA that are based largely on multiple-choice questions. Two notable examples of this type of tests are the SAT II Chinese with Listening Subject Test (the SAT II Chinese Test hereafter) developed by the College Board and the Chinese Proficiency Test (CPT) developed by the Center for Applied Linguistics (CAL). As standardized tests, these tests are easy to be administered and scored. However, a limitation is also noted in that they focus on receptive skills (i.e., listening and reading) rather than productive skills (i.e., speaking and writing), which suggests that students' oral or written responses to real-world communication problems cannot be elicited and assessed.

The SAT II Chinese with Listening Subject Test

SAT scores are a widely used standard for college admission and college course replacement or selection in the USA. As one of the SAT subjects, the SAT II Chinese Test assesses the ability to understand spoken and written Mandarin

Chinese in the context of contemporary Chinese culture. It was first launched in 1999. The targeted test-takers are students who have no Chinese background but have learned Chinese for two to four years in high school or the equivalent in the USA.

The SAT II Chinese Test is one hour long, and it consists of 85 multiple-choice questions, including 30 listening comprehension questions, 25 usage questions, and 30 reading comprehension questions. The listening section asks students to first listen to spoken statements, dialogues, or monologues and then answer some questions printed on the test paper. The usage section consists of a number of incomplete sentences, each of which has four possible answers. Students have to choose one answer that best completes the sentence structurally and logically. The reading section has various types of reading passages, and these passages are written in both traditional and simplified characters. Comprehension questions are written in English. The test is first graded in raw score based on the following rules: (1) the full score is 85; (2) each correct answer is 1 point; (3) each wrong answer for the first 15 questions will have negative point of $-1/2$; and (4) each wrong answer for question 16 to question 85 will have negative point of $-1/3$. Then, raw scores will be converted into reported score. The full reported score is 800.

According to the most recent report on test characteristics of SAT subject tests, the SAT II Chinese Test had 1812–2533 test-takers and the average score was 729–746 (about 74–80 in raw scores) in 2013 (College Board 2014). Note that the College Board originally aimed to use the subject test to assess the achievement of learners without Chinese background. Yet, the majority of these test-takers were likely Chinese heritage language learners, as McGinnis (2010) pointed out "the SAT II never really moved beyond providing primary service to the Chinese Heritage Language Learners community" (p. 205).

The Chinese Proficiency Test (CPT)

Supported by the US Department of Education, the Center for Applied Linguistics (CAL) developed the CPT with collaboration of Chinese language scholars at the University of Hawaii in 1986. The test is designed to measure the general proficiency in listening and reading attained by English-speaking learners of Mandarin in 9–12 grades, college learners, or adult learners. According to the introductions on CAL's Website, the CPT lasts for about 2 h and 30 min. Similar to the SAT II Chinese Test, the CPT uses multiple-choice questions to assess students' competences in listening, reading, and grammar. The listening section includes two-speaker and single-speaker passages (such as news broadcasts and public announcements). The Structure section asks students to recognize correct syntactic patterns in written Mandarin. The Reading section measures students' reading comprehension ability.

Review of Studies on Assessments in Chinese

In this part, we review a small number of studies that either aimed to validate some of the tests reviewed above or used the tests as research instruments. This review will help us further understand the nature of the tests and inform us of the current developments in Chinese language assessment research in the USA. It is hoped to help us identify issues or topics that need to be addressed in future research.

Studies on Test Validation

During the past few decades, a number of studies have been conducted to validate the OPI (e.g., Hallek 1992, 1995, 1996; Liskin-Gasparro 2003; Magnan 1987; Surface & Dierdorff 2003; Swender 2003; Thompson 1995), the OPIc (Surface et al. 2008), the WPT (Surface & Dierdorff 2004), the SOPI (Clark & Li 1986; Kenyon & Tschirner 2000; Shohamy et al. 1989; Stansfield & Kenyon 1992, 1993), the COPI (Kenyon & Malabonga 2001; Malabonga et al. 2005), and the AP language tests (Baum 2007a, b; Baum & Nuessel 2007; Bischof 2005; Chen 2011; Lokai et al. 2004; Marshall 2010). However, only a very small number of them specifically examined the tests in Chinese or involved Chinese together with multiple other languages, and they almost exclusively focused on the OPI, the SOPI, and the AP Chinese Test. So far, little research has been published to provide validation evidence for the OPIc, the COPI, the WPT, and the AAPPL in Chinese.

Surface and Dierdorff (2003), for example, examined the reliability of the ACTFL OPI in Mandarin Chinese and 18 other languages. Results revealed very high inter-rater reliability with r ranging from 0.96 to 0.98; the overall inter-rater agreement was 80.97% for all tested languages. Specifically for Mandarin Chinese, the inter-rater reliability was 0.989 and the inter-rater agreement was 86.31%. The study thus suggested that the ACTFL OPI was a reliable assessment to examine speaking proficiency in those 19 languages, including Mandarin Chinese. However, this study did not explain why and how raters disagreed for the 13.69% of the Mandarin OPI cases. Such information is important because it could help us understand the potential difficulties in rating Chinese OPIs.

This study also found that 58.5% of the disagreements between raters were within the same major level, which indicates that determining the sublevels is difficult. Another interesting finding was that the third rater tended to agree with the second rater for the cases that the first rater and the second rater disagreed on. Given that the first rater was the OPI tester and the second rater (and the third rater in this study) did not have face-to-face contact with an examinee, this finding suggests that the interview experience with an examinee, or lack thereof, may have an influence on how the examinee's oral proficiency level is rated. This apparently has implications for OPI rater training.

Clark and Li (1986) developed four forms of the SOPI in Chinese and then administered them together with an OPI to 32 students of Chinese at two American universities. Each test was double scored by two raters, and then the two scores on the SOPI and the OPI were statistically compared. A significant correlation of 0.93 was found between these two types of tests, which indicated that the SOPI was a valid assessment for Chinese oral proficiency like the OPI. Similar studies have also been conducted and strong correlations found between the two tests in other languages, such as Hebrew (Shohamy et al. 1989), Indonesian and Hausa (Stansfield & Kenyon 1992, 1993), German (Kenyon & Tschirner 2000), and Portuguese (Stansfield et al. 1990).

The College Board conducts college-grade comparability studies every five to seven years to make sure that the final AP grades earned by test-takers reflect the standards and practices of colleges and universities and the expectations of the parallel course they offer. So far, such comparability studies have also been conducted in a number of languages, including Mandarin Chinese (Baum 2007a) as well as French, German, and Spanish (Bischof 2005), Italian (Baum & Nuessel 2007), Japanese (Baum 2007b), and Russian (Marshall 2010).

Baum (2007a) administered a shortened AP Chinese Test to 353 students enrolled in Chinese language and culture courses that were parallel to the AP Chinese course at 17 colleges or universities. These students had completed at least 300 h of college-level Chinese language study. A group of college professors and AP teachers scored the students' college examinations and their AP Chinese Test together using the same scoring rubrics. Then, a composite score of the AP test obtained by combining scores on each section was used in combination with course grades to determine cutoff points for different AP final grade levels 1–5. It was found that high school AP students' minimum composite scores for each AP final grade were comparable to the average course grade of college students in the corresponding college level. This led to the conclusion that the AP Chinese Test was valid in reflecting the standards and expectations of the parallel course offered at colleges and universities.

There was, however, a concern about such AP college comparability studies in that using final course grades could be very subjective and unreliable because different college professors might have different criteria for those grades (Marshall 2010). Moreover, in the case of Chinese, course requirements between AP Chinese courses are different from their parallel college courses. One notable difference is that high school students are not often required to write by hand in AP courses; it is fine for them to type on computer when taking AP courses or taking the AP Chinese Test. Yet, Chinese courses at colleges and universities all typically require students to write by hand for their homework or examinations. In this aspect, there tends to be misalignment between what an AP grade can attest to about one's proficiency and the standards and practices of colleges and universities and the expectations of the parallel courses offered there.

Studies Using the Tests as Research Instruments

In addition to the aforementioned studies that aimed for test validation, there were a few other studies that used some of these tests to measure learners' Chinese proficiency with varied research purposes (e.g., Glisan et al. 2013; Ke & Reed 1995; Liu 2010; Swender 2003; Thompson et al. 2014).

One of the research objectives was to investigate learners' language development in study-abroad and immersion contexts. For example, Ke and Reed (1995) investigated 122 adult learners' language development in an intensive summer program in the USA. The students were tested with the OPI and the CPT at the beginning and at the end of the program. A moderate correlation was found between the students' OPI scores and CPT scores. After nine weeks of intensive learning, half of the students improved on the OPI, and nearly all of the students improved on the CPT. Those who improved on the OPI tended to have higher CPT scores than those who did not improve on the OPI. As the authors noted, the moderate correlation between the OPI and the CPT indicated that one's performance in one test would not necessarily predict how well he/she would perform in the other test. Therefore, it may not be appropriate to use a student's OPI rating in Chinese as his/her general Chinese proficiency or use CPT score to represent the test-taker's oral proficiency in Chinese.

Liu (2010) assessed students' language proficiency gains in a Chinese learning program that included an at-home preparation intensive summer program (8 weeks in the USA) and a short-term study abroad summer program (4 weeks in China). Eleven students' pre- and post-program SAT II Chinese scores and their Chinese OPI ratings were compared. Results showed that all students' SAT scores increased, and their performances in the OPI were positively correlated with their SAT scores. The students whose SAT scores were between 520 and 630 before the program were likely to achieve an average SAT score of 750 and an OPI rating at the advanced level after the program. However, the findings of this study need to be taken cautiously due to its small number of participants.

Assessments such as the OPI and the SOPI have also been used to provide descriptive evidence for undergraduate learners' Chinese learning outcomes. For example, Swender (2003) reported a study of 501 official OPI ratings collected between 1998 and 2002 in 7 languages including Mandarin Chinese. The students tested were junior or senior foreign language majors from five liberal arts colleges in the USA. This study only included 10 Chinese major students, and their OPI ratings were in the range of intermediate low to advanced mid. Only 4 of them got a rating above the advanced level. Despite its small sample size, this study provided helpful information for Chinese language programs to set up a reasonable goal of language learning outcomes for their majors. The low percentage of students with advanced ratings is noteworthy and suggests that college Chinese language major education needs to be improved.

Using the SOPI, Thompson et al. (2014) assessed undergraduate students' oral proficiency in Mandarin Chinese as well as French, German, and Spanish.

About 76% of the students were found to meet or exceed the intermediate-mid level, which was their university's desired foreign language learning outcome. This evidence suggested that the university had set up a reasonable goal for undergraduate students' foreign language outcome. However, this study did not specifically report how many of Chinese-learning students met or exceeded the foreign language requirement. Moreover, as the authors admitted, this study failed to provide much information that could be used for course improvements at different levels, especially for specific language programs.

Lastly, oral proficiency tests such as the OPI have also been used in assessing to what extent teacher candidates can meet the oral proficiency requirement for Chinese teacher certification. The ACTFL/NCATE (The National Council for Accreditation of Teacher Education) Program Standards for the Preparation of Foreign Language Teachers (2002) established the minimum oral proficiency levels for teacher candidates based on the ACTFL Proficiency Guidelines-Speaking (ACTFL 2012a). Many states in the USA require OPI and/or WPT tests for teacher certification. For less commonly taught languages, such as Chinese, the minimum proficiency standard is advanced low or intermediate high.

Glisan et al. (2013) examined teacher candidates' OPI data in 11 different languages, including Mandarin Chinese, to find out to what extent teacher candidates had met the minimum oral proficiency standard in the USA. The study showed that 54.8% of the candidates met the required standard of advanced low or intermediate high in Arabic, Chinese, Japanese, and Korean between 2006 and 2012. This finding echoed a study conducted by Swender and her collegues in 2007 (cited in Glisan et al. 2013), in which 59.5% of teacher candidates met the ACTFL/NCATE requirements in 7 languages including Chinese. Specifically with respect to Chinese, Glisan et al. (2013) reported that 88.7% of the teacher candidates had met the requirement of intermediate high, but all candidates were reported to meet this standard in the study conducted by Swender and her collegues. Due to the lack of report on the teacher candidates' demographic information, the two studies could not be directly compared to explain the gap in the findings, but the possibly differential levels of representation of native speakers or heritage language speakers of Chinese in the pools of candidates might be a reason.

Conclusions and Implications

This chapter provided an overview of Chinese language assessments in the USA. It first introduced the theoretical bases, structures, administration, and scoring of nine major Chinese tests, including the OPI, the OPIc, the SOPI, the COPI, the WPT, the AAPPL, the AP Chinese Test, the SAT Chinese II, and the CPT. It then reviewed a small number of research studies that validated some of the tests or used them to measure learners' Chinese proficiency for various research purposes.

The majority of the Chinese assessments reviewed in this chapter were developed on the basis of standards such as the ACTFL Proficiency Guidelines and the

Foreign Language Standards. With the advance of technology, most of these assessments can be delivered on computer, which makes it more convenient for test-takers to access and for raters to score. However, computerized tests have some limitations that need to be noted. For example, computerized oral tests such as the OPIc and the COPI may not be able to capture the characteristics of natural real-life interactions. Moreover, computerized writing tests such as the WPT in Chinese and the writing part of the AP Chinese Test, which require students to type on computer, tend to neglect the importance of character writing in assessing Chinese writing proficiency. Therefore, it is important for test-takers and language practitioners to weigh the advantages and disadvantages of computerized testing before making a decision for test selection.

Assessments such as the AP Chinese Test and the SAT II Chinese Test are intended to be used as important standards for college admission and college course replacement or selection. Scores of the two tests, however, tend to provide limited evidence for such purposes. Because of their reliance on multiple-choice questions, these tests cannot properly assess learners' proficiency to use Chinese, especially the writing proficiency. Because the requirements for high school AP course are different from those of college Chinese courses, it is in a great need that new assessments are developed to show alignment with skills taught in college Chinese language programs. In addition, as presented earlier in this chapter, the majority of the test-takers of these two tests are found to be heritage language learners, who have been reported to easily achieve very high scores; yet the tests are intended for all types of learners of Chinese, including learners without any Chinese background. So far there has not been any published research that examined whether these tests will have testing bias for different groups of learners, but it is certainly an issue that warrants attention in the future.

There has been an increasing attention to assessment of Chinese at the PreK-12 levels, but we still know little about how assessment could inform instruction to support young learners' learning. ACTFL's most recently developed assessment, AAPPL, for example, is specifically designed for young learners and assesses what they can do with Chinese in terms of all four skills. It provides students with a detailed score description and some suggestions for future improvement. With such information, test-takers can have a better idea about what they can do with the language and what to be improved in the future, and the information is arguably helpful to teachers as well. In this respect, AAPPL provides positive wash-back effects on language instruction and learning. On the other hand, there is little research evidence on how AAPPL could support classroom instruction and student learning. Recently CAL also developed two assessment tools for K-12 students. One is Student Oral Proficiency Assessment (SOPA) targeting for Grades 2–8 learners. The other is Early Language Listening and Oral Proficiency Assessment (ELLOPA) targeting at Grades PreK-2. Both of them are currently available in Chinese and six other languages. Yet, there is little research on them. Overall, assessments and research studies on assessment for young learners are currently very limited in number, which cannot satisfy the great assessment need resulted from the increasing Chinese language course enrollments at PreK-12 levels (see also Teng, this volume; Sun et al., this volume). Future studies on these assessments are greatly needed so that assessment and classroom instruction can be better aligned to support young students' Chinese language learning.

References

ACTFL. (1987). ACTFL Chinese proficiency guidelines. *Foreign Language Annals, 20*(5), 471–487.

ACTFL. (1999). *ACTFL proficiency guidelines-speaking.* Yonkers, NY: ACTFL Inc.

ACTFL. (2002). *ACTFL/NCATE program standards for the preparation of foreign language teachers.* Yonkers, NY: ACTFL.

ACTFL. (2012a). *ACTFL proficiency guidelines 2012.* Retrieved October 15, 2015, from http://www.actfl.org/sites/default/files/pdfs/public/ACTFLProficiencyGuidelines2012FINAL.pdf

ACTFL. (2012b). *ACTFL performance descriptors for language learners.* Retrieved October 15, 2015, from http://www.actfl.org/sites/default/files/pdfs/ACTFLPerformance-Descriptors.pdf

ACTFL. (2015). *AAPPL score descriptions for interpersonal listening/speaking.* Retrieved October 15, 2015, from http://aappl.actfl.org/sites/default/files/AAPPL/AAPPL%20Scores%20Interpersonal.pdf

ACTFL (American Council on the Teaching of Foreign Languages). (1986). *ACTFL proficiency guidelines-speaking.* Retrieved February 14, 2016, from http://www.actfl.org/sites/default/files/pdfs/public/ACTFLProficiencyGuidelines1986.pdf

Baum, D. (2007a). *Establishing AP Chinese language and culture exam validity using college professors' grading standards.* Retrieved January 2, 2016, from http://www.apcentral.org/apc/.../collegeCompStudy_chineseLang.pdf

Baum, D. (2007b). *Establishing AP Japanese language and culture exam validity using college professors' grading standards.* Retrieved January 2, 2016, from http://apcentral.collegeboard.com/apc/public/repository/collegeCompStudy_japaneseLang_07.pdf

Baum, D., & Nuessel, F. (2007). *Establishing AP Italian exam validity using college professors' grading standards.* Paper presented at the annual meeting of the American Council on the Teaching of Foreign Languages, Henry B. Gonzalez Convention Center, San Antonio, TX.

Bischof, D. L. (2005). Validating the AP German language exam through a curricular survey of third-year college language courses. *Teaching German, 38*(1), 74–81.

Canale, M., & Swain, M. (1980). Theoretical bases of communicative approaches to second language teaching and testing. *Applied Linguistics, 1*(1), 1–47.

Center for Applied Linguistics. (2008). *Foreign language teaching in U.S. schools: Results for the national K-12 foreign language survey.* Washington, D.C: Author. Retrieved July 18, 2015, from http://www.cal.org/what-we-do/projects/national-k-12-foreign-language-survey

Chan, M. Y. (1982). Statistics on the strokes of present-day Chinese script. *Chinese Linguistics, 1,* 299–305.

Chen, Y. F. (2011). An analysis of the 2007-2010 AP Chinese exam results: Compared with the results of AP exams of other world languages. *Korean Journal of Chinese Language and Literature, 40*(1), 191–210.

Clark, J. L. D., & Li, Y. C. (1986). *Development, validation, and dissemination of a proficiency-based test of speaking ability in Chinese and an associated assessment model for other less commonly taught languages.* Washington, DC: Center for Applied Linguistics.

College Board. (2014). *The 10th annual AP report to the nation.* Retrieved July 18, 2015, from http://media.collegeboard.com/digitalServices/pdf/ap/rtn/10th-annual/10th-annual-ap-report-to-the-nation-single-page.pdf

Glisan, E. W., Swender, E., & Surface, E. (2013). Oral proficiency standards and foreign language teacher candidates: Current finding and future research directions. *Foreign Language Annals, 46*(2), 264–289.

Goldberg, D., Looney, D., & Lusin, N. (2015). *Enrollments in languages other than English in United States institutions of higher education, Fall 2013*. Retrieved March 15, 2016, from http://www.mla.org/pdf/2013_enrollment_survey.pdf

Halleck, G. B. (1992). The oral proficiency interview: Discrete point test or a measure of communicative language ability? *Foreign Language Annals, 25*(3), 227–231.

Halleck, G. B. (1995). Assessing oral proficiency: A comparison of holistic and objective measures. *Modern Language Journal, 79*(2), 223–235.

Halleck, G. B. (1996). Interrater reliability of the OPI: Using academic trainee raters. *Foreign Language Annals, 29*(2), 223–238.

Ke, C., & Reed, D. (1995). An analysis of results from the ACTFL oral proficiency Interview and the Chinese proficiency test before and after intensive instruction in Chinese as a foreign language. *Foreign Language Annals, 28*(2), 208–222.

Kenyon, D. M., & Malabonga, V. M. (2001). Comparing examinees' attitudes toward a computerized oral proficiency assessment. *Language Learning and Technology, 5*, 60–83.

Kenyon, D. M., & Tschirner, E. (2000). The rating of direct and semi-direct oral proficiency interviews: Comparing performance at lower proficiency levels. *Modern Language Journal, 84*(1), 85–101.

Kramsch, C. (1989). New directions in the study of foreign language. *ADFL Bulletin, 27*(1), 4–11.

Kuo, J., & Jiang, X. (1997). Assessing the assessments: The OPI and the SOPI. *Foreign Language Annals, 30*(4), 503–512.

Liskin-Gasparro, J. (2003). The ACTFL proficiency guidelines and the oral proficiency interview: A brief history and analysis of their survival. *Foreign Language Annals, 36*(4), 483–490.

Liu, J. (2010). Assessing students' language proficiency: A new model of study abroad program in China. *Journal of Studies in International Education, 14*(5), 528–544.

Lokai, D., Baum, D., Casabianca, J. M., Morgan, R., Rabiteau, K. A., & Tateneni, K. (2004). Validating AP modern foreign language examinations through college comparability studies. *Foreign Language Annals, 37*(4), 616–622.

Magnan, S. S. (1987). Rater reliability of the ACTFL oral proficiency interview. *The Canadian Modern Language Review, 43,* 267–276.

Malabonga, V. A., Kenyon, D. M., & Carpenter, H. (2005). Self-assessment, preparation and response time on a computerized oral proficiency test. *Language Testing, 22*(1), 59–92.

Malone, E. M. (2003). Research on the oral proficiency interview: Analysis, synthesis, and future directions. *Foreign Language Annals, 36*(4), 491–497.

Marshall, C. (2010). Examining the validity of the 2010 prototype AP Russian exam through a college comparability study. *Russian Language Journal, 60,* 319–331.

McGinnis, S. (2010). Heritage is not enough: The changing demographics of the Chinese language field in the United States. *Russian Language Journal, 60,* 201–214.

National Standards Collaborative Board. (2015). *World-Readiness standards for learning languages* (4th ed.). Alexandria, VA: Author.

National Standards in Foreign Language Education Project. (1996). *Standards for foreign language learning in the 21st century (SFFLL)* (1st ed.). Lawrence, KS: Allen Press.

National Standards in Foreign Language Education Project. (1999). *Standards for foreign language learning in the 21st century (SFFLL)* (2nd ed.). Lawrence, KS: Allen Press.

National Standards in Foreign Language Education Project. (2006). *Standards for foreign language learning in the 21st century (SFFLL)* (3rd ed.). Lawrence, KS: Allen Press.

Norris, M. J. (2001). Concerns with computerized adaptive oral proficiency assessment. *Language Learning and Technology, 5*, 99–105.

Perkins, A. J. (1979). Report of the President's commission on foreign language and international studies. *Foreign Language Annals, 12*(6), 457–464.

Savignon, S. J. (1972). *Communicative competence: An experiment in foreign-language teaching*. Philadelphia: The Centre for Curriculum Development Inc.

Shohamy, E., Gordon, C., Kenyon, D. M., & Stanfield, C. W. (1989). The development and validation of a semi-direct test for assessing oral proficiency in Hebrew. *Bulletin of Hebrew Higher Education, 4,* 4–9.

Stansfield, C. W., & Kenyon, D. M. (1992). The development and validation of a simulated oral proficiency interview. *Modern Language Journal, 76*(2), 129–141.

Stansfield, C. W., & Kenyon, D. M. (1993). Development and validation of the Hausa speaking test with the ACTFL proficiency guidelines. *Issues in Applied Linguistics, 4*(1), 5–31.

Stansfield, C. W., Kenyon, D. M., Paiva, D., Doyle, F., Ulsh, I., & Cowles, M. A. (1990). Development and validation of the Portuguese speaking test. *Hispania, 73,* 641–651.

Surface, E. A., & Dierdorff, E. C. (2003). Reliability and the ACTFL oral proficiency interview: Reporting indices of interrater consistency and agreement for 19 languages. *Foreign Language Annals, 36*(4), 507–519.

Surface, E. A., & Dierdorff, E. C. (2004). *Preliminary reliability and validity findings for the ACTFL writing proficiency test.* SWA Technical Report 2004-C04-R01.

Surface, E. A., Poncheri, R. M., & Bhavsar, K. S. (2008). *Two studies investigating the reliability and validity of the English ACTFL OPIc with Korean test takers: The ACTFL OPIc validation project technical report.* Retrieved July 15, 2015, from http://www.languagetesting.com/wp-content/uploads/2013/08/ACTFL-OPIc-English-Validation-2008.pdf

Swender, E. (2003). Oral proficiency testing in the real world: Answers to frequently asked questions. *Foreign Language Annals, 36*(4), 520–526.

Swender, E., & Vicars, R. (2012). *ACTFL oral proficiency interview tester training manual.* Alexandria, VA: American Council on the Teaching of Foreign Languages.

Thompson, I. (1995). A study of interrater reliability of the ACTFL oral proficiency interview in five European languages: Data from ESL, French, German, Russian, and Spanish. *Foreign Language Annals, 28*(3), 407–422.

Thompson, L. G., Cox, L. T., & Knapp, N. (2016). Comparing the OPI and the OPIc: The effect of test method on oral proficiency scores and student preference. *Foreign Language Annals, 49* (1), 75–92.

Thompson, R. J., Walther, E., Tufts, C., Lee, K. C., Paredes, L., Fellin, L. … Schlosberg, L. (2014). Development and assessment of the effectiveness of an undergraduate general education foreign language requirement. *Foreign Language Annals, 47*(4), 653–668.

Wang, W., & Ruan, J. (2016). Historical overview of Chinese language education for speakers of other languages in China and the United States. In J. Ruan, J. Zhang, & C. Leung (Eds.), *Chinese language education in the United States* (pp. 1–28). Switzerland: Springer.

Chapter 4
Developments in Research on Testing Chinese as a Second Language

Dongbo Zhang

Abstract This chapter provides an overview of developments in research on testing Chinese as a Second Language (CSL), with a focus on four language skills (listening, speaking, reading, and writing) and two types of language knowledge (vocabulary and grammatical knowledge). It aims to make CSL testing research, which has almost all been published in Chinese, accessible to non-Chinese-speaking scholars who might have become interested in Chinese testing and assessment as the popularity of the language grows. It is also hoped to make scholars of CSL testing aware of the research limitations so that more high-quality research, especially original research on issues that specifically pertain to Chinese testing, could be conducted in the future.

Keywords Chinese as a second language · Testing · Review

Introduction

Along with the increase of China's global influence, the Chinese language, a part of the country's soft power, has also gained unprecedented popularity around the world. The global "Hanyu Re" or craze for learning Chinese as a Second Language[1] (CSL) has been evident not only from an increasingly large number of foreign students coming to study in China, but also the fast expansion of Chinese programs outside of China (Chinese Ministry of Education 2014; Furman et al. 2010;

---

[1]Chinese as a Second Language (CSL) is used as a broad term to refer to the language learned and tested as an additional or non-primary language. CSL learners or test-takers, therefore, include not only non-native speakers of Chinese studying abroad in China or domestically in their own country, but also minority students in China and ethnic Chinese speaking Chinese as a heritage language.

D. Zhang (✉)
Michigan State University, East Lansing, MI, USA
e-mail: zhangdo6@msu.edu

© Springer Nature Singapore Pte Ltd. 2017
D. Zhang and C.-H. Lin (eds.), *Chinese as a Second Language Assessment*,
Chinese Language Learning Sciences, DOI 10.1007/978-981-10-4089-4_4

Hanban/Confucius Institute Headquarters 2010). The popularization of learning Chinese has promoted the testing and assessment of the language. A variety of tools have been developed, and new ones keep emerging, to address diverse purposes of CSL testing and assessment.

In China, for example, the Hanban/Confucius Institute Headquarters (hereafter, Hanban) administers the New HSK (新汉语水平考试 Hanyu Shuiping Kaoshi or Chinese Proficiency Test), the HSKK (汉语水平口语考试 Hanyu Shuiping Kouyu Kaoshi or Chinese Speaking Proficiency Test), the New YCT (新中小学生汉语 考试 Youth Chinese Test), and the BCT (商务汉语考试 Business Chinese Test) (see Teng, this volume). All these tests serve foreign learners. To differentiate those learners from ethnic minority students in China who are also CSL learners and specifically serve the need of testing minority students' Chinese proficiency, the MHK (民族汉语水平考试 Minzu Hanyu Shuiping Kaoshi or Test of Chinese Proficiency for Minorities) was developed by the Minorities Education Division of the Chinese Ministry of Education. In Taiwan, the Steering Committee for the Test of Proficiency-Huayu (SC-TOP) established by the Taiwanese Ministry of Education administers the TOCFL (華語文能力測驗 Test of Chinese as a Foreign Language), a standardized test for non-native speakers of Chinese with four sub-tests that are aligned with the Common European Framework of References for Languages (CEFR) and tests the four skills of listening, reading, speaking, and writing, respectively (see Chang, this volume). In non-Chinese-speaking countries, a number of Chinese tests and assessment tools have also been developed and promulgated for a variety of purposes. For example, in Japan, the Society for Testing Chinese Proficiency conducts the Test of Chinese Proficiency for Japanese learners. In the USA, there is the Oral Proficiency Interview or OPI, which was developed in alignment with the ACTFL (American Council on Teaching of Foreign Languages) Proficiency Guidelines to test oral proficiency in foreign languages, including Chinese (Liskin-Gasparro 2003; Liu, this volume). ACTFL recently also developed the ACTFL Assessment of Performance toward Proficiency in Languages with Chinese as one of the target languages. Two other major tests of Chinese in the USA are the AP (Advanced Placement) Chinese Language and Culture Exam and the Chinese Subject Test of the SAT, both of which are administered by the College Board (see Liu, this volume).

Along with the booming growth of test development, research on CSL testing has also experienced fast growth. However, reports on CSL testing were largely written and published in Chinese, which makes the development in the field hardly accessible to the international community. It is with this gap in mind that this chapter is written to provide an overview of research on Chinese testing. Given the vast scope of language testing research (Fulcher and Davison 2012; Kunnan 2014), it is beyond the limit of a single paper to have every topic of L2 Chinese testing reviewed. Consequently, this chapter restricts its review to four skills (i.e., listening, speaking, reading, and writing) and two types of language knowledge (i.e., vocabulary and grammar), the areas where most empirical studies were reported.

To prepare for the review, a list of keywords in Chinese and English was first generated to conduct a broad search of research published in full papers on CSL testing and assessment. The Chinese keywords included *hanyu*, *huayu*, and *zhongwen*, which all mean Chinese: *kaoshi* and *ceshi* (test/testing); *pinggu* (assess/assessing/assessment); and *dier yuyan* (second language) and *waiyu* (foreign language). The English keywords were *Mandarin/Chinese*, *test/testing*, *assess/assessing/assessment*, and *second/foreign language*. The search with Chinese keywords on CAJ, or China Academic Journals,[2] returned a few hundred titles in the past 20 years (1994–2014), most of which were discussion papers or papers that aimed to introduce an area of language testing to Chinese readers (e.g., Fang 2007). Only a few dozen met the inclusion criterion by reporting on empirical studies with CSL testing or assessment as the research focus. A majority of them were published in such major Chinese testing or applied linguistics journals as 中国 考试 *Zhongguo Kaoshi* (*China Examinations*), 语言教学与研究 *Yuyan Jiaoxue Yu Yanjiu* (*Language Teaching and Linguistic Studies*), 世界汉语教学 *Shijie Hanyu Jiaoxue* (*Teaching Chinese in the World*), and 华语教学与研究 *Huawen Jiaoyu Yu Yanjiu* (*Teaching Chinese to Speakers of Other Languages [TCSOL] Studies*). The search with the English keywords without year constraint on ERIC and Linguistics and Language Behavior Abstracts, supplemented by a search on Google Scholar, returned no more than a dozen English papers where empirical studies were reported on CSL testing and assessment (e.g., Ke and Reed 1995; Jin and Mak 2012). Most of the studies reported in those English papers were conducted in the USA (e.g., Clark 1988; Ke and Reed 1995; Surface and Dierdorff 2003) with a few in a Chinese context (e.g., Chan 2008; Jin and Mak 2012).

Overall, the Chinese and English papers with an empirical focus covered a variety of topics of CSL testing and assessment, from validation of standardized proficiency tests (e.g., Fu et al. 2013; Zhang and Li 2009) and examination of their washback effects (e.g., Huang 2013; Tu 2011) to explorations of alternative assessments (e.g., Wang 2012a, b, 2005). However, most examined the testing of different types of knowledge and skills of Chinese. To limit the scope of the review in this chapter, only those papers where an empirical study was reported specifically on listening, speaking, reading, writing, vocabulary, or grammatical knowledge were included. The references of the included papers were also checked so that any studies missed in the searches were also included.

Listening

The appearance of listening in standardized testing of Chinese dates back to as early as the early 1980s when the HSK (Elementary/Intermediate), the predecessor of the New HSK, was first developed that used multiple-choice questions to test sentence

---

[2]CAJ is "the most comprehensive, full-text database of Chinese journals in the world." The information retrieved on September 15, 2015 from the Web site of CAJ (http://oversea.cnki.net/kns55/brief/result.aspx?dbPrefix=CJFD) showed that it had a collection of 10,016 Chinese academic journals and 52,614,141 full-text papers.

as well as short and long dialogue comprehension. Listening is now an integral component of all major CSL tests. For example, all six bands of the New HSK have a section that tests various listening skills, such as a simple task of judging whether a word heard twice matches a given picture and more complex ones like long dialogue/monologue comprehension. Despite the relatively long history of listening in CSL testing, only recently has there been research that empirically examined issues of testing CSL listening. However, fast-developing interests have been witnessed among CSL testing scholars whose research has covered a variety of issues of listening testing, such as question types and response formats, item characteristics and item difficulty, and factor structure of CSL listening comprehension.

Huang (2010) investigated the psychometric properties of a new component introduced as the third part of the listening section of the HSK (Revised, Intermediate) (refer to Teng, this volume for the differences between the HSK, the HSK [Revised], and the New HSK). Different from the second part of the listening section, which uses multiple-choice questions for long dialogues/monologues, the third part includes eight choices for five questions for each long monologue. The analyses of three HSK (Revised, Intermediate) tests revealed that the second and the third parts had a similar level of item difficulty (P from 0.50 to 0.65) and item discrimination (rpb from 0.46 to 0.51); the two sections also showed similar internal consistency reliability (α from 0.79 to 0.84). The guessing parameter of a three-parameter logistic IRT (item response theory) model analysis, however, indicated that across the three tests, the third part (C from 0.12 to 0.14) was significantly better than the second part (C from 0.17 to 0.24).

How item characteristics influence the difficulty of listening, which has interested English language testing researchers (e.g., Kostin 2004), also received attention in CSL testing research. Based on Kostin (2004), Chan (2008) conducted a study on the short dialogue part of the listening section of the TOP-Huayu (Advanced), the predecessor of the TOCFL (refer to Chang, this volume, for the historical development of the TOP-Huayu and the TOCFL). The author identified 17 variables of three categories (i.e., word, sentence, and task processing) that might affect the difficulty level of the short dialogue listening (e.g., number of negatives in utterances and use of rhetorical questions). Interestingly, none of the linguistic factors at the word and the sentence levels significantly correlated with the b parameter or item difficulty from IRT analysis. Regression analysis using the stepwise method left only two task-processing variables, including "the proposition of the key is opposite to the one of any of the three distractors" and "the propositions of any two of the three distractors are opposite," in the model that significantly explained about 33% of the variance in item difficulty. Such a result seems to be surprising given that previous studies did document significant, albeit weak, correlations of some word and sentence-level features with listening item difficulty (e.g., number of dependent clauses in total dialogue in Kostin 2004). The gap of findings, according to Chan (2008), might be related to the exploratory nature of his study, which was based only on a small number of short dialogue items (35 in contrast to 365 in Kostin 2004).

The construct validity of listening comprehension has also been an interest of CSL testing researchers. Huang and Wang (2013) examined the underlying structure of CSL listening comprehension with a focus on the listening section (and the reading section; reviewed later in Reading) of the HSK (Advanced). The HSK (Advanced)'s multiple-choice listening (and reading) comprehension questions were classified into three categories that measured three aspects of comprehension processes, including main idea, details, and inferencing. Confirmatory factor analyses (CFA) tested a one-factor model; a two-factor model (main idea and details loaded on a factor of comprehension of explicit messages and inferencing on the other factor of comprehension of implicit messages); and a three-factor model. Both the two- and the three-factor models, with a second-order factor of listening comprehension, produced acceptable model fit; the three-factor model, however, was much better; the one-factor model showed very poor model fit.

A few studies of an experimental nature addressed whether manipulation of task-related variables or listening conditions affects listening performance. In Zhang's (2006) Study 1, intermediate learners in the control group listened to long dialogues with three types of multiple-choice questions corresponding to the three categories of comprehension processes in Huang and Wang (2013). The experimental group listened to the same materials and answered the same questions, but was exposed to a brief introduction of each dialogue prior to the test. In addition to a significant main effect of both group and question type, a significant interaction effect was found, and the pattern of the interaction effect seemed to be moderated by topic familiarity of the listening materials. When the topics were familiar, the experimental group only outperformed the control group on the questions that required making textual inferences. When the topics were unfamiliar, however, the experimental group's advantage was found in both main idea and inferencing questions.

Zhang's (2006) Study 2 focused on question previewing in listening comprehension. Intermediate learners in one condition previewed the test questions before each long dialogue was played. In the other condition, learners first listened to each long dialogue and did not have access to the test questions until after the dialogue was played. No main effect of question preview was found, for materials both familiar and unfamiliar to the learners. Like in Study 1, a significant group X question type interaction effect was found, and the interaction effect showed different patterns for materials with familiar and unfamiliar topics. For familiar topics, question preview led to a performance advantage only for the questions that required attention to details, whereas for unfamiliar topics, a performance advantage was found of question preview for all three types of questions.

In Yang and Wen (2012), the listening sections of two parallel tests of the New HSK (Band 4), which included three parts (i.e., sentence, short and long dialogue comprehension), were administered to the same group of intermediate learners, with one test conducted in the form of "semi-listening" (choices presented on paper) and the other "full-listening" (choices presented orally). While sentence and short dialogue listening did not show any significant differences between the two test conditions, the "full-listening" performance was significantly better than that of "semi-listening" on long dialogue listening. The authors interpreted the significant difference as that learners in the "full-listening" condition tended to utilize all of their mental resources for each long dialogue, as they knew that they would not be able to access any information of the test questions while the listening materials were being played.

CSL testing researchers also explored the implications of listening testing to listening instruction. Adopting the rule space model, Xu (2010) diagnosed the listening abilities of test-takers of the C.Test (Test of Practical Chinese; often nicknamed "Chinese TOEIC") (http://www.c-test.org.cn) (see also Li and Wang this volume). Based on a survey with expert teachers of Chinese, nine sub-skills of listening comprehension were identified. Test-takers' responses to short and long dialogue comprehension questions were categorized into 68 response patterns; three major patterns were identified across two groups of test-takers at different testing times. A diagnostic report was generated for each test-taker that consisted of the mastery pattern, fluent listening skills, skills that require further practice, strategies for improving those skills, and ability level. The author noted that test-takers having the same ability level might well show different mastery patterns and suggested that teachers offer differentiated instruction to improve their listening ability.

The review above shows diverse research interests of CSL scholars in listening testing. However, many issues of L2 listening testing (see Vandergrift 2007) are yet to be addressed or expanded in CSL research, for example, whether different types of visual support may or may not enhance listening comprehension (Ginther 2002). Some issues that specifically pertain to CSL listening have also received little research attention. For example, the listening section of the lower bands of the New HSK (e.g., Band 2) contains comprehension questions with four choices appearing in both Chinese characters and pinyin (i.e., an alphabetic system that is used to facilitate the pronunciation of Chinese characters), which is not the case in the higher bands and other CSL tests (e.g., the TOCFL-Listening). Empirically, a question remains as to which condition, character only, pinyin only, or character and pinyin, would result in the best listening performance and whether the availability of pinyin would create testing bias among different types of test-takers.

Speaking

Speaking did not receive as much attention as did other skills, such as listening and reading, in the early development of standardized testing of Chinese. For example, in the HSK, the predecessor of the New HSK, only at the Advanced level was a speaking component included (see also Teng, this volume). Such a situation, however, has dramatically changed in recent CSL testing development. Not only do all major current CSL tests have a speaking component (e.g., the HSKK and the TOCFL-Speaking), but also there have been fast-growing research interests in testing CSL speaking. Overall, the studies included in this review addressed five broad issues pertaining to CSL-speaking testing, including test validity, test reliability, comparison of different forms of testing spoken Chinese, comparison of scoring methods, and automated scoring of speaking.

The first group of studies examined the extent to which test-takers' performance on a speaking test is related to that on another test of speaking or other abilities (i.e., concurrent or criterion-related validity). In Clark's (1988) study, Chinese learners took, in addition to an ACTFL interview, four alternate forms of the Chinese Speaking Test (CST): personal conversation (listening and responding to conversational questions pre-recorded on a tape), single-picture description (answering questions about a single picture), picture sequence (narrating based on a sequence of pictures), and English-cued discourse (producing a long Chinese discourse with a written English prompt). Students' responses to all CST forms and the ACTFL interview were tape-recorded and scored by two raters. Very strong correlations were found between the ratings of different CST forms and, more importantly, between the four forms of the CST test and the interview across the two raters, which indicated high concurrent validity of the CST test. Ke (1993, cited in Ke 2012) examined the relationship between learners' performance on the OPI and its alternative test, the Simulated Oral Proficiency Interview (SOPI). The SOPI is a semi-direct speaking test that elicits oral speech by asking an examinee to respond to test questions or descriptions printed in a booklet, making it different from the OPI, which involves a face-to-face interview with a certified examiner (see also Liu, this volume). The examinees' responses were scored following the ACTFL proficiency guidelines for both tests. Actual ratings of the SOPI and the OPI were very close, and a very strong correlation was also found between the two speaking tests, which suggested that the SOPI might be able to serve as a substitute for the OPI for some testing needs, as it is obviously logistically more manageable. Ke and Reed (1995) administered the OPI and the Chinese Proficiency Test (CPT) to American college students prior to and after intensive Chinese instruction to assess the effect of the type of instruction on Chinese learning. Only moderate correlations were found of students' OPI level with their total CPT score and the scores of the listening, reading, and grammar sections of the CPT, even though the correlations between the OPI and the CPT and CPT components became stronger after the intensive instruction. The lack of a strong correlation between the OPI and the CPT led the authors to caution against the use of CPT as a substitute for indexing Chinese oral proficiency.

The second group of studies focused on inter-rater reliability analysis. To examine the reliability of the ACTFL OPI after the ACTFL Proficiency Guidelines —Speaking were revised in 1999, Surface and Dierdorff (2003) conducted an inter-rater reliability analysis of 5881 OPI interviews of 19 languages, including 241 interviews of Mandarin. Like other languages, across different indices, Mandarin showed very high inter-rater reliability. A large majority of the Mandarin interviews (about 86%) showed absolute agreement between the tester (the interviewer or the first rater) and the second rater who rated the audio recordings of the interviews. The rest of the interviews showed a difference of only one proficiency category between the tester and the second rater. No interviews had a difference of two or more proficiency categories. Taken together, these findings suggested high inter-rater reliability of the ACTFL OPI. Chai (2003) examined the reliability of the speaking section of the HSK (Advanced), which is a semi-direct test of speaking with scoring done on the tape-recording of an examinee's read-aloud of a passage and spoken answers to two written questions. In the study, four groups of three raters were asked to rate holistically a sample of examinees' responses to the test. Significant inter-rater reliability was found between the three raters in each group as well as between the four groups of raters. In addition, the two sets of ratings given by the same rater with an interval of half a year also showed a very strong correlation for all four groups.

The third group of studies compared different forms of tests for spoken Chinese and examined their psychometric properties. Wang (2007) administered to beginning learners a speaking test with four tasks: answering questions (two parts, each with 10 items), detecting differences in two pictures (two parts, each with 10 items), repeating after listening (two items), and speaking based on a sequence of pictures (two items). With all tasks scored with a 0/1 scoring method, G-theory analysis revealed that for the two parts of the first as well as the second task, the variance accounted for by P (examinee) was similarly small and that by I (item) was even smaller; most variance was accounted for by $P \times I$ interaction. For the second task, with the number of items kept constant (i.e., 10), one rater already led to satisfactory generalizability coefficients; adding more raters would not improve the coefficients much. Separate analyses showed that for the four items of the third and the fourth tasks, P accounted for more than 90% of the total score variance, and one rater already led to very high generalizability coefficients. The scores of all four tasks significantly correlated with learners' self-assessed speaking competence, and their speaking and listening as well as the total scores of their final examination. Wang (2011) further examined those four forms of speaking test focusing on their criterion-related validity. All forms significantly and moderately correlated with learners' speaking and listening as well as the total scores of their final examination. Their correlations with learners' self-assessed speaking competence were also significant.

The fourth group of studies focused on different scoring methods. In proposing a model of fuzzy scoring (later called confidence scoring in Jin et al. 2011), Jin et al. (2008) suggested that methods for scoring spoken language could be analyzed on three dimensions: holistic versus analytic, subjective versus objective, and precise versus fuzzy. Jin et al. (2008) explored fuzzy, holistic, and analytic scoring by human raters (i.e., subjectively). Two raters scored intermediate learners' responses to a speaking test holistically as well as analytically on pronunciation, content, accuracy, and fluency, using a fuzzing scoring method on a five-point scale, that is, they used a score of 1–100 to show scoring confidence in any level from 1 to 5 (e.g., 0 for 1, 10 for 2, 60 for 3, 20 for 4, and 10 for 5). Two overall scores of each learner were calculated from the scores on the four features using a rule-based reasoning method and a weighted average method, respectively. No significant difference was found between the two overall scores and a holistic fuzzy score, and all scores correlated highly with the learners' speaking scores in their midterm examination.

Jin et al. (2011) further developed a complex confidence scoring algorithm (CSA), which could translate the confidence scores of two adjacent levels to an exact score for three scales (i.e., delivery, language use, and topic development). Examinees listened to a passage and orally summarized the passage with supporting details. Oral responses were scored by two raters on the three five-point scales and also coded on their coverage of the 20 key message points (KMPs) identified based on native speakers' benchmarked responses. To perform confidence scoring, raters split a total score of 10 to two adjacent levels for each scale, such as three for Level 3 and seven for Level 4 for language use. Using the CSA, an exact confidence score was generated for an examinee based on the confidence scores assigned to the three scales. In addition, a traditional score was also calculated, that is, the average of the levels assigned to the three scales. G-theory analysis revealed that the confidence scoring method resulted in better dependability than the traditional one, whether there was a single rater or two raters. In addition, the confidence scores produced a much higher correlation with the KMP-based coding scores than did the traditional scores, although both correlations were significant.

Wang (2002) compared holistic (subjectively by a human rater) and analytic (objectively with quantified indexes of language features) scoring for three speaking tasks: answering questions (providing a short answer to a question heard), sentence repetition (repeating a short sentence heard), and oral report (giving an oral report on a given topic). The first two tasks were scored using a 0/1 scoring method and the third on a rating scale. All tasks were assigned objective indexes of pronunciation, grammar, and fluency. The rated scores and the objective indexes significantly correlated with teachers' ratings of the learners' speaking ability as well as the learners' self-assessed speaking competence. Such a finding was true of all three tasks, which seemed to suggest that using objective indexes of pronunciation, grammar, and fluency might be as reliable and valid a way to represent one's speaking ability as a holistic score from a rater. Further Multitrait-Multimethod (MTMM) analysis, however, indicated that this was not the case: Human holistic rating showed better convergent validity than objective indexes. As a comparison between the three tasks, the study found that the first had the highest convergent validity with the second in the middle; oral report had the lowest convergent validity, even though it is often believed to have the highest face validity.

Jin and Mak (2012) administered to advanced learners a speaking test with three tasks: listening to a conversation and expressing an opinion, listening to a speech or lecture and summarizing the topic, and giving a talk on a social phenomenon. Learners' responses were coded on seven distinguishing features of four categories, including pronunciation (target-like syllables), fluency (speech rate and pause time), vocabulary (word types and tokens), and grammar (grammatical accuracy and complexity). In addition, two raters rated the responses holistically with a rubric that focused only on degrees of communicative effectiveness and task fulfillment. Corroborating Wang (2002), all features correlated significantly with the raters' scores, word types, and tokens being the strongest and grammatical complexity the least strong correlates. Because word tokens and word types showed multi-collinearity, two separate multiple regression analyses were conducted with either one in combination with other features predicting the raters' holistic scores. In both regression models, speech rate and grammatical complexity were not significant after accounting for the other four variables. In the model where word token was a predictor, pause time was not a significant predictor either.

The last group of studies examined automated scoring of speaking. In Zhang (2011), nine human raters and an automated system scored the read-aloud and the closed question sections of the MHK (Band 3) speaking test. The correlation between the automated scores and the average scores of human raters was small for the closed question section but high for the read-aloud section; in addition, the automated scoring system and the human raters showed an absolute or adjacent agreement on the scores of almost all examinees. Li and Li (2014) reported the development of the Spoken Chinese Test (SCT) by Peking University (PKU) in collaboration with Pearson. The SCT, which is conducted through Pearson's Versant Test system, is a fully automated and adaptive test with a number of sections, including naming words and phrases, reading sentences aloud, repeating sentences heard, antonyms of words heard, short questions and answers, tone perception (isolated words), tone perception (in a sentence context), sentence building (reordering words/phrases to make a sentence), and retelling short narra-tive and expository passages. They address five aspects of Chinese-speaking ability: grammar, vocabulary, fluency, pronunciation, and tones. The SCT showed very strong split reliability (r from 0.87 for tone to 0.98 for overall score) and test–retest reliability (r from 0.74 for tone to 0.96 for grammar). A very high inter-rater reliability was found between the automated scores and the scores of human raters (r from 0.89 for fluency to 0.99 for grammar). The test also showed very good concurrent validity, having a correlation of 0.79 with the OPI and 0.86 with the HSKK (Intermediate) (see Teng, this volume, for more information about the HSKK).

Research on CSL-speaking testing has witnessed rapid progress in the most recent decade, despite the relatively short history of speaking in CSL testing. Some research, such as Jin and associates' research on fuzzy or confidence scoring (Jin et al. 2008, 2011), has made a significant contribution to testing of spoken lan-guage. On the other hand, plenty of issues still remain unaddressed. For example, current speaking tests of CSL (e.g., the HSKK and the TOCFL-Speaking) are largely semi-direct that do not involve any co-construction of language of a test-taker with an examiner and/or a peer, such as repeating a sentence, reading aloud or retelling a passage, describing a picture or a video, or answering printed questions. While presentation-based testing of speaking avoids a possible influence of an examiner or partner on a test-taker's speaking performance (Brown 2003), direct, interaction-based forms certainly deserve a space in testing speaking (Galaczi 2010).

Reading

Reading occupies a significant place in all current large-scale tests of Chinese and their predecessors (e.g., the New HSK and the HSK, the TOCFL, and the TOP-Huayu). For example, in the New HSK, not only do all six bands have a reading section, but the listening and writing sections also involve reading (e.g., choices of listening questions presented in print and rewriting a reading material). The HSKK, a test of spoken Chinese, also involves reading aloud materials. Despite the important place of reading in CSL tests, there are surprisingly few studies that examined the testing of reading. The two studies included in this review examined a cloze test of Chinese reading and the factor structure of reading comprehension in Chinese, respectively.

Liu (1995) administered an open cloze test where every 7th character was deleted, and learners' answers were scored using both the semantically acceptable scoring method (SEMAC) and the exact replacement scoring (ERS) method . Under the SEMAC method, the characters deleted and their synonyms or non-synonymic characters that semantically make sense in the context of the text are both considered acceptable responses, whereas under the ERS method, only the exact characters deleted are considered acceptable. The study found that the SEMAC produced a slightly higher score than the ERS; the internal consistency reliability of the test was high based on both scoring methods. The two scoring methods produced an extremely high correlation, and both had similarly moderate to high correlations with learners' listening comprehension ability, grammatical knowledge, and multiple-choice passage comprehension ability. Based on these findings, the author suggested that teachers consider the SEMAC method, because it would not be as time-consuming to use it in classroom assessment as it would in a large-scale test, and more importantly, students should be encouraged to demonstrate their command of knowledge and skills when working on a cloze instead of being asked to find the exact words of a passage. Liu (1995) also raised a few questions for researchers of Chinese assessment: Should the character or the word, which can be multiple characters, be the unit of deletion in Chinese cloze test? If the character is the unit, should the first or the second character be deleted from a two-character compound word? To what extent is cloze a reliable test of reading in Chinese? Surprisingly, little research has been published since Liu's (1995) study that further addressed cloze in CSL assessment, despite its wide use in past (e.g., the HSK) and current CSL tests (e.g., the New HSK and the TOCFL).

As reviewed earlier in the Listening section, Huang and Wang (2013) examined the factor structure of both the listening and the reading sections of the HSK (Advanced). Multiple-choice questions of reading comprehension were classified into three categories that measured understanding of main ideas, attention to details, and textual inferencing, respectively. CFAs showed that the two-factor model, which included a factor of comprehension of explicit information (main idea and details as two indicators) and a second one of comprehension of implicit information (inferencing as the only indicator), with a second-order factor of reading comprehension produced acceptable model fit; the model fit of the three-factor model (three comprehension skills as three separate factors) was reasonable but not as good as that of the two-factor one. The one-factor model showed very poor model fit. The lack of good model fit of the three-factor model marks a contrast to the authors' finding of listening comprehension where the three-factor model showed very good model fit. One reason for the difference, according to the authors, might be that in reading, learners could read a passage ideally as many times as they want to pay attention to details as well as summarize the main idea of that passage with the help of the details, which might blur the distinction between attention to main ideas and details. Due to the nature of a listening test, however, in no way could one re-listen to test materials; consequently, it seems hardly possible that one could rely on scattering details he/she has gathered to get the main idea of a long dialogue.

It is apparent that many research issues remain to be examined in CSL reading testing, despite the great effort of using a variety of methods to test reading in such tests as the New HSK and the TOCFL. For example, what is the construct of reading in Chinese, a language with a logographic writing system; and what are the skills and knowledge underlying CSL reading comprehension and reading fluency? Are short answer questions, which involve handwriting or typing Chinese characters, reliable and valid in testing reading in comparison with multiple-choice questions? What is the possible influence of embedding a picture (or other types of visual support) into a passage (e.g., in the New HSK) on the validity of a passage comprehension task and the performance of different types of test-takers?

Writing

Writing is included in almost all major CSL tests or bands of a CSL test. It first appeared in large-scale testing of CSL in the 1990s when the HSK (Advanced), which included testing of essay writing, was developed. A few current writing tests, such as the TOCFL-Writing, are computer-based and require test-takers to type Chinese characters to complete the tests. Writing is also tested in a variety of forms across (bands of) current CSL tests, such as writing a character with pinyin support, sentence construction, keywords or picture writing, rewriting, and letter or essay writing. The studies reviewed below generally addressed three major areas of CSL writing testing, including rater background effects on essay scoring, comparison of different forms of testing writing, and algorithms for automated scoring of Chinese essays.

Bo (2005) compared essay scoring by human raters of different backgrounds. Two groups of raters rated essays of the HSK (Advanced) holistically with consideration of five features (i.e., content, grammar, vocabulary, handwriting, and coherence), and took note of three primary criteria they followed in assigning a score. The professional group was graduate students who majored in CSL Studies and had experiences in CSL teaching and scoring HSK essays; the non-professional group was graduate students whose majors had no relevance to CSL. No significant difference was found between the two groups in their mean ratings, and there was a very strong agreement on their rank order of rated essays. G-theory analysis, however, revealed that the professional group's generalizability and dependability coefficients were far better than those of the non-professional group. The two groups also displayed different patterns of primary criteria. For example, grammar was noted the most times as a primary criterion by the professional group, whereas in the non-professional group, it was least frequently noted. Such a finding tends to corroborate those of some previous studies that examined the effect of raters' disciplinary background on rating of writing in English as a Second Language (ESL). For example, Weigle et al. (2003) found that raters from the English department seemed to be most concerned with grammar, whereas those from the psychology department regarded content as the most important criterion. On the other hand, it seems to differ from a more recent study where experienced ESL raters tended to refer more frequently to ideas than language errors (Barkaoui 2010). A single study like Bo's (2005) certainly cannot be conclusive on raters' background effect on their rating of CSL writing. Certainly, more research is needed in the future.

A few studies compared different forms of testing CSL writing. In Zhao and Xie (2006), foreign learners and minority college students in China took three writing tasks: topic writing, picture writing, and multiple-choice writing (e.g., choosing a connective for a blank in a sentence or paragraph). In both learner groups, the first two writing tasks, as opposed to the third one, significantly correlated with the students' writing ability rated by their teachers. Picture writing had the highest correlation, which seems to justify that a few standardized tests recently adopted it to test L2 Chinese writing (i.e., the New HSK and the MHK). Li and Zhao (2012) administered to CSL learners two picture writing tasks. In one, a single picture was provided in between an introductory and a concluding paragraph and test-takers were to fill in missing details to complete a story; in the other, a series of pictures was provided with no words. While both forms significantly correlated with teachers' ratings of the learners' writing ability and overall Chinese proficiency, the form with a series of pictures produced much higher correlations, particularly with teachers' ratings of writing ability.

Zhu et al. (2013) developed two mock writing tests following the specifications of Band 5 of the New HSK, the band with the most diverse types of tasks to assess writing, including sentence construction (i.e., rearranging words/phrases to make a sentence; eight items), keywords writing (one item), and picture writing (one item). Separate univariate G-theory analyses revealed that for the sentence construction task, the variance of person, item, as well as rater was minimal. The dependability of the task barely rose when the number of raters increased from 1 to 10; on the other hand, it could be raised to around 0.8 when the items increased from 8 to 20. For the keywords writing, the variance of person was the largest, that of item was very small, and that of rater was negligible. D Study revealed that with one item, the dependability coefficient increased from 0.57 to 0.63 when the number of rater increased from one to four; with two raters, and with the item increased from one to four, the dependability increased from 0.61 to 0.85. For the picture writing task, the variance of person was also the largest, that of rater was very small, and that of item was minimal. D Study indicated that with one item, and the number of rater increased from one to four, there was an increase of the dependability from 0.52 to 0.61; a significant increase of the dependability was observed from 0.57 to 0.82 when, with two raters, the number of items increased from one to four.

Additional multivariate G-theory analysis found that the variance of the composite score of the writing section was largely explained by the keywords writing task (51.20%) and the picture writing task (44.45%), that explained by the sentence construction task was very small (about 4.35%), which led the authors to suggest that it be removed from the writing section of Band 5 of the New HSK, even though the dependability of this task could be significantly increased by adding substantially more items as revealed in the aforementioned univariate G-theory analysis. If 0.85 is set as an acceptable level of composite dependability, the authors suggested, with the sentence construction task removed, increasing keywords writing items to two and picture writing items to three with the same three raters or two different pairs of raters.

Most research on Chinese writing testing focused on developing an algorithm or system for automated essay scoring. Zhang and Ren (2004), for example, extracted 17 features from 700 essays of Band 3 of the MHK, a test targeting ethnic minority students learning Chinese as a non-native language in China. All features were surface ones, such as the total numbers of Chinese characters, (different types of) words, and sentences; the mean length of sentences; and the number of grammatical errors. Quantitative indexes of those features were then used to predict the average of three human raters' scores. A regression model was later determined with five features, such as the total number of sentences and grammatical errors and the type frequency of Chinese characters. Ren's (2004) study on the HSK (Advanced) adopted a similar method. The 37 features extracted were largely similar to those in Zhang and Ren (2004), with the exception of some quantitative indexes based on some keywords identified by the researchers as topically related to target essays. In both studies, the established models were then applied to scoring other MHK (Band 3) or HSK (Advanced) essays, and the automated scores had moderate or high correlations with human raters' scores (r from 0.75 to 0.84). In a similar vein, Huang et al. (2014) correlated quantified indexes of 107 features of six categories (i.e., essay length, handwriting of Chinese characters, lexical use, grammar, discourse, and formality) with human raters' scores of a large number of HSK essays. A regression model was constructed with 19 features of five categories that showed a correlation of 0.3 or higher with human raters' scores (e.g., the numbers of characters, words of different frequency levels, and sentences). Interestingly, the model was only robust for scoring essays whose scores were in the middle range of HSK scores as opposed to those on the high end.

While the aforementioned studies focused on determining features of different categories to build a model for automated essay scoring, a few studies focused on how a particular category of features should be important and be employed to develop an algorithm for automated scoring. Feng et al. (2008), for example, explored formality of Chinese writing, which, according to Prosodic Grammar of Chinese (Feng 2005), covers at least three features: monosyllabic words used in disyllabic templates, disyllabic words used in disyllabic copulates, and formal sentence patterns in written Chinese. A program of degree of formality that considered five features was developed and applied to a large sample of HSK essays that covered four levels. A close correspondence was found between the writing levels assigned by human raters and the degree of formality generated by the automated scoring program. Cai et al. (2011) found that a significant proportion of minority students' MHK essays deviated from the topics, which led the authors to believe that an automated scoring system should consider features related to topic relevance over and above discrete low-level features. To this end, the authors combined the technology of statistical natural language processing and information retrieval (e.g., term frequency and PageRank) to extract topic features, and proposed a statistical model called Triple Segmented Regression (TSR). The essay scoring program based on the TSR reached a very high level of agreement with a human rater when scoring essays of the MHK, with about 97% precision and a correlation of about 0.92.

If using the synthesis of L2 writing assessment research in Leki et al. (2008) as a reference, there are clearly plenty of issues yet to be examined about testing of CSL writing. In addition to many issues that have interested ESL researchers, there are also ones that specifically pertain to assessing Chinese writing that have received little research attention. For example, Chinese has a logographic writing system. It is required that test-takers handwrite Chinese characters to complete a writing task in traditional paper-and-pencil tests. In the digital age, some CSL tests, such as the TOCFL-Writing, are now computer-based and require typewriting. There are different types of Chinese character input methods that vary in the level of learning challenges and input efficiency (Wong et al. 2011). Consequently, a question to ask about CSL writing testing is how digital literacy, like the skill to input Chinese characters, is related to test-takers' performance on a writing test and how computer-based testing of Chinese writing might lead to testing bias among test-takers in comparison with traditional paper-and-pencil testing (see Liu, this volume, for a similar discussion).

Vocabulary and Grammatical Knowledge

Major current CSL tests do not have a section specifically for testing vocabulary knowledge. The HSK (Elementary/Intermediate) used to include a separate section for testing grammatical structure, but it was abandoned in the New HSK. Testing of grammatical knowledge does not seem to disappear though. For example, the first part of the reading section of the New HSK (Band 6) asks test-takers to identify erroneous sentences, which essentially involves test-takers' grammatical competence, even though that part is used as an assessment of reading skills.

There has been a lot of discussion among CSL researchers on how many words students need to know to pass a certain band of a test (e.g., Zhai 2012). However, little research has been conducted that aimed to directly test vocabulary knowledge. Qian (2002) developed two tests of vocabulary breadth with 300 target words sampled from the 3051 words of Levels 1 and 2, the two lower levels in the *Outline of Graded Words and Characters for Chinese Proficiency* (OGWCCP), which was developed by the then Testing Center of the National Chinese Proficiency Testing Committee and includes 8822 most commonly used words at four levels. One test asked learners to provide a meaning definition in their native language for each word; the other was modeled on Nation's (1990) Vocabulary Levels Test (VLT): the 300 words were divided into 50 groups, each group with six words and three meaning explanations in Chinese; learners were to match the meaning explanations with three of the six words in each group. Results showed that the Chinese VLT test produced a much higher proportion of correct answers than did the translation test. Learners' performance on the two tests also strongly correlated.

Ren (2011) developed an active vocabulary test for foreign learners studying in China where in a written sentence, either a single-character word was removed with the initial of its pinyin syllable provided, or a multiple-character word was removed with the pinyin of the first morpheme provided. Learners were to use the given initial or syllable to write the character(s) of the removed word to fill in the blank. Sixty target words were sampled from the 3052 Levels 1 and 2 words from the OGWCCP. The test result led to an estimate that first-year learners' active vocabulary size was 638 and second-year learners' 1520. Those numbers suggested that they had not reached the size of active vocabulary required of them (993 and 1756, respectively) by the *Teaching Syllabus of Chinese for Foreign Students of Chinese Major in Higher Educational Institutions* (hereafter, *Syllabus for Foreign Students*), a document developed by the then National Committee on Teaching Chinese as a Foreign Language, the predecessor of the Hanban, to guide the teaching of Chinese to foreign students with a Chinese major in colleges in China.

Chinese uses a character-based writing system, which makes it different from alphabetic languages like English, which follow the rule of Grapheme-to-Phoneme Correspondence (GPC). To facilitate the pronunciations of Chinese characters in children's early literacy development, pinyin, an alphabetic system, is adopted in mainland China to annotate characters, and it is also commonly introduced to L2 learners of Chinese. Given the unique representation of Chinese words in print, there has been a natural research interest in the phonological as well as orthographic dimensions of Chinese words in addition to the semantic dimension when L2 Chinese vocabulary acquisition and assessment are examined. Zhao (2003), for example, asked beginning learners to write the pinyin of characters sampled from their textbooks and use the characters to create compound words. The two tasks showed a very strong correlation. Li's (2003) study was similar and included a third task that asked learners to write out a target character that appeared in the context of a multiple-character word with pinyin provided. Not surprisingly, advanced learners outperformed intermediate learners on all three tasks. What is interesting is that there was an unbalanced development of the three types of knowledge/skills—both groups of learners performed the best on providing pinyin for the target characters and the worst on writing the characters. The ability to recognize and write Chinese characters certainly has broad implications for CSL testing beyond being an aspect of Chinese word knowledge itself. Recently, a few standardized tests (e.g., the New HSK and the TOCFL) intentionally reduced the involvement of Chinese character recognition and/or writing in their lower bands that target beginning learners. However, as pointed out earlier at the end of the earlier review sections, the implications are yet to be studied empirically in CSL testing.

In comparison with vocabulary knowledge, research on assessment of grammatical knowledge has almost been overlooked in the CSL community, despite researchers' strong interests in learners' interlanguage grammar and grammatical teaching. Ren (2007) designed a test of grammar as a simplified placement test for foreign students studying Chinese in a university in China. The timed multiple-choice test, which covered major sentence structures stipulated in the *Syllabus for Foreign Students*, demonstrated high internal consistency reliability and correlated highly with the learners' HSK scores and their total score of a department-level placement test that covered vocabulary, grammar, reading, and writing.

Conclusions

Given that the research on CSL testing has been largely reported in Chinese and published in Chinese venues, which has prevented the international language testing community from knowing recent development in the field, this paper provided a review of major studies on CSL testing with a focus on four skills and two types of language knowledge (i.e., vocabulary and grammar). The review has shown fast growth of Chinese scholars' interests in CSL testing along with the development of standardized tools to measure students' Chinese proficiency. However, limitations are also apparent. In addition to the ones highlighted in each review section, it is clear that existing research shows an unbalanced attention to different issues. While speaking testing and automated essay scoring have attracted a lot of research attention, testing of grammatical knowledge and reading, for example, has been relatively under-researched. There are also issues specifically pertaining to L2 Chinese that remain to be addressed or expanded in research, such as the involvement of pinyin in testing reading and computer-mediated testing of Chinese writing.

A limitation of this review is noted. When preparing for this review, we restricted our search of the literature to full papers published in Chinese and English where empirical studies were reported. This means that those works published in other languages or unpublished research studies, such as those presented at conferences without a full paper, were necessarily not included. Such an inclusion criterion by no means indicated an inclination to devaluing the importance of those types of scholarly work. In addition, when we selected Chinese papers to be included in the review, we relied on CAJ, the largest database of papers published in Chinese academic journals in China. Such a decision means that some important work written in Chinese but published in venues outside of China could have been missed in the literature research. It is, therefore, admitted that the review in this paper does not necessarily represent a full spectrum of existing research on CSL testing.

Despite the above limitation, it is hoped that this chapter has achieved its purpose of providing international readers with an overview of major studies on the testing of Chinese skills and knowledge, and making scholars interested in the field aware of the research limitations so that more high-quality research could be conducted to address them. It is also our hope that more original research on issues that specifically pertain to Chinese testing could be conducted so that existing theories and models, which have largely been built on the basis of English language testing, could be refined and enriched to advance the field of language testing as a whole.

References

(References marked with * indicate articles reviewed in this paper)

Barkaoui, K. (2010). Do ESL essay raters' evaluation criteria change with experience? A mixed-methods, cross-sectional study. *TESOL Quarterly, 44,* 31–57.

*Bo, L. (2005). *Scoring essays of the HSK (Advanced): A comparison between scorers with different background* (Unpublished Master's Thesis). Beijing Language and Culture University (in Chinese).

Brown, A. (2003). Interview variation and the co-construction of speaking proficiency. *Language Testing, 20,* 1–25.

*Cai, L., Peng, X., & Zhao, J. (2011). An assisted scoring system for the MHK. *Journal of Chinese Information Processing, 5,* 120–125 (in Chinese).

*Chai, S. (2003). Theoretical analysis and empirical research on rater reliability of oral proficiency test in Chinese. *Language Teaching and Linguistic Studies, 4,* 69–77 (in Chinese).

*Chan, Y.-C. (2008). *Factors affecting the difficulty of short dialogue listening items of Test of Proficiency-Huayu.* Paper presented at the Annual Conference of the American Council on the Teaching of Foreign Languages. November 21–23, Orlando, Florida.

Chinese Ministry of Education (2014). *Statistics on overseas students in China in 2013.* Retrieved January 10, 2015, from http://www.moe.gov.cn/publicfiles/business/htmlfiles/moe/s5987/201402/164235.html (in Chinese).

*Clark, J. L. D. (1988). Validation of a tape-mediated ACTFL/ILR-scale based test of Chinese speaking proficiency. *Language Testing, 5,* 187–205.

Fang, X. (2007). The implications of CEFR to Chinese language testing. *Teaching Chinese in the World, 20,* 136–143. (in Chinese).

Feng, S. (2005). *Chinese prosodic grammar.* Beijing: Peking University Press (in Chinese).

*Feng, S., Wang, J., & Huang, M. (2008). An automatic feature checking algorithm for degree of formalities in written Chinese. *Language Sciences, 7*, 113–126 (in Chinese).

*Fu, H., Zhang, J., Li, Y., Li, P., & Zhang, T. (2013). Validity of the New HSK (Band 5). *China Examinations, 3*, 65–69 (in Chinese).

Fulcher, G., & Davison, F. (Eds.). (2012). *The Routledge handbook of language testing*. New York: Routledge.

Furman, N., Goldberg, D., & Lusin, N. (2010). *Enrollments in languages other than English in United States Institutions of higher education, Fall 2009*. Retrieved January 10, 2015, from http://www.mla.org/pdf/2009_enrollment_survey.pdf

Galaczi, E. D. (2010). Paired speaking tests: An approach grounded in theory and practice. In J. Mader & Z. Urkun (Eds.), *Recent approaches to teaching and assessing speaking (IATEFL TEA SIG Famagusta Conference Proceedings)*. Canterbury, UK: IATEFL Publications.

Ginther, A. (2002). Context and content visuals and performance on listening comprehension stimuli. *Language Testing, 19*, 133–167.

Hanban/Confucius Institute Headquarters. (2010). *About 40 million people are studying Chinese outside China*. Retrieved January 10, 2015, from http://www.hanban.edu.cn/article/2010-06/25/content_150854.htm (in Chinese).

*Huang, C. (2013). Washback effect of the HSK on Chinese learners' learning behaviors. *Journal of Yunnan Normal University (Chinese as a Second Language Teaching and Research), 1*, 10–17 (in Chinese).

*Huang, J., & Wang, J. (2013). Factor structure of L2 comprehension among advanced Chinese learners: A structural equation modeling approach. *TCSOL Studies, 2*, 24–35 (in Chinese).

*Huang, T. (2010). A study on the criterion-related validity of the listening section of the HSK (Revised, Intermediate). *China Examinations, 9*, 33–37 (in Chinese).

*Huang, Z., Xie, J., & Xun, E. (2014). Feature extraction for automated scoring of HSK essays. *Computer Engineering and Applications, 50*(8), 118–122 (in Chinese).

Jin, T., & Mak, B. (2012). Distinguishing features in scoring L2 Chinese speaking performance: How do they work? *Language Testing, 30*, 23–47.

*Jin, T., Mak, B., & Zhou, P. (2011). Confidence scoring of speaking performance: How does fuzziness become exact. *Language Testing, 29*, 43–65.

*Jin, T., Wang, Y., Song, C., & Guo, S. (2008). A fuzzy method for scoring spoken language test. *Modern Foreign Languages, 31*, 157–164.

Ke, C. (2012). Research in second language acquisition of Chinese: Where we are, where we are going? *Journal of the Chinese Language Teachers Association, 47*, 43–113.

*Ke, C., & Reed, D. J. (1995). An analysis of results from the ACTFL oral proficiency interview and the Chinese proficiency test before and after intensive instruction in Chinese as a foreign language. *Foreign Language Annals, 28*, 208–222.

Kostin, I. (2004). *Exploring item characteristics that are related to the difficulty of TOEFL dialogue items*. Princeton, NJ: ETS.

Kunnan, A. (Ed.). (2014). *The companion to language assessment*. Boston, MA: Wiley.

Leki, I., Cumming, A., & Silva, T. (2008). *A synthesis of research on second language writing in English*. New York: Routledge.

*Li, D. (2003). Character breadth of intermediate and advanced foreign learners of Chinese. *TSCOL Studies, 2*, 12–18 (in Chinese).

*Li, J., & Zhao, J. (2012). Two picture-based tests of writing in Chinese as a second language. *TCSOL Studies, 3*, 38–43 (in Chinese).

*Li, X., & Li, J. (2014). Validity of the spoken chinese test (SCT). *Teaching Chinese in the World, 1*, 103–112 (in Chinese).

Liskin-Gasparro, J. E. (2003). The ACTFL proficiency guidelines and the oral proficiency interview: A brief history and analysis and their survival. *Foreign Language Annals, 36*, 483–490.

*Liu, S. (1995). Developing a cloze test for Chinese as a second language. *Teaching Chinese in the World, 2*, 85–93 (in Chinese).

Nation, I. S. P. (1990). *Teaching and learning vocabulary*. New York: Newbury House Publishers.

*Qian, X. (2002). An exploratory study of assessing Chinese vocabulary size. *Teaching Chinese in the World, 4*, 54–62 (in Chinese).

*Ren, C. (2004). Objective scoring of HSK essays. *Chinese Language Learning, 6*, 58–67 (in Chinese).

*Ren, C. (2007). Developing a simplified placement test for Chinese as a second language. *Language Teaching and Linguistic Studies, 6*, 45–50.

*Ren, C. (2011). Measuring controlled productive vocabulary of learners of Chinese as a second language. *Applied Linguistics, 4*, 110–115 (in Chinese).

*Surface, E. A., & Dierdorff, E. C. (2003). Reliability and the ACTFL oral proficiency interview: Reporting indices of interrater consistency and agreement for 19 languages. *Foreign Language Annals, 36*, 507–519.

*Tu, H. (2011). Washback effect of the MHK on minority students' Chinese learning. *Language and Translation, 3*, 69–72 (in Chinese).

Vandergrift, L. (2007). State of the art: Recent developments in second and foreign language listening comprehension research. *Language Teaching, 40*, 191–210.

*Wang, D. (2012a). Self-assessment of oral presentation in advanced Chinese class. *Journal of Shenyang Aerospace University, 6*, 57–60 (in Chinese).

*Wang, J. (2002). Scoring three forms of Chinese speaking test. *Teaching Chinese in the World, 4*, 63–77 (in Chinese).

*Wang, J. (2005). Validity of self-assessment of second language ability. *Language Teaching and Linguistic Studies, 5*, 60–68 (in Chinese).

*Wang, J. (2007). Application of G-theory in testing elementary learners' Chinese speaking. *Journal of Yunnan Normal University (Chinese as a Second Language Teaching and Research), 2*, 31–37 (in Chinese).

*Wang, J. (2011). Different forms for testing elementary spoken Chinese. *Examinations Research, 5*, 67–76 (in Chinese).

*Wang, J. (2012b). Development of the language ability self-assessment scale for intermediate Chinese learners. *China Examinations, 11*, 11–16 (in Chinese).

Weigle, S. C., Boldt, H., & Valsecchi, M. I. (2003). Effects of task and rater background on the evaluation of ESL student writing: A pilot study. *TESOL Quarterly, 37*, 345–354.

Wong, L.-H., Chai, C.-S., & Gao, P. (2011). The Chinese input challenges for Chinese as a second language learners in computer-mediated writing: An exploratory study. *Turkish Online Journal of Educational Technology, 10*, 233–248.

*Xu, S. (2010). A study of diagnostic assessment of Chinese. *China Examinations, 7*, 12–16 (in Chinese).

*Yang, W., & Wen, Y. (2012). Semi-listening and full-listening testing for elementary Chinese learners. *Applied Linguistics, 3*, 107–116 (in Chinese).

Zhai, Y. (2012). On the development of word lists for teaching Chinese to beginning level learners. *TCSOL Studies, 3*, 52–59 (in Chinese).

*Zhang, J. (2006). Two factors influencing foreign students' performance on long dialogue/monologue listening. *Applied Linguistics, 1*, 99–106 (in Chinese).

*Zhang, J. (2011). Validity of computer-assisted scoring of the speaking test of the MHK (Band 3). *Examinations Research, 5*, 51–58 (in Chinese).

*Zhang, J., & Li, Y. (2009). Reliability and validity of the YCT. *TCSOL Studies, 3*, 40–45 (in Chinese).

*Zhang, J., & Ren, J. (2004). A study on electronic rating of Chinese essays. *China Examinations, 10*, 27–32 (in Chinese).

*Zhao, G. (2003). Productivity of characters in forming words and the acquisition of characters among beginning CSL learners. *Applied Linguistics, 3*, 106–112 (in Chinese).

*Zhao, L., & Xie, X. (2006). Different forms of assessing writing in Chinese as a second language. In X. Xie & J. Zhang (Eds.), *Studies on testing* (Vol. III, pp. 117–133). Beijing: Economic Sciences Press (in Chinese).
*Zhu, Y., Fung, S.-L., & Xin, T. (2013). Improving dependability of the New HSK writing test score: A G-theory based approach. *Journal of Psychological Science, 36,* 479–488 (in Chinese).

Part II
Assessing Orthography, Vocabulary, and Grammar

Chapter 5
How Ethnic Minority Students Perceive Patterns in Chinese Characters: Knowledge of Character Components and Structures

Elizabeth K.Y. Loh, Loretta C.W. Tam, Cally P.T. Lau and Shing On Leung

Abstract This chapter assesses ethnic minority (EM) adolescent Chinese as a second language (CSL) learners' perception of visual patterns in Chinese characters and examines the role of component and structural knowledge in CSL beginner- and intermediate-level curricula. In this exploratory mixed-methods study, 213 Grades 7–11 EM students of different ethnic origins in Hong Kong and Macau without prior training in components and spatial configurations of Chinese characters completed a set of tests that measured their character component and structural knowledge, including (i) the Separation of Character Components Test, (ii) the Constitution of Character Components Test, and (iii) the Character Structure Test. Five ways of componential analysis of Chinese characters, namely (1) unanalytical agglomeration of strokes; (2) agglomeration of sequenced strokes; (3) arbitrary repetition of (parts of) component; (4) hybrid agglomeration of strokes and components; and (5) agglomeration of components, were identified to be used by the participants. The participants' television-viewing habits had a significant effect on their performance on the test; however, overall, their demographic background and after-school activities had no significant effects on their test performance. With reference to the findings, recommendations on enhancing EM adolescent CSL learners' orthographic awareness for literacy success are given toward the end of the chapter. In particular, An Integrative Perceptual Approach for Teaching Chinese Characters (Tse et al. 2007) is recommended for teaching orthographic knowledge in a way that is beneficial to students' all-round second language (L2) development.

E.K.Y. Loh (✉) · L.C.W. Tam · C.P.T. Lau
The University of Hong Kong, Pok Fu Lam, Hong Kong, China
e-mail: ekyloh@hku.hk

S.O. Leung
University of Macau, Macau, China

© Springer Nature Singapore Pte Ltd. 2017
D. Zhang and C.-H. Lin (eds.), *Chinese as a Second Language Assessment*,
Chinese Language Learning Sciences, DOI 10.1007/978-981-10-4089-4_5

Keywords Chinese as a second language (CSL) · Ethnic minority (EM) students · Orthographic awareness · Chinese character components · Learning strategies

Introduction

There are about 28,854 ethnic minority (EM) students in Hong Kong (approximately 3.6% of the overall student population) studying in local public sector and directly subsidized schools (hereafter referred to as "local schools") (Education Bureau (EDB) of the Government of the Hong Kong SAR 2016), and 3,782 non-Chinese residents aged between 0 and 19 in Macau (approximately 1.2% of the overall student population) according to the 2011 Population Census (Direcção dos Serviços de Estatística e Censos de Macau 2011). These EM students are mostly descendants of migrants from India, Pakistan, Nepal, and the Philippines, with a small number of them being Caucasian, Eurasian, or immigrants from other parts of the world. Past research (EDB of the Government of the Hong Kong SAR 2008) indicated that EM students encounter difficulties in learning Chinese as a second language (CSL), particularly in character writing and reading. Lacking the automatic character recognition ability that characterizes efficient readers of Chinese (Leong et al. 2011), most EM students studying in local schools with compulsory Chinese curricula are facing enormous difficulties in mastering the language (Tsung et al. 2013). Such learning difficulties are often complicated by the huge diversity among EM students in local schools in terms of the number of years spent learning Chinese and the actual level of Chinese language proficiency. While some EM students were born in Hong Kong/Macau and started learning Chinese when they were young, others are new immigrants who only started learning the language upon their arrival in Hong Kong and Macau.

Geographically proximate to each other, both Hong Kong and Macau have been seeking solutions to confront the existing challenges of catering for individual learning needs of EM students. In Hong Kong, for example, streaming is a common practice in schools admitting EM students. EM students from different "streams" often show significant differences among themselves in trajectories of Chinese learning; as an effort to bridge the gaps in CSL learning among EM students, differentiation is being introduced to Chinese instruction in academically and ethnically mixed Chinese language classrooms. Schools in Macau tend to follow a different approach, encouraging EM students to learn Chinese in classrooms together with their ethnic Chinese counterparts, in hopes that they will integrate into the host society upon acquisition of the lingua franca "like a native speaker."

Given the fact that most teachers in both special administrative regions (SARs) are not trained in teaching Chinese as a second language, many of them adhere to the pedagogies they have been using for teaching native speakers in their classroom with EM students. Such a practice can be problematic as EM students' learning needs, ways of thinking and trajectory of Chinese development (esp., literacy) can be extremely different from those of their fellow Chinese-speaking counterparts

(Leong et al. 2011). As an example of their instructional practice, these teachers tend to spend little time teaching component- and spatial configuration-based orthographic knowledge; instead, they often go straight to text-based reading and writing practice (Loh et al. 2015a), overlooking the importance of direct instruction to help learners develop their orthographic knowledge (Chang 2009). Tsung et al. (2013) reported that Chinese character learning was considered by the teachers interviewed in Hong Kong as the major obstacle to CSL learning for EM students, who were frustrated and tended to give up quickly. In light of this challenge of Chinese characters for EM students, there is a pressing need to develop new pedagogies, curricula, and materials for teaching them Chinese characters, which could be based on cognitive processes of Chinese character recognition.

To this end, we conducted the present study that examined how EM students visually perceived patterns of Chinese characters. Specifically, it aimed to address the following two research questions. It is hoped that the findings could shed light on EM students' orthographic knowledge development for the teaching and learning of CSL in Hong Kong and Macau.

1. How do EM students without specific training in component- and spatial configuration-based orthographic knowledge in Chinese visually perceive Chinese characters?
2. How do EM students' demography and after-school activities relate to their visual perceptions of Chinese characters?

Character Components (Bùjiàn) and Orthographic Knowledge

As pointed out by Liu et al. (2007), Lee and Kalyuga (2011), second language (L2) learning in Chinese is a complex and challenging task, particularly for learners with an alphabetic language background. Given that the Chinese language is logographic without explicit phonetic hints like in alphabetic languages, character recognition is an essential skill that any learner of Chinese needs to have to access word meanings and comprehend texts.

The highly sophisticated orthographic system of the Chinese language often puzzles its L2 learners, including EM students in Hong Kong who mostly speak their heritage language and/or English at home and learn Chinese as a second language through formal instruction in school. Certain Chinese characters (字$zì$) are pictographs resembling physical objects, with 人 ("human") as an example, and evolving through time into their current orthographic forms. However, single-unit characters (獨體字) that have a pictographic origin are very small in number; most characters in modern Chinese are made up of multiple, reusable components or *bùjiàn* (部件)—estimated to be about 540—that fit well into the square space allocated for each character within a text (or 合體字, compound characters).

The majority of compound characters are phonetic-radical compound characters (形聲字) with a component providing partial information about the sound (i.e., phonetic) and another component about the meaning (i.e., semantic radical or simply radical) of the host character (Taylor and Taylor 1995). Competent Chinese language users would be able to guess the meaning or sound of a character based on the hints provided by its components (Zhang 1987).

Chinese radicals, estimated to be about 214 (Chinese National Language Committee 1998), are a centuries-old system for accessing dictionaries that can be dated back to the second century, as detailed in the philological work *Shuowen Jiezi* (*Analytical Dictionary of Characters*) by Xu Shen (58–147 AD). The long-established radical system finds its roots in Chinese etymology and semantics. More modern interest in the component system of Chinese characters places an emphasis not only on the phonetic and semantic information or "clues" as displayed in individual characters but also on the structural configurations and composition rules of the components.

Overall, the compositions of Chinese characters can be classified into 15 spatial configurations of structural components/*bùjiàn* (Ki et al. 2003; Tse 2000; Wong 2009), namely:

1. **single component (square)** 日 [sun];
2. **single component (triangle)** 上 [above];
3. **left-right** 日 [sun] + 月 [moon] = 明 (bright);
4. **upper-lower** 小 [small] + 大 [big] = 尖 [sharp];
5. **diagonal** 夕 [half moon] + 夕 [half moon] = 多 [many];
6. **left-middle-right** 彳 [walking slowly] + 圭 [jade] + 亍 [stop walking] = 街 [street];
7. **top-middle-bottom** 亠 [high] + 口 [mouth] + 小 [small] = 京[capital];
8. **top (left-right)-down** 竹 [bamboo] + 夭 [dog] = 笑 [smile];
9. **top-down (left-right)** 口 [mouth] + 口 [mouth] + 口 [mouth] = 品 [commodity];
10. **left-right (top-down)** 氵 [water] + 垰 [born] + 丹 [red] = 清 [clear];
11. **surrounding** 囗 [boundary] + 大 [big] = 因 [reason];
12. **outer-inner** 木 [wood] + 口 [mouth] = 束 [bundle];
13. **half-surrounding (top-down)** ⺈[rack] + 㐫[knot & death] = 罔 [net] or **(bottom-up)** 乂 [entangle] + 凵[trap] = 凶 [danger] or **(left-right)** 匚[ruler] + 口 [mouth] = 叵 [improbable];
14. **inclusive structure (left-bottom)** 走 [walk] + 丩 [join] = 赳 [valiant] or **(left-top)** 尸 [corpse] + 肖 [small] = 屑 [small pieces] or **(right-top)** 戈 [weapon] + 廾 [two hands] = 戒 [get rid of];
15. **eudipleural** 大 [big] + 人 [human] + 人 [human] = 夾 [hold].

Tse (2002) found that 77 of the most commonly used components constitute 1200 high-frequency Chinese characters. Forty-eight of them are single-component characters themselves (e.g., 人 person), of which 26 are commonly used with such good configuration ability (as deformable components [變形部件] when combined with other components (e.g., 人 and 亻) that they construct one-third of essential Chinese characters. Wong (2009) reported that most of traditional Chinese characters are constructed by two to eight components (with five as the average number). As a result, the memory load for memorizing components is lower than strokes. (The average number of stokes of characters is about 12, and there is no meaningful relationship between the different strokes as opposed to components.) Character learning could thus be possibly enhanced by acquiring these single-component characters with high occurrence and good configuration ability (Tse 2002; Zhang 2012), as the components involved are meaning carriers and thus making better sense to learners.

Previous studies showed that orthographic awareness enhances character learning among Chinese-speaking students (e.g. Shu et al. 2000). This kind of sensitivity has also been found to benefit the learning of characters among second language learners of Chinese, including kindergarteners (e.g., Loh et al. 2013; Tse and Loh 2014), primary school students (Tse et al. 2012), secondary school students (Lee and Kalyuga 2011) as well as adult learners (e.g., Liu et al. 2007). However, L2 studies on learners' orthographic knowledge are still limited. In addition, these existing studies only addressed a limited number of components (Shu and Anderson 1997) or structures (e.g., Loh et al. 2013; Shu et al. 2003). A complete understanding of L2 learners' knowledge of diverse spatial configurations of components is yet to be achieved. To this end, the current study examined the perceptions of the 26 most commonly used components with high configuration ability and 15 spatial configurations among EM students learning CSL in Hong Kong and Macau. By prioritizing essential Chinese components and identifying the effect, if any, of sociocultural factors on orthographic knowledge acquisition among secondary EM students, the authors also aimed to propose a number of feasible solutions to the challenges faced by adolescent CSL learners in Hong Kong and Macau in their character learning.

Methods

Participants

One hundred and fifty-one EM students (49 males and 102 females) from a local secondary school in Hong Kong and 62 EM students (34 males and 28 females) from a local secondary school in Macau took part in the study as a closed cohort through convenience sampling. Both schools were EM-dominated mission schools adopting the Hong Kong Chinese language curriculum teaching the Traditional Chinese script and spoken Cantonese. Among them, 141 of them were lower secondary students and 72 of them were upper secondary students (see Table 5.1).

Among the 213 EM students, four major ethnic groups were identified, including Filipinos ($N = 80$), Pakistanis ($N = 66$), Nepalese ($N = 30$), and Indians ($N = 21$). There were also 14 participants from other ethnic groups (see Table 5.2); most of

Table 5.1 Distribution of participants with different years of study in school (*N* = 213)

Year of study	*N*	Percentage
Grade 7	52	24.40
Grade 8	47	22.10
Grade 9	42	19.70
Grade 10	33	15.50
Grade 11	39	18.30

Table 5.2 Overview of participants' ethnicities (*N* = 213)

Ethnicity	*N*	Percentage
Filipino	80	37.6
Pakistani	66	31
Nepalese	30	14.1
Indian	21	9.9
Others	14	6.6
Missing	2	0.9

Table 5.3 Age of participants at the time of migration to Hong Kong/Macau (*N* = 213)

Time of migration to Hong Kong/Macau	*N*	Percentage
Born in Hong Kong/Macau	136	36.8
0–3 years old	18	8.5
3–6 years old	18	8.5
After 6 years old	41	19.2

them were Asian (4 Thais, 2 Myanmarese, 2 overseas Chinese, 1 Korean), with 1 Australian, 1 Portuguese, 1 Irish, 1 Kazakh, and 1 African. Ethnicity information was not available for two students.

Most of the participants (*N* = 136) were born in their place of residence (i.e., Hong Kong/Macau), with 36 moving to Hong Kong/Macau between 0 and 6 years old, and 41 after six years old (see Table 5.3).

Research Instruments

Three tasks, designed by the research team on the basis of the *Chinese Language Assessment Tool for Non-Chinese Speaking Students* (Education Bureau of the Government of the Hong Kong SAR 2010), were adopted in this study to examine the orthographic awareness of the participants. The tasks aligned with the basic requirements for the first stage in reading in both the Chinese as the first language (CL) primary curriculum (Curriculum Development Council of the Hong Kong SAR 2008) and the CSL general curriculum (Education Bureau of the Government of the Hong Kong SAR 2014), i.e., "ability to recognize and read aloud commonly used characters," with orthographic knowledge as the prerequisite or an integral part of the curriculum. In addition, a language use survey was administered.

Separation of Chinese Character Components Test

This instrument assessed the participants' awareness of Chinese character components, more specifically, whether they were able to separate various components from a character. It covered 26 randomly ordered compound characters constituted by the 26 most commonly used components (which were themselves single-component characters) with high configuration ability.

Each participant was required to list the components embedded in their host compound characters so as to break the characters down into individual components. Each compound character (i.e., each item) with all components correctly listed was awarded 1 mark, the full mark of each item. A partial mark was also awarded with one or more but not all components correctly listed. For each item, the partial mark is equal to the number of components identified divided by the total number of components. Regardless of partial or full mark, each Chinese character, or each item, is scored with the range 0–1. The maximum raw score possible for this task was 26. The final scores were reported in decimal form representing a proportion (i.e., total raw score divided by 26).

E.g., 倡 = 亻 (or 人) + 日 + 日

Constitution of Chinese Character Components Test

This instrument assessed the participants' ability to use the components commonly used in their curricular materials to construct Chinese characters. Based on seven of the most commonly used single-unit components (i.e., 人, 心, 女, 口, 木, 目 and 子), it required the EM students to compose as many legitimate characters as possible. With these seven components, the theoretical total number of legitimate characters is 39. For each participant, the individual score was the total number of characters composed divided by 39. Each possibly composed character was considered an item. For each item, the item score was the total number of participants who composed that character divided by the total number of participants.

Chinese Character Structure Test

This instrument assessed the participants' awareness of 15 types of spatial configurations of Chinese characters via 30 multiple-choice-type items. It required the participants to identify the structure of each of the 30 target characters by circling the correct choice among the four given options. The 30 randomly ordered characters were selected from the list of *Frequency Statistics of Commonly Used Modern Chinese Characters* (Ho and Kwan 2001). Each correct answer would be awarded one mark. The maximum raw score for this test was 30. The final scores were reported in decimal form representing the proportion of correct choices.

E.g., 多   A. ⊟   B. ◩   C. ⊟   D. ⊡

(The correct answer is B)

Survey on Participants' Language Use

The survey consisted of 10 multiple-choice questions. It covered the students' ethnic and sociolinguistic backgrounds, language domains, as well as their television-viewing, reading, and Chinese language learning habits. It helped us examine the relationship between the students' after-school activities and their performance on the aforementioned three tasks, with an objective to identify factors affecting CSL literacy development in informal contexts. Up to 5 options were given in each of the multiple-choice questions; the students were asked to choose the option that best described their background or after-school activities.

For example, 你每星期花多少時間溫習中文? How much time do you spend every week studying Chinese?

A. 沒有時間 No time
B. 1小時以下 Less than one hour
C. 1至3小時 One to three hours
D. 3至7小時 Three to seven hours
E. 其他Others
   (請註明Please specify: _____)

Data Collection

Multiple one-hour on-site, pencil-and-paper assessment tests took place in the participating schools. The participants were given detailed instructions and allowed to raise queries about the tests before they took them. At least, one research team member was sent to each test site as an invigilator.

Analytical Tools/Methods

The data collected were analyzed both qualitatively and quantitatively. The quantitative analysis was conducted with SPSS (e.g., ANOVA), whereas the qualitative data were examined in the form of typological analysis. The participants' patterns of deciphering the spatial configurations of Chinese characters were identified by categorizing their answers for Task 1 according to the basic unit(s) they opted for (e.g., components, strokes) and the combinations formed.

Results

Task 1: Separation of Chinese Character Components Test

The mean and standard deviation of the 213 participants' scores for Task 1 were 0.79 and 0.123, respectively. Cronbach's alpha was 0.84, indicating a good level of reliability. The results showed that the participants, who had not received systematic, formal training in Chinese character components and their spatial configurations, overall possessed a certain, yet limited, level of knowledge of them. Out of the 213 participants, 122 (or about 57.9%) scored 0.80 or above, among whom 17 (about 8.1% of all 213 participants) earned 0.90 or above, and the scores of the other 105 (about 49.8% of all participants) fell into a range of 0.80–0.89. Only five participants (2.3% of the cohort) earned 0.30 or below.

For item-level analysis, the mean score for each item in Task 1 fell within a range of 0.62–0.94. The items with the largest number of correct responses were "災" (lit. "disaster," 91.1% correctness out of 213 responses), "初" (lit. "beginning," 89.2% correctness), "想" (lit. "to think," 87.3% correctness), "蝴" (lit. one of the characters in the word "butterfly," 82.6% correctness), and "霜" (lit. "frost," 82.2% correctness). The items with the smallest number of correct responses included "藥" (lit. "medicine," 36.6% correctness), "糕" (lit. "cake," 34.7% correctness), "臉" (lit. "face," 34.3% correctness), "晴" (lit. "sunny," 33.3% correctness), and "問" (lit. "to ask," 25.5% correctness).

There were multiple ways in which the EM students in Hong Kong and Macau visually perceived Chinese characters when asked to break the target characters down to their components. Based on the analysis of the scripts produced by the participants for Task 1, five ways were identified. They included unanalytical agglomeration of strokes, agglomeration of sequenced strokes, arbitrary repetition of (parts of) component, hybrid agglomeration of sequenced strokes and components, and agglomeration of components, which we describe in detail below.

1. Unanalytical agglomeration of strokes (see Fig. 5.1)

In the above example, the character "做" (lit. "to do") was split into eight individual parts, displaying the stroke sequence by adding a new stroke to a set of repeated strokes in the preceding space. Interestingly, it shows close resemblance to how

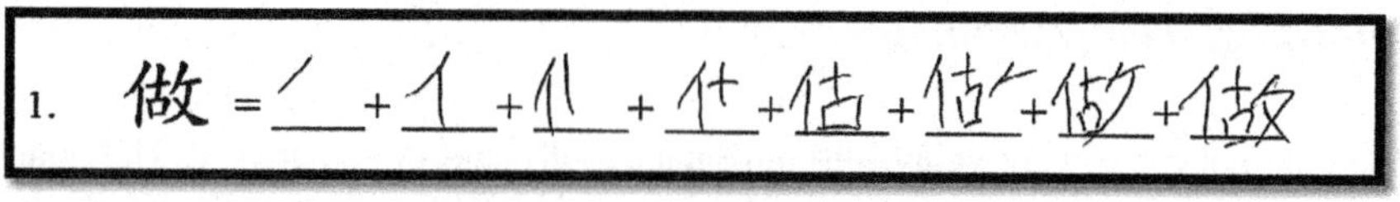

Fig. 5.1 Chinese character splitting—unanalytical agglomeration of strokes

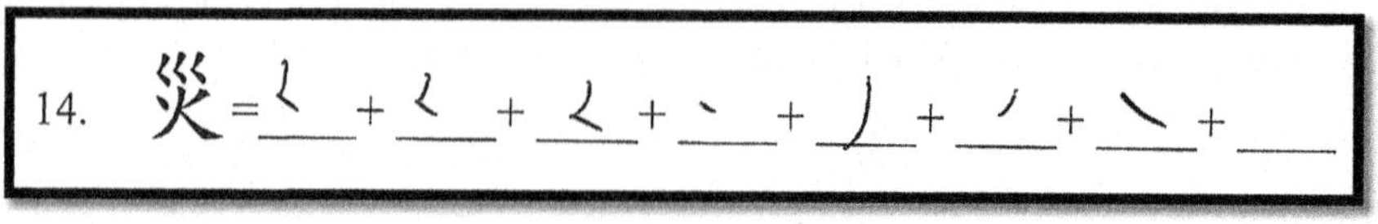

Fig. 5.2 Chinese character splitting—agglomeration of sequenced strokes

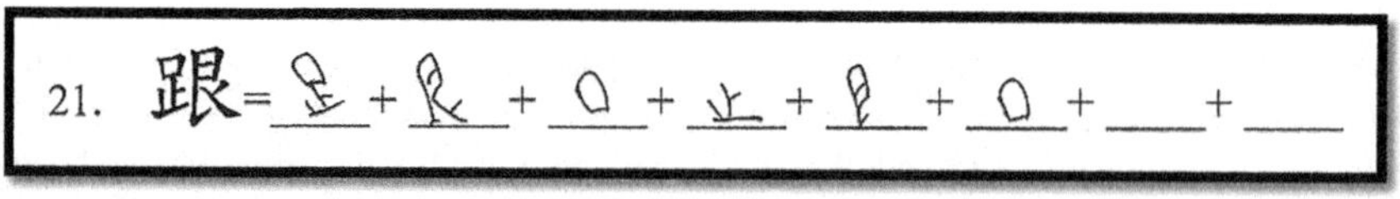

Fig. 5.3 Chinese character splitting—arbitrary repetition of (parts of) component

learners of Chinese, including CSL learners, typically practice character writing in their exercises, which do not have a focus on breaking down characters into their constituent components or *bùjiàn*. Apparently the participant whose pattern of breaking down 做 in the example given did not have a clear concept of character component—he/she made a guesstimate that showed a confusion between stroke and bùjiàn in written Chinese. In other words, the structure of the character was visually perceived by the participant as an unanalytical agglomeration of strokes showing little concept of component constitution of characters.

2. Agglomeration of sequenced strokes (see Fig. 5.2)

In the above example, the character "災" (lit. "disaster") was split into seven individual parts, all of which were individual strokes making up the character. Apparently the participant did not have a clear concept of character components. Like the participant who produced the example shown in Fig. 5.2, he/she seemed to be confused between the smallest written unit (i.e., stroke) and the smallest meaningful unit (i.e., bùjiàn or component) in written Chinese. As a result, the participant gave an incorrect answer in which the visual structure of the character was presented simply as an agglomeration of strokes in a sequence he/she was used to writing the character.

3. Arbitrary repetition of (parts of) component (see Fig. 5.3)

In the above example, the character "跟" (lit. "heel"; "to follow") was split into six individual parts. The participant seemed to display a certain level of awareness of character component with the two components of 跟 correctly produced (the first and second parts in Fig. 5.3). However, it does not seem clear if his/her awareness was intact or he/she might still be confused about what constitutes components, as he/she further split the two components into stoke combinations that are not necessarily meaningful (see, in particular, the fifth part on his/her list). Eventually, the answer was only partially correct in that the visual structure of the character was presented as only an arbitrary repetition of parts of components in a sequence he/she was used to when writing the character.

4. Hybrid agglomeration of sequenced strokes and components (see Fig. 5.4):

In the above example, the character "灾" (lit. "disaster") was split into four individual parts, three of which were individual strokes making up the top half of the character, whereas the remainder was the component "火" (lit. "fire") making up the bottom half of the character. Like his/her peer who produced in the example shown in Fig. 5.3, this participant seemed to have developed a certain level of awareness of character components giving him/her discernment of "火" from the overall structure of 灾 as a correct component, yet his/her orthographic knowledge did not seem to be sufficient for him/her to discern "巛" (archaic; lit. "river") as another component of the target character. In other words, he/she still seemed to be confused between stroke and component in written Chinese. As a result, his/her answer was only partially correct in that the visual structure of the character was perceived as a hybrid agglomeration of three strokes (in a sequence, he/she might be used to when writing the character) and a component (i.e., 灾 having four parts rather than being composed of two components).

5. Agglomeration of components (see Fig. 5.5):

In the above example, the character "霜" (lit. "frost") was split into three individual parts, namely "雨" (lit. "rain"), "木" (lit. "wood") and "目" (lit. "eye"). The participant offered the correct answer by identifying the character as an agglomeration of the three components.

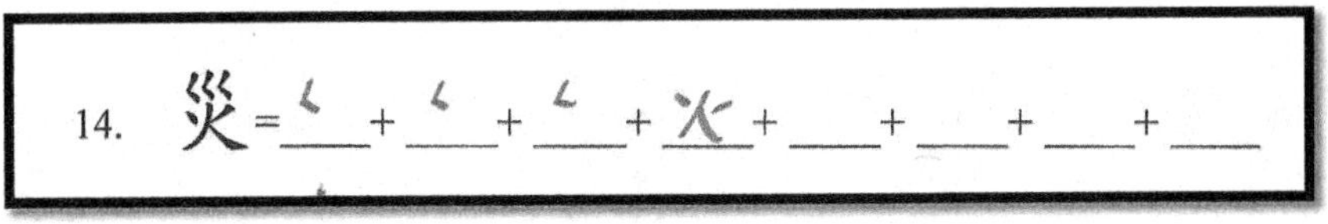

Fig. 5.4 Character splitting—hybrid agglomeration of strokes and components

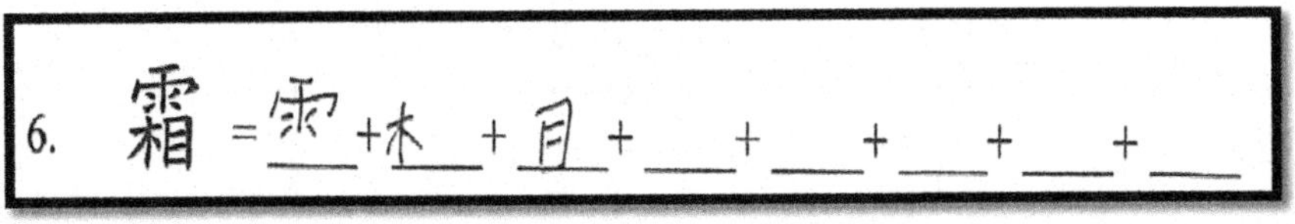

Fig. 5.5 Chinese character splitting—agglomeration of components

Task 2: Constitution of Chinese Character Components Test

Thirty-nine legitimate characters were created by the participants using the seven components provided in the task. These characters are listed below in a descending order of occurrence (more specifically, the proportion of the 213 participants who produced each character) (see Table 5.4).

The ten most frequently occurring characters were "想" (lit. "want," "think"), "好" (lit. "good"), "如" (lit. "if"), "相" (lit. "inspect," "together"), "林" (lit. "forest"), "森" (lit. "forest"), "仔" (lit. "son," "small," "young"), "休" (lit. "stop," "rest"), "品" (lit. "taste," "quality") and "李" (lit. "plum," and a common family name too). Among them, six carried the component "木" (lit. "wood") and three carried the component "子" (lit. "child"), with left-right (6 characters) and top-down (4 characters) spatial configurations (3 characters with a combination of both) as the most frequently occurring ones. All of the aforementioned characters were commonly used in both Hong Kong and Macau and were relatively familiar to the participants (e.g., 87.3% participants answered the Task 1 question on "想" correctly).

Table 5.4 List of legitimate Chinese characters created with the given components by the participants (in descending order)

Character created with given components (ranked 1–20)	Frequency of occurrence (proportional to 213 participants)	Character created with given components (ranked 21–39)	Frequency of occurrence (proportional to 213 participants)
1. 想	0.859	21. 伈	0.089
2. 好	0.728	22. 呌	0.085
3. 如	0.685	23. 伙	0.075
4. 相	0.653	24. 叺	0.075
5. 林	0.549	25. 孖	0.052
6. 森	0.547	26. 怒	0.042
7. 仔	0.514	27. 呼	0.038
8. 休	0.423	28. 囡	0.033
9. 品	0.413	29. 孟	0.033
10. 李	0.380	30. 惢	0.028
11. 困	0.239	31. 惏	0.028
12. 回	0.197	32. 众	0.023
13. 杍	0.178	33. 囚	0.023
14. 杏	0.156	34. 杺	0.023
15. 保	0.155	35. 从	0.019
16. 呆	0.150	36. 团	0.014
17. 姦	0.131	37. 田	0.005
18. 恕	0.113	38. 弄	0.005
19. 忎	0.103	39. 杲	0.005
20. 來	0.099		

The ten least frequently occurring characters were "惢" (lit. "suspicious"), "㤝" (lit. "violent"), "众" (lit. "crowd"), "囚" (lit. "to imprison"; "the imprisoned"), "杺" (lit. "a type of tree with yellow heartwood"), "从" (lit. "to follow," "belonged to"), "囝" (lit. "child"), "昍" (lit. "bright"), "孨" (lit. "weak," "cowardly"), and "喿" (lit. "chirping of birds"). Among them, only "众", "囚", "从", and "囝" are considered commonly used characters, with "众" and "从" as simplified equivalents of "眾" and "從", respectively. Three of them carried the component "心" (lit. "heart"); another three carried the character/component "木" (lit. "wood"), with left-right and top-down combined (5 characters), left-right (3 characters), and surrounding (2 characters) as the most frequently occurring spatial configurations. Given that all of the aforementioned characters were rarely used in both Hong Kong and Macau (and thus unlikely taught in school curriculum), it is highly likely that they were guesses made by the participants using their orthographic knowledge of spatial configurations.

Task 3: Chinese Character Structure Test

The mean and standard deviation of the 213 participants' performance on the Character Structure Test were 0.65 and 0.129, respectively. Cronbach's alpha was 0.623, indicating an acceptable level of reliability. Among the 213 participants, 28 of them (13.1%) earned 0.80 or above, whereas 23 of them (12.3%) earned lower than 0.50. Most participants fell into the 0.50–0.77 range (76.1%). Only 4 participants scored 0.30 or below, making up a mere 1.9% of the cohort. These findings seem to suggest that the participants as a group possessed a certain level of awareness in spatial configurations of character components despite a lack of formal training in orthographic structure of characters.

Our item-level analysis revealed that the five target characters (out of 30) with the largest number of correct responses from the 213 participants were "做" (lit. "to do") (left-right; 93.9% correctness); "的" (lit. "something/somebody's") (left-right; 91.5% correctness); "和" (lit. "and," "peace") (left-right; 91.5% correctness); "晶" (lit. "crystal") (top-down and left-right; 88.7% correctness); and "月" (lit. "moon") (single component; rectangle; 86.4% correctness). The five characters with the smallest number of correct responses were "我" (lit. "I", "me") (single component; square; 39.0% correctness); "問" (lit. "ask") (half-surrounding and top-down; 34.7% correctness); "時" (lit. "time") (left-right; 28.6% correctness); "爲" (lit. "for") (diagonal; 19.7% correctness); and "喉" (lit. "throat") (left-right; 15.0% correctness).

Relationship of Participants' Demography and After-School Activities with Orthographic Knowledge

As shown in Table 5.5, among the four major ethnic groups (i.e., the Filipinos, Pakistanis, Nepalese and Indians), based on the sample means, the Filipinos appeared to score the highest whereas the Indians the lowest for Task 1. For Task 2, the Pakistanis appeared to score the highest whereas the lowest-scoring group was the Filipinos. The Filipinos appeared to score the highest for Task 3, with the Indians as the lowest-scoring group (see Table 5.5). Results of the ANOVA for each task, however, showed that ethnicity had a significant effect on the learners' performance on Task 2 only ($F = 5.679$, $p < 0.001$); no significant differences among the four ethnic groups were observed for Tasks 1 and 3.

For all three of the tasks, ANOVA revealed no significant effect of the age at which the participants arrived in Hong Kong or Macau (see Table 5.6).

We also analyzed if the participants' television (TV)-viewing habits would have any effect on their performance on Tasks 1 to 3. As shown in Table 5.7, the mean scores of the participants who reported watching TV after school appeared to outperform those who did not on all three tasks. Further t tests, however, showed that participants who have more TV viewing performed significantly better in Task 2 only, and there was no significant effect of TV viewing on the performance on Tasks 1 and 3.

Table 5.5 Mean scores of Tasks 1–3 according to ethnic groupings

Student ethnicity	M of Task 1 (SD)	M of Task 2 (SD)	M of Task 3 (SD)
Filipino	0.803 (0.087)	0.162 (0.105)	0.653 (0.128)
Pakistani	0.783 (0.167)	0.237 (0.103)	0.627 (0.126)
Nepalese	0.786 (0.135)	0.208 (0.121)	0.651 (0.129)
Indian	0.766 (0.094)	0.227 (0.111)	0.625 (0.156)
Others	0.820 (0.067)	0.253 (0.092)	0.68655 (0.116)
F value	F (4, 204) = 0.673, $p = 0.611$	F (4, 204) = 5.679***, $p < 0.001$	F (4, 206) = 0.603, $p = 0.661$

*** $p < 0.001$

Table 5.6 Mean scores of Tasks 1–3 according to age of arrival in Hong Kong or Macau ($N = 213$)

Time of migration to Hong Kong/Macau	M of Task 1 (SD)	M of Task 2 (SD)	M of Task 3 (SD)
Born in HK/Macau	0.790 (0.128)	0.211 (0.114)	0.640 (0.121)
0–3 years old	0.797 (0.072)	0.219 (0.131)	0.633 (0.149)
3–6 years old	0.793 (0.118)	0.171 (0.081)	0.665 (0.125)
After 6 years old	0.797 (0.130)	0.193 (0.101)	0.655 (0.146)
F value	F (3, 207) = 0.040, $p = 0.989$	F (3, 207) = 0.972, $p = 0.407$	F (3, 209) = 0.388, $p = 0.762$

Table 5.8 further shows the mean scores of those TV-watching students (168 in total) as related to the language of the TV programs they watched (i.e., if they watched TV programs in Chinese/with Chinese subtitles or programs not in Chinese). The sample means in Table 5.8 appeared to suggest that watching Chinese TV programs or TV programs with Chinese subtitles helped to improve the participants' ability of using given character components to construct Chinese characters (i.e., Task 2), and there did not appear to be any effect on their ability of separating the components for characters (Task 1) or identifying the spatial configurations of characters (Task 3) (see Table 5.8). Further t tests confirmed that the participants who watched Chinese TV programs performed significantly better in Task 2 only.

Finally, ANOVA revealed that the participants' time spent on studying Chinese outside of class did not have a significant effect on their performance on any one of the three tasks. However, based on the sample means presented in Table 5.9,

Table 5.7 Mean scores of Tasks 1–3 as related to participants' television-viewing habits ($N = 213$)

TV-watching habits after school	N	M of Task 1 (SD)	M of Task 2 (SD)	M of Task 3 (SD)
Yes	168	0.793 (0.125)	0.213 (0.110)	0.651 (0.124)
No	45	0.788 (0.118)	0.174 (0.110)	0.632 (0.145)
T value		$t (1, 209) = 0.233$, $p = 0.816$	$t (1, 209) = 2.092*$, $p = 0.038$	$t (1, 211) = 0.896$, $p = 0.371$

* $p < 0.01$

Table 5.8 Mean scores of Tasks 1–3 as related to participants' choice of television programs ($N = 166$)

Watching Chinese TV programs after school	N	M of Task 1 (SD)	M of Task 2 (SD)	M of Task 3 (SD)
Yes	68	0.787 (0.144)	0.237 (0.115)	0.635 (0.124)
No	98	0.798 (0.110)	0.197 (0.104)	0.662 (0.123)
T value		$t (1, 164) = 0.555$, $p = 0.580$	$t (1, 162) = 2.335*$, $p = 0.021$	$t (1, 166) = 1.375$, $p = 0.171$

* $p < 0.01$

Table 5.9 Mean scores of Tasks 1–3 as related to time spent on studying Chinese ($N = 213$)

Time spent on studying Chinese	Mean of Task 1 (SD)	Mean of Task 2 (SD)	Mean of Task 3 (SD)
No time	0.790 (0.085)	0.210(0.121)	0.649 (0.150)
Less than 1 hour	0.790 (0.118)	0.204 (0.117)	0.651 (0.120)
1–3 hours	0.785 (0.137)	0.201 (0.098)	0.640 (0.137)
3–7 hours	0.801 (0.165)	0.213 (0.099)	0.643 (0.103)
More than 7 hours	0.856 (0.014)	0.372 (0.091)	0.683 (0.024)
F value	$F (4, 201) = 0.205$, $p = 0.936$	$F (4, 201) = 1.420$, $p = 0.224$	$F (4, 203) = 0.119$, $p = 0.976$

it appeared that there was some positive effect on their Chinese orthographic knowledge at or beyond the 3-h threshold in a week. Those participants who reported having spent three to 7 hours per week studying Chinese appeared to earn the highest mean scores for Tasks 1 and 2, namely 0.801 (Task 1) and 0.213 (Task 2), respectively. No such tendency, however, was found for Task 3, in which the "More than 7 hours" group appeared to earn the highest mean score (i.e., 0.683).

Discussion

Participants' Task Performance

To answer the first research question, despite the lack of systemic, formal training in component-related orthographic knowledge, there was a relatively high percentage of the participants earning 0.8 or above (57.9%) for Task 1 (i.e., Separation of Character Components). We argue that this fairly good performance among the participants might be attributed to their knowledge of Chinese (semantic) radicals, which teachers from both schools claimed as an essential part of their Chinese language (CL) curricula. The students' prior training in Chinese radicals might have played a role in enhancing their orthographic awareness with respect to character components in general. At the item level, the fact that they carry common components with simple spatial configurations such as top-down, left-right, and left-middle-right seemed reasonable for the largest number of correct responses to occur for characters such as "災", "初", "想", "蝴" and "霜". Likewise, the less common components and relatively sophisticated, multi-tiered spatial configurations of the characters such as "藥", "糕", "臉", "晴", and "問" might explain the finding that they received the smallest number of correct responses.

As for Task 2 (Constitution of Chinese Character Components Test), the results showed that the participants were able to create at least a few characters from the list of common components with which the students should be rather familiar. The top ten characters produced by the students (see Table 5.4) were actually basic vocabulary items in CSL beginners' curricula; their frequent appearance seemed to indicate that the participants' mental lexicon was accessed during the test. Among the 10 characters, six were of a left-right structure and four a top-down structure (three actually involved a combination of both), which seems to suggest that it was easier for the participants to master these two spatial configurations of components.

One should note that obsolete or rarely used characters also came up on the list of legitimate characters produced by the participants in Task 2. Their frequency of appearance, however, was very low (see Table 5.4). Given that these characters are either rare characters seldom used in daily life or simplified Chinese characters, they were supposed to be totally new to the participants. It seemed evident that they were educated guesses of those who produced them. On the other hand, the guesses might constitute a good piece of evidence that supports the active use of orthographic knowledge among those students. In other words, the fact that these characters are legitimate ones suggests the active engagement of some EM students, albeit small in number, with the components they were familiar with as well as their knowledge of common spatial configurations of components of Chinese characters (e.g., left-right and top-down or a combination of them).

Results of Task 3 (Chinese Character Structure Test) showed that the participants as a whole group seemed to possess a considerable level of structural awareness of Chinese orthography, which tends to support some of the evidence obtained from their performance on the other two tasks discussed earlier. Although knowledge of spatial configurations was not formally taught in either school, the students overall displayed a considerable level of ability (with 87.8% of them earning a score of 0.50 or above) to discern different spatial configurations.

On the other hand, it is interesting to note that all the items that most participants got correct were highly frequent characters that were supposed to have been learnt by the participants at the elementary level with relatively simple and easily recognizable spatial configurations. The five items that most participants failed to get correct, on the contrary, appeared to have ambiguous character components and spatial configurations (e.g., "我", "問", "時", "爲", and "喉"). Thus, the participants' prior character knowledge and the complexity of spatial configurations of character components seemed to be a major contributing factor of their achievement in Task 3.

Influence of Demography and After-School Activities

To answer the second research question, with reference to the sample mean scores (see Table 5.5), it appeared that the Filipinos scored the highest in Task 1 and the Indians the lowest; the Pakistanis scored the highest and the Filipinos the lowest in Task 2; and the Filipinos scored the highest in Task 3, and the Indians the lowest. However, ANOVA revealed that ethnicity actually did not have any significant effect on Tasks 1 and 3 as opposed to Task 2. Because of a lack of information about the specific formal and informal Chinese learning experiences of these ethnic groups, it was unclear to us why such patterns existed.

The age at which the participants arrived in Hong Kong or Macau did not have any statistically significant effect on their mean scores of the three tasks. Based on the mean scores, it seemed that the participants who immigrated to Hong Kong/Macau between "0 and 3 years old" scored the highest in Task 2; the participants who immigrated to these two places between "0 and 6 years old" scored highest in Task 3; and the participants who immigrated between "3 and 6 years old" scored the highest in Task 1. However, no between-group differences can be found from the ANOVA results. It suggests that in these places, age of arrival might not be a good indicator of immigrant students' actual exposure to the target language or general language proficiency in Chinese and, consequently, did not show any effect on actual performance on the three tasks. The development of Chinese orthographic knowledge or overall Chinese proficiency might well be the result of classroom instruction in Hong Kong and Macau. Such a speculation also seems to agree with the findings discussed below that after-school or informal experiences with Chinese to a larger extent did not have any significant effect on the participants' measured orthographic competencies in this study.

With regard to the participants' TV-viewing habits, the t tests indicated that those who watched TV programs, especially those with Chinese subtitles, performed significantly better in Task 2, but not Tasks 1 and 3. In other words, watching TV programs with Chinese subtitles helped to improve the participants' ability to use components to construct Chinese characters, but not breaking whole characters down into components and identifying spatial configurations. This finding might be explained by the different nature of the tasks. More specifically, Task 2 was based on orthographic sensitivity and mental lexicon, both of which could be possibly enhanced via TV viewing, whereas Tasks 1 and 3 seemed to require systematic input on orthographic knowledge, which is not possible to deliver in the form of self-learning in informal contexts through TV captions.

Time spent studying Chinese outside of class did not have a significantly positive effect on student performance, even though based on the sample mean scores (see Table 5.9), those who spent 3 hours or more studying Chinese outside of class appeared to have greater performance than their counterparts in Tasks 1 and 2, and those who spent "more than 7 hours" studying Chinese outside of class appeared to perform the best across all of the three tasks. The fact that no systematic training on Chinese orthographic knowledge had been provided to the cohort before the assessments might explain why the time spent studying Chinese outside of class did not show any statistical significance related to mean scores. It also seems to suggest that language input from their self-study, as opposed to classroom instructional experience, might not be directly related to the students' orthographic knowledge being tested in the three tasks.

Implications for CSL Teaching and Learning

Traditionally, Chinese character teaching tends to place a lot of emphasis on "roots" (i.e., radicals) based on a classification system that used to be indispensable for dictionary use, "stroke order" based on a set of ancient calligraphic principles, as well as the etymology of single-component characters. Radicals are, by no means, equivalents of components in a strict sense, as the indexicality of radicals lies in the etymology that serves lexicographical purposes, whereas that of components lies in the structural functionality that serves pedagogical purposes. The traditional pedagogy, which lacks explicit attention to spatial configurations of the components in multi-component characters, however, fails to address the needs of CSL learners, particularly EM students with diverse sociolinguistic backgrounds, who often lack the level of exposure to print and cultural input that their native-speaking peers commonly have. Another reason that the radical-oriented traditional pedagogy of character teaching might not be as productive to EM students is that certain radicals in the Traditional Chinese script can be highly complicated in form (extreme examples include "龍" [lit. "dragon"] and "龜" [lit. "tortoise"]), which are not easily identified or deciphered by CSL learners. Thus, teaching the skills related to spatial configurations of character components (such as those featured in the present study) seems a comparatively sustainable approach to the learning and teaching of Chinese characters among CSL learners.

Preliminary findings from Loh, Mak, and Tam (2015b) indicated that students with low Chinese proficiency possess a number of characteristics: (1) they cannot discriminate between the structures and components of Chinese characters and only rely on their intuition for random speculation; (2) due to their poor knowledge of character structures and components, they tend to mix up components with similar visual characteristics, while using wrong components to construct wrong characters; and (3) they see Chinese characters as individual images, while selecting parts of a character they like most and making free or even random associations in an attempt to analyze the orthographic structure. On the contrary, students with good Chinese language proficiency possess a different set of characteristics: (1) they are able to discern between various character components and even identify the phonetic and the (semantic) radical components in a character; (2) they tend to be able to make use of their knowledge of phonetic and radical components to construct new characters; and (3) they are able to accurately identify spatial configuration of Chinese characters.

The findings of the current study seem to echo the aforementioned research. The high-scoring participants in Task 1 could discern between different components and even show a good concept of Chinese orthographic structures beyond strokes and stroke sequences without formal, systematic training in Chinese components. Task 2 was the most difficult one among the three, yet the high-scoring participants were able to apply their prior knowledge (including mental lexicon and their vague concept of spatial configurations) to create characters, which was well-supported by the list of archaic, yet legitimate, characters in the answers which might not be understood by the participants themselves. The same applies to Task 3 in which high-scoring participants did not receive any formal training in Chinese spatial configurations prior to the study, and there appears to be a widespread use of common sense and visual matching when tackling the easily recognizable items.

In light of the above studies, and the different learning needs of L1 and L2 learners of the Chinese language, specific curricula and teaching materials that enable systematic acquisition of Chinese orthographic knowledge based on L2 learners' level of proficiency and stage of learning would be highly desirable. These findings also suggest that formal training in character components and their spatial configurations could show great potential to reinforce L2 learners' orthographic knowledge and would equip EM students, and learners in general, with the skills and awareness they need for learning to read and write in their target language. In what follows, we propose a few specific recommendations for teaching Chinese orthographic knowledge to EM learners or CSL learners, who typically do not receive any formal training in the discernment and application of character components and their spatial configurations:

Teaching Chinese Character Components in a Systematic and Contextualized Manner

As indicated earlier in this chapter, the Chinese radical system was originally devised for L1 learners to study etymology. Radicals include not only components but also whole characters, which can easily confuse CSL learners as they do not have an equal Chinese culture input as their L1 counterparts. Teaching CSL learners systematically about character components and spatial configurations instead would help learners acquire advanced orthographic knowledge at large, which is essential for achieving higher levels of Chinese proficiency. Such advanced orthographic knowledge includes the relationship between orthographic form, sound, and meaning, as well as the proportion, symmetry, and size of a component as constituting parts of Chinese characters. Based on the hypothesis of comprehensible input (Krashen 1982) and variation theory (Marton and Booth 1997; Marton et al. 2004), Tse et al. (2007) proposed the Integrative Perceptual Approach to Teaching Chinese Characters, which highlights the importance of systematic training on Chinese orthographic knowledge (inclusive of character components and spatial configurations), which is essential for the automatization of Chinese character recognition and a prerequisite for the development of Chinese reading ability. Such an approach would be a good starting point for relating the teaching of Chinese characters' components to students' mental lexicon and everyday life along with their development of all four skills in CSL learning.

Enhancing Students' Orthographic Awareness with Exercises Based on the Components that Have Been Covered in Their CL Lessons

Most EM CSL learners are L1 speakers of alphabetic languages. Their knowledge components, such as vocabulary, are built up step-by-step. Component-related exercises could strengthen students' character writing skills; and exercises with component constitution games, such as component cards, flash cards, and access to mental lexicon (Loh et al. 2015; Tse 2000) could also elevate their levels of motivation and confidence in learning Chinese through peer collaborative learning and communicative language teaching in the CSL classroom.

Teaching Students About Spatial Configurations of Chinese Characters with Special Reference to Component Position, Symmetry, and Proportion

While teaching Chinese components to EM CSL learners, it would be important to start introducing the two levels of spatial configurations specific to Chinese characters (Kao and Chen 2012), at an early stage to enhance their understanding of the orthographic concepts for the Chinese language. The two levels of spatial configurations are namely (1) the relationship among strokes in a component or single character (e.g., "士" vs. "土" with different lengths of strokes signifying different things) and (2) the relationship among components in a character (e.g., the ways in which different forms of the same component "人" are used for different positions in a character). With reference to the findings of the current study, particularly the most frequently occurring characters in Task 2, we have identified certain common components (e.g., "木" and "子") and spatial configurations (i.e., left-right and top-down) more easily recognized by the participants. Teachers may consider introducing the concept of spatial configurations in Chinese orthography for CSL beginners with the aforementioned configurations and components to facilitate better learning for their students, such as teaching the left-right configurations with common components "木", "女", and "子" (as in "林" and "好") instead of starting with the less easily recognized ones (e.g., half-surrounding and top-down) with more complicated components (e.g., "門", as in "問").

Conclusion

In this chapter, we reported a study on the orthographic knowledge among EM students at various levels in Hong Kong and Macau who learned Chinese as a second language. The participants overall performed better on separating characters into their constituent components (Task 1) and identifying the spatial configurations of characters (Task 3), which tapped their passive knowledge of Chinese orthography, than on producing characters with given character components (Task 2), which required more active knowledge of applications of character components. The current findings on the patterns in EM adolescent CSL learners' perception of Chinese characters also echoed with our previous research on Chinese reading strategies used by learners with different proficiency levels (Loh et al. 2015). Without the ability to discern among different levels of Chinese orthographic structures, it would be difficult for low-level or beginning CSL learners to develop effective reading strategies, which might cause them to resort to random association of images with specific (parts of) characters.

This study sheds light on curriculum development and pedagogies for cultural and academically diverse EM CSL learners, especially with respect to effective approaches to teaching orthographic knowledge for learners with different proficiency levels in CSL classrooms. The results on the students' orthographic knowledge project their basic competency required for reading in the current CL and CSL curricula, and pave the way for an ongoing study on the relationship between orthographic knowledge and students' performance in Chinese learning. Teaching of character components and their spatial configurations, as revealed in this chapter, would be an essential scaffold in EM CSL curricula for reinforcing learners' orthographic awareness before extensive text-based reading and writing practice. In this spirit, the Integrative Perceptual Approach for Teaching Chinese Characters is recommended for beginner- and intermediate-level CSL teaching.

References

Chang, C.-L. (2009). Exploring the results of foreign students' reading and writing capacities taught by the strategy differentiating Chinese character range between reading and writing: Teaching experiments based on the foreign beginners without knowledge of Chinese characters. *Chung Yuan CSL Bulletin, 3,* 55–74.

Chinese National Language Committee. (1998). *Information processing using GB13000.1character symbol anthology.* Beijing: Beijing Language Institute Press (in Chinese).

Curriculum Development Council of the Hong Kong SAR. (2008). *Suggested learning objectives for primary school Chinese language (Tentative).* Hong Kong: Curriculum Development Council of the Hong Kong SAR. (in Chinese).

Direcção dos Serviços de Estatística e Censos de Macau. (2011). *2011 Population census.* Macau: The Government of the Macau SAR.

Education Bureau (EDB) of the Government of the Hong Kong SAR. (2008). *Executive summary of the study report on tracking the adaptation & development of non-Chinese speaking children in mainstream schools.* Hong Kong: The Government of the Hong Kong SAR. (in Chinese).

Education Bureau (EDB) of the Government of the Hong Kong SAR. (2010). *Chinese language assessment tool for non-Chinese speaking students.* Hong Kong: The Government of the Hong Kong SAR.

Education Bureau (EDB) of the Government of the Hong Kong SAR. (2014). *Chinese language curriculum second language adapted learning framework.* Hong Kong: The Government of the Hong Kong SAR. (in Chinese).

Education Bureau (EDB) of the Government of the Hong Kong SAR. (2016). *Audit of expenditure 2015-16: Primary and secondary schools included Government, Aided, Caput and Direct-Subsidy schools (Doc. No. EDB219).* Hong Kong: Hong Kong Legislative Council Finance Committee.

Ho, S. W., & Kwan, C. W. (2001). *Frequency statistics of commonly used Modern Chinese characters.* Hong Kong: CUHK.

Kao, C.-H., & Chen, C.-C. (2012). Seeing visual word forms: Spatial summation, eccentricity and spatial configuration. *Vision Research, 62,* 57–65.

Ki, W. W., Lam, H. C., Chung, A. L. S., Tse, S. K., Ko, P. Y., Lau, C. C., et al. (2003). Structural awareness, variation theory & ICT support. *L1 Educational Studies in Language & Literature, 3,* 53–78.

Krashen, S. D. (1982). *Principles and practice of second language acquisition.* Oxford: Pergamon.

Lee, C. H., & Kalyuga, S. (2011). Effectiveness of different pinyin presentation formats in learning Chinese characters: A cognitive load perspective. *Language Learning, 61*(4), 1099–1118.

Leong, C. K., Tse, S. K., Loh, E. K. Y., & Ki, W. W. (2011). Orthographic knowledge important in comprehending elementary Chinese text by users of alphasyllabaries. *Reading Psychology, 32*(3), 237–271.

Liu, Y., Wang, M., & Perfetti, C. A. (2007). Threshold-style processing of Chinese characters for adult second language learners. *Memory & Cognition, 35*(3), 471–480.

Loh, E. K. Y., Ki, W. W., Kwan, C. Y., & Tam, L. C. W. (2015). *Reading strategies of rthnic minority adolescent CSL learners: A think aloud study.* Paper presented at the Society for the Scientific Study of Reading Twenty-Second Annual Meeting. Kona, HI: Hapuna Beach Prince Hotel.

Loh, E. K. Y., Mak, M. T. F., & Tam, L. C. W. (2015b). The road to successful Chinese language learning: Effective strategies for teaching and learning Chinese characters. In I. Hill & M. S. K. Shum (Eds.), *Infusing IB philosophy and pedagogy in Chinese language teaching* (pp. 174–194). Suffolk, UK: John Catt.

Loh, E. K. Y., Tse, S. K., & Tsui, V. S. K. (2013). A study of the effectiveness of a school-based Chinese character curriculum for non-Chinese speaking kindergarteners: Hong Kong experience. *Journal of Han Character & Han Writing Education, 30*, 277–323. (in Chinese).

Marton, F., & Booth, S. (1997). *Learning and awareness*. Mahwah, NJ: Lawrence Erlbaum.

Marton, F., Tsui, A. B. M., & Chik, P. P. M. (2004). *Classroom discourse and the space of learning*. London: Taylor & Francis.

Shu, H., & Anderson, R. C. (1997). Role of radical awareness in the character & word acquisition of Chinese children. *Reading Research Quarterly, 32*(1), 78–89.

Shu, H., Anderson, R. C., & Wu, N. (2000). Phonetic awareness: Knowledge of orthography-phonology relationships in the character acquisition of Chinese children. *Journal of Educational Psychology, 92*, 56–62.

Shu, H., Chen, X., Anderson, R. C., Wu, N., & Xuang, Y. (2003). Properties of school Chinese: Implications for learning to read. *Child Development, 74*(1), 27–47.

Taylor, I., & Taylor, M. (1995). *Writing and literacy in Chinese, Korean and Japanese*. Amsterdam: John Benjamins.

Tse, S. K. (2000). *Pleasurable learning of Chinese characters*. Hong Kong: Education Bureau of the Government of Hong Kong SAR. (in Chinese).

Tse, S. K. (2002). *Comprehensive and effective teaching & learning of Chinese characters*. Hong Kong: Greenfield. (in Chinese).

Tse, S. K., & Loh, E. K. Y. (Eds.). (2014). *Effective teaching and learning of Chinese characters for non-Chinese speaking kindergarten students*. Beijing: Beijing Normal University Press. (in Chinese).

Tse, S. K., Marton, F., Ki, W. W., & Loh, E. K. Y. (2007). An integrative perceptual approach for teaching Chinese characters. *Instructional Science, 35*(5), 375–406.

Tse, S. K., Wong, M. Y., & Loh, E. K. Y. (2012). Non-Chinese speaking primary school students learning Chinese reading in a differentiated approach: A case study. In S. K. Tse, W. W. Ki, & M. S. K. Shum (Eds.), *The Chinese language learning and teaching of non-Chinese speaking: Curriculum, teaching materials, teaching strategies & assessment* (pp. 57–67). Hong Kong: HKU Press. (in Chinese).

Tsung, T. H., Shum, M. S. K., Ki, W. W., & Zhang, K. (2013). *Studies of teaching Chinese as a second language to ethnic minority students in Hong Kong: Theories, challenges, & practices*. Hong Kong: HKU Press. (in Chinese).

Wong, P. W. (2009). *The theory & practice of Chinese character teaching*. Taipei: Joyful Learning Press.

Zhang, T. R. (2012). *Literacy focused learning, mass reading, step-by-step writing*. Beijing: Central Compilation & Translation Press (in Chinese).

Zhang, Z. G. (1987). Chinese characters & reading. *Reading News, 8*, 7–8.

Chapter 6
Developing a Word Associates Test to Assess L2 Chinese Learners' Vocabulary Depth

Dongbo Zhang, Xuexue Yang, Chin-Hsi Lin and Zheng Gu

Abstract This chapter reports on our development and initial validation of a Word Associates Test (WAT) for assessing the depth of vocabulary knowledge of Chinese as Second/Foreign Language learners. The validation study revealed the Chinese WAT (WAT-C) to be a reliable and valid test. Specifically, the WAT-C's medium-sized correlations with a vocabulary size measure and its unique predictive effect on reading comprehension suggested that the test, as intended, assessed a distinct aspect of vocabulary knowledge (i.e., depth). Learners' performance on the WAT-C was significantly better when they were informed on the number of associates (informed condition) than when they were not (uninformed condition). The scores of the WAT-C produced by three different scoring methods consistently predicted reading comprehension significantly in the informed condition as opposed to the uninformed condition. Taken together, these findings suggest that the informed condition may be preferred for administering the WAT-C. Finally, in both conditions, the All-or-Nothing scoring method, which awards a point only if all associates but no distractors are selected, consistently predicted reading comprehension significantly and uniquely, and it also tended to explain more variance in reading comprehension than the One-Point method (i.e., one point awarded for each associate without considering distractor selection) and the Correct-Wrong (i.e., one point awarded for selecting an associate as well as non-selection of a distractor). With consideration of both the strength of predictive validity and the complexity of scoring, the All-or-Nothing method was evaluated to be the best for scoring the WAT-C. Some remaining issues for the future and the implications of the reported work for instruction and classroom assessment of Chinese L2 learners are discussed.

Keywords Chinese as a second/foreign language · Vocabulary depth · Word associates test · Vocabulary size · Reading comprehension

D. Zhang (✉) · X. Yang · C.-H. Lin · Z. Gu
Michigan State University, East Lansing, MI, USA
e-mail: zhangdo6@msu.edu

© Springer Nature Singapore Pte Ltd. 2017
D. Zhang and C.-H. Lin (eds.), *Chinese as a Second Language Assessment*,
Chinese Language Learning Sciences, DOI 10.1007/978-981-10-4089-4_6

Introduction

This chapter reports on our development and initial validation of a Word Associates Test (WAT) for assessing the depth of vocabulary knowledge of Chinese as a Second/Foreign Language (CSL/CFL; hereafter L2) learners. In what follows, we first discuss the multiple dimensions of vocabulary knowledge, focusing on the oft-recognized dimensions of size/breadth and depth. In particular, we discuss the word associates format, which is perhaps the best-known method for the assessment of vocabulary depth. We then present how we developed a 40-item WAT for L2 learners of Chinese (WAT-C) and report a small-scale study that provided preliminary validation evidence for the WAT-C. The validation study aimed to examine whether the WAT-C indeed tapped a dimension of knowledge distinct from vocabulary size, whether or not learners were informed on the number of associates for a target word had any influence on the WAT-C, and what scoring method was the best for the WAT-C. In the discussion and conclusion sections, we make sense of the findings of the validation study, note some limitations of our work and remaining issues for the future, and discuss some implications of the WAT-C for classroom assessment and instruction for L2 learners of Chinese.

Vocabulary Depth and Its Assessment

Dimensions of Vocabulary Knowledge

Vocabulary knowledge is one of the most important competencies that learners need to develop in the acquisition of a language. Extant research has been conducted and discussions made on what the nature of vocabulary knowledge is (e.g., Henriksen 1999; Nagy and Scott 2000; Richards 1976), how vocabulary knowledge is acquired and how it can be appropriately assessed (e.g., Milton 2009; Read 2000), what best vocabulary instruction should be like (e.g., Schmitt 2008), and how vocabulary knowledge is closely related to the development of various language and literacy skills (e.g., Grabe 2009; Nation 2001, 2005; Milton 2013).

One of the notable findings from the literature is that vocabulary knowledge is multi-dimensional and entails different aspects of knowledge about words (Henriksen 1999; Nagy and Scott 2000; Nation 1990, 2001). Broadly, knowing a word means knowing its form, meaning, as well as use; the knowledge can be receptive (i.e., recognizing a word and accessing its meaning[s]) or productive (i.e., producing a word to fulfill communicative functions), active or passive, and related to the oral or the written modality (Laufer and Paribakht 1998; Melka 1997; Nation 1990, 2001; Richards 1976). Among the various conceptualizations of dimensions of vocabulary knowledge, a popular one addresses how many words one knows and how well one knows those words (Anderson and Freebody 1981). The former is known to pertain to size or breadth of vocabulary knowledge and the latter depth of vocabulary knowledge (Anderson and Freebody 1981; Read 2000, 2004; Schmitt 2014; Wesche and Paribakht 1996). In the literature on vocabulary acquisition and assessment, a lot of attention has been paid to the size dimension (Read 2000; Schmitt 2014). This prioritized attention seems to be commonsensical as words are the building blocks of language, and thus, presumably the more words one knows, the better s/he could comprehend and use a language. Numerous studies have shown a high correlation between learners' vocabulary size and various language skills, notably reading comprehension (e.g., Qian 1999, 2002; Zhang 2012), and there is general agreement that a lexical coverage would need to be at least 98% for L2 learners to have adequate comprehension of a printed text (Hu and Nation 2000).

On the other hand, researchers argue that a focus on the size dimension alone could be very limiting (Read 1993, 1998, 2000, 2004; Webb 2013; Wesche and Paribakht 1996). As a learner gets to know more and more words, it is important that we understand how these words are organized and how word meanings are related in the learner's lexical repertoire. This is an issue of vocabulary depth. A large number of words, particularly high-frequency words, tend to have multiple meanings and uses; thus, focusing on a specific definitional meaning, as how vocabulary size is typically assessed, would not capture the quality of the knowledge that learners have about words.

Assessing Vocabulary Depth

Commonsensically, when one gets to know more words in the process of L2 learning, s/he will also be learning more about those words and the links between them. Thus, there was a concern that the parallel development of size and depth suggests they are closely related and may not constitute distinct dimensions (Vermeer 2001). Empirically, this concern means that the construct of vocabulary depth will need to be assessed and validated. A big challenge to assessing vocabulary depth is to define what exactly constitutes this dimension of knowledge or what specific aspects of knowledge depth entails (Henriksen 1999; Milton 2009; Read 2004; Vermeer 2001). Read (2004), for example, distinguished between several meanings of depth, including precision of meaning ("the difference between having a limited unclear idea of what a word means and having much more specific knowledge of its meaning"), comprehensive word knowledge ("knowing the semantic feature of a word and its orthographic, phonological, morphological, syntactic, collocational, and pragmatic characteristics"), and network knowledge ("the incorporation of the word into its related words in the schemata, and the ability to distinguish its meaning and use from related words") (pp. 211–212).

Vocabulary Knowledge Scale (VKS)

One major line of work on assessing vocabulary depth was conducted by Paribakt and Wesche, who developed the Vocabulary Knowledge Scale (VKS) following a "developmental" approach which manifests the nature of incrementality of vocabulary acquisition (Wesche and Paribakht 1996). Initially developed for intermediate university English as a Second Language (ESL) students, the VKS involves learners reporting on their knowledge of a given word by responding to the following statements: (I) I haven't seen this word before; (II) I have seen this word before, but I don't know what it means; (III) I have seen this word before, and I think it means _____ (synonym or translation); (IV) I know this word. It means _____ (synonym or translation); and (V) I can use this word in a sentence: _____. Their responses to each word are then scored 1–5 based on the following VKS scoring categories.

1. The word is not familiar at all.
2. The word is familiar, but its meaning is not known.
3. A correct synonym or translation is given.
4. The word is used with semantic appropriateness in a sentence.
5. The word is used with semantic appropriateness and grammatical accuracy in a sentence.

The VKS covers a mixture of aspects of knowledge about a word with respect to its form, meaning, and use; it involves receptive as well as productive aspects, with learners' ability to productively use a word in a semantically and grammatically correct way constituting the greatest depth of the word.

Although the VKS is a popularly known method for assessing vocabulary depth, there has been little effort to validate it in the L2 vocabulary literature. Wesche and Paribakht (1996) reported test–retest correlations of over 0.80 for the VKS. The VKS also showed moderate correlations (about 0.53) with the Eurocentres Vocabulary Size Test (Meara and Jones 1990), which suggested that the two measures, while showing some commonality, touched on distinct aspects of vocabulary knowledge. Stewart et al. (2012), based on a study on Japanese-speaking learners of English as a Foreign Language, found high reliability of the VKS (over 0.90). However, the assumption for the unidimensionality of the VKS was not confirmed, suggesting that the scale may not be assessing a single aspect of vocabulary knowledge. Nevertheless, the authors noted that the scale may still be used as a unidimensional measurement model if misfitting test words are removed with care.

Despite the aforementioned evidence that tends to support the VKS as a reliable and valid tool for assessing vocabulary depth, it has notable limitations (Bruton 2009; Nation 2001; Read 1997; Webb 2013). Nation (2001), for example, pointed out that the different aspects of knowledge (e.g., receptive vs. productive) about a word actually "do not fit comfortably into one scale" (p. 357). A learner may be able to use a word in a sentence without having the full knowledge of the meaning repertoire of the word. Thus, it is questionable whether being able to use the word correctly would suggest that the learner has the greatest depth of knowledge of the word. In addition, the five levels in the scale do not necessarily "represent five key stages in the acquisition of a word or they form an equal-interval scale" (Read 1997, p. 317). From a psychometric perspective, Stewart et al. (2012) found that Stages 3 and 4 in the scale are indistinct. There are also questions about whether providing a synonym or translation and composing a sentence would be the most appropriate ways for learners to demonstrate their knowledge of the word (Read 1997). Similar discussions were also made by Bruton (2009), who raised concerns about scoring for the VKS; for example, the same total score of two learners may be the result of diverse response patterns for test words.

Word Associates Test (WAT)

The best-known method for assessing vocabulary depth is perhaps the Word Associates Test (WAT) developed by Read (1993, 1998) through the word associates format (WAF), which is based on the concept of word association and primarily focuses on learners' network knowledge (Read 2004). As Read (2004) pointed out:

As a learner's vocabulary size increases, newly acquired words need to be accommodated within a network of already known words, and some restructuring of the network may be needed as a result. This means that depth can be understood in terms of learners' developing ability to distinguish semantically related words and, more generally, their knowledge of the various ways in which individual words are linked to each other. (p. 219)

The WAT was initially designed to assess vocabulary learning of university English learners. It is essentially a test of receptive knowledge of words without requiring learners to have the full meaning repertoire of a target word. Typically, in a WAT item, a target word is followed by six or eight other words, half of which are semantically associated with the target word (i.e., associates) and the other half are not (i.e., distractors). The associates have two primary types of relationships with a target word: paradigmatic and syntagmatic. The former type of relationship pertains to an associate from the same word class and performs the same grammatical function as the target word in a sentence, such as a synonym; the latter pertains to an associate that bears a sequential relationship to the target word in a sentence and is usually a word from a different word class, such as a collocate. Figure 6.1 shows an example of the typical format of a WAT item (Read 1998). The target word *sudden* is an adjective followed by two boxes of four words. The four words on the left are all adjectives with associates being synonymic to *sudden* (i.e., *quick* and *surprising*), and the four words on the right are all nouns with associates being collocates of *sudden* (i.e., *change* and *noise*). The other four words (e.g., *thirsty* and *school*) are semantically unrelated. Note that in this particular example, there are two associates in each box; however, to prevent learners from guessing, a target word could also have one associate on the left and three on the right or three on the left and one on the right (Read 1998, 2004).

Ever since Read (1993, 1998) developed the prototype of WAT, various other forms of the test have been developed in different languages, depending on specific designing features (Greidanus et al. 2004, 2005; Greidanus and Nienhuis 2001; Qian and Schedl 2004; Shoonen and Verhallen 2008). Overall, evidence has been accumulated that WAF tests are reliable and valid in assessing learners' vocabulary depth. In his initial validation study, Read (1993) reported that the two forms of an earlier version of the WAT demonstrated a very good level of reliability (at least 0.90). Both forms also demonstrated correlations of over 0.70 (0.76–0.81) with another vocabulary test which asked learners to match words with given meaning definitions and mimicked the Vocabulary Levels Test (VLT) (Nation 1990; Schmitt et al. 2001) for testing vocabulary size. This result pointed to a substantial relationship between the two vocabulary tests, but also indicated that the WAT tapped a distinct aspect of vocabulary knowledge than the criterion vocabulary test. A revised version of the WAT, which covered 40 adjectives as target words, was later developed and validated in Read (1998). Like in Read (1993), the revised WAT showed a very high reliability of 0.93, and the strong correlations with a word matching test (0.82–0.86) and an interview that adopted an expanded VKS scale (0.76) also pointed to the WAT's good criterion validity. Using the VLT (Nation 1990) as the vocabulary size measure and Read's (1998) new version of WAT to measure vocabulary depth, Qian (1999, 2002) found university ESL learners' vocabulary depth, while strongly correlated with vocabulary size (r ranging from 0.70 and 0.82 in the two studies) significantly predicted their reading comprehension after accounting for the influence of vocabulary size, which provided clear evidence that size and depth are two distinct dimensions of vocabulary knowledge.

Additional evidence that supports the WAT as a reliable and valid measure of depth of vocabulary knowledge also came from studies on learners of languages other than English, including young L2 learners. Schoonen and Verhallen (2008), for example, used the WAF to create a test to measure the vocabulary depth of primary school students learning Dutch as a Second Language (DSL). The Dutch WAT, different from Read's (1993, 1998) WAT (see Fig. 6.1), adopted a word Web format; each target word has three associates and three distractors. Children were informed on the number of associates and asked to draw lines to link the associates and a target word. It was found that children's WAT performance was strongly correlated with their performance on a word definition task (about 0.75), and a large amount of variance (about 55–56%) was shared between the two measures; yet, the substantial difference between them meant that they did not measure the same construct. Greidanus et al. (2004) reported their development of a WAF test for Dutch university students learning French as a Foreign Language (i.e., Deep Word Knowledge or DWK test) and found consistently very good reliability of the test for students in different years of studying French at their respective university (Cronbach's alpha ranging from 0.84 to 0.89). The students' DWK performance also showed a strong correlation with their performance on a test that

sudden

| beautiful *quick* *surprising* thirsty | | *change* doctor *noise* school |

Fig. 6.1 Example of WAT item (Read 1998, p. 46). Note *Bold* and *italicized* words are correct answers

measured their vocabulary breadth (about 0.80), which suggested that there was a close relationship yet significant difference between the two tests to show that they did not assess exactly the same type of knowledge.

Overall, the aforementioned research findings support the WAT as a reliable and valid measure of vocabulary depth. However, like the VKS, there were also some concerns (Read 1993, 1998; Schmitt et al. 2011). In Read's (1993) initial validation study, the verbal reports from students suggested that higher proficiency learners were more willing to guess than less proficient learners, believing that "guess has some chance but not guess-nothing!" (p. 365), and interestingly, their guesses (for target words unknown) were often quite successful. Those guesses would of course end up overestimating learners' actual knowledge and threaten the validity of the test (Schmitt et al. 2011). In addition, there was a concern that the syntagmatic and paradigmatic aspects of the associative relationships measured may address disconnected aspects of vocabulary knowledge. In other words, the "synonymic" knowledge tested through syntagmatic associates and the "collocational" knowledge tested through paradigmatic associates may tap distinct aspects of depth of vocabulary knowledge (Batty 2012; Read 1998).

What's more, there are several issues related to the WAF that have received little attention in the literature. One pertains to the scoring for the WAT. In the initial validation of the WAT, Read (1993) reported that students were encouraged to select as many associates as possible (the number of associates was four), even if they were not sure about any of them; their responses were scored on the associates only, which means selection of a distractor would not be penalized. Such a scoring method, which was called the One-Point method by Schmitt et al. (2011), was also adopted in a few studies that employed the WAT (e.g., Qian 1999, 2002). However, a concern is that if test-takers are informed on this scoring method prior to testing, it would be possible that they strategically select as many associates as possible to boost their scores instead of actively engaging their network of knowledge to select the associates while avoiding the distractors. Such a concern promoted some researchers to adopt a scoring method which gives credit to the selection of associates as well as the non-selection or avoidance of distractors (e.g., Greidanus et al. 2004, 2005; Zhang 2012). This method, which was called the Correct-Wrong method by Schmitt et al. (2011), is notably more complex and tedious, if not necessarily more accurate, than the One-Point method. A third and also the simplest and strictest method, which has also been used to counteract guessing, is what Schmitt et al. (2011) termed the All-or-Nothing method. It awards a test-taker a point for a response only if it precisely matches the correct answer (i.e., selection of all associates but not any distractors) (Schoonen and Verhallen 2008). As Schoonen and Verhallen (2008) argued, their DWK test based on the word Web format should be considered as a whole item. "Treating each stimulus word—associate word relation ... as a separate item," such as in the case of the Correct-Wrong and One-Point methods described above, "causes unwanted interdependence between the items which might inflate reliability estimates" (p. 221).

While all three methods seem to have a good rationale with respect to simplicity and/or control for guessing, empirically to what extent one might be preferred over the other has received little attention in the literature. In a recent validation study with university ESL students, Schmitt et al. (2011) reported that for the WAT with six options (three associates and three distractors), the All-or-Nothing method produced the largest correlation (0.884) with learners' scores of an interview, which was believed to elicit more accurately learners' knowledge of associative relationships of target words. The One-Point and Correct-Wrong methods produced correlations of 0.871 and 0.877, respectively. For the WAT with eight options (four associates and four distractors), the One-Point method produced the strongest correlation (0.885), and the correlations were 0.855 and 0.871 for the Correct-Wrong and the All-or-Nothing method, respectively. While the three methods, overall, seemed to produce comparable results without substantial difference, Schmitt et al. (2011) concluded that the Correct-Wrong method could be discounted as it is much more complicated than the other two methods without yielding more encouraging results, and the All-or-Nothing might be better for the 6-option format and the One-Point for the 8-option format.

Another issue of WAF tests that has received little attention is the condition in which the tests are administered, particularly whether or not learners are informed on the number of associates. When Read (1993) validated his English WAT, learners were encouraged to select as many options as they believe could be associates without knowing the correct number of associates for all items was four. In Greidanus et al.'s (2004) French WAT, learners were informed that the number of associates varied across items (two or four), but did not know which items had two associates and which ones had four. In Schoonen and Verhallen (2008), young Dutch L2 learners were told to choose a fixed number of associates for each target word (i.e., three). So far, no studies seem to have directly tested if the conditions of administering the WAT, informed or uninformed (on the number of associates), would have any influence on the test.

WAT for Chinese Learners

The review above suggested that the WAF has established itself as a reliable and valid way for assessing vocabulary depth and has been widely used in various language contexts. However, there are still some issues that remain to be further studied. In the literature on Chinese L2 acquisition and assessment, while some research has been conducted on vocabulary size (Ke 2012; see also Zhang, this volume), vocabulary depth has barely received any attention, not to mention the development of a Chinese WAT and validation of it as a measure of vocabulary depth. To examine the development of different types of association knowledge among L2 learners of Chinese, Jiang (2002) developed a WAT in an aural/oral response format which asked L2 learners with varied levels of Chinese proficiency (and native speakers) to verbally provide an associate for each one of the 100 stimulus words heard. Their responses were then categorized in accordance with different types of associative relationships (i.e., syntagmatic, paradigmatic, clang/phonological, no response, and other); the percentages of those types of relationships in different groups of learners were then analyzed and compared. Despite some interesting findings about Chinese learners' association knowledge, such as an increase in the percentage of paradigmatic responses with increasing Chinese proficiency, there was no effort to validate the WAT as a measure of vocabulary depth, and nothing was known about the reliability and validity of the tool. It was thus our purpose to develop and validate a WAT for Chinese L2 learners and address some of the aforementioned issues that need to be further addressed about the WAF for assessing vocabulary depth.

Developing a Chinese Word Associtation Test

Our development of a Chinese Word Associates Test (hereafter, WAT-C) involved several phases and took into consideration a number of issues and principles related to word selection and target group(s) of learners, among others. One of the most important considerations we had was what words to include for the test and whom the test is for. As it is clear from our earlier discussion, WAT has a heavy involvement of words in that each target word typically goes with six or eight other words. A critical consideration for developing a WAT is that the basic meanings of all words should be known to target group(s) of learners so that learners' performance on the test would reflect their actual association knowledge without confounding from guessing due to their lack of knowledge about the meaning of a word (Read 1993, 1998). Consequently, we decided that beginning learners who have very limited vocabulary and low-frequency words would not fit our purpose for developing a WAT-C.

Eventually, we decided to focus on high-frequency words and Chinese learners at the intermediate level or higher. Intermediate-level learners were defined as those who have a level of Chinese proficiency equivalent to two years of formal learning at the college level in a foreign language context (e.g., the USA) or one year of learning in a study-abroad context (e.g., China). To select an initial pool of words for constructing the WAT-C, we referred to the *Graded Chinese Syllables, Characters and Words for the Application of Teaching Chinese to Speakers of Other Languages* (hereafter, GCSCW-TCSOL) developed by China's State Language Commission (2011), which is a unit of the Chinese Ministry of Education charged with policy and planning for Chinese language and orthography in China. The graded lists in the GCSCW-TCSOL were developed based on the largest dynamic corpus of Chinese with three billion Chinese characters. The graded words consist of three levels that cover 11,092 words, including 2245 for Level 1, 3211 for Level 2, and 5636 for Level 3. Level 1 words are the lowest level with highly frequent words for low-level learners of Chinese.

Formal development of the WAT-C began with our preliminary selection of 40 verbs (e.g., 忘记 *forget*) and 40 adjectives (e.g., 便宜 *cheap*) from the 2245 Level 1 words. We followed the general principles highlighted by Read (1998) for target word selection and also used our expert knowledge about L2 Chinese curriculum, target group(s) of learners, and the utility of Chinese words (Read 2004).[1] We considered both verbs and adjectives, instead of focusing only on adjectives as in Read's (1998) revised WAT, because we wanted to have a better representation of the network knowledge that learners have about words of different word classes.

All of the words (and their corresponding associates and distractors) were two-character compound words, because words of this type are the most dominant in modern Chinese in general and in the GCSCW-TCSOL in particular. Finding four options for paradigmatic relationships and another four for syntagmatic relationships for the 80 words was not easy, as many words turned out to have a restricted range of uses, and consequently, it was impossible to make sure four associates could be found for all the words. Such a challenge was also reported in Read (1993) in his pioneering development of the WAT for English learners. In addition, having 80 target words would mean to find another 640 different words (nouns, adjectives, and verbs) from the 2245 Level 1 words, which turned out to be virtually impossible. Given those challenges, we decided that each WAT-C item would have six choices instead of eight. As reviewed earlier, the six-choice format has also been used in previous studies and validated as measuring depth of vocabulary knowledge reliably and validly (e.g., Greidanus and Nienhuis 2001; Greidanus et al. 2004, 2005; Schoonen and Verhallen 2008). Additionally, we removed those target words that we found difficult to come up with even six choices (three for syntagmatic and three for paradigmatic relationships). We also decided to have a fixed number of associates for all target words. This is not only a common practice in the literature (e.g., Schoonen and Verhallen 2008; Read 1993, 1998), but it would also allow us to easily compare how different conditions of administering the test (i.e., whether or not learners are informed on the number of associates) might have an influence on the WAT-C (see the validation study reported later).

Consequently, an initial version of the WAT-C was constructed that included 25 target adjectives, each of which was followed by three adjectival choices and three noun choices, and 25 target verbs, each of which went with three verbal choices and three noun choices. The response patterns varied across items: either there was one syntagmatic associate (i.e., collate) or two paradigmatic associates (i.e., synonym or antonym) or vice versa, with a total of three associates.

---

[1] All four of the authors are native Chinese speakers and had extensive experience of teaching Chinese at various levels in a Second and/or Foreign Language context.

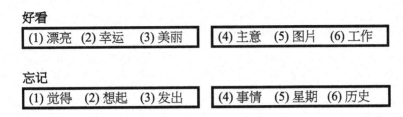

好看
| (1) 漂亮 (2) 幸运 (3) 美丽 | (4) 主意 (5) 图片 (6) 工作 |

忘记
| (1) 觉得 (2) 想起 (3) 发出 | (4) 事情 (5) 星期 (6) 历史 |

Fig. 6.2 Examples of WAT-C items

To pilot the test, this 50-item WAT-C was administered to 20 native Chinese-speaking undergraduate students in China. They were not informed on the number of associates; instead, they were asked to choose as many words as they believed to be appropriate. Based on the responses from those students, we removed those items where there was a notable pattern of associates failing to be selected or distractors being selected or replaced some choice words with more appropriate ones. For example, the target word 参加 (*to participate*) had three paradigmatic choices, including 退出 (*to withdraw*), 旅游 (*to travel*), and 看到 (*to see*). Only 退出 was the associate. However, seven of the 20 students also selected 旅游 as an associate of 参加, which might be because 旅游 could be also a noun in Chinese, and consequently, they might have thought that it could go with 参加, even though in modern Chinese, 旅游 is not usually considered a collocate of 参加. Nevertheless, we replaced the word 旅游 with 上学 (*to go to school*) so that any potential confusion among L2 learners could be avoided.

Our final version of the WAT-C consisted of 40 target words, including 20 adjectives and 20 verbs. Two examples, one for an adjectival item and the other for a verbal item, are given below. To illustrate, 好看 is an adjective which means *good-looking* or *pretty* and has 漂亮 (*pretty*) and 美丽 (*pretty/beautiful*), but not 幸运 (*lucky*), as their paradigmatic associates; it also has 图片 (*picture*), but not 主意 (*idea/thought*) and 工作 (*job*), as a syntagmatic associate. 忘记 is a verb which means *forget* and should have 想起 (*to recall* or *to come back to memory*), but not 觉得 (*to think/believe/gather*) and 发出 (*to send out* or *to issue*) as the paradigmatic associate, and 事情 (*things*) and 历史 (*history*), but not 星期 (*week*), as the syntagmatic associates (Fig. 6.2).

Validating the WAT-C

In what follows, we report a study with adult CFL learners that aimed to validate the WAT-C. As discussed earlier, among the many issues explored in the literature on WAF tests are whether or not test-takers should be informed on the number of associates and how students' responses are best scored. Existing studies did not seem to have come to an agreement on those issues. It was thus our interest in this study to further address them with a Chinese WAT. Specifically, we aimed to answer the following three questions.

1. Does the WAT-C, which was designed to measure depth of vocabulary knowledge, indeed measure a dimension of vocabulary knowledge that is distinct from vocabulary size?
2. Does informing learners on the number of associates have an impact on the WAT-C?
3. What is the preferred method for scoring the WAT-C?

Participants

The participants taking part in the validation study were 21 students from various countries (mostly Russia, Thailand, and Korea) who were studying at a university in China at the time of the study. None of them were heritage learners of Chinese. They included two males and nineteen females with an average age of about 22.5 years. According to a background survey, about 76% of them ($N = 16$) had studied Chinese in their home country for about two years or more, and about 86% ($N = 18$) had studied in China for about a year. The only student who had not learned any Chinese in her own country reported having studied Chinese for more than three years in China. Given those years of studying Chinese, particularly the study-abroad experience in China, most of the students were likely intermediate or advanced learners. No information, however, was elicited about their exact proficiency level in Chinese. Most of the students were studying in China for the enhancement of their Chinese proficiency instead of having a specific major at the host university; a few, however, had teaching Chinese as a Foreign Language as their major.

Instruments

In addition to a background survey, the participants were administered the WAT-C, a picture selection task which aimed to assess their vocabulary size, and a short passage comprehension task which assessed their reading comprehension.

WAT-C

The final version of the WAT-C described earlier was administered to measure the learners' depth of vocabulary knowledge. The 40 items were randomly assigned into two sets of 20 items, with each set consisting of 10 adjectives and 10 verbs. Set A was administered first in a condition in which the learners were informed that in each of the two boxes of three words, at least one word was related to the target word, and were asked to select as many words as they believed to be appropriate. Set B was administered afterward where the learners were told that each box had one or two words related to the target word, and the total number of words to be selected should be three.

The items in both sets of the WAT-C were scored with three methods. Following Schmitt et al. (2011), we call those three methods the All-or-Nothing (Schoonen and Verhallen 2008), the One-Point (Read 1993, 1998), and the Correct-Wrong method (Greidanus and Nienhuis 2001; Greidanus et al. 2004, 2005; Zhang 2012), respectively. Specifically, the All-or-Nothing method scored responses with an option of 1 or 0. If all three associates, but not any distractors, were selected, 1 was awarded; missing any associates or having any distractors selected would result in a 0. The One-Point method awarded 1 point for each selected associate; distractors were not considered in scoring. The Correct-Wrong method awarded 1 point for each selected associate; in the meantime, it also awarded 1 point for each distractor not selected. For all scoring methods, no response was recorded as 0. Based on these scoring schemes, the ranges of scores for the three methods would be 0–20, 0–60, and 0–120 points, respectively, for each set of the WAT-C.

Vocabulary Size

According to Messick (1995), the distinctness from measures of other constructs is an important piece of evidence in construct validation. Thus, it is no surprise that a vocabulary size measure has been typically included in the literature for deciding whether WAT measures a distinct aspect of vocabulary knowledge. To this end, we administered a picture selection task that aimed to measure the learners' vocabulary breadth. The task included five single-character and 25 two-character words of various frequency levels with reference to the Modern Chinese Frequency Dictionary (Beijing Language Institute 1986). Each word was followed by four pictures. The learners were to select a picture that best represented the meaning of the word. One point was awarded for each correct picture selection. The total score for this task was 30. Note that this test was not meant to provide an estimate for the actual size of vocabulary knowledge of the learners; rather, it was to help us identify any individual differences in the number of words that the learners could possibly know.

Reading Comprehension

Reading comprehension has been a widely used criterion variable for the validation of measures for assessing the construct of depth of vocabulary knowledge, including the WAT (e.g., Qian 1999, 2002). To provide evidence for the predictive validity of the WAT-C, we included a short passage comprehension task to measure the learners' reading comprehension. Altogether, there were 15 passages; each passage was comprised of only a small number of sentences, which tended to be simple lexically and grammatically. Each passage was followed by a question which required inference-making. For example, 我去年春节去过那个小镇, 今年再去的时候, 经过那条街道, 我几乎不认识了。(*I was in the small town during the Spring Festival last year. This year when I was there and passing that street, I could barely recognize it anymore.*). Based on this passage, learners were asked to select an appropriate inference about the town: (1) 春节很热闹 (*Spring Festival was exciting*), (2) 变化很大 (*There were huge changes*), and (3) 人很热情 (*People were very nice*). The correct answer should be (2). The total score for this task was 15.

Results

Table 6.1 shows the means and standard deviation (SD) of learners' performance and the internal consistency reliability (i.e., Cronbach's α) of all the measures. As Table 6.1 shows, the reliability of all the measures was very high, and there did not appear to be any notable differences between the two conditions of administering the WAT-C with respect to the reliability of the test. For both Set A and Set B, the α values produced using the scores of the three different scoring methods also appeared to be comparably high. However, the learners' performance on the WAT-C was significantly greater for Set B (i.e., the informed condition) than for Set A (i.e., the uninformed condition), which was true for all three scoring methods: $t(20) = -6.654$ $(p < 0.001)$, $t(20) = -6.552$ $(p < 0.001)$, and $t(20) = -3.653$ $(p = 0.002)$ for the three methods, respectively.

Correlations

Table 6.2 shows the correlations between all of the measures, including the three different scores for each set of the WAT-C. Vocabulary size correlated significantly

Table 6.1 Learners' performance on the tests and test reliabilities

Variables		Maximum score	Mean (SD)	Reliability (α)
Vocabulary size		30	20.71 (6.03)	0.942
Reading comprehension		15	12.76 (1.30)	0.861
WAT-C Set A	All-or-Nothing	20	6.62 (5.40)	0.904
	One-Point	60	43.43 (8.47)	0.895
	Correct-Wrong	120	97.00 (12.38)	0.886
WAT-C Set B	All-or-Nothing	20	12.67 (5.70)	0.912
	One-Point	60	50.81 (7.32)	0.895
	Correct-Wrong	120	103.05 (13.25)	0.879

Table 6.2 Correlations between all measures

		1	2	3	4	5	6	7	8
1	VocabSize	–							
2	Reading	0.501*	–						
3	SetA_M1	0.658***	0.620**	–					
4	SetA_M2	0.629**	0.546**	0.946***	–				
5	SetA_M3	0.735***	0.553**	0.920***	0.963***	–			
6	SetB_M1	0.610**	0.629**	0.720***	0.812***	0.832***	–		
7	SetB_M2	0.620**	0.626**	0.695***	0.796***	0.832***	0.981***	–	
8	SetB_M3	0.620**	0.616**	0.719***	0.790***	0.827***	0.959***	0.975***	–

Note VocabSize = vocabulary size; Reading = short passage comprehension; SetA_M1 = Set A, All-or-Nothing; SetA_M2 = Set A, One-Point; SetA_M3 = Set A, Correct-Wrong; SetB_M1 = Set B, All-or-Nothing; SetB_M2 = Set B, One-Point; SetB_M3 = Set B, Correct-Wrong. $* p < 0.05$ $** p < 0.01$ $*** p < 0.001$

with reading comprehension ($r = 0.501$, $p < 0.05$), which was not a surprise, given the previously confirmed importance of vocabulary breadth to reading comprehension. Vocabulary size also significantly correlated with all three scores for each set of the WAT-C, although the correlations appeared to be slightly stronger for Set A (r from 0.619 to 0.735) than for Set B (r from 0.610 to 0.620) (all $ps < 0.01$ or 0.001).

More importantly, all WAT-C scores, regardless of the condition in which the test was administered, significantly correlated with reading comprehension, with r ranging from 0.546 to 0.620 for Set A and from 0.616 to 0.629 for Set B (all $ps < 0.01$). These correlations were overall medium in strength. Within each set of the WAT-C, particularly Set B, the three scores were very highly correlated, with the smallest being 0.920 between the All-or-Nothing and the Correct-Wrong methods for Set A, and the greatest being 0.981 between the All-or-Nothing and the One-Point methods for Set B (all $ps < 0.001$). This appeared to suggest that the three methods may have substantial overlap. However, correlations of such great strength did not happen to any one of the methods between Set A and Set B: $rs = 0.720$, 0.796, and 0.827, respectively, for the three methods (all $ps < 0.001$). While these correlations were overall strong, they also suggested some notable differences between the two test conditions for each of the methods.

We further conducted two sets of hierarchical regression analyses to examine how effectively the three scores in each test condition of the WAT-C would predict reading comprehension. In both sets of analyses, the orders of entry for vocabulary size and the three WAT-C scores into regression equations were switched to test their independent contribution to and relative strength of predicting reading comprehension.

As shown in Table 6.3, for Set A, as the first variable entered into the regression equation, vocabulary size significantly predicted reading comprehension and explained about 25.1% of the variance in the comprehension task. Over and above vocabulary size, the scores produced by the All-or-Nothing method explained about 14.9% additional variance in reading comprehension, and this unique effect was

Table 6.3 Predicting the contribution of the WAT-C to reading comprehension

Step	Predictor	WAT-C Set A[a]			WAT-C Set B[b]		
		R^2	ΔR^2	ΔF	R^2	ΔR^2	ΔF
1	VocabSize	0.251	0.251	6.358*	0.251	0.251	6.358*
2	WAT_M1	0.400	0.149	4.477*	0.418	0.167	5.162*
1	WAT_M1	0.385	0.385	11.888**	0.396	0.396	12.456**
2	VocabSize	0.400	0.015	0.453	0.418	0.022	0.672
1	VocabSize	0.251	0.251	6.358*	0.251	0.251	6.358*
2	WAT_M2	0.339	0.088	2.401	0.412	0.161	4.935*
1	WAT_M2	0.298	0.298	8.062**	0.391	0.391	12.214**
2	VocabSize	0.339	0.041	1.116	0.412	0.021	0.632
1	VocabSize	0.251	0.251	6.358*	0.251	0.251	6.358*
2	WAT_M3	0.325	0.074	1.986	0.403	0.152	4.574*
1	WAT_M3	0.306	0.306	8.372**	0.380	0.380	11.630**
2	VocabSize	0.325	0.019	0.515	0.403	0.023	0.689

Note. [a]Results of regression analysis with Set A scores as predictors. [b]Results of regression analysis with Set B scores as predictors. VocabSize = vocabulary size; WAT_M1 = All-or-Nothing method; WAT_M2 = One-Point method; WAT_M3 = Correct-Wrong method. * $p < 0.05$ ** $p < 0.01$

significant ($p < 0.05$). The scores of the other two methods, however, did not predict reading comprehension significantly ($\Delta R^2 = 0.088$, $p = 0.509$ and $\Delta R^2 = 0.074$, $p = 0.176$, respectively, for the One-Point and the Correct-Wrong methods); the proportion of variance in the comprehension task explained by those two methods was also notably smaller than that by the scores of the All-or-Nothing method.

When the order of entry for the predictors was switched, some different patterns were revealed. When entered as the first predictor, all three WAT-C scores significantly predicted reading comprehension. The All-or-Nothing method obviously had the greatest effect on the criterion variable; it explained about 38.5% of the variance in reading comprehension ($p < 0.01$). The One-Point and the Correct-Wrong methods explained about 29.8 and 30.6% of the variance in reading comprehension, respectively, both $ps < 0.01$. However, after controlling for vocabulary depth, vocabulary size did not significantly predict reading comprehension; it explained minimal additional variance in reading comprehension (about 1.5–4.1%), which was true when any of the three WAT-C scores was the first predictor.

The same procedure of regression analysis was followed to predict reading comprehension with vocabulary size and depth for Set B of the WAT-C. As shown in Table 6.3, similar as well as different results were found for the predictive effects of vocabulary size and depth. Specifically, over and above vocabulary size, all three WAT-C scores, as opposed to the scores of the All-or-Nothing method only as in the case of Set A, had a significant and unique effect on reading comprehension.

Like for Set A, the All-or-Nothing method explained the largest amount of additional variance in reading comprehension (about 16.7%, $p < 0.05$). This effect, however, did not seem to show any substantial difference from the other two methods, which explained about 16.1 and 15.2% of the variance in reading comprehension, respectively (both $ps < 0.05$). Also similar to Set A, all three WAT-C scores were significant predictors when entered into the regression equations before vocabulary size, and vocabulary size did not significantly and uniquely predict reading comprehension and explained only minimal additional variance (2.1–2.3%). Based on the proportion of variance explained in reading comprehension, the three scoring methods did not seem to show substantial difference, though the All-or-Nothing method appeared to show the largest proportion (about 39.6%, $p < 0.01$) compared to the One-Point (about 39.1%, $p < 0.01$) and the Correct-Wrong (about 38.0%, $p < 0.01$) methods.

Discussion

Distinctness of Vocabulary Depth and Size

Our first question for the validation study asked whether the WAT-C we developed indeed measured an aspect of vocabulary knowledge (i.e., depth) distinct from vocabulary size. To answer this question, the medium-sized correlations (r from 0.610 to 0.735; see Table 6.2) suggested that the WAT-C and the picture selection task had significant overlap in measuring learners' vocabulary competence; yet there was substantial difference or independence between the two that make them tests of distinct aspects of that competence. The hierarchical regression analysis further confirmed that over and above vocabulary size, vocabulary depth also explained a significant amount of unique variance in reading comprehension. This was true for all three scores of Set B and for the All-or-Nothing scores of Set A, confirming a distinct aspect of vocabulary knowledge tapped by the WAT-C.

We also found that vocabulary depth had a more dominant effect on reading comprehension than vocabulary size. A similar finding was also reported in Qian's (1999) study on adult ESL learners. Interestingly, however, our validation study revealed that after depth was in the regression model, size was no longer a significant predictor. It would of course be spurious to interpret this result as vocabulary size being unimportant to Chinese reading. We conjecture that the lack of a unique effect of vocabulary size might be related to the nature of the reading comprehension task used in the validation study. As noted earlier, all our passages were very short and tended to be lexically (and grammatically) simple, compared to the typical passages used for testing reading comprehension (e.g., the reading comprehension section of the TOEFL as used in Qian's (1999) study). Thus, they did not seem to require a breadth of knowledge as great as what is typically required for advanced learners' reading in an academic context. Overall, it seems that the relative importance of vocabulary size and depth in reading comprehension may be sensitive to how we measure learners' reading comprehension (or, the textual properties of a reading task). This definitely warrants attention in the future for validation of depth of vocabulary knowledge measures on the one hand and the vocabulary demand of reading comprehension on the other hand.

Test Condition

The second question for the validation addressed whether the condition under which WAT-C was administered would have an influence on the WAT-C. The answer was obviously yes based on our findings. The influence on the WAT-C was manifested in several ways. To begin with, we found learners' performance was significantly greater on the WAT-C when they were informed on the number of associates than when they were not. Such a result may be understood with reference to the argument Schoonen and Verhallen (2008) made when they decided to have a fixed number of associates for their Dutch WAT; specifically, as the authors argued:

> It is important that the number of required associations is fixed and specified for the test-takers, because association is a relative feature. Depending on a person's imagination or creativity, he/she could consider all distractors to be related to the target word. A fixed number is helpful in the instruction because it forces test-takers to consider which relations are the strongest or most decontextualized. (p. 218)

Thus, having a fixed number of choices reported to test-takers can refrain them from using wild imagination to choose as many words as they believe to be associates and consequently making their choices more precise. Logically, having learners informed on the number of choices could also help them make an easier decision in challenging situations such as when they are debating with themselves whether a fourth associate should be circled and when they are inclined to choosing only one or two associates. This also seemed to agree with our observation that learners' responses were almost all three in the informed condition (Set B),[2] whereas in the uninformed condition (Set A), besides correct selection of three associates, a large majority of the other responses included only two choices with a small number of one or four choices.

The aforementioned results appeared to favor the informed condition. However, it would be premature to conclude that the informed condition is necessarily better and more valid simply because it can boost learners' test performance. To make an evaluation, we need to look at other types of evidence. For example, the size of the correlations between the two conditions for each of the three scoring methods ($rs = 0.720$, 0.796, and 0.827; see Table 6.2) suggested some notable difference

---

[2]There were a few two-associate responses, which might be because the learners were so unsure about the choices other than those two selected that they were hesitant to mark a third choice based on pure guessing.

between the two conditions in addition to a significant overlap. More importantly, the consistently significant and unique effects of all three scores on reading comprehension in WAT-C Set B, as opposed to only the All-or-Nothing method having a significant and unique effect in Set A (see Table 6.3), also suggested that when learners were informed on the number of associates, WAT-C tended to have more consistent predictive effects on the criterion variable. Thus, from the perspective of predictive validity, it seems more desirable to make sure test-takers know the number of associates for WAT items.

Preferred Scoring Method

The last question for the validation asked about the best method for scoring the WAT-C. While all three methods showed very strong correlations among themselves, disregarding how the WAT-C was administered, some variations were observed when they were used to predict learners' reading comprehension. In both conditions, the scores of the All-or-Nothing method were a significant, unique predictor of reading comprehension over and above vocabulary size; it also appeared that they explained the largest proportion of variance in reading comprehension whether the WAT-C was entered before or after vocabulary size into the regression equations. The scores of the other two methods only significantly and uniquely predicted reading comprehension in the informed condition as opposed to the uninformed condition.

Previously, the Correct-Wrong method was argued to have the capability for controlling for guessing (Greidanus et al. 2004, 2005; Zhang 2012), if informed to test-takers before they took the WAT, because selecting an incorrect choice that one is unsure of through guessing would mean to lose a point (that would otherwise be earned) and another point for a correct choice failing to be selected.[3] Given the complexity of scoring and the lowest effect size of prediction (see Table 6.3), the Correct-Wrong method, thus, did not seem to be a preferred method for scoring. While the One-Point method was simpler than the Correct-Wrong method in that scoring only needs to reward correctly selected associates (without needing to consider selection of distractors), it is still more complex than the All-or-Nothing method yet without achieving any larger predictive effect. Thus, the One-Point method, compared to the All-or-Nothing method, may not be a preferred method, either. To conclude, the All-or-Nothing method seemed to be the best method for scoring the WAT-C.

Such a conclusion also agrees with that of Schmitt et al. (2011) where they found that for their six-option format, which was the format used in the present study, the

---

[3]This is because the learner might believe s/he has already come up with three choices, including that wrongly selected one, and thus, there is no need to go deeper with the analysis of the other choices.

All-or-Nothing method produced the highest correlation with the interview scores of WAT words. It also seems to support the earlier decision of Schoonen and Verhallen (2008) for choosing this method for scoring their WAF test for young DSL learners, although the authors' concern that the other two methods might inflate reliability estimates as a result of the "unwanted interdependence" between the associative relations of a target word with all its associates caused by the two methods was not supported in our study. As shown in Table 6.1, for both sets of the WAT-C, compared to the All-or-Nothing method, the other two methods consistently showed the lowest level of consistency reliability, although the reliabilities of all three methods did not seem to show substantial difference.

On the other hand, we agree with Schmitt et al. (2011) that an evaluation of scoring methods also needs to consider the purpose of the assessment. If the purpose is to know how a student(s) stands in the level of vocabulary depth knowledge compared to his/her peers in a class, then the All-or-Nothing would give the quickest result; on the other hand, if the purpose is to diagnose the specific associates which learners have mastered or where they may display poor knowledge, the One-Point or the Correct-Wrong method would be a better choice to give more specific information of diagnosis. The complexity of scoring in the last two methods should not be interpreted as a lack of validity. After all, they were also significant and unique predictors of reading comprehension over and above vocabulary size when learners were informed on the number of associates (see Table 6.3).

Retrospection and Directions for Future Research

As we retrospect on our development of the WAT-C and the initial validation, it seems fit to say that more questions are left unaddressed than answered. There are some issues and limitations that warrant future attention for revising, updating, and further validating the WAT-C. The first issue pertains to word frequency. We followed the general practice in the field to select high-frequency words for constructing the WAT-C (Read 1993, 1998; Schoonen and Verhallen 2008). However, Greidanus and colleagues (Greidanus and Nienhuis 2001; Greidanus et al. 2004, 2005) found that the actual frequency levels of stimulus words could be an important issue, as it is possible that the more frequent a word is, the more likely the learner would have better knowledge of different aspects of the word. It thus appears that making sure all words are high frequency without considering variations in their actual frequency levels and possible effect on response behaviors may limit our knowledge about the WAT. Another influence of the lack of attention to actual word frequency in our validation study is the compatibility of words in the two random sets of the WAT-C, which might have some influence on the comparisons we made between the two sets.

The second issue that we failed to consider is how distractor properties might influence the WAT-C. Read (1998) argued that distractors should be semantically irrelevant to the stimulus word, a principle we adopted in developing the WAT-C.

Read's (1998) argument, however, was not always endorsed and followed in the literature. Schoonen and Verhallen (2008), for example, in their development of a Dutch WAT actually used semantically related distractors rather than completely semantically irrelevant ones. Greidanhus and Nienhuis (2001) specifically tested how different types of distractors would have an influence on the DWK they developed for Dutch university learners of French. Using the Correct-Wrong scoring method, Greidanhus and Nienhuis (2001) found that learners with different years of learning French showed consistently better scores for test items with distractors unrelated to the stimulus words. This finding did not appear to be a surprise, given that semantically unrelated distractors are much easier to eliminate than related ones and given the scoring method values non-selection of distractors.

On the other hand, the fact that items with semantically related distractors favored learners does not necessarily indicate that it should be a more preferred item design for WAT. As noted by Read (1998), more proficient readers may use the relationships between options, or the lack thereof, to make guesses on associates for an unknown target word. In other words, a test with semantically related distractors may make guessing harder. Schmitt et al. (2011) found distractors with no semantic relationships (0.776) produced a less strong correlation with interview scores than semantically related distractors (0.910) in the situation of a six-option WAT, whereas in the case of an eight-option WAT, the reverse pattern was found (0.912 and 0.813, respectively). Taken together, these studies and discussions suggest that the influence of types of distractors on the WAT, if any, could be much more complex than we thought.

The third issue that we did not attend to in the validation study is that the WAT-C, which was designed to measure the network aspect of learners' depth knowledge (Read 2004), requires learners to be able to recognize all the characters for accessing the meaning of each word. If any character is not recognized in a word, which means word meaning cannot be (effectively) accessed, the validity of the WAT-C may be threatened. In alphabetic languages (particularly languages with very transparent grapheme-to-phoneme mapping relationships such as Dutch and Italian), which were the focus of almost all previous studies on WAT (and other tests of vocabulary knowledge), orthographic processing is rarely considered as a factor separate from meaning when L2 vocabulary knowledge is assessed. This might be because the test developers adopted a view of integrated assessment of form and meaning, or there might be an assumption that orthographic processing skills would not affect meaning access for words in a test because of the alphabetic nature of the target language. Such an assumption, if valid at all, would not be as straightforward in Chinese, because of its unique orthography (Taylor and Taylor 2014).[4] Given that the primary purpose of the WAT-C is to assess network

---

[4]It is well known that Chinese characters are very challenging to learners from alphabetic language backgrounds. Chinese characters usually have a very salient place in L2 curriculum and classroom instruction. They are also an important aspect of word knowledge that is commonly tested in Chinese (e.g., Zhao 2003; see also Zhang this volume). In teaching syllabuses or documents that guide the development of curriculum and testing for Chinese learners, such as the

knowledge about word meanings, failure to recognize any characters in the WAT-C may threaten the validity of the test. This might be a reason why Jiang (2002) adopted the aural/oral modality (i.e., learners listened to target words and orally provided associates) when he developed the productive word association test for Chinese L2 learners. In the future, it might be interesting to compare whether learners would perform differently between an aural–oral and a written condition, or how adding *pinyin* to all words might or might not have any influence on the WAT-C. These issues may be particularly important to the assessment of the depth knowledge of heritage language learners, who typically have significant oral language experiences in Chinese (hence, a presumably significant network knowledge developed out of those experiences) but have challenges with respect to Chinese orthography and characters. In other words, without appropriate control, the WAT-C, if used for heritage learners, might underestimate their association knowledge.

The fourth issue is whether the syntagmatic and paradigmatic aspects of associative relationships measured in the WAT-C may address a single dimension or disconnected aspects of vocabulary knowledge. Read (1998) voiced a concern that the "synonymic" knowledge tested through syntagmatic associates and the "collocational" knowledge tested through paradigmatic associates may tap distinct aspects of depth of vocabulary knowledge. Batty's study (2012) tested three different hypothetical models about the factor structure of an English WAT with respect to different association relationships. Neither the one-factor model, which hypothesized that all the WAT items loaded on a general vocabulary factor, nor the two-factor model, which hypothesized that the syntagmatic and paradigmatic associates formed two separate but correlated factors, showed satisfactory model fits. The third model, a bifactor model which hypothesized that all WAT items loaded on a single general factor (of vocabulary depth) while the syntagmatic and paradigmatic associates additionally loaded on two separate, smaller factors, exhibited the best fit. These findings suggested that a simple aggregation of the scores for different association relationships, which is often the case in the literature and is also the case in our study, may not be a preferred practice.

Finally, we need to admit that the small sample size is also a limitation of the study. In addition, we did not interview the learners on word associations and did not have any verbal report from them on their decision-making while working on the WAT-C to elucidate patterns of their responses. Consequently, a lot of the issues as reported in Read (1998) and Schmitt et al. (2011) about the qualitative nuances and variations in students' response processes and patterns (e.g., in relation to distractor type, guessing and use of other strategies, etc.) could not be revealed. As Read (1998) alluded to in his validation of the revised English WAT:

(Footnote 4 continued)

GCSCW-TCSOL (State Language Commission 2011), there are often graded character lists in addition to graded word lists.

Validation involves the accumulation of various kinds of evidence to support the desired interpretations of the test scores under the general rubric of construct validity … several forms of evidence (content analysis, item analysis and reliability statistics, verbal reports from test-takers, and criterion-related data) to investigate the meaning of the test scores with respect to the underlying construct of vocabulary knowledge (p. 42).

With reference to this comment, the validation evidence from our study for the WAT-C was certainly limited.

Conclusions

In this chapter, we reported our development and validation of a WAF test to assess Chinese L2 learners' vocabulary depth. We found the WAT-C to be reliable and valid. It not only demonstrated high internal consistency reliability but also was shown to measure an aspect of vocabulary knowledge distinct from vocabulary breadth. Based on the learners' greater performance and the consistently significant predictive effects of all WAT-C scores on reading comprehension, we concluded that it may be more desirable to administer the WAT-C with learners informed on the number of associates. In addition, we concluded that the All-or-Nothing method may be the best method for scoring the WAT-C, given its simplicity of scoring in comparison with the other two methods. We believe our work not only produced a useful assessment tool for future research concerning vocabulary depth of Chinese L2 learners but also enriched our knowledge about the WAT in assessing depth of vocabulary knowledge in general.

Our hope for the use of the WAT-C goes beyond research purposes. It is our belief that appropriately modified and used, the WAT-C could also be a useful tool for teachers to formatively assess their students' vocabulary knowledge, in conjunction with other methods that we commonly use in classroom assessment (e.g., L1 translation, dictation, multiple-choice questions). Given that vocabulary knowledge development is incremental in nature, it is clear that a deep understanding of how the meaning of a word is organized and related to other words in the mental lexicon is much more important than knowledge of the basic, definitional meaning of a word. Yet, recent analyses of ESL and foreign language textbooks revealed that the two aspects of vocabulary knowledge that received the most attention were often word forms and meanings (i.e., helping learners to establish form-meaning connections) with critical aspects of vocabulary depth, like associations, minimally covered (Brown 2011; Neary-Sundquist 2015). While there is no similar report on Chinese textbooks, there have been constant reports that Chinese learners, even advanced ones, tend to show a lack of fine-grained understanding of word meanings, such as the nuanced meanings of synonyms and their distinct collocation patterns (e.g., Li 2016; Zhou 2016). As Schmitt (2008, p. 339) argued, while the initial form-meaning connection is an important first step, the goal of vocabulary instruction should go far beyond it. From a curricular and pedagogical perceptive, "more exposure, attention, manipulation, or time spent on lexical items," which is referred to by Schmitt as "engagement" with words, are essential not only for consolidating the form-meaning relationships but also for providing opportunities for the development of other types of vocabulary knowledge (Schmitt 2008). Thus, it cannot be too important for teachers to facilitate students' development of a deeper knowledge of various aspects of words. On the other hand, effective instruction and instructional accommodation come from effective assessments to diagnose the strengths and learning needs of students (Katz and Gottlieb 2013; see also Sun et al., this volume). To this end, we hope the WAT-C could be a useful tool for teachers as well.

References

Anderson, R. C., & Freebody, P. (1981). Vocabulary knowledge. In J. T. Guthrie (Ed.), *Comprehension and teaching: Research reviews* (pp. 77–117). Newark, DE: International Reading Association.

Batty, A. (2012). Identifying dimensions of vocabulary knowledge in the word associates test. *Vocabulary Learning and Instruction, 1,* 70–77.

Beijing Language Institute. (1986). *Modern Chinese frequency dictionary.* Beijing: Beijing Language Institute Press.

Brown, D. (2011). What aspects of vocabulary knowledge do textbooks give attention to? *Language Teaching Research, 15,* 93–97.

Bruton, A. (2009). The vocabulary knowledge scale: A critical analysis. *Language Assessment Quarterly, 6,* 288–297.

Grabe, W. (2009). *Reading in a second language: Moving from theory to practice.* NY: Cambridge University Press.

Greidanus, T., Beks, B., & Wakely, R. (2005). Testing the development of French word knowledge by advanced Dutch- and English-speaking learners and native speakers. *The Modern Language Journal, 89,* 221–233.

Greidanus, T., Bogaards, P., van der Linden, E., Nienhuis, L., & de Wolf, T. (2004). In P. Bogaards & B. Laufer-Dvorkin (Eds.), *Vocabulary in a second language: Selection, acquisition, and testing* (pp. 191–208). Amsterdam: John Benjamins.

Greidanus, T., & Nienhuis, L. (2001). Testing the quality of word knowledge in a second language by means of word associations: Types of distractors and types of associations. *The Modern Language Journal, 84,* 567–577.

Henriksen, B. (1999). Three dimensions of vocabulary development. *Studies in Second Language Acquisition, 21,* 303–317.

Hu, M. H.-C., & Nation, I. S. P. (2000). Unknown vocabulary density and reading comprehension. *Reading in a Foreign Language, 13,* 403–430.

Jiang, S. (2002). Chinese word associations for English speaking learners of Chinese as a second language. *Journal of the Chinese Language Teachers Association, 37*(3), 55–70.

Katz, A., & Gottlieb, M. (2013). Assessment in the classroom. In C. Chapelle (Ed.), *The encyclopedia of applied linguistics.* Oxford: Blackwell Publishing.

Ke, C. (2012). Research in second language acquisition of Chinese: Where we are, where we are going. *Journal of the Chinese Language Teachers Association, 47*(3), 43–113.

Laufer, B., & Paribakht, T. S. (1998). Relationship between passive and active vocabularies: Effects of language learning context. *Language Learning, 48,* 365–391.

Li, S. (2016). A corpus-based analysis of collocational errors by American learners of Chinese and its implications for the teaching of vocabulary. *Chinese as a Second Language, 51,* 62–78.

Meara, P., & Jones, G. (1990). *Eurocentres vocabulary size test 10Ka*. Zurich: Enrocentres Learning Services.

Melka, F. (1997). Receptive vs. productive aspects of vocabulary. In N. Schmitt & M. McCarthy (Eds.), *Vocabulary: Description, acquisition and pedagogy* (pp. 84–102). Cambridge: Cambridge University Press.

Messick, S. (1995). Validity of psychological assessment: Validation of inferences from persons' responses and performances as scientific inquiry into scoring meaning. *American Psychologists, 50,* 741–749.

Milton, J. (2009). *Measuring second language vocabulary acquisition*. Bristol: Multilingual Matters.

Milton, J. (2013). Measuring the contribution of vocabulary knowledge to proficiency in the four skills. In C. Bardel, C. Lindqvist, & B. Laufer (Eds.), *L2 vocabulary acquisition, knowledge and use: New perspectives on assessment and corpus analysis* (pp. 57–78). Euro SLA.

Nagy, W. E., & Scott, J. (2000). Vocabulary processes. In M. Kamil, P. Mosenthal, P. D. Pearson, & R. Barr (Eds.), *Handbook of reading research* (Vol. III, pp. 269–284). Mahwah, NJ: Lawrence Erlbaum Associates.

Nation, I. S. P. (1990). *Teaching and learning vocabulary*. New York: Newbury House.

Nation, I. S. P. (2001). *Learning vocabulary in another language*. Cambridge: Cambridge University Press.

Nation, I. S. P. (2005). Teaching and learning vocabulary. In E. Hinkel (Ed.), *Handbook of research in second language teaching and learning* (pp. 581–595). Mahwah, NJ: Lawrence Erlbaum.

Neary-Sundquist, C. A. (2015). Aspects of vocabulary knowledge in German textbooks. *Foreign Language Annals, 48,* 68–81.

Qian, D. D. (1999). Assessing the roles of depth and breadth of vocabulary knowledge in reading comprehension. *Canadian Modern Language Review, 56,* 282–307.

Qian, D. D. (2002). Investigating the relationship between vocabulary knowledge and academic reading performance: An assessment perspective. *Language Learning, 52,* 513–536.

Qian, D. D., & Schedl, M. (2004). Evaluation of an in-depth vocabulary knowledge measure for assessing reading performance. *Language Testing, 21,* 28–52.

Read, J. (1993). The development of a new measure of L2 vocabulary knowledge. *Language Testing, 10,* 355–371.

Read, J. (1997). Vocabulary and testing. In N. Schmitt & M. McCarthy (Eds.), *Vocabulary: Description, acquisition and pedagogy* (pp. 303–320). Cambridge: Cambridge University Press.

Read, J. (1998). Validating a test to measure depth of vocabulary knowledge. In A. J. Kunnan (Ed.), *Validation in language assessment* (pp. 41–60). Mahwah, NJ: Lawrence Erlbaum Associates.

Read, J. (2000). *Assessing vocabulary*. Cambridge: Cambridge University Press.

Read, J. (2004). Plumbing the depths: How should the construct of vocabulary knowledge be defined. In B. Laufer & P. Bogaards (Eds.), *Vocabulary in a second language: Selection, acquisition and testing* (pp. 209–227). Amsterdam: John Benjamins.

Richards, J. C. (1976). The role of vocabulary teaching. *TESOL Quarterly, 10,* 77–89.

Schmitt, N. (2008). Instructed second language vocabulary learning. *Language Teaching, 12,* 329–363.

Schmitt, N. (2014). Size and depth of vocabulary knowledge: What the research shows. *Language Learning, 64,* 913–951.

Schmitt, N., Ng, J. W. C., & Garras, J. (2011). The word associates formats: Validation evidence. *Language Testing, 28,* 105–126.

Schmitt, N., Schmitt, D., & Clapham, C. (2001). Developing and exploring the behaviour of two new versions of the vocabulary levels test. *Language Testing, 18,* 55–88.

Schoonen, R., & Verhallen, M. (2008). The assessment of deep word knowledge in young first and second language learners. *Language Testing, 25,* 211–236.

State Language Commission. (2011). *Graded Chinese syllables, characters and words for the application of teaching Chinese to speakers of other languages.* Beijing: State Language Commission, Chinese Ministry of Education.

Stewart, J., Batty, A. O., & Bovee, N. (2012). Comparing multidimensional and continuum models of vocabulary acquisition: An empirical examination of the vocabulary knowledge scale. *TESOL Quarterly, 46,* 695–721.

Taylor, I., & Taylor, M. M. (2014). *Writing and literacy in Chinese, Korean and Japanese.* Philadelphia, PA: John Benjamins.

Vermeer, A. (2001). Breadth and depth of vocabulary in relation to L1/L2 acquisition and frequency of input. *Applied Psycholinguistics, 22,* 217–234.

Webb, S. (2013). Depth of vocabulary knowledge. In C. Chapelle (Ed.), *The encyclopedia of applied linguistics.* Oxford: Blackwell Publishing.

Wesche, M., & Paribakht, T. S. (1996). Assessing second language vocabulary knowledge: Depth vs. breadth. *Canadian Modern Language Review, 53,* 13–39.

Zhang, D. (2012). Vocabulary and grammatical knowledge in L2 reading comprehension: A structural equation modeling study. *The Modern Language Journal, 96,* 554–571.

Zhao, G. (2003). Productivity of characters in forming words and the acquisition of characters for CSL beginners. *Applied Linguistics, 3,* 106–112.

Zhou, Y. (2016). A corpus-based study on the semantic collocation between disyllabic emotional psychological verbs and noun objects in Mandarin Chinese. *Studies in Chinese Learning and Teaching,* (2), 29–45.

Chapter 7
Can Grammatical Knowledge Predict Chinese Proficiency?

Liu Li

Abstract This study explored how to assess the explicit and implicit grammatical knowledge of learners of Chinese, and their relationship to learners' overall Chinese language proficiency. The participants were 85 learners of Chinese as a foreign language (CFL) at universities in the USA. A test battery included three parts: (1) a timed grammaticality judgment test (GJT) and an oral repetition task for implicit grammatical knowledge; (2) an untimed GJT and an error correction task for explicit grammatical knowledge; and (3) a general language proficiency test. A set of correlation coefficients were computed to explore the contributions of implicit and explicit grammatical knowledge to overall proficiency. The results showed that there was no statistically significant correlation between the CFL learners' implicit grammatical knowledge and their proficiency scores, but there was a strong relationship between their explicit grammatical knowledge and their general proficiency. Further multiple regression analyses demonstrated that explicit knowledge better predicted the CFL learners' general L2 proficiency. These findings are discussed in light of how the relationship of implicit and explicit grammatical knowledge with general proficiency might be influenced by learners' actual level of proficiency or learning stage and how general proficiency is tested. Pedagogical implications are also discussed.

Keywords Implicit grammatical knowledge · Explicit grammatical knowledge · Language proficiency · Assessment · Chinese as a foreign language

Introduction

Grammar is an integral component of Chinese as a Foreign Language (CFL) curriculum and pedagogy, and a large amount of instructional time is usually spent on grammar to promote CFL learners' grammatical competence (Xing 2006). Despite its

L. Li (✉)
Ball State University, Muncie, USA
e-mail: lli5@bsu.edu

© Springer Nature Singapore Pte Ltd. 2017   141
D. Zhang and C.-H. Lin (eds.), *Chinese as a Second Language Assessment*,
Chinese Language Learning Sciences, DOI 10.1007/978-981-10-4089-4_7

important status in Chinese teaching and learning, grammar has rarely become a direct and legitimate topic in Chinese assessment; there has been little attempt in the CFL community to study the assessment of grammatical knowledge (Jin et al. 2012).

To fill this gap in CFL assessment, we conducted a study that assessed CFL learners' grammatical knowledge and examined its relationship with learners' overall Chinese proficiency. There were two major objectives of the study. First, we aimed to develop and validate measures to assess CFL learners' grammatical knowledge. In alignment with the recent development of research on acquisition of second language (L2) grammar (N. Ellis 2008; R. Ellis 2005), we differentiated between implicit and explicit knowledge of grammar, and assessed both types. Second, previous studies on L2 grammatical knowledge have produced mixed findings about the relative importance of implicit and explicit knowledge to L2 proficiency (e.g., R. Ellis 2006; D. Zhang 2012). Therefore, it was also an objective of the present study to examine how implicit and explicit grammatical knowledge would (differentially) predict L2 proficiency with a focus on CFL learners.

Implicit and Explicit Knowledge of Grammar and L2 Proficiency

Grammatical knowledge consists of two types of knowledge, implicit and explicit. Many studies have found that implicit and explicit grammatical knowledge are different, and they play different roles in second language acquisition (SLA) (e.g., Elder and Ellis 2009; R. Ellis 2004, 2005, 2006; Green and Hecht 1992; Philp 2009). Implicit knowledge is the unconscious knowledge of knowing how to use a language, and speakers of the language cannot explain such knowledge with explicit statements (Cleeremans et al. 1998). Implicit knowledge, therefore, is unconscious and intuitive. R. Ellis (2004, 2006) argued that once implicit knowledge is absorbed into a learner's inter-language, it becomes highly systematic. L2 learners usually are unconsciously guided by this system while processing the language. In contrast to implicit knowledge, explicit knowledge is the knowledge that learners can explicitly explain with grammatical rules or statements (Dienes and Perner 1999). With explicit knowledge, learners consciously know some facts or information about the related L2 grammar aspects or features. But these explicit grammatical facts may not be systematically connected. Therefore, the knowledge of these facts may not constitute as stable system as implicit knowledge of proficient L2 users does. In this sense, explicit knowledge is less structured than implicit knowledge. Because of their differences, learners may use explicit and implicit knowledge differently when they deal with different grammar tasks (R. Ellis 2004). Consequently, how to measure L2 learners' implicit and explicit grammatical knowledge becomes an important topic in the field of L2 assessment, because such an understanding will have significant contributions to the development and assessment of general L2 proficiency (R. Ellis 2006).

Previous studies have found that both implicit and explicit knowledge play an important role in achieving L2 proficiency (e.g., N. Ellis 2008; R. Ellis 2006). Among these studies, Han and Ellis (1998) examined the relationship between explicit and implicit knowledge, and their relationship with general language proficiency among advanced adult learners of English from different backgrounds in the USA. The test included five tasks focusing on complement clauses in English. The three tasks to assess grammar knowledge were as follows: (1) an oral production test (OPT); (2) a grammaticality judgment test (GJT) given three times (first two were timed and the last one was not); and (3) an interview. The proficiency tasks included the Test of English as a Foreign Language (TOEFL) and the Secondary Level English Proficiency Test (SLEP). The measures resulting from grammar knowledge tests were grouped into a factor analysis that produced two significant factors, one for implicit knowledge and the other one for explicit knowledge. These two types of grammatical knowledge were positively correlated with each other as well as with the two measures of language proficiency (i.e., TOEFL and SLEP tests). The results demonstrated that both implicit and explicit L2 knowledge could play a role in general L2 proficiency.

R. Ellis (2006) further examined to what extent L2 proficiency can be properly explained by implicit and explicit grammatical knowledge. In this study, R. Ellis attempted to find out why some L2 grammatical structures are more difficult to learn than others. Using a battery of tests that were designed to measure implicit and explicit L2 grammatical knowledge of 17 grammatical structures, R. Ellis (2006) investigated the learning difficulty in relation to these two types of knowledge. The results showed that structures that were easy in terms of implicit knowledge were often difficult in terms of explicit knowledge and sometimes vice versa. Overall, there was no correlation between the rank orders of difficulty of the 17 grammatical structures for implicit and explicit knowledge. However, a correlational analysis showed when the structures varied as to whether it was implicit or explicit knowledge, they were correlated to a measure of general language proficiency. These findings indicated that there existed a correlation between grammar scores and general proficiency scores. A regression analysis demonstrated that both types of knowledge predicted general language proficiency. However, as far as the distinction was concerned, the implicit and the explicit measures of the same structure were not equally correlated with proficiency. In other words, the implicit measures of one set of structures and the explicit knowledge of another set were found to relate to the general language proficiency measures. He concluded that the distinction between implicit and explicit knowledge contributed to the level of learning difficulty in L2 grammar learning.

Elder and Ellis (2009) further investigated the extent to which implicit and explicit L2 knowledge of specific grammatical features related to general L2 proficiency. The same 17 grammatical structures used in R. Ellis's study (2006) were employed in this study. Four measures were used to measure the participants' implicit and explicit linguistic knowledge, including the elicited imitation test (EIT), timed grammatical judgment test (TGJT), untimed grammatical judgment test (UGJT), and metalinguistic knowledge test (MKT). Participants' scores from the International English Language Testing System (IELTS) test measuring their L2 proficiency were also obtained. A key finding in this study was that both the implicit and explicit measures of the same structure were not related to proficiency. The results of a series of correlation and multiple regression analyses also displayed that the measures of both implicit and explicit knowledge predicted IELTS participants' total scores. Implicit knowledge was found to be a significant predictor of both speaking and writing, whereas explicit knowledge predicted both listening and reading.

With a large sample pool, D. Zhang (2012) was able to employ structural equation modeling analysis to examine the contribution of vocabulary and grammatical knowledge to second language reading comprehension among advanced Chinese EFL learners. In his study, the implicit grammatical knowledge was measured with a timed grammaticality judgment task. The explicit knowledge was measured with a grammatical error correction task. It was found that the two types of grammatical knowledge only showed a weak contribution to reading comprehension. Through further analysis, it was found that the learners' implicit knowledge of grammar had a stronger relationship to reading comprehension than explicit knowledge. Zhang's findings in this regard differed from Elder and Ellis's study (2009), in which explicit knowledge predicted reading.

A few studies also attempted to explore the relationship between explicit grammatical knowledge and general language proficiency in languages other than English. For example, Elder and Manwaring (2004) found that although explicit knowledge of the Chinese grammatical system was a good predictor of overall course performance, it was associated with better performance in a Chinese language course for some of the groups, but not for others. Their findings also revealed that some aspects of this knowledge are more critical than others, and the relationship between explicit grammar knowledge and proficiency varied in strength according to the nature of the assessment task and learners' prior experience of language study. Roehr (2008) examined the relationship between explicit knowledge of L2 German and L2 proficiency measured as knowledge of grammar and vocabulary, and found a strong positive correlation between the two. However, neither study looked into the relationship between implicit knowledge and the general L2 proficiency.

Although the findings of the reviewed studies overall supported the viewpoint that general L2 proficiency is associated with implicit and/or explicit L2 knowledge, they only afforded limited empirical support for it. First, most of those studies focused on European languages, especially English as a second/foreign language (ESL/EFL). Little effort was made to examine less commonly taught languages. Second, some studies examined only explicit grammar knowledge and its relationship with overall proficiency. Implicit knowledge was not in the picture. Third, the findings sometimes showed some discrepancies. For example, Elder and Ellis's study (2009) found that explicit knowledge predicted reading, whereas in D. Zhang's study (2012), it was found that the learners' implicit knowledge of grammar had a stronger relationship to reading comprehension.

These problems indicate that more research is needed on how the two different types of grammatical knowledge could be assessed in various languages and how they might contribute differentially to L2 proficiency in these languages. Particularly, since most empirical studies done so far have focused on English as a second/foreign Language, the relationship between implicit/explicit L2 knowledge and general L2 proficiency among less commonly taught languages urgently needs further empirical investigation.

To this end, we conducted the present study with a focus on adult CFL learners to further explore the nature of L2 grammatical knowledge, the relationship between implicit and explicit knowledge, and the relationship of the two types of knowledge with general L2 proficiency. It is hoped that the study will be illuminating for both SLA research and the teaching and testing practice of L2 Chinese grammatical knowledge.

Acquisition of L2 Chinese Grammar

In contrast to the importance attached to the teaching and learning of grammar in any Chinese program, there is a disappointing fact that little attention has been given to the assessment of grammatical knowledge in L2 Chinese. This is evident not only from a lack of direct assessment of grammatical knowledge in major standardized tests but also from the little empirical effort of scholars to address issues of grammar in research on Chinese assessment. So far, most of the research on explicit and implicit grammatical knowledge has been done among learners of English, Spanish, or other European languages (e.g., R. Ellis 2005, 2006; Mirzaei et al. 2011). Little attention has been paid to less commonly taught languages such as Chinese. According to the report released by the Modern Language Association on enrollments in languages other than English in United States' Institutions of Higher Education (Furman et al. 2010), there has been an increasing number of learners studying Chinese in recent years. It is thus worth examining how CFL learners develop grammatical knowledge and how their grammatical knowledge is related to their overall Chinese proficiency development.

Chinese language is typologically different from English in terms of grammar (Jiang 2009; Xing 2006). From a grammatical perspective, there are some specific challenges to learners of Chinese, who usually have a different path of development for different grammatical features. For example, Y. Zhang (2001) has developed a sequential hierarchy of eight Chinese morphemes in L2 acquisition of the language based on the Processability Theory, which are as follows:

1. Adjective marker—de 的 (e.g., 漂亮的 pretty),
2. Possessive marker—de 的 (e.g., 我的 mine),
3. Attributive marker—de 的 (e.g., 北京的天气 weather in Beijing),
4. Experiential marker—guo 过 (e.g., 看过 has/have seen),

5. Progressive marker—zhe 着 (e.g., 躺着 be lying),
6. V-complement marker—de 得 (e.g., 走<u>得</u>很慢 walk slowly)
7. Classifier (e.g.,一张纸 a piece of paper)
8. Relative clause marker—de 的 (妈妈做<u>的</u>饭很好吃 The meal that mom cooked was delicious).

Following Y. Zhang's (2001) research, Gao (2005) conducted a similar study between two groups of Chinese L2 learners. She identified similar findings with Y. Zhang's (2001) and also found several grammatical structures at the syntactic level that were challenging to L2 learners, such as the *ba* 把 structure and topicalization in Chinese. In Y. Zhang (2008), the proposed hierarchy of processing in L2 Chinese in Zhang (2001) was extended to the following syntactic aspects:

1. Topicalization: OSV, SOV

> e.g., 1）机票　　　我 买好了。
> Flight tickets I already bought.
> 2）我什么水果都吃。
> I　any fruit all eat.

2. Adv-fronting and subordinate clause: XP SV(O)/S XP VO

> e.g.,慢慢地 他 走　　进了　　教室。
> Slowly　he walked into the classroom.

3. Canonical SV(O): declaratives and interrogatives (y/n, wh-question, and intonation).

> e.g., 1)我学　　中文。
> I study Chinese.
> 2)你　学　什么？
> You study what?

However, Y. Zhang's (2008) data came from elicitation tasks, which seemed less natural than spontaneous conversation. In addition, her research participants had been taught the aspects of grammar through a sequence that followed the processing hierarchy she proposed. Therefore, we cannot rule out the possibility that learners might reveal different acquisition sequences if they were taught grammar structures in different orders.

In order to develop a set of stages that L2 learners follow in acquisition of Chinese grammar and with the gaps of previous studies discussed above addressed, Wang (2013) extended and tested the processing hierarchy (Gao 2005; Y. Zhang 2001, 2008) in a different group of Chinese L2 learners. Wang's study attempted to demonstrate the emergence sequence of a number of core structures in L2 Chinese. Previously, most studies on L2 Chinese focused on a single structure or a very limited set of them. Wang's study had a much wider scope and covered both morphological level and syntactical level. Therefore, it can be used to serve as a good base for future experimental designs. Wang collected spontaneous and prompted oral data through semi-structured interviews at an interval of 2 or

Table 7.1 Learning stages in Chinese grammar (Wang 2013)

Stages	Processing procedure	Information exchange	Morpheme	Syntax
5	S-bar procedure	Main and sub-clause	/	ba structure
4	S-procedure	Inter-phrasal information	Relative clause marker de	Topicalization: OSV, SOV
3	Phrasal procedure	Phrasal information	Classifier V-Comp marker —de	XP SV(O)/S XP VO: adv-fronting, subordinate clause
2	Category procedure	Lexical morphology	Possessive marker —de Adjective marker —de Attributive marker —de Progressive marker zhengzai Experiential marker—guo	Canonical SV(O): declaratives, interrogatives (y/n, wh-, intonation)
1	Word	Words	Invariant forms: Single words/constituents	Formulaic expressions

3 weeks over 38 weeks from 8 undergraduate students, who had diverse language learning experiences and backgrounds. The speech data were transcribed into text, resulting in a 30,000-word corpus for the study. Overall, Wang's (2013) study confirmed the previous findings by Y. Zhang (2001, 2008) and Gao (2005) that L2 learners do tend to follow a set of stages in their acquisition of Chinese grammar. She summarized CFL learners' grammar acquisition order in the following table.

Table 7.1 provides a relatively complete picture of the acquisition sequence of grammar for Chinese L2 learners. The hierarchy provides teachers with a useful framework to understand the typical developmental path and direction that learners with typologically different L1 backgrounds go through in acquiring L2 Chinese grammar. It also offers us a practical framework to sample grammatical features for assessing L2 learners' Chinese grammatical competence in the present study.

Research Questions

As mentioned previously, most existing studies on implicit and explicit grammatical knowledge (and their relationships with L2 proficiency) focused on English, Spanish, or other commonly taught languages. There has been little research to study the two dimensions of grammatical knowledge among learners of Chinese. Previously, a number of tasks have been developed and implemented to examine L2 learners' implicit and explicit grammatical knowledge. Therefore, an objective of the present study was to find out whether these tasks would also be reliable and valid measures of grammatical knowledge in L2 Chinese. Specifically, the study aimed to address the following research questions:

1. Is there any significant correlation between implicit and explicit grammatical knowledge of CFL learners and their general L2 proficiency?
2. Which type of grammatical knowledge, implicit or explicit, better predicts the general L2 proficiency of CFL learners?

Methods

Participants

The participants in this study were adult CFL learners studying Chinese at two universities in Indiana, USA. The two universities used the same textbooks (*Integrated Chinese*). The pace of instruction and the benchmark set for each proficiency level (beginning, intermediate, and advanced) were similar. At each university, one class of students was randomly chosen from all the classes at the beginning, intermediate, and advanced level, respectively. Altogether, there were six classes of students; in each class, only native English speakers were recruited. In the final pool of participants, there were 85 students (47 males and 38 females) with an average age of 20.5 years. They had studied Chinese for 1–3 years in correspondence to the level of their Chinese class.

Instruments and Procedures

The participants first completed a language background questionnaire. The questionnaire provided personal information about the participants, as well as the information about their language background and exposure to Chinese language.

There were five tests for participants to take in order to assess their grammatical knowledge and general Chinese proficiency. Based on previous research (R. Ellis 2005; Mirzaei et al. 2011), a timed GJT and an oral repetition task were administered to measure the participants' implicit grammatical knowledge, whereas an untimed GJT and an error correction task were used as measures of explicit knowledge. A fifth test was administered to measure the overall Chinese proficiency of the participants.

The timed GJT included 40 sentences, 20 grammatical ones and 20 ungrammatical ones. For example, both Sentences (1) and (2) below use the—ba structure. The second one is grammatically correct; the first is not because the aspectual marker—le is missing.

(1) Gāo Wénzhōng bǎ dàngāo chī.
　　高　文中　把　蛋糕　吃。
(2) Wáng Péng bǎ gōngkè zuò le.
　　王　　朋　把功课　做　了。

All 40 sentences were presented on PowerPoint with both characters and pinyin and played automatically to learners with an interval of 10 s. This task was group administered to learners in their regular Chinese classes. The timed GJT was designed following R. Ellis's (2004, 2005, 2006) guidelines. The participants were required to select the correct sentence from among the two parallel grammatical and ungrammatical sentences within the time limit of 10 s for each slide. The participants were reminded of the speeded nature of the test and were instructed to indicate whether the sentences were grammatical or ungrammatical on an answer sheet as fast as they could. The reliability of the test was estimated through Cronbach's alpha, which was found to be 0.69, suggesting that the test was acceptable in reliability.

The oral repetition task was administered individually. The participants listened to a recording of 20 sentences and repeated each one of them one by one, for example:

(3) Dàngāo bèi shāfā yā huài le.
　　蛋糕　被　沙发　压　坏　了。
　　The cake was crushed by the couch.

Students' repetition was recorded for analysis. A repeated sentence was scored as correct only if all sentence elements were repeated in a correct order; pronunciation errors were not considered. Cronbach's alpha of this task was 0.78, suggesting that it was also acceptable in reliability.

The untimed GJT asked the learners to indicate if a Chinese sentence was grammatically correct. Like the timed GJT, it also included 20 pairs of short Chinese sentences (one grammatical and the other ungrammatical, altogether 40 sentences) printed on paper with both characters and pinyin. But there was no time limit to complete it. The reliability of this task was 0.74, suggesting that it was acceptable.

The error correction task contained 20 ungrammatical sentences covering the same grammatical structures as the GJTs. The error correction task was also printed on paper with both characters and pinyin, each of which had four underlined places with one containing a grammatical error. The learners needed to first identify the place with an error and then correct that error. For example, in Sentence (4) below, there is an error in A. Learners should first identify A, and then correct it as "请你吃饭的" to make it a grammatically appropriate modifier of 男人. The reliability of this task was 0.67, suggesting that it was acceptable.

(4) qǐng nǐ chī fàn nán rén shì shuí?
　　请 你吃饭 男 人　是　谁？
　　A　　　B　C　D

In addition to the four grammatical knowledge measures, the learners also took a researcher-developed Chinese proficiency test. This test was a simulation of the standardized measure of L2 Chinese proficiency HSK, which is an official proficiency test for Chinese as an L2 developed by China's Hanban (see Teng, this volume). It consisted of three sections that covered listening, reading, and writing, respectively. In the listening section, the learners were to listen to two audio files and then respond to 10 multiple-choice comprehension questions for each file. Among the two audio files, one contained 10 mini-dialogues between a man and a woman; the other was a narrative. The reading section contained two passages for each of which the learners had to answer 10 multiple-choice questions regarding their comprehension of the passage. The writing section asked the learners to write a short essay in response to one of the two given topics. The total score was 50 points. The proficiency test was group administered in several Chinese classes after the learners completed the grammatical knowledge tasks. Data collection was completed in about a month. Cronbach's alpha of the proficiency test was 0.80, which means that it was a very reliable test.

Scoring Procedures

The responses to the timed and the untimed GJTs were scored in terms of correct and incorrect answers. Each correct response received 1 point, and an incorrect or unanswered response received 0 points. The total score for each task was 20 points (one point for each item). The oral repetition task was also scored in terms of correct or incorrect answers. The total score was 20 points (one point for each item). The total score of the error correction task was also 20 points. If a student identified an error and corrected it, he/she received one point. If an error was only identified, but failed to be corrected, he/she would receive a half point.

The listening and reading sections of the general proficiency test were scored on the basis of correct or incorrect responses depending on whether the learners correctly answered the multiple-choice questions. A correct answer to a question received one point; a wrong answer or no choice made did not receive any points. The total score for both the listening and the reading section was 20. The writing section of this test received a holistic score (0–10) with consideration of topic content, text organization, language use (vocabulary and grammar), as well as mechanics. Two college professors of Chinese with more than 10 years of experience of teaching Chinese in a university setting independently rated the essays of the participants. Inter-rater agreement was 93.02%, and all disagreements were resolved through discussions. The maximum score possible for the general proficiency test was 50 points.

Results

Table 7.2 shows the descriptive statistics of the five tests. Following R. Ellis (2005), we first conducted exploratory factor analysis on the total scores of the four tasks of grammatical knowledge to examine the factor structure of L2 Chinese grammar before we examined their relationships with general L2 proficiency. Two factors were extracted. As shown in Table 7.3, the timed GJT and the oral repetition task were loaded on a factor of implicit knowledge; and the untimed GJT and the error correction task on that of explicit knowledge. Detailed results of this analysis are shown in Table 7.3. This two-factor solution lends support to the claim that these tests provided relatively separate measures of implicit and explicit knowledge in L2 Chinese as they did in L2 English.

To answer the first research question, the relationship between the participants' implicit and explicit grammatical knowledge and their general L2 proficiency was examined through the bivariate correlations using the IBM SPSS software. Implicit knowledge was represented by the total scores of the timed GJT and the oral repetition task, and explicit knowledge by those of the untimed GJT and the error correction task. The correlations are shown in Table 7.4. There was no significant correlation between the scores of the CFL learners' implicit knowledge and their general L2 proficiency scores, $r = 0.21$; but the correlation between the scores of

Table 7.2 Descriptive statistics of the test scores

Knowledge	Task	Mean score	SD
Implicit knowledge	Timed GJT	10.6	2.98
	Oral repetition task	9.7	4.88
Explicit knowledge	Untimed GJT	15.8	3.76
	Error correction task	11.3	5.09
General proficiency		37.8	14.9
	Listening	13.2	4.96
	Reading	18.5	3.43
	Writing	6.1	2.82

Table 7.3 Results of exploratory factor analysis on grammatical knowledge tests

Components	Total	% of variance	Cumulative %
1	3.881	58.389	58.386
2	1.014	32.813	33.920
Test		Component 1	Component 2
Repetition task		0.725	
Timed GJT		0.792	
Untimed GJT			0.801
Error correction			0.787

Table 7.4 Correlations between implicit/explicit knowledge and general L2 proficiency

Correlations	r	p	N
Implicit and General proficiency	0.210	0.398	85
Explicit and General proficiency	0.515***	0.000	85

***$p < 0.001$

Table 7.5 Correlations between implicit and explicit grammatical knowledge and the sub-components of the general language proficiency test

Sub-components	Implicit Knowledge		Explicit knowledge		N
	r	p	r	p	
Listening	0.076	0.328	0.321***	0.000	85
Reading	0.053	0.271	0.406***	0.000	85
Writing	0.009	0.862	0.198*	0.026	85

*$p < 0.05$ *** $p < 0.001$

Table 7.6 Standard multiple regression analysis predicting general L2 proficiency

Model	R	R squared	Adjusted R squared	Std. error of the estimate
1	0.541	0.298	0.291	13.98

the CFL learners' explicit knowledge test scores and their general L2 proficiency scores was significant ($r = 0.515$, $p < 0.001$).

Table 7.5 shows the bivariate correlations between CFL learners' implicit and explicit grammatical knowledge and the three sub-components of their general L2 proficiency (i.e., listening, reading, and writing). As shown in the table, none of the sub-components of CFL learners' overall proficiency was significantly correlated with their implicit grammatical knowledge: listening comprehension ($r = 0.076$, $p = 0.328$), reading comprehension ($r = 0.053$, $p = 0.271$), and writing ($r = 0.009$, $p = 0.862$). In contrast, the correlational relationships between explicit knowledge and all three sub-components of the proficiency test were significant. Specifically, the correlations between explicit knowledge and listening comprehension, reading comprehension, and writing were $r = 0.321$ ($p < 0.001$), $r = 0.406$ ($p < 0.001$), and $r = 0.198$ ($p < 0.05$), respectively.

To answer the second research question, a multiple regression analysis was conducted to examine how implicit and explicit grammatical knowledge as two independent variables predicted learners' general L2 proficiency. It was found that the two types of grammatical knowledge together explained about 29% of the variance in the learners' general Chinese proficiency; such a predictive effect was significant, $F(2, 84) = 18.40$, $p < 0.001$. Table 7.6 shows the results of model summary of standard multiple regression analysis.

Further hierarchical regression analyses were conducted to examine how explicit and implicit grammatical knowledge independently or uniquely contributed to general L2 proficiency. It was found that CFL learners' implicit grammatical

Table 7.7 Hierarchical regression analysis predicting general L2 proficiency

Model	Unstandardized coefficients		Standardized coefficients	t	Sig.	Collinearity statistics			
	B	Std. error	Beta			Partial	Part	Tolerance	VIF
(Constant)	9.985	7.097		1.981	0.209				
Implicit knowledge	0.698	0.541	0.102	1.573	0.114	0.177	0.152	0.231	0.086
Explicit knowledge	1.791	0.296	0.473	6.704	0.000	0.563	0.548	0.997	1.003

knowledge, as the first variable entered into the regression equation, did not significantly predict their general L2 proficiency. Over and above implicit knowledge, learners' explicit grammatical knowledge stood as a unique and significant predictor of their general proficiency. Table 7.7 shows the results of hierarchical regression analysis.

In the above model, the regression coefficients or standard betas of implicit and explicit knowledge were 0.102 and 0.473 ($p < 0.001$), respectively, which suggests that the participants' explicit grammatical knowledge made a significantly higher contribution to their general proficiency. We also switched the order of entry of the two grammatical knowledge predictors in the regression equation. This time, explicit knowledge was entered first, followed by the implicit knowledge. The overall pattern remained the same showing a significant and stronger predictive effect of explicit knowledge.

Discussion

The study reported a significant correlation between the CFL learners' explicit grammatical knowledge and general Chinese proficiency, and the former was also a significant predictor of the latter. On the other hand, the implicit grammatical knowledge of CFL learners was not a significant correlate of their general Chinese proficiency (and its sub-components; see Tables 7.4 and 7.5). In addition, explicit knowledge was found to have a larger predictive effect on learners' general proficiency.

An explanation for the above pattern of relationships between implicit and explicit grammatical knowledge and L2 proficiency found on Chinese learners might pertain to how Chinese is typically learned in the USA or the type of exposure that the learners in the study had to the target language. Chinese is a less commonly taught language in the USA; and there is not a big Chinese community in Indiana where the learners were sampled. The students in this study, all of whom were native English speakers, learned Chinese almost exclusively in the classroom context through explicit instruction on language structures and rules and had very little exposure to and practice of Chinese (written or spoken) outside of the classroom to enhance their implicit knowledge of Chinese grammar. Consequently, it seemed reasonable that the Chinese learners relied primarily on their explicit knowledge when they worked on the general proficiency tasks. The fairly strong relationship between L2 Chinese explicit grammatical knowledge and Chinese proficiency seemed to corroborate previous research findings on ESL/EFL learners (e.g., Elder and Ellis 2009; R. Ellis 2006).

In addition to the nature of L2 Chinese learning, we need to consider the learning experiences of the students in this study as well. The lack of a significant relationship between implicit knowledge and L2 proficiency seemed to contradict those findings of some previous studies (e.g., Elder and Ellis 2009) that often showed a close relationship between ESL/EFL learners' implicit knowledge and general English proficiency or a sub-component of that proficiency. We speculate this might be due to the limited experience (and hence limited proficiency) of the participants in this study. The participants of the current study had studied Chinese for only 1–3 years (with an average of about 1.9 years). Such a short period of time of studying Chinese indicates that the actual proficiency level of the learners could be very low. Chinese is one of the most difficult languages for native English speakers to learn. The American Council on the Teaching of Foreign Language (ACTFL) has found that English speakers can reach ACTFL Oral Proficiency Interview (OPI) (see Liu, this volume, for more information about the OPI) intermediate-low or intermediate-mid level after about 240 class hours of learning a European language. However, it takes native English speakers 480–720 class hours to reach the same proficiency level in Chinese. According to the list created by the Foreign Service Institute on the approximate time, an English speaker needs to learn a specific language, learners of Spanish, after spending 575–600 h, could reach "Speaking 3: General Professional Proficiency in Speaking" and "Reading 3: General Professional Proficiency in Reading." However, learners of Chinese would have to spend approximately 2200 h. Therefore, the actual (low) proficiency level of the students in this study might have led to a limited involvement of implicit knowledge in the general proficiency test. In other words, learners' actual proficiency or stage of learning might moderate how implicit knowledge (and explicit knowledge) would be related to L2 listening, reading, and/or writing. In the present study, given the small number of participants at each Chinese course level (i.e., beginning, intermediate, and advanced), we did not compare how the relational patterns might differ across these levels. It would certainly be interesting in future research to further explore such an issue with learners at diverse stages of their Chinese learning.

Another possible explanation for the pattern of the findings of this study (especially the lack of significant relationship of implicit knowledge with Chinese proficiency) and its difference from previous studies on English might be related to how the L2 proficiency test was conducted. It is worth noting that in some, if not all, previous studies (e.g., R. Ellis 2006), learners' L2 proficiency data were drawn from a testing context where learners tended to have a pressure to complete their test within a stipulated period of time; therefore, it seems reasonable that implicit knowledge, which implies efficiency of language processing, emerged as a significant and more important predictor of the performance on a proficiency test. To mark a contrast, the proficiency test was conducted in the learners' natural Chinese classes in this study instead of a real testing situation. This seemed to have allowed for more active involvement of explicit knowledge of grammatical rules for monitoring their work on the proficiency test.

Conclusions and Implications

With a focus on learners studying in a university context and using researcher-developed tasks, this study tested CFL learners' implicit as well as explicit grammatical knowledge and explored the relationship of these two dimensions of grammatical knowledge and their general Chinese proficiency development. It was found that implicit knowledge was not significantly correlated with general proficiency (and its sub-components). However, a significant, positive correlation was found of explicit knowledge and general proficiency. As a result of these correlational patterns, it was not surprising that hierarchical regression analysis revealed explicit knowledge as a significant and better predictor of CFL general proficiency.

Previous findings about the relationships of different types of grammatical knowledge to L2 proficiency came largely from research on ESL learners. With a focus on Chinese, a less commonly taught language, the present study enriches our understanding about the role of grammar in L2 proficiency development. Pedagogically, the findings recognize the importance of explicit knowledge in language learning, especially in CFL settings. While a significant relationship of implicit knowledge with Chinese proficiency development did not emerge, it does not necessarily follow that implicit knowledge is not important. As explained earlier, such a pattern might be due to the sensitivity of the relationship to developmental stage or testing condition. The most important insight that can be gained from this study is perhaps that a balanced approach needs to be adopted by L2 teachers in Chinese classrooms between the time devoted to the development of L2 learners' explicit grammatical knowledge through teaching explicit rules and the time specialized to the real communicative use of L2, which can help with the development of both CFL learners' implicit knowledge and their general L2 proficiency.

References

Cleeremans, A., Destrebecqz, A., & Boyer, M. (1998). Implicit learning: News from the front. *Trends in Cognitive Sciences, 2*, 406–417.

Dienes, Z., & Perner, J. (1999). A theory of implicit and explicit knowledge. *Behavioural and Brain Sciences, 22*, 735–808.

Elder, C., & Ellis, R. (2009). Implicit and explicit knowledge of an L2 and language proficiency: Applying the measures of implicit and explicit L2 knowledge. In R. Ellis et al. (Eds.), *Implicit and explicit knowledge in second language learning, teaching, and testing* (pp. 167–193). UK: Multilingual Matters.

Elder, C., & Manwaring, D. (2004). The relationship between metalinguistic knowledge and learning outcomes among undergraduate students of Chinese. *Language Awareness, 13,* 145–162.

Ellis, N. (2008). Implicit and explicit knowledge about language. In J. Cenoz & N. H. Hornberger (Eds.), *Encyclopedia of language and education Volume 6: Knowledge about language* (2nd ed., pp. 119–131). New York: Springer.

Ellis, R. (2004). The definition and measurement of L2 explicit knowledge. *Language Learning, 54*(2), 227–275.

Ellis, R. (2005). Measuring implicit and explicit knowledge of a second language: A psychometric study. *Studies in Second Language Acquisition, 27,* 141–172.

Ellis, R. (2006). Modeling learning difficulty and second language proficiency: The differential contributions of implicit and explicit knowledge. *Applied Linguistics, 27,* 431–463.

Furman, N., Goldberg, D., & Lusin, N. (2010). *Enrollments in languages other than English in United States Institutions of Higher Education, Fall 2009*. Retrieved from https://www.mla.org/content/download/2872/79842/2009_enrollment_survey.pdf

Gao, X. D. (2005). *Noun phrase morphemes and topic development in L2 mandarin Chinese: A processability perspective*. Unpublished doctoral dissertation: Victoria University of Wellington.

Green, P., & Hecht, K. (1992). Implicit and explicit grammar: An empirical study. *Applied Linguistics, 13*(2), 168–184.

Han, Y., & Ellis, R. (1998). Implicit knowledge, explicit knowledge and general language proficiency. *Language Teaching Research, 2,* 1–23.

Jiang, W. (2009). *Acquisition of word order in Chinese as a Foreign Language*. Germany: De Gruyter Mouton.

Jin, L., Oh, L. B., & Razak, R. (2012). C-LARSP: Developing a Chinese grammatical profile. In M. J. Ball, D. Crystal, & P. Fletcher (Eds.), *In assessing grammar: The languages of LARS* (pp. 208–229). New York: Multilingual Matters.

Mirzaei, A., Domakani, M., & Shakerian, Z. (2011). Differential accessibility of implicit and explicit grammatical knowledge to EFL learners' language proficiency. *Iranian Journal of Applied Linguistics, 14*(2), 111–143.

Philp, J. (2009). Pathways to proficiency: Learning experiences and attainment in implicit and explicit knowledge of English as a second language: Applying the measures of implicit and explicit L2 knowledge. In R. Ellis et al. (Eds.), *Implicit and explicit knowledge in second language learning, testing and teaching* (pp. 194–215). UK: Multilingual Matters.

Roehr, K. (2008). Metalinguistic knowledge and language ability in university-level L2 learners. *Applied Linguistics, 29,* 173–199.

Wang, X. (2013). *Grammatical development of Chinese among non-native speakers: From a processability account*. Newcastle: Cambridge Scholars Publishing.

Xing, J. Z. (2006). *Teaching and learning Chinese as a foreign language: A pedagogical grammar*. Hong Kong: Hong Kong University Press.

Zhang, D. (2012). Vocabulary and grammatical knowledge in L2 reading comprehension: A structural equation modeling study. *The Modern Language Journal, 96,* 554–571.

Zhang, Y. Y. (2001) *Second language acquisition of Chinese grammatical morphemes: A processability perspective*. Unpublished doctoral thesis, Australian National University.

Zhang, Y. Y. (2008) Adverb-placement and wh-questions in the L2 Chinese of English speakers: Is transfer a structural property or a processing constraint? In J. Kessler (Ed.), *Processability approaches to second language development and second language learning*. Newcastle: Cambridge Scholars Publishing.

Part III
Assessing Language Skills

Chapter 8
What Standard and Whose Standard: Issues in the Development of Chinese Proficiency Descriptors in Singapore

Guowen Shang and Shouhui Zhao

Abstract In language assessment, the assessors often need to judge whether certain language forms produced by students are correct or acceptable. This seemingly easy procedure may be at stake in situations where the *de jure* language standard is unspecified. Drawing upon the challenges we encountered in developing proficiency descriptors for Chinese language (CL) in Singapore, this study attempts to examine the impact and implications of lacking an officially endorsed standard and norm for CL education and assessment. To resolve the dilemmas in pedagogy and assessment, we suggest that the value of the indigenized CL variety be recognized and more focus be put on communicative competency rather than language forms. Understanding language tests and their effects involves understanding some of the central issues and processes of the whole society, and thus, decision makers have to be well versed in sociolinguistics and be able to elaborate on the consequences of tests in broader sociopolitical settings.

Keywords Proficiency descriptors · Language assessment · Chinese language · Standard · Huayu · Putonghua

Introduction

In recent years, there has been a growing interest in the development and utilization of proficiency descriptors (or proficiency scales) as a guidance and/or benchmark in language learning and teaching (e.g., Fulcher et al. 2011). Some well-received language proficiency descriptors developed in worldwide context include, among

G. Shang
Zhejiang University, Hangzhou, China

S. Zhao (✉)
University of Bergen, Bergen, Norway
e-mail: Shouhui.Zhao@uib.no

© Springer Nature Singapore Pte Ltd. 2017   159
D. Zhang and C.-H. Lin (eds.), *Chinese as a Second Language Assessment*,
Chinese Language Learning Sciences, DOI 10.1007/978-981-10-4089-4_8

many others, the Common European Framework of Reference for Languages (CEFR), American Council on the Teaching of Foreign Languages (ACTFL) guidelines, World-class Instructional Design and Assessment (WIDA), PreK-12 English Language Proficiency Standards, and Canadian Language Benchmarks (CLB). These endeavors correspond with the call for a performance-based assessment, which emphasizes the evaluation of learners' ability to apply content knowledge to critical thinking, problem solving, and analytical tasks in the real world throughout their education (Rudner and Boston 1994; Darling-Hammond and McCloskey 2008). Language proficiency descriptors usually consist of a successive band of descriptions of the language knowledge and skills learners are expected to attain at certain learning stages. These descriptors are established to reflect the language learners' real-life competencies or interaction abilities (Bachman 1990) and are intended to be instrumental in identifying language learners' proficiency levels and helping teachers consistently assess and track students' learning progression. As encapsulated by North and Schneider (1998), proficiency descriptors or scales can be used to fulfill a number of functions, such as to provide "stereotypes" for learners to evaluate their position or to enhance the reliability of subjectively judged ratings with a common standard and meaning for such judgments. In other words, a common metric or yardstick enables comparison between systems or populations. Owing to the proliferation of potential pedagogical benefits, numerous language proficiency descriptors have been developed worldwide. With carefully established proficiency descriptors, the operationalization of classroom authentic assessment of language proficiency in a specific language-in-use context is becoming more target-oriented.

In general, proficiency level descriptors are designed to show the progression of second language acquisition from one proficiency level to the next and serve as a road map to help language teachers to instruct content commensurate with students' linguistic needs. Language learners may exhibit different proficiency levels within the domains of listening, speaking, reading, and writing. In the development of proficiency descriptors, the linguistic competence, namely the knowledge of, and ability to use, the formal resources to formulate well-formed, meaningful messages (Council of Europe 2001), is one of the key components to be scaled. This competence sets out to define learners' phonological, orthographic, semantic, lexical, and grammatical knowledge of the target language as well as their ability to use them accurately and properly. For example, the language outputs of advanced learners are expected to be closely approximate to the standard forms or conventions, thus the descriptors for this proficiency level tend to contain descriptions such as "free of error" and "consistently correct."

However, the linguistic competence can become an intricate part of the development of proficiency descriptors as well as in the implementation of assessment due to the nature of the language tests as a social practice (McNamara 2001). Many scholars in recent years have pointed out the complex link between language policies and standardized testing. Shohamy (2007), for instance, notes that "the introduction of language tests in certain languages delivers messages and ideologies about the prestige, priorities and hierarchies of certain language(s)" (p. 177). This is because when the assessment framework is used to determine the educational outcomes, the tests have an "encroaching power" in influencing national language policy (McNamara 2008). That is, the criteria of proficiency descriptors used for judging language competence via rating scales would inevitably bring about sociopolitical ramifications. Unfortunately, the social and political functions of tests "are neglected in most of the texts on language testing" (McNamara 2008, p. 416).

As a guide for language assessment, proficiency descriptors are supposed to define clearly the achieving standards for each key stage. However, there are cases where the establishment of specific standards can be a hard decision to make due to the tremendous sociopolitical implications that they may engender. In this chapter, we look into the development of Chinese language (CL) proficiency descriptors in Singapore, a polity renowned for its linguistic diversity, with a purpose to demonstrate how language assessment can be thwarted by the tensions between language use and language standard.

Focusing on the percept-practice gap in the development of proficiency descriptors, this chapter examines the challenges in setting up standards for second language assessment in a politically sensitive society in order to showcase the effect of tacit language policy on language assessment. The organization of this chapter is as follows. We begin by offering a brief introduction to the sociolinguistic milieu in Singapore and the rationale of developing curriculum-based CL proficiency descriptors. Then, we present some entrenched usages of Singaporean Mandarin in students' output, on which CL proficiency descriptors are based. Next, we provide a discussion of the difficulties we encountered in the development of CL proficiency descriptors and an elaboration of the challenges these difficulties may pose in CL teachers' instructional practice from the perspective of language acquisition planning. Finally, possible solutions are proposed to overcome any pedagogical dilemmas that may be caused by the lack of universally accepted assessment criteria. The concluding section critically reflects on the implications of Singapore experience for the assessment and other relevant issues in other places of the Chinese-speaking world and beyond.

Developing CL Proficiency Descriptors in Singapore: Background and Rationale

In Singapore, in order to provide an evaluative instrument with comparability across schools and eventually to replace the more traditional school-based tests, a set of Mother Tongue Language (MTL) proficiency descriptors has been developed recently as a common reference for learners, teachers, curriculum planners, and assessment officers. In this way, MTL learning expectations can be better defined and goals of attainment more easily gauged (MTLRC 2011). In this section, the rationale and process of developing proficiency descriptors are illustrated in detail.

Singapore's Language Environment and Education

Singapore is a multiracial and multilingual city state in Southeast Asia. It has a total population of 5.47 million, of which Chinese, Malays, Indians, and others account for 74.26, 13.35, 9.12, and 3.27%, respectively (Department of Statistics 2014). English, Mandarin, Malay, and Tamil are established as four official languages, with English being the working language as well as the *lingua franca* of the residents, and the other three being the designated mother tongues of the major ethnic groups. In light of its bilingual education policy, all school students must learn English as the first language and their mother tongue languages (MTLs) as second languages, despite their *bona fide* linguistic backgrounds.

In view of the dominant role and overriding significance of English in the society, the past two decades have witnessed a marked and steady change of frequently used home language from mother tongues to English in Singapore. For instance, a survey conducted by the Ministry of Education (MOE) showed that ethnic Chinese students with English as the most frequently used home language increased from 28% in 1991 to 59% in 2010 (MTLRC 2011). This rapid home language shift has brought about far-reaching implications for MTL education (Zhao and Liu 2010). To ensure MTL education, including CL education, continues to stay relevant to learners' daily life and effective in teaching approaches, the MOE has reviewed and reformed the MTL curriculum and pedagogy on a periodic basis. In the latest endeavor, the MTL Review Committee, commissioned by the MOE in January 2010, conducted a comprehensive evaluation of MTL teaching and testing in Singapore schools, and thereafter proposed some practical recommendations to enhance MTL education. One of the key recommendations made by the MTL Review Committee was to develop proficiency descriptors to aid teachers in aiming for observable outcomes in teaching, and also to motivate students at different learning stages to progress accordingly (MTLRC 2011, p. 13).

MTL Proficiency Descriptors: What and Why

There has been an agreed-upon belief among language educators and scholars that the expectations of learners should be stated clearly at different phases of learning so that teaching, learning, and assessment can be well guided (Wang et al. 2014). In view of this, proficiency descriptors for each of the three MTLs in Singapore were recommended to be developed by educational authorities. This recommendation on developing proficiency descriptors also tallies with a major objective of MTL education, i.e., to develop proficient users who can communicate effectively using the language in authentic contexts and apply it in interpersonal communication, as highlighted in MTLRC (2011). Through school curriculum, students are expected to learn to apply and use MTL in their lives, and these expectations need to be scoped into clearly defined performance objectives at progressive levels.

In order to spell out the attainment goals for a wide range of real-life communications, proficiency descriptors of six core language skills in MTL, namely listening, speaking, reading, writing, spoken interaction, and written interaction,[1] have been articulated by the curriculum officers at MOE. The introduction of interaction (spoken and written) descriptors is based on the fact that many real-life situations require spontaneous two-way interaction (e.g., listening and responding orally during a conversation or reading and responding in written form such as an e-mail). To help students cope with communication in such interactive settings, it is necessary for school curriculum to emphasize spoken and written interaction skills to enhance their ability to use the language meaningfully and effectively in daily communications.

The MTL proficiency descriptors can fulfill three purposes, as indicated in MTLRC (2011). First, the proficiency descriptors can help MTL teachers target observable outcomes and tailor their teaching, classroom activities, and assessments to create more opportunities for students to practice and use their MTLs in specific ways. With clearer goals for students to achieve, the teachers can also implement new instructional materials and learning resources based on the proficiency descriptors. Second, for the students, the breaking down of goals can bolster their confidence and inspire their learning. Proficiency descriptors spell out more explicitly the language skills and levels of attainment students should achieve at various key stages of learning. With clearer goals, learners can be better motivated to progress from one level to the next. In addition, in the proficiency descriptors, the use of everyday situations and contexts, current affairs, and contemporary issues as well as authentic materials (e.g., reports and news articles) will provide real-world context for classroom learning. This will allow students to see the relevance of MTLs in their daily lives and enable them to achieve practical language competence. Third, MTL assessments will be better targeted. With proficiency descriptors serving as an array of definite progressive criteria, assessments can be aligned with the content and objectives of the curriculum.

Development of Chinese-Speaking Proficiency Descriptors

The development of the MTL proficiency descriptors[2] was undertaken by the Curriculum Planning and Development Division (CPDD) of MOE from 2011 to 2014 (Wang et al. 2014). As CPDD's collaborators, the two authors were commissioned to lead a research team to conduct a project that aimed to develop proficiency descriptors for CL speaking and oral interaction. Since speaking and

---

[1]For the differences between speaking and spoken interaction and between writing and written interaction, please see Zhu (2014).

[2]The full title of the project was "Development of the Proficiency Descriptors Framework of the Teaching, Learning and Assessment of Mother Tongue Languages in Singapore." The Chinese part was the prototype for the other two MTLs, i.e., Malay and Tamil languages.

interaction are two closely related oral skills and the proficiency descriptors development processes are similar, for sake of convenience, we hereafter just focus on the development of CL speaking proficiency descriptors, which encapsulate CL learners' ability to communicate orally in clear, coherent, and persuasive language appropriate to purpose, occasion, and audience.

As part of our effort to develop CL speaking proficiency descriptors, Singaporean Chinese students with average CL speaking aptitude[3] at some key learning stages from elementary and secondary school to junior college or high school (e.g., primary 2, primary 4, primary 6, and secondary 2; or Grades 2, 4, 6, and 8) were selected to perform a diverse range of speaking tasks as a means of soliciting oral speech, such as show-and-tell, picture description, and video description/comment. The speaking activities were video-recorded, and thereafter, some video clips containing performances commensurate to specific speaking levels were transcribed and linguistic features were analyzed in detail. Based on the students' performance, nine levels of proficiency descriptors were developed for CL speaking skills. The speaking proficiency descriptors comprise a scale of task-based language proficiency descriptions about what individual learners can speak in spontaneous and non-rehearsed contexts and serve as a guide to the teaching and assessment of CL learners over the course of 12 years (from Primary 1 or Grade 1 to Junior College 2nd year or Grade 12) in Singapore. They describe CL learners' successive levels of speaking achievement. After the proficiency descriptors for CL speaking were established, a validation session was administered by MOE among CL practitioners, and for a reference purpose, two to three video clips were selected as exemplars of each speaking level (for more about the sampling process and project implementation, please see Wang et al. 2014). Now, the CL proficiency descriptors have been incorporated in the new CL syllabus (CPDD 2015), serving as a guide for curriculum development, teaching, and assessment.

In the formulation of specific performance levels, a range of well-recognized proficiency descriptors or scales, such as HSKK (*Hanyu Shuiping Kouyu Kaoshi* or Oral Chinese Proficiency Test) (see Teng, this volume), CEFR, ACTFL Proficiency Guidelines (see Liu, this volume), were closely referenced. In the established CL speaking proficiency descriptors, five aspects of speaking competence have been factored into the assessment: topic development, organization, vocabulary, grammar, and articulation, with the latter three concerned with language forms. In terms of vocabulary, frequency level of words featured in a student's discourse was taken as an indicator of vocabulary advancement. For instance, the vocabulary used by lower level speakers was mainly confined to high-frequency words. For higher level speakers, they tended to use a significant amount of low-frequency or advanced

---

[3]This selection criterion was set up with a purpose to screen out students with extremely high or extremely low CL proficiencies so that the participants represented the normal and average level of CL speaking for each stage. This selection was mainly done by the CL teachers in the participating schools according to their prolonged observation to the students' daily performance in CL speaking. In addition, the research team also sifted out obviously unsuitable participants during the tasks.

vocabulary, and the use of rhetoric devices such as idiomatic language or figures of speech was also expected. A mix of high-frequency and lower frequency words typically would appear in medium level speakers' oral discourse. Grammatically, the use of simple or complex sentence structures was the major criterion. With the progression of speaking competence, students' sentence structures would become more syntactically complicated. For articulation, the dimensions that were scaled included correctness of pronunciation and intonation and naturalness and fluency of speech. For instance, with respect to naturalness and fluency of speech, lower level speakers would have many pauses, whereas higher level speakers could present more naturally and fluently.

A keen awareness we fostered in the process of developing the speaking CL proficiency descriptors was that proficiency descriptors formulated by educational experts, researchers, and teaching professionals must be customized to accommodate Singaporean students' abilities and learning needs. In this regard, one crucial factor that held sway in the development process was students' actual language practice in Singapore's Mandarin-speaking environment. In the next section, we examine some language use features of Huayu (i.e., Singapore Mandarin) that constituted an important basis on which we considered the relevance and adequacy of speaking proficiency descriptors to Singapore students. Through the discussion of the differences between Huayu and Putonghua (standard Mandarin in Mainland China), we aim to unravel the importance of attending to issues of what standard and whose standard in CL assessment, in particular, the discrepancies that often exist between what is imposed through language policy making and how language is actually used in the society.

Huayu Usage in Spoken Language: Students' Output

Huayu and Its Subvarieties

Huayu is a term used in Singapore to refer to Mandarin, the designated mother tongue of Singaporean Chinese. Huayu is often recognized as a new variety of Modern Chinese developed in Singapore's particular pluralinguistic environment (Chew 2007; Shang and Zhao 2013; Wang 2002). It is a unique product of its long-term close contact with different languages, such as English, Malay, and various Chinese regionalects. In the early years after Singapore's independence, most ethnic Chinese Singaporeans spoke Southern Chinese dialects, e.g., Hokkien, Cantonese, Teochew, Hakka, and Hainanese, which were mutually unintelligible. Mandarin, which features totally different pronunciations from the regional dialects, was merely a minority CL variety with relatively few native speakers in Singapore then. In order to facilitate communicative intelligibility among different dialectal groups and to create an environment conducive for children's CL learning, the government launched the Speak Mandarin Campaign in 1979, which has institutionalized as an annual event to promote the use of Mandarin (Bokhorst-Heng 1999; Newman 1988). In light of this initiative, many dialect speakers have switched to Mandarin as their most oft-used home language. However, the dialects, as substratum languages, have exerted continuous influence on the Mandarin that Chinese Singaporeans are using. In addition, due to its constant contact with English, the language of wider communication in the country, Huayu has also incorporated some linguistic features of English. Generally speaking, Huayu is similar to other Chinese varieties, such as Putonghua in Mainland China and Guoyu in Taiwan, though it has some idiosyncratic linguistic features that make it distinct from other Chinese varieties[4].

In fact, Huayu, as a new variety of Modern Chinese, is a heterogeneous variety in itself. Based on the widely cited postcreole continuum in sociolinguistics (Platt and Weber 1980), three subvarieties of Huayu can be identified according to their linguistic convergence with Putonghua: acrolect, basilect and mesolect.[5] The acrolect is closely approximate to Putonghua in all linguistic aspects; it is typically found in CL textbooks, mass media, and print publications and used by most highly proficient CL speakers in formal contexts. Except for some lexical items uniquely found in Singapore, the phonology, vocabulary, and grammar of the acrolect of Huayu are in compliance with the Putonghua norm. In news broadcasting, for instance, except some vocabulary signifying items of local reference (e.g., *Zuwu* signifying government-constructed economic flats, *Yongchezheng* signifying the license to own a car), language forms of Huayu are nearly indiscernible even for Putonghua speakers from Mainland China. Undeniably, one reason for this is that a number of the Chinese newscast anchors in MediaCorp, the official broadcasting company in Singapore, are immigrants from Mainland China. When it comes to CL textbooks, it is found that many retroflex ending sounds, which Singaporeans rarely produce in their oral language, are actually annotated (Shang and Zhao 2013).

---

[4]Whether there are significant differences between Singaporean Huayu and other varieties, particularly Taiwan Guoyu, is a complicated issue. Admittedly, many of the so-called Singapore-specific or unique linguistic features that are noted by researchers are also squarely shared by Taiwan Guoyu. The main reason for the high-level similarities between Singaporean Huayu and Taiwan Guoyu might be due to the fact that the bulk of the population in both polities are originally native speakers of Hokkien, a Southern Chinese dialect that exerts considerable influence on Mandarin. Other reasons may include the strong presence of Taiwan Guoyu speakers in local media before the 1980s (Kuo 1985, pp. 115, 131) and the popularity in Singapore of TV drama series and recreational programmes produced in Taiwan. A detailed discussion on how and why Taiwan Guoyu and Singapore Huayu share a lot of similarities would take us too far afield from the focus of this chapter. Interested readers may refer to Guo (2002), Li (2004) and Khoo (2012).

[5]In a creole continuum, acrolect is the variety that approximates most closely the standard variety of a major international language, as the English spoken in Guyana or Jamaica; basilect is the variety that is most distinct from the acrolect; and mesolect is any variety that is intermediate between the basilect and the acrolect.

The basilect Huayu, by contrast, is the variety that diverges most from Putonghua. It is not only heavily accented by dialectal usages, but also characterized by frequent code switching and heavy code mixing between Mandarin and dialects, English, Malay, and so forth. This subvariety, or "Chap Chye" (stir-fried mixed vegetables) Mandarin as dubbed by the former Prime Minister Goh Chok Tong (Goh 1999), is often found in the colloquial language of those who have a fairly low proficiency of Mandarin. Due to its heavy code-mixing, people may doubt whether this colloquial form should be categorized as Huayu.

Finally, the mesolect is a variety between the acrolect and the basilect, which is widely used by those Singaporeans proficient in the language and in mass media as well. In other words, mesolect Huayu is the daily language for most Chinese speakers in Singapore. Albeit the differences in pronunciation, vocabulary, and grammar from Putonghua, it is generally intelligible to Chinese speakers in other regions. The examples given in the following section are essentially mesolect usages produced by Singaporean students.

Huayu in Practice: Students' Entrenched Usage

In this section, some Huayu usages in Singapore are presented in order to demonstrate part of the entrenched linguistic features of this new CL variety. The examples given below were taken from the output elicited by the speaking tasks of those students who participated in the aforementioned project that we conducted to develop the CL speaking proficiency descriptors. Therefore, they may represent the localized usages that have been internalized into young Chinese speakers' linguistic system. Since Putonghua is widely recognized as the dominant variety of Chinese language currently used across the world, the Huayu usages are examined below with reference to it in order to show the extent to which Singapore Huayu is deviant from Putonghua.

Pronunciation

Huayu in Singapore is different from Putonghua in a number of phonetic distinctions (for a comprehensive investigation, see Li 2004). The discussion here focuses on only one aspect: lexical weak stress. Chinese is a tonal language, and tones have a function of distinguishing word meanings (Chao 1968). Apart from four basic tones specified in the lexicon, a prominent feature of Putonghua pronunciation is the wide use of *qingsheng* or neutral tone, i.e., unstressed syllables that do not bear any of the four tones. In Huayu, however, there is minimal use of *qingsheng* in pronunciation. One case is that in Putonghua, the second syllable of some words is pronounced in neutral tone, whereas in Huayu, such syllables are pronounced in their original, non-neutral tones. For instance,

1)

Huayu: ...Yīnwèi nàlǐ bǐjiào **rènào**.

Putonghua: ...Yīnwèi nàlǐ bǐjiào **rènao**.

因为 那里 比较 热闹。

English: ...because that place is more bustling.

In this example, it can be seen that the word in bold—*rènao* (bustling)—contains a syllable that is usually pronounced in neutral tone in Putonghua. The neutral-tone syllables are usually pronounced in their original tones in other contexts, such as when they stand alone or appear in the initial position of a word. By contrast, de-neutralization takes place in Huayu pronunciation. That is, Singaporean students tend to pronounce the neutral-tone syllables in Putonghua as their original tones.

Moreover, the suffix of a word is, more often than not, pronounced in a neutral tone in Putonghua.[6] However, it is very common to hear Singaporean Chinese students pronounce such suffixes as non-neutral tones, as shown in the following examples.

2)

Huayu: Wǒ **juédé tāmén** dōu méiyǒu cuò.

Putonghua: Wǒ **juéde tāmen** dōu méiyǒu cuò.

我 觉得 他们 都 没有 错。

English: I think none of them are wrong.

3)

Huayu: Nàshí wǒ yào zū yīgè **fángzǐ**.

Putonghua: Nàshí wǒ yào zū yīgè **fángzi**.

那时 我 要 租 一个 房子。

English: At that time I need to rent a house.

In Putonghua, the verbal suffix *de* and nominal suffix *zi* are usually pronounced as neutral tones, and the plural suffix *men* is an unconditionally neutral-tone syllable or is pronounced as neutral tone in any circumstances in oral communication. In Huayu, however, these syllables are often pronounced as non-neutral tones.

In addition, orientation verbs used immediately behind core verbs are often pronounced in neutral tone in Putonghua. This contrasts with Huayu, wherein the original tones of orientation verbs are pronounced. See the following example produced by Singaporean students,

---

[6]This refers mainly to inflection-like suffixes in Chinese. There are derivation-like suffixes in Chinese that are not pronounced in neutral tone, such as 者 zhe and 家 jia.

4)

Huayu:	Zhuàng **shàng** tā de nà liàng chēzǐ tíng le **xiàlái**.
Putonghua:	Zhuàng **shang** tā de nà liàng chēzi tíng le **xiàlai**.
	撞　　上 他的那 辆 车子 停 了 下来。
English:	The car that knocked her down finally stopped.

In this case, Singaporean students pronounce the orientation verbs shàng (to go up) and lái (to come) as their original tones, which deviate from the neutral-tone pronunciations in Putonghua.

Vocabulary

With regard to vocabulary, some objects in the physical world are lexicalized differently in Huayu and Putonghua. For instance, Putonghua uses *càishìchǎng*, *gōngjiāochē* and *chūzūchē* to denote vegetable market, bus, and taxi, respectively, while in Huayu, the corresponding lexical forms are *bāshā*, *bāshì*, and *déshì*, respectively, which are the phonetic loans of Malay/English words *pasar*, *bus*, and *taxi* (dialect transliteration), respectively. Such terms have taken root in Singapore Mandarin and have become essential vocabulary of the Chinese community in Singapore. Apart from these words, some other commonly used lexical forms in Huayu also appeared in the oral speech of the students who participated in our project. In the following examples, the lexical items in bold mark some differences of the vocabulary between Huayu and Putonghua.

5)

Huayu:	Wǒ měitiān hěn **chí** cái líkāi **zuògōng** de dìfāng.
	我 每天 很 迟 才 离开 做工 的 地方。
Putonghua:	Wǒ měitiān hěn **wǎn** cái líkāi **gōngzuò** de dìfang.
	我 每天 很 晚 才 离开 工作 的 地方。
English:	I leave the workplace very late every day.

6)

Huayu:	Nǐ **jǐshí** bǎ dōngxī jiāo gěi wǒ ne?
	你 几时 把 东西 交 给 我 呢？
Putonghua:	Nǐ **shénme shíhou** bǎ dōngxi jiāo gěi wǒ ne?
	你 什么 时候 把 东西 交 给 我 呢？
English:	When will you give the purchase to me?

7)

Huayu:	shàng gè **bàiwǔ**, wǒmen yījiā rén qù wàimiàn chī wǎncān le.
	上 个 拜五，我们 一家人 去 外面 吃 晚餐 了。
Putonghua:	shàng gè **lǐbàiwǔ**, wǒmen yījiā rén qù wàimiàn chī wǎncān le.
	上 个 礼拜五，我们 一家人 去 外面 吃 晚餐 了。
English:	Last Friday, our whole family went outside to eat supper.

In the above examples, it can be seen that Putonghua tends to use *wǎn* (late), *shénme shíhou* (when), *gōngzuò* (to work), and *lǐbàiwǔ* (Friday), whereas Singaporean students, following the habitual usages of Huayu, used *chí*, *jǐshí*, *zuògōng*, and *bàiwǔ*, respectively.

8)

Huayu:	Wǒ jiù qù **bāngmáng** nà wèi nánshēng.

我 就去　 帮忙　那 位　男生。

Putonghua: Wǒ jiù qù **bāngzhù** nà wèi nánshēng.

我 就 去 帮助　那 位　男生。

English:	I then went to help the boy student.

9)

Huayu:	yīnwèi wǒ xǐhuan wán yóuxì, bàba jiù hěn **shēngqì** wǒ.

因为 我 喜欢 玩 游戏，爸爸 就 很 生气 我。

Putonghua: yīnwèi wǒ xǐhuan wán yóuxì, bàba jiù **duì** wǒ hěn **shēngqì**.

因为 我 喜欢 玩 游戏，爸爸 就 对 我 很 生气。

English:	Because I like playing games, my father is very angry at me.

10)

Huayu:	Suǒyǐ hěn duō rén huì bǐjiào **lǎnduò** yīdiǎn.

所以 很 多 人 会 比较　懒惰　一点。

Putonghua: Suǒyǐ hěnduō rén huì bǐjiào **lǎn** yīdiǎn.

所以 很 多 人 会 比较 懒 一点。

English:	So many people are relatively a bit lazy.

In these examples, the same vocabularies have very different usages in Putonghua and Huayu. For instance, *bāngmáng* (to help) (in contrast to the transitive verb *bāngzhù* in example 8) and *shēngqì* (to get angry) in Putonghua are intransitive verbs, yet in Huayu they are used as transitive verbs; *lǎnduò* (laziness) in Putonghua is a noun (in contrast to the adjective form *lǎn*), while in Huayu it is used as an adjective.

Grammar

In terms of grammar, Huayu also shows some deviances from Putonghua (see Chen 1986; Goh 2010; Lu et al. 2002). For instance, Lu et al. (2002) state that the grammatical features of Huayu are generally identical to those in Putonghua, yet there are some nuanced differences between the two varieties. The following sentences were produced by Singaporean students when performing the speaking tasks.

11)

Huayu: Bìxū **gěi duō** yīdiǎn qián.

必须 给 多 一点 钱。

Putonghua: Bìxū **duō gěi** yīdiǎn qián.

必须 多 给 一点 钱。

English: You must give more money.

12)

Huayu: Wǒ bù cháng qù, dàn wǒ **yǒu qù** kuàicān diàn

我 不 常 去，但 我 有 去 快餐 店。

Putonghua: Wǒ bù cháng qù, dàn wǒ **qù guò** kuàicān diàn

我 不 常 去，但 我 去 过 快餐 店。

English: I did go to fast food store, though not often.

13)

Huayu: Bàba ràng wǒ chī wán **cái** huíqù.

爸爸 让 我 吃 完 才 回去。

Putonghua: Bàba ràng wǒ chī wán **zài** huíqù.

爸爸 让 我 吃 完 再 回去。

English: Dad told me to go home only after I finished eating.

14)

Huayu: Yīdìng yào qù **chángcháng yīxià**, cái huì zhīdào.

一定 要 去 尝尝 一下 才 会 知道。

Putonghua: Yīdìng yào qù **chángcháng**, cái huì zhīdào.

一定 要 去 尝尝 才 会 知道。

English: You won't know (its real flavour) until you take a bite of it.

15)

Huayu: Māmā shuō zhèxiē shíwù tài yóunì, **bù kěyǐ** duō chī.

妈妈 说 这些 食物太 油腻 不 可以 多 吃。

Putonghua: Māma shuō zhèxiē shíwù tài yóunì, **bù néng** duō chī.

妈妈 说 这些 食物太 油腻 不 能 多 吃。

English: Mum said that the food is too oily, and I must not eat too many of them.

In Example 11, the relative position of the adverb *duo* (much/many, more) and the verb modified differs in Huayu and Putonghua. The adverb is put behind the verb in Huayu, and this word order might have resulted from the influence of English (i.e., the English structure *give more* ….). In Example 12, the verb *you* (to have) is used as a perfective aspectual marker in Huayu, while this usage of *you* is unacceptable in Putonghua, wherein the auxiliary *guo* tends to be used to fulfill this function. In Example 13, the adverb *cai* (only) in Putonghua is used to refer to an action that has been completed and there is often an emphasis on the temporal lateness of the action. When referring to an action that has yet to be performed, the adverb *zai* needs to be used instead of *cai*. In Huayu, by contrast, the adverb *cai* is used to refer to the occurrence of an action following another action, regardless of the actual completion state of the action. In Example 14, the verb in reduplication form can be followed by *yixia* (one time) to indicate a tentative action or an attempt, while in Putonghua, the juxtaposition of reduplication form and *yixia* is ill-formed. In Example 15, *bu keyi*, namely the negative form of the modal verb *keyi* (can), can be used in Huanyu to modify the verb indicating a purpose, whereas in Putonghua, only *buneng* is acceptable in this circumstance (Lü 1999).

We have demonstrated that the pronunciation, vocabulary and grammar of Huayu used in Singapore exhibit some idiosyncratic features vis-à-vis their Putonghua counterparts. Growing up in a Huayu-speaking society, Singaporean students may feel it comfortable to project Huayu usages in the community into their CL learning. Should such Huayu usages be taken as errors? Due to the lack of specific educational policy hitherto regarding CL norms, CL educators and assessors are often found in a dilemma. In the following section, we turn to discuss the difficulties or challenges we encountered in the process of developing CL proficiency descriptors in Singapore due to the tacitness of the policy for CL standards and norms implemented in the educational system.

Challenges for the Development of CL Proficiency Descriptors

The CL proficiency descriptors that we developed in Singapore are different from those specifically for proficiency testing in that they serve as an official guideline for overall CL education with a broader significance; in other words, the knowledge and skill requirements established for different proficiency levels represent the attainment goals for CL teachers as well as CL learners. Therefore, the establishment of proficiency descriptors must take into account the overall language education policy in Singapore, which also regulates the other two MTLs as well as their feasibility for target learners.

In this spirit, one of the issues that we, as developers and evaluators of the CL proficiency descriptors, could not shun away from was determining what standard and whose standard of CL should serve as a benchmark for CL education in Singapore. The issue, however, was particularly precarious given the fact that in the Singapore context, no official CL standards concerning the norms of phonology, vocabulary, and grammar have ever been promulgated. The challenges we encountered were, to a large extent, attributed to the lack of a legitimized CL standard in Singapore.

In fact, the endonormative versus exonormative competition has long been a central concern in Singapore, a place dubbed as "Sociolinguistic Laboratory" (e.g., Xu and Li 2002). Chen (1999), for instance, reviews some early academic works that discussed sociolinguistic differences between the two norms in the 1980s and 1990s. Wee (2003) discussed the dilemmas in choosing a standard in Singapore's language policy development. It seems that Putonghua, the most prestigious CL variety in Mainland China and the dominant standard among Chinese community, is often taken as the official standard in Singapore's practice. However, even though Putonghua is often regarded as the de facto standard for Singapore's CL teaching and learning, it has never been an officially sanctioned standard (Shang and Zhao 2013). A recent study affirms Putonghua's position "as the standard language holding unwavering prestige and power" and "as a variety associated with status, education and economic advantage" (Chong and Tan 2013, p. S 134). On the other hand, there are also advocacies for official recognition of the type of Huayu usages as we exemplified in Section "Huayu Usage in Spoken Language: Students' Output" (Lu et al. 2002; Xu and Wang 2004). As such, giving precedence to either Putonghua standard or Huayu idiosyncrasies would cause a lot of resistance. Cognizant of this contested issue, we, as developers, carefully sought to generate CL proficiency descriptors through observing and analyzing Singaporean Chinese students' actual usages, and organized the knowledge and skill requirements within an integrated framework that took into consideration the educational principles as well as guidelines stipulated in official curricular documents. However, challenges were still inevitable.

To illustrate, in our analysis of the students' spoken language outputs, which, as indicated earlier, formed the basis for the formulation of the speaking proficiency descriptors, there was an issue of determining whether certain Huayu forms were acceptable in both lower and higher speaking levels. We realized that a judgment was far from easy to be made in the Singapore context where language issues are often heavily politically tinted (Zhao and Liu 2010). This is because there exists a longstanding tension between language standard in practice and actual usages in the society. As shown earlier in Singaporean students' CL speech samples, there are a number of language forms in Singaporean Huayu that are deviant from their Putonghua counterparts, yet those forms are widely used and quite acceptable for local Huayu speakers. For example, should the neutral tone be taken as a criterion to determine Huayu proficiency? To date, how to deal with such deviance in CL learning, teaching, and assessment is still a matter of debate in Singapore. If the indigenized Huayu practice is followed, those expressions would be quite acceptable. On the other hand, if Putonghua is taken as a standard or benchmark, those Huayu usages, due to their deviation from such a standard, should be considered as errors in CL education, including assessment. The crux of the matter is that there has been no explicit official policy or fiat to institutionalize the implementation of Huayu or Putonghua norms in the education domain. As a result, how to treat Huayu-specific pronunciation, vocabulary, and grammar forms constituted a tremendous challenge when we were developing the CL speaking proficiency descriptors.

In Can-Do statements of proficiency descriptors, accuracy, which is concerned with how well language functions are performed or to what extent a message is found acceptable among native speakers (Ramírez 1995), is usually encompassed as a key category to characterize proficiency levels. Taking the ACTFL speaking proficiency descriptors for instance, the guideline delineates that speakers at the Superior level "are able to communicate with accuracy and fluency", and "demonstrate no pattern of error in the use of basic structures" (ACTFL 2012, p. 5). However, in the CL speaking proficiency descriptors, with particular consideration of their implications for assessing students' language performance, we were very cautious to use terms such as "error" or "accurate" and avoided, wherever possible, those expressions that tended to value a single standard of language. Our decision-making was careful and strategic because a linguistic standard or norm remains undefined in official discourse. In cases where descriptors seemed to require a standard-oriented expression, we deliberately left any relevant standard unspecified. For instance, one of the descriptors for Level 5 Pronunciation is as follows.

Pronunciation is clear and comprehensible.

Here, we did not specify the standard, either Putonghua or Huayu, for correctness. This is a compromise we decided to make under the sociopolitical constraint to keep proficiency descriptors uncontroversial regarding the issue of standard and ensure wide acceptance of them among CL practitioners and scholars. We admit that if one raises the question of clarifying the standard against which "correctness" is defined and measured, it would be a challenge that is hard to be responded by us. As a matter of fact, standard-related issues were also recognized as a flammable topic by our MOE collaborators (i.e., curriculum officers of the CPDD) when we sought advice from them during our development of the CL speaking proficiency descriptors.

Pedagogical Dilemmas for CL Teaching

The tacit policy of CL standard in Singapore not only baffled us proficiency descriptor developers and assessors, but also seemed to cause tremendous confusion for frontline teachers. In this section, we take a look at the pedagogical consequences associated with the lack of an explicit CL standard in Singapore.

In any language community, there are always language varieties other than the standard one used by different sub-groups of the community, yet formal policies regulating these non-standard varieties are rare in educational systems (Corson 2001). Earlier in this chapter, we have seen that Huayu usages which deviate from the Putonghua standard abound in Singaporean students' CL speech. Given the idiosyncrasies of Huayu, one may wonder how CL teachers, as the final gatekeeper of CL standard if any, deal with the discrepancies between Huayu and Putonghua in their teaching and assessment of students' CL abilities. This is an issue that warrants serious explorations. One thing that merits attention is that in CL classrooms, due to ignorance of the difference between Putonghua and Huayu, teachers sometimes become norm-breakers rather than norm-makers of the exonormative standard (Pakir 1994). In other words, the local teachers may also find themselves more comfortable with the localized usages in their spoken language. To illustrate, on the basis of our previous experience with CL teachers through observing their classroom teaching and assessment practices, it is fairly common to see the permeation of Huayu usages, suggesting that unofficial and covert Putonghua norms could be hard for teachers to follow in practice despite Putonghua's prevalent influence in the Chinese-speaking world.

On the other hand, in our informal communications with CL teachers, it was revealed that some teachers were very concerned with students' CL use deviant from Putonghua norms, and they felt frustrated by prevailing Huayu idiosyncrasies in students' spoken language (and written work) and were often at a loss about how to deal with them. Some CL teachers mentioned to us that in their teaching of vocabulary or grammatical structures, Putonghua norms were often imparted to students. It appeared that most teachers tended to emphasize to students that to play safe in examinations, either school-based or in a high-stakes testing context, the usages in Putonghua should be followed even though there had never been an official declaration on Putonghua norms in the educational discourse in Singapore. In the oral tasks designed to elicit speech samples for our project to develop the speaking proficiency descriptors, we did notice that some students stopped intermittently to adjust or repair their Huayu pronunciations or vocabulary so as to accord with Putonghua usages, even though these unnatural pauses for repair purposes jeopardized the fluency of their overall speech. Such an intriguing observation seems to suggest that students, like their teachers, were also struggling between the two norms; and the rule of thumb for examination purposes reiterated by their teachers, i.e., Putonghua usage is a much safer choice, exerted an influence on their critical awareness of the issue of standard and compelled them to reconcile in this regard.

It also appeared that many teachers showed intolerance to Huayu usages in students' oral or written works and tended to provide corrective feedback according to Putonghua norm. However, they also complained that their corrections were often to no avail. In view of the reality of students' persistent Huayu usages against Putonghua norm, some teachers pinpointed the unfairness and implausibility of stigmatizing Singaporeans' own variety. In other words, the teachers felt that it was hard to convince students that the Huayu they were acquiring and using daily with their family members, friends, and community members in Singapore was a substandard variety teemed with errors. Particularly, the teachers failed to justify themselves when students (or parents sometimes) refuted their corrective feedback by arguing that "everybody in Singapore speaks Huayu in this way, so how can you say it is wrong? For your corrected form, we never use it." Therefore, teachers were eager to be informed of more explicit and effective strategies to deal with Huayu usages in CL education in Singapore. In addition, given the fact that a significant proportion of CL teachers working in Singapore's public schools are recruited by MOE from mainland China, Taiwan, and Malaysia, they come along with different language ideologies, which makes the issue of "who speak the best Chinese" even more intricate and complex (Zhao and Shang 2013; Zhao and Sun 2013).

Toward a Solution to the Dilemmas

CL standard or norm has long been a perplexing and controversial issue in Singapore, and empirical evidence shows that there are distinct differences between the perceptions of Huayu and Putonghua in Singaporeans (Chong and Tan 2013). This standard-related issue usually does not interrupt the linguistic life of the general public, but conflict arises when the assessment of language proficiency in the education domain is at stake. We have illustrated in this chapter that the lack of an officially endorsed standard in Singapore's CL education resulted in a dilemma for the development of speaking proficiency descriptors that we undertook, and the discrepancies in Huayu and Putonghua norm have fettered CL education, engendering a tremendous challenge to language educators, assessors as well as us proficiency descriptor developers. It is, therefore, important that interventional measures at the policy level be taken to address the dilemmas in CL learning, teaching, and assessment.

In reference to Kachru's (1985) three-circle model of world Englishes, Huayu in Singapore is often categorized as a variety in the Outer Circle of Chinese (Goh 2010). Looking at the issues of standard and norm from a broad perspective, we may find that controversies over what standard and whose standard are not unique to CL education in general and CL education in Singapore in particular, but rather prevalent for second language teaching and assessment in most Outer Circle countries where pluricentric languages (Clyne 1992) are used (e.g., Gupta 1994; Mufwene 2001; Newbrook 1997). In such contexts, the exonormative standard, often prescribed as an official norm, tends to be in tension with local usages, and the advocacy of endonormative or exonormative standards has constituted a seemingly everlasting debate in many educational systems (e.g., Bex and Watts 1999; Bruthiaux 2006; Newbrook 1997).

Back to CL language standard in Singapore, it is clear that feasible and applicable language norms should be established for the good of CL education and assessment. The questions are as follows: who should set the norm for Huayu and which standard or norm will be the most suitable and beneficial?

For the norm-setting in Singapore as to whether conducted by educational authorities or policy-makers in government agencies, we contend that educated and proficient Huayu speakers rather than Putonghua speakers should be committed to this function. As Mufwene (1997, 2001) argued, reliance on native language speakers to set norms for second language learners is undesirable, and proficient local speakers should serve as the arbiter of a community norm. With respect to the standard variety, Corson (2001) suggests that we should promote a variety "that is widely used, provides a more effective means of communication across contexts than non-standard varieties. ...it meets the acquired interests of and expectations of many groups, rather than just the interests of its more particular speakers" (p. 76). In light of this, the promotion of Putonghua standard in the Singapore Chinese community does not seem feasible in that the exonormative standard stands aloof of the expressive needs of Huayu speakers. An endonormative standard might be more relevant in this regard.

In order to establish a feasible endonormative standard, as Gupta (1986) suggests, three criteria need to be considered: (1) local prestige usage (written, not informal), (2) usage not locally stigmatized, and (3) usage not internationally stigmatized. In our view, the acrolect variety of Huayu can meet the criteria, thus can be a possible candidate to serve as CL standard in Singapore Chinese community. However, before codifying the acrolect and employing it as a major pedagogical vehicle in education, more research is needed to find out the habitual and generally accepted usages found in the local community, and integrate them into the indigenized norm. In addition, perceptions of CL speakers in the Singapore Chinese community toward Putonghua and Huayu should be explored to find out their desirability as CL norms in Singapore. When a consensus has been reached concerning the standardization of the acrolect of Huayu, the government should endorse its function as a standard for CL. After all, an indigenized standard with official authority is the ultimate solution to the dilemmas emerging in CL education. Specifically in the domain of assessment, we argue that language assessment should focus more on students' communicative ability than accuracy of language forms; language features that do not conform to Putonghua norm should not be penalized in CL assessment as long as they cause no harm to intelligibility or communication of meanings. This argument also seems to align with the CL curriculum in Singapore where willingness to communicate is privileged over language forms.

Concluding Remarks

Language is rooted in social life and nowhere is this more apparent than in the ways in which language proficiency is assessed. As Li (2010) indicates, language assessment is in itself a social phenomenon, and assessing an individual's language abilities inevitably involves making assumptions of what is expected to be the standard. Standards have long been used to enforce social values throughout educational systems, and tests are the instruments that operationalize and implement standards. In other words, the social and political functions of standard and standardization not only constitute an aspect of identity, but also serve as the point of insertion of power, or in Foucault's term, they can be experienced as exercises in subjection to power (Foucault 1983). Standard is about "who set the rule of the game" (Smith 1997) and all language tests have implications of value and social consequences (Hubley and Zumbo 2011).

Previous discussions about language assessment tended to be fundamentally asocial and treated language competence as individual cognition that can be simply subject to psychometrics, ignoring the facts that language is rooted in society and language assessments play a role in implementing policies on education in a particular social setting. In a multilingual community, which language variety is more prestigious, and thus more correct (or standard), than others is both sociopolitically and pedagogically complex and sensitive. In Singapore, an increasingly postmodern society, CL classes in schools are attended by learners with diversifying backgrounds (e.g., immigrants from China and other Chinese-speaking polities as well as locally born Singaporean students), which has inevitably come forward as a big concern for both CL assessors and classroom teachers with a language standard or norm remaining undefined in the education domain.

Singapore is the only polity outside of the Greater China where Mandarin is designated by state as an official language, which shows its significant position in the linguistic life and education in the nation (Ang 1999). Putonghua, as an exonormative standard, has been tacitly taken as the benchmark for CL education in Singapore. However, due to concerns that pertain to political sensitivity, neither the Singapore government nor educational authorities in the country have legitimized the adoption of either Putonghua or indigenized Huayu as a standard in CL education and assessment. Without an officially sanctioned standard in place, students' CL outputs flavored with idiosyncratic Huayu usages are hard to be assessed in due terms, which was a big hurdle for our development of CL proficiency descriptors.

In this paper, with speech examples extracted from students' performance on oral tasks, we showcased some discrepancies between Huayu and Putonghua usages. On the basis of the comparisons between the two CL varieties, we shared the confusions we had and the compromises we made to accommodate concerns about issues of what standard and whose standard in our development of CL speaking proficiency descriptors. We also discussed how the lack of clearly stated CL standard posed challenges to CL educators and assessors. To establish an appropriate and accessible CL standard, we called for more open acceptance of local habitual usages, and suggested that the acrolect variety of Huayu be taken as the standard for Singaporean CL community. In other words, we argued that the CL standard in Singapore should be derived from the usages of its speakers instead of being forced to be benchmarked on Putonghua. Moreover, we suggested that endeavors should also be made to codify the entrenched acrolect. This is because people are inclined to refer to the codified variety as a reliable source. As Milroy and Milroy (1985) indicate, "[t]he attitudes of linguists (professional scholars of language) have little or no effect on the general public, who continue to look at dictionaries, grammars and handbooks as authorities on 'correct' usage" (p. 6). Thus, an endonormative standard accommodating local usages, once established, would be able to resolve the prolonged dilemmas in CL learning, teaching, and assessment in Singapore. Currently, there are no governmental or educational institutions in Singapore that assume responsibility or govern language use in the educational domain. We contend that such official agencies should be established and more tolerant and pluralist approaches be taken toward CL standardization.

Finally, we discussed that the issues associated with exonormative and endonormative standards are not unique to CL education and assessment in Singapore, but rather have wider implications for Chinese diaspora all over the world and are also relevant to other societies where there is a precept-practice gap with respect to the issue of standard in language education and assessment. This research should be helpful for understanding the standard-related problems involved in second language education and assessment and contribute to the satisfactory solution toward resolving the controversies.

Acknowledgements The authors wish to express their appreciation for the comments from the anonymous reviewers on an earlier draft of this article. All errors and omissions in this version are, of course, our own.

References

American Council on the Teaching of Foreign Languages [ACTFL]. (2012). *ACTFL proficiency guidelines 2012*. Alexandra, VA: ACTFL Inc.

Ang, B. C. (1999). The teaching of the Chinese language in Singapore. In S. Gopinathan (Ed.), *Language, society and education in Singapore: Issues and trends* (pp. 333–352). Singapore: Times Academic Press.

Bachman, L. F. (1990). *Fundamental considerations in language testing*. Oxford: Oxford University Press.

Bex, T., & Watts, R. (1999). *Standard English: The widening debate*. London: Routledge.

Bokhorst-Heng, W. (1999). Singapore's Speak Mandarin Campaign: Language ideological debates in the imagining of the nation. In J. Blommaert (Ed.), *Language ideological debates* (pp. 235–266). New York: Mouton de Gruyter.

Bruthiaux, P. (2006). Restandardizing localized English: Aspirations and limitations. *International Journal of Sociology of Language, 177*, 31–49.

Chao, Y. R. (1968). *A grammar of spoken Chinese*. Berkeley: University of California Press.

Chen, C. Y. (1986). Xinjiapo Huayu Yufa Tezheng (Syntactic features of Singapore Mandarin). *Yuyan Yanjiu (Studies in Language and Linguistics), 1*, 138–152.

Chen, P. (1999). *Modern Chinese: History and sociolinguistics*. Cambridge: Cambridge University Press.

Chew, C. H. (2007). Lun quanqiu yujing xia huayu de guifan wenti (Standardization of the Chinese language: A global language). *Yuyan Jiaoxue Yu Yanjiu (Language Teaching and Research), 4*, 91–96.

Chong, R. H. H., & Tan, Y. Y. (2013). Attitudes toward accents of Mandarin in Singapore. *Chinese Language & Discourse, 4*(1), 120–140.

Clyne, M. (1992). *Pluricentric languages: Different norms in different nations*. Berlin: Mouton de Gruyter.

Corson, D. (2001). *Language diversity and education*. Mahwah, NJ: Lawrence Erlbaum Associates Publishers.

Council of Europe. (2001). *Common European framework of references for languages: Learning, teaching, assessment*. Cambridge: Cambridge University Press.

CPDD (Curriculum Planning and Development Division). (2015). *2015 syllabus Chinese language primary*. Singapore: Ministry of Education.

Darling-Hammond, L., & McCloskey, L. (2008). *Benchmarking learning systems: Student performance assessment in international context*. Stanford, CA: Stanford University.

Department of Statistics. (2014). *Population trends 2014*. Singapore: Department of Statistics.

Foucault, M. (1983). The subject and power. In H. Dreyfus & P. Rabinow (Eds.), *Michel Foucault: Beyond structuralism and hermeneutics* (pp. 208–226). Chicago: The University of Chicago Press.

Fulcher, G., Davidson, F., & Kemp, J. (2011). Effective rating scale development for speaking tests: Performance decision trees. *Language Testing, 28*(1), 5–29.

Goh, C. T. (1999). Speech by Prime Minister Goh Chok Tong at the 70th Anniversary Celebration Dinner of the Teochew Poit Ip Huay Kuan on Saturday, September 4, 1999 at 7:45 PM at the

Neptune Theatre Restaurant. *Press Release*. Singapore: Singapore Ministry of Information and the Arts.

Goh, Y. S. (2010). *Hanyu Guoji Chuanbo: Xinjiapo Shijiao (Global spread of Chinese language: A perspective from Singapore)*. Beijing: Commercial Press.

Guo, X. (2002). Yu neiwai Hanyu xietiao wenti chuyi (A rudimentary suggestion on integration of Mainland China and overseas Mandarin). *Applied Linguistics (Yuyan Wenzi Yingyong), 3*, 34–40.

Gupta, A. F. (1986). A standard for written Singapore English. *English World-Wide, 7*(1), 75–99.

Gupta, A. F. (1994). *The step-tongue: Children's English in Singapore*. Clevedon: Multilingual Matters.

Hubley, A. M., & Zumbo, B. D. (2011). Validity and the consequences of test interpretation and use. *Social Indicators Research, 103*, 219–230.

Kachru, B. B. (1985). Standards, codification and sociolinguistic realism: The English language in the outer circle. In R. Quirk & H. Widdowson (Eds.), *English in the world: Teaching and learning the language and literatures* (pp. 11–30). Cambridge: Cambridge University Press.

Khoo, K. U. (2012). Malaixiya yu Xinjiapo Huayu cihui chayi jiqi huanjing yinsu (Malaysia and Singapore Mandarin lexical differences and the environmental factors). *Journal of Chinese Sociolinguistics (Zhongguo Shehui Yuyanxue), 12*, 96–111.

Kuo, E. C. Y. (1985). *Languages and society in Singapore (Xinjiapo de Yuyan yu Shehui)*. Taipei: Zhengzhong Press.

Li, C. W.-C. (2004). Conflicting notions of language purity: The interplay of archaising, ethnographic, reformist, elitist, and xenophobic purism in the perception of standard Chinese. *Language & Communication, 24*(2), 97–133.

Li, W. (2010). The nature of linguistic norms and their relevance to multilingual development. In M. Cruz-Ferreira (Ed.), *Multilingual norms* (pp. 397–404). Frankfurt: Peter Lang.

Lu, J. M., Zhang, C. H., & Qian, P. (2002). Xinjiapo Huayu Yufa De Tedian (The grammatical features of Singapore Mandarin). In C.-H. Chew (Ed.), *Xinjiapo Huayu Cihui Yu Yufa (Vocabulary and grammar in Singapore Mandarin)* (pp. 75–147). Singapore: Lingzi Media.

Lü, S. X. (1999). *Xiandai Hanyu Babai Ci (Eight hundred words in modern Chinese)*. Beijing: Commercial Press.

McNamara, T. (2001). Language assessment as social practice: Challenges for research. *Language Testing, 18*, 333–349.

McNamara, T. (2008). The socio-political and power dimensions of tests. In E. Shohamy & N. Hornberger (Eds.), *Encyclopedia of language and education: Language testing and assessment* (pp. 415–427). New York: Springer Science+Business Media L.L.C.

Milroy, J., & Milroy, L. (1985). *Authority in language*. London: Routledge and Kegan Paul.

MTLRC (Mother Tongue Language Review Committee). (2011). *Nurturing active learners and proficient users: 2010 Mother Tongue Languages Review Committee report*. Singapore: Ministry of Education.

Mufwene, S. (1997). Native speaker, proficient speaker, and norm. In R. Singh (Ed.), *Native speaker: Multilingual perspective* (pp. 111–123). New Delhi: Sage Publications.

Mufwene, S. (2001). New Englishes and norm-setting: How critical is the native speaker in linguistics. In E. Thumboo (Ed.), *The three circles of English* (pp. 133–141). Singapore: Unipress.

Newbrook, M. (1997). Malaysian English: Status, norms, some grammatical and lexical features. In E. Schneider (Ed.), *Englishes around the world, Vol 2: Caribbean, Africa, Asia, Australia* (pp. 229–256). Amsterdam: John Benjamins.

Newman, J. (1988). Singapore's speak Mandarin campaign. *Journal of Multilingual and Multicultural Development, 9*, 437–448.

North, B., & Schneider, G. (1998). Scaling descriptors for language proficiency scales. *Language Testing, 15*(2), 217–263.

Pakir, A. (1994). English in Singapore: The codification of competing norms. In S. Gopinathan, A. Pakir, W. K. Ho, & V. Saravanan (Eds.), *Language, society and education in Singapore: Issues and trends* (pp. 92–118). Singapore: Times Academic Press.

Platt, J. T., & Weber, H. (1980). *English in Singapore and Malaysia: Status, features, functions.* Kuala Lumpur: Oxford University Press.

Ramírez, A. G. (1995). *Creating contexts for second language acquisition: Theory and methods.* London: Longman.

Rudner, L. M., & Boston, C. (1994). Performance assessment. *ERIC Review, 3*(1), 2–12.

Shang, G. W., & Zhao, S. H. (2013). Huayu Guifanhua De Biaozhun Yu Luxiang: Yi Xinjiapo Huayu Weili (The standard and direction of Huayu codification: A case study of Singapore Mandarin). *Yuyan Jiaoxue Yu Yanjiu (Language Teaching and Research), 3,* 82–90.

Shohamy, E. (2007). Language tests as language policy tools. *Assessment in Education, 14*(1), 117–130.

Smith, M. J. (1997). Policy networks. In M. Hill (Ed.), *Policy process: A reader* (pp. 76–86). New York: Routledge.

Wang, C. M., Lee, W. H., Lim, H. L., & Lea, S. H. (2014, 5). Development of the proficiency descriptors framework for the teaching, learning and assessment of mother tongue languages in Singapore. Paper presented in 40th IAEA (International Association for Educational Assessment) Annual Conference. Singapore.

Wang, H. D. (2002). Xinjiapo Huayu Teyou Ciyu Tanwei (An investigation of the Singapore Mandarin vocabulary). In C.-H. Chew (Ed.), *Xinjiapo Huayu Cihui Yu Yufa (Vocabulary and grammar in Singapore Mandarin)* (pp. 75–147). Singapore: Lingzi Media.

Wee, L. (2003). Linguistic instrumentalism in Singapore. *Journal of Multilingual and Multicultural Development, 24*(3), 211–224.

Xu, D., & Li, W. (2002). Managing multilingualism in Singapore. In W. Li, J. D. Marc, & A. Housen (Eds.), *Opportunities and challenges of bilingualism* (pp. 275–295). Berlin: Mouton de Gruyter.

Xu, J., & Wang, H. (2004). *Xiandai Huayu Gailun (Introduction to modern Huayu).* Singapore: Global publishing.

Zhao, S. H., & Liu, Y. B. (2010). Chinese education in Singapore: The constraints of bilingual policy from perspectives of status and prestige planning. *Language Problems and Language Planning, 34*(3), 236–258.

Zhao, S. H., & Shang, G. W. (2013, 7). "Who speaking Chinese best": Reflections and suggestions for the issues emerging from developing exemplars of the education oriented speaking and spoken interaction proficiency descriptors in Singapore. Paper presented at the 10th International Symposium of Teaching Chinese to Foreigners. Hohhot, China: Inner Mongolia Normal University.

Zhao, S. H., & Sun, H. M. (2013, 7). Chinese language teachers from China and Chinese language in Singapore: Towards an integration of the two. Paper presented at the 10th International Symposium of Teaching Chinese to Foreigners. Hohhot, China: Inner Mongolia Normal University.

Zhu, X. H. (2014). Jiangou cujin xuexi de yuwen lingting, shuohua yu kouyu hudong de pingjia Tixi (A system of assessing students' listening, speaking and oral interaction skills for implementing assessment for learning (AfL) in Chinese language education). *Huawen Xuekan (Journal of Chinese Language Education), 6*(1), 1–21.

Chapter 9
Diagnostic Assessment of L2 Chinese Learners' Reading Comprehension Ability

Shuai Li and Jing Wang

Abstract This study explored the feasibility of applying the Rule Space Method (RSM) to diagnosing the strengths and weaknesses of reading ability among learners of Chinese based on their performance on the reading comprehension section of a standardized Chinese proficiency test, the C. Test. Combining literature review, instructor coding, and expert judgment, we finalized a set of eight attributes measured by 30 multiple-choice reading comprehension test items. Eight hundred and fifty-seven (857) examinees took the above-mentioned test, and their responses to the 30 test items were used for statistical analyses. The results showed that 90.54% of the examinees were successfully classified into one of the pre-specified attribute mastery patterns, based on which we were able to offer detailed diagnostic reports to individual examinees regarding their mastery/non-mastery of the attributes.

Keywords Diagnostic language assessment · Rule Space Method · L2 Chinese · Reading ability

Introduction

Diagnostic language assessment (DLA), understood as the "processes of identifying test-takers' (or learners') weakness, as well as their strengths, in a targeted domain of linguistic and communicative competence and providing specific diagnostic feedback and (guidance for) remedial learning" (Lee 2015, p. 5), has attracted a lot of attention in applied linguistics. For example, the 2015 special issue of *Language Testing* and the 2009 special issue of *Language Assessment Quarterly* were devoted to understanding the various approaches to DLA and their applications to second

S. Li (✉)
Georgia State University, Atlanta, USA
e-mail: sli12@gsu.edu

J. Wang
Kennesaw State University, Kennesaw, USA

© Springer Nature Singapore Pte Ltd. 2017
D. Zhang and C.-H. Lin (eds.), *Chinese as a Second Language Assessment*,
Chinese Language Learning Sciences, DOI 10.1007/978-981-10-4089-4_9

language (L2) assessment. The surge of interest and empirical effort in DLA is in response to the growing demand from practitioners and stakeholders of language teaching and learning calling for refined assessment techniques that are able to provide individualized diagnoses of test takers' mastery and non-mastery of knowledge and skills in order to guide subsequent teaching and learning (Jang 2009a; Kim 2015; Lee 2015). In this regard, traditional language assessment techniques, such as those informed by classical testing theories, which typically report examinees' standardized total test scores and section scores (e.g., for reading and listening), are not able to meet this demand. In fact, it is possible that two test takers with different underlying skill/knowledge profiles receive identical total/section scores based on their test performance (Tatsuoka 2009). Hence, unless there is a means to detect the mastery/non-mastery of latent knowledge/skills, we are not able to conduct individualized remedial teaching and learning for test takers.

The Rule Space Method (RSM) (Tatsuoka 1983, 1995, 2009), a psychometrically based technique for tapping latent cognitive attributes (defined as knowledge and cognitive processing skills), provides a viable solution to the aforementioned problem. As a statistical method of pattern recognition and classification, the RSM aims to classify examinees' observable test item response patterns into a set of predetermined attribute mastery/non-mastery patterns, called knowledge states. In so doing, it can provide fine-grained diagnostic information for individual test takers regarding their strengths and weaknesses in the knowledge and cognitive skills assessed by a test. In the field of second language assessment, the RSM and related methods (e.g., the Fusion Model) have been used to diagnose the knowledge states of examinees as they respond to test items assessing listening and reading comprehension (e.g., Buck and Tatsuoka 1998; Buck et al. 1997; Jang 2009a, b; Kim 2015). Previous studies have mostly relied on existing tests (e.g., TOEIC, LanguEdge, TOEFL iBT), and it is interesting that among those studies targeting the same language skill (e.g., reading), the attributes identified and the knowledge states examined were often different and dependent on the particular test items under investigation. Research is thus needed to examine additional tests to evaluate the generalizability of previous research findings. A related issue is that, because previous studies have exclusively focused on English as the target language, it is critical to expand this line of research to other, particularly those typologically different, languages such as Chinese.

This study is an effort in this direction. It explored the feasibility of using the RSM for conducting diagnostic assessment of test takers' strengths and weaknesses in reading ability as they responded to a standardized Chinese proficiency test, the C. Test. The following sections will first introduce the rationale and procedures of the RSM, followed by a discussion of the applications of the RSM to L2 assessment.

Rule Space Method (RSM): Rationale and Procedures

The Rule Space Method (RSM) (Tatsuoka 1983, 1995, 2009) was developed with the purpose of reporting fine-grained information about an individual examinee's mastery/non-mastery of specified latent attributes (i.e., knowledge and cognitive skills) based on his/her performance on a set of test items. The rationale is that a correct (or incorrect) response to a test item entails the mastery (or non-mastery) of certain latent attribute(s). Therefore, a specific test item can be described by the latent attribute(s) that it measures, and a specific set of test items can be described by different combinations (or patterns) of latent attributes that they measure. Hence, ideally, by examining an individual test taker's observable item response patterns, one can identify his/her (unobservable) attribute mastery pattern (i.e., knowledge state) by means of pattern recognition. In reality, however, test takers' performance on test items are influenced not just by those specified latent attributes, but also by many other factors (e.g., carelessness). Therefore, the RSM also involves a pattern classification procedure which is probability-based. In other words, as Tatsuoka (2009) summarizes, "RSM converts students' item response patterns into attribute mastery probabilities" (p. xii).

The application of RSM involves three phases (Buck and Tatsuoka 1998; Buck et al. 1997; Gierl 2007): (1) identifying attributes and determining ideal knowledge states; (2) formulating a classification space (or rule space); and (3) classifying examinee responses. During the first phase, test items are analyzed to identify the attributes that need to be mastered for correct responses.[1] This analysis typically involves domain experts' evaluation of test items based on relevant theories and empirical results, occasionally supplemented by an examination of test takers' verbal protocols (e.g., Jang 2009b). The hierarchical relations (if any) among the identified attributes are then described. For example, Fig. 9.1 illustrates the hierarchical structure of a hypothetical set of five attributes assessed by a collection of test items. As can be seen, the mastery of attribute A1 serves as the prerequisite for the mastery of attribute A2; the mastery of attribute A2, in turn, is the prerequisite for the mastery of attribute A4.

With the above information, we can construct an adjacency matrix (A) where all (unidirectional) direct relations among the attributes are represented by "1" and the lack of such relation by "0" (Table 9.1). Through Boolean addition and multiplication based on the A matrix (Tatsuoka 2009), one can obtain a reachability matrix (R) where all (unidirectional) direct and indirect relations among the attributes are represented by "1" and the lack of such relation by "0" (Table 9.2). Note that each attribute is by default related to itself (e.g., A1 is related to A1).

---

[1]As Sawaki et al. (2009) summarized, there are three approaches to identifying attributes: (a) by examining surface test item characteristics, (b) by referring to theoretical taxonomies of language ability, and (c) by analyzing test takers' reported skills and processes. The current study adopted the first approach because it was based on an existing test.

Fig. 9.1 Hierarchical structure of five hypothetical attributes assessed by a test

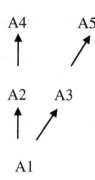

Table 9.1 An adjacency matrix (A) based on five attributes

	A1	A2	A3	A4	A5
A1	0	1	1	0	0
A2	0	0	0	1	0
A3	0	0	0	0	1
A4	0	0	0	0	0
A5	0	0	0	0	0
A5	0	0	0	0	0

Table 9.2 A reachability matrix (R) based on five attributes

	A1	A2	A3	A4	A5
A1	1	1	1	1	1
A2	0	1	0	1	0
A3	0	0	1	0	1
A4	0	0	0	1	0
A5	0	0	0	0	1

The next step involves determining the allowable item types (i.e., potential attribute combinations) based on the specified attributes and their relations. Initially, an incident matrix (Q) can be made where the columns represent possible combinations of attributes and the rows represent the specified attributes. In the our example involving five attributes, the number of potential combinations is 31 (that is, $2^5 - 1$) should there be no hierarchical relations among the attributes. However, because of the hierarchy of attributes (Fig. 9.1), not all potential combinations are allowed. For example, an item type that only involves attributes A1 and A4 is not allowed because it is impossible to tap attribute A4 without tapping attribute A2. By removing those unallowable item types, one can obtain a reduced incident matrix (Q_r). The reduced Q matrix for our example will look like the following (Table 9.3), where each column represents one allowed item type and each row represents one attribute.

In an ideal scenario where test takers' item responses fully conform to the specified attributes and their hierarchical structure, the 10 item types illustrated in Table 9.3 can also be seen as test takers' ideal item response patterns. Because the

Table 9.3 A reduced incident matrix (Q_r) based on five attributes

Attributes	Item types									
	i1	i2	i3	i4	i5	i6	i7	i8	i9	i10
A1	1	1	1	1	1	1	1	1	1	1
A2	0	1	0	1	1	1	0	1	1	1
A3	0	0	1	1	0	1	1	0	1	1
A4	0	0	0	0	1	1	0	0	0	1
A5	0	0	0	0	0	0	1	1	1	1

Table 9.4 Ideal response matrix (E) based on five attributes

Attribute mastery patterns (or knowledge states)					Ideal response patterns (item types)									
A1	A2	A3	A4	A5	i1	i2	i3	i4	i5	i6	i7	i8	i9	i10
1	0	0	0	0	1	0	0	0	0	0	0	0	0	0
1	1	0	0	0	1	1	0	0	0	0	0	0	0	0
1	0	1	0	0	1	0	1	0	0	0	0	0	0	0
1	1	1	0	0	1	1	1	1	0	0	0	0	0	0
1	1	0	1	0	1	1	0	0	1	0	0	0	0	0
1	1	1	1	0	1	1	1	1	1	1	0	0	0	0
1	0	1	0	1	1	1	0	0	0	1	0	0	0	0
1	1	0	0	1	1	1	1	1	0	0	1	1	0	0
1	1	1	0	1	1	1	1	1	0	0	1	1	1	0
1	1	1	1	1	1	1	1	1	1	1	1	1	1	1

Note For the "Attribute mastery patterns" section, "1" denotes mastery of an attribute and "0" denotes non-mastery; for the "Ideal response patterns" section, "1" denotes correct response(s) and "0" denotes incorrect response(s)

response patterns entail specific combinations of attribute mastery/non-mastery, these patterns represent examinees' various knowledge states. With this understanding, we can construct an ideal response matrix (E) where the columns represent different item types and the rows represent test takers' various knowledge states (Table 9.4). This matrix shows the mappings between test takers' attribute mastery patterns (or knowledge states) and ideal item response patterns (or item types). For example, a test taker mastering attributes A1, A2, and A3 is expected to respond correctly to item types i1, i2, i3, and i4 (please also refer to the reduced Q matrix in Table 9.3); however, this test taker is not expected to have correct responses to item type i5, which requires the mastery of attribute A4 for correct response, nor is he/she expected to respond correctly to item type i9 because that requires the mastery of attribute A5 in addition to A1, A2, and A3.

With the ideal response matrix (E), we can infer test takers' latent attribute mastery patterns (i.e., knowledge states) based on their observable item response patterns (i.e., test performance). Note that what is described here assumes an ideal situation where test takers do not produce atypical item responses that do not conform to their attribute mastery patterns (or inconsistent with the attributes that an item is designed to measure). An example of atypical item response is for an examinee mastering only attribute A1 to get correct responses to item type i2. In reality, the ideal situation, as illustrated by the ideal response matrix (E), is virtually impossible to exist, as test takers can always be expected to produce unexpected responses (e.g., a low-ability examinee responds correctly to a high-difficulty item). Hence, there needs to be a means to take into consideration examinees' atypical responses when inferring their latent knowledge states. This brings us to the next phase of the RSM: formulating a classification space.

During the second phase, the formulation of a classification space (or rule space) relies on the calculation of two sets of coordinates: examinees' IRT-based estimation of ability level (or θ) as well as an index indicating how atypical their item response patterns are (or ζ). The classification space can thus be visualized as consisting of a set of ideal points (θ_R, ζ_R) based on the ideal item response patterns, as well as a set of non-ideal points (θ_x, ζ_x) for all test takers based on their actual item response patterns. Each ideal point represents a pre-specified knowledge state, and each non-ideal point represents an examinee's observed pattern of item responses.

In the last phase (i.e., classifying test taker responses into pre-specified knowledge states), Mahalanobis distances (i.e., a statistic used to measure the likelihood ratio between a sample and a population) are calculated between each non-ideal point (θ_x, ζ_x) and each ideal point (θ_R, ζ_R), and the Bayes classification rule for minimum error is applied to determine which pre-specified knowledge state (represented by the corresponding ideal point) a test taker (represented by the corresponding non-ideal point) belongs to. In this way, individual test takers' mastery and non-mastery of attributes can be diagnosed for subsequent remedial teaching and learning.

Rule Space Method and Its Application to L2 Assessment

The RSM and other diagnostic language assessment methods (e.g., the Fusion Model) have been applied to educational assessment (e.g., math) in order to diagnose learners' mastery of latent cognitive skills and knowledge. In the field of L2 assessment, the application of the RSM and related techniques remains very limited, with a few studies examining L2 learners' knowledge states as they respond to test items assessing reading (Buck et al. 1997; Jang 2009a, b; Kim 2015), listening (Buck and Tatsuoka 1998), or both skills (Lee and Sawaki 2009; Sawaki et al. 2009).

In a pioneering study, Buck et al. (1997) applied the RSM to diagnosing the sub-skills involved in responding to the reading comprehension section of a TOEIC test among 5000 Japanese examinees. Based on literature review and test item analyses, the researchers identified 27 potential attributes (e.g., the ability to recognize relevant information, the ability to identify the gist of a passage, the ability to use a word-matching strategy in selecting the correct option, and the knowledge of low-frequency vocabulary). Through four rounds of statistical analyses, 24 attributes were retained for examinee classification. Ninety-one percent (91%) of the examinees were successfully classified into one of the knowledge states consisting of the 24 attributes and those attributes together accounted for 97% of the variances in test performance.

Focusing on the reading comprehension sections of two forms of the *LanguEdge* assessment (part of a courseware for preparing the TOEFL iBT), Jang (2009a, b) combined examinee verbal protocol analysis and statistical analysis to identify nine attributes assessed by the reading comprehension test items (e.g., deducing the meaning of a word or a phrase by searching and analyzing a text and by using contextual clues appearing in the text, read carefully or expeditiously to locate relevant information in a text and to determine which information is true or not true). Those nine attributes were used to develop the Q matrix. The *LanguEdge* tests were administered to 2703 test takers. Different from Buck et al.'s (1997) study, Jang (2009a) applied the Fusion Model for statistical analysis to classify the examinees to three categories (i.e., mastery, non-mastery, and undetermined) for each attribute.[2] The average classification rates were 90% for test Form One and 88% for test Form Two. Jang also reported, among other things, the varying levels of diagnostic capacity of individual test items as well as the usefulness of diagnostic feedback on improving subsequent teaching. In another study focusing on the TOEFL iBT, Sawaki et al. (2009) relied on expert judgment to identify and code the attributes assessed by two forms of the reading (and listening) comprehension section of the test. A total of 441 examinees completed both forms of the test. After applying the Fusion Model, the researchers finalized a set of four attributes for developing the Q matrix for the reading section (and another four attributes for developing the Q matrix for the listening section). The results showed that, across the two test forms, 76.2% of the examinees were consistently classified into their respective attribute mastery states (for all attributes, or all but one attribute) for the reading section (and 79.6% for the listening section).

In a more recent study focusing on an English placement test, Kim (2015) combined literature search and instructor coding to identify the attributes involved in the reading comprehension section of the test. Ten attributes (e.g., strategy of finding information, strategy of inferencing, knowledge of lexical meaning, and knowledge of sentence meaning) were identified for constructing the Q matrix for subsequent statistical analysis. Similar to Jang's (2009a, b) studies cited above, Kim's analysis focused on the mastery probabilities of individual attributes and reported varied levels of mastery (e.g., ranging from 51.5% to 71.2% across the

---

[2]The Fusion Model and the RSM are similar in that they are both probabilistic models that decompose examinee abilities into cognitive attributes based on a Q Matrix. They are different in terms of assumptions of attribute structure, flexibility of handling items scored polytomously, and parameter estimation methods. Interested readers can refer to Lee and Sawaki (2009) for comparing the features of various cognitive diagnostic models.

attributes). The attribute mastery probabilities also differed significantly across beginner, intermediate, and advanced proficiency groups. Finally, the study provided diagnostic reports for individual examinees regarding the degree of mastery of the 10 attributes.

Three observations can be made after summarizing this limited body of empirical research on diagnostic assessment of reading ability. First, although utilizing existing tests may bring concerns of generalizability because researchers need to accommodate the specifics of a particular set of test items in the process of identifying relevant attributes, it remains a common practice in the literature. Second, a related observation is the lack of agreed-upon methods/procedures for identifying attributes. As the above summaries can show, expert judgment, literature search, examinee protocol analysis, and sometimes a combination of these procedures have been adopted by researchers. The consequence, however, is very different sets of attributes even for the same language skill (e.g., reading) assessed by similar tests (e.g., comparing Jang's (2009a, b) studies and Sawaki et al.'s (2009) study). The question, therefore, is to what extent the identified set of attributes an artifact of the research procedures involved. Because an ultimate goal of diagnostic language assessment is to provide individual examinees with detailed information regarding knowledge/skill mastery for the purpose of remedial learning/instruction, it is important that the attribute mastery reports closely reflect their true ability rather than being influenced by extraneous factors. Finally, previous research has exclusively focused on English as the target language, and it is desirable to extend this line of research to other languages for generalizability considerations. In practice, Chinese is an ideal candidate language, thanks to the growing worldwide popularity of the language. Earlier estimations reported that approximately 30 million people were studying Chinese as a second language around the world (Xu 2006), and over 3000 institutions of higher education were offering Chinese courses (China Educational Newspaper 2009, September 30). This huge demand in Chinese language learning calls for effective means of assessment that can provide fine-grained information for learners in order to enable sustained learning effort. To this end, this study represents an exploratory effort in the field of L2 Chinese assessment.

Research Question

This study aimed to apply the RSM to analyzing L2 Chinese test takers' responses to the reading comprehension test items of a standardized Chinese proficiency test (i.e., the C. Test). The research question was as follows: Is it feasible to use the RSM to conduct diagnostic assessment of examinees' reading ability in L2 Chinese?

Method

Participants

On December 2, 2007, the C. Test (A-D level) was officially administered to 857 test takers globally. All those test takers became our participants. There were 668 Japanese test takers, 139 Koreans, 36 Chinese (ethnic minorities in China with Chinese as their second language), two Filipinos, two Vietnamese, two Malaysians, two Cambodians, two Indians, one Russian, one Australian, one Polish, and one Mauritius. Among these examinees, 681 took the test in Japan, 109 in South Korea, and the remaining 67 in China. The mean test score of the examinee sample was 67.66 (out of 160), and the standard deviation (SD) was 27.99. The mean score of the reading comprehension section (detailed below) was 13.51 (out of 30) with an SD of 5.16.

Instrument

The C. Test, or Test of Practical Chinese "实用汉语水平认定考试", is a standardized Chinese proficiency test developed by the Chinese Proficiency Test Center of Beijing Language and Culture University and was launched in 2006. The test has two different proficiency levels, namely E-F (Elementary) and A-D (Intermediate to Advanced).[3] The instrument used in this study was the reading comprehension section of the C. Test (A-D) officially administered on December 2, 2007. In this version of the test, there were six reading comprehension texts each with five multiple-choice questions (each contained four options) for a total of 30 items. The texts were 714–803 characters in length, and the content did not require specialized knowledge. Readers interested in accessing the test items can refer to HSK Center (2008).

---

[3]The C. Test (A-D) includes two main components: listening comprehension (70 items) and integrated skill use (90 items). The listening comprehension component further includes four sections: (a) graph-based listening comprehension (10 items), (b) short-dialogue-based listening comprehension (20 items), (c) extended-dialogue-based listening comprehension (10 items), and (d) listening comprehension and note-taking (20 items). The integrated skill use component includes six sections: (1) vocabulary/structure (10 items), (2) word order (20 items), (3) reading comprehension (30 items), (4) error identification (10 items), (5) passage-based blank filling (10 items), and (6) passage-based sentence making (10 items). The allowable time for completing the entire test is 150 min (i.e., 50 for listening and 100 for integrated skill use).

Procedures

Attribute identification involved several procedures. The researchers first consulted published empirical research on diagnostic assessment of L2 reading ability and theories of reading comprehension to prepare a list of potentially relevant attributes. This list and the 30 test items were then forwarded to two domain experts in L2 Chinese reading comprehension, who identified nine attributes that were assessed by the test items. Afterward, the researchers recruited 10 Chinese language instructors with minimally five years of teaching experience to review and code the test items according to the nine attributes. Following Kim (2015), an attribute with over 60% agreement among the coders for each test item was considered essential and subsequently retained. As it turned out, one attribute, the ability to apply background knowledge, was measured by less than three items. Following Kim (2015), this attribute was removed from the original attribute list. Table 9.5 shows the remaining eight attributes with their corresponding item characteristics. Finally, the eight attributes and the item codings were reviewed by the two domain experts, who discussed and finalized the attribute hierarchy illustrated in Fig. 9.2.

Following the procedures outlined in the literature review section, we constructed the adjacency matrix (A), the reachability matrix (R), the incident matrix (Q), the reduced incident matrix (Q_r), and the ideal response pattern (E). Because there were eight attributes involved, the incident matrix (Q) included $2^8 - 1 = 255$ possible combinations of attributes; however, because of the hierarchical structure among the attributes (Fig. 9.2), only 52 of the 255 combinations were allowed. These 52 combinations were included in the reduced incident matrix (Q_r) shown in Table 9.6. Then, a 52×52 ideal response pattern (E) was developed with the rows

Table 9.5 Attribute list for the C. Test reading comprehension section

Attribute	Item characteristics coded
A1. Ability to recognize characters and words	Correct response to the item entails appropriate knowledge of Chinese characters and words
A2. Ability to hold information in memory	The options tend to be long, and/or the necessary information spreads over two sentences
A3. Ability to use given information as a basis for searching the text	The necessary information or information in options is easy to locate
A4. Ability to understand explicitly stated information	The item requires understanding of literal meaning of words and sentences
A5. Ability to understand the gist of a passage	The item is a "main idea" item
A6. Ability to recognize relevant information	The necessary information occurs out of item order, and/or the necessary information is scattered across the text
A7. Ability to understand implicit/implied meaning and/or attitude	The necessary information (e.g., meaning and/or attitude) is not explicitly stated and needs to be inferred
A8. Ability to infer word meaning in context	The item asks for the meaning of a specific word and/or phrase appeared in the text

Fig. 9.2 Hierarchical
structure of eight attributes
assessed by the reading
comprehension section of the
C. Test

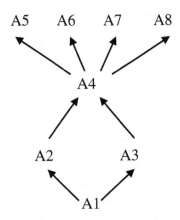

representing possible knowledge states of examinees and the columns representing different item types.

The next step was to calculate a set of coordinates consisting of examinees' IRT-based estimation of ability level (or θ) and their atypical response index (or ζ). Because IRT-based parameter estimation cannot be made for examinees who answer all items correctly or incorrectly as well as for items that all examinees answer correctly or incorrectly (Hambleton et al. 1991), the first and last rows and the first and last columns of the ideal response pattern (E) were removed, resulting in 50 rows and 50 columns in the ideal response pattern (E) for subsequent statistical analyses. We calculated 50 ideal points (θ_R, ζ_R) based on the ideal item response patterns as well as 857 non-ideal points (θ_x, ζ_x) based on the examinees' actual item response patterns.

Finally, in order to classify the examinees into the 50 pre-specified knowledge states, we calculated Mahalanobis distances (D^2) between each non-ideal point (θ_x, ζ_x) and each ideal point (θ_R, ζ_R). Because Mahalanobis distances (D^2) follow the X^2 distribution with two degrees of freedom (Tatsuoka and Tatsuoka 1987), D^2 less than 5.99 is considered to be valid for classification. For an examinee who met this criteria (i.e., D^2 less than 5.99), he/she was classified into the nearest pre-specified knowledge state based on the smallest D^2.

Results

The results showed that 776 of the 857 test takers' Mahalanobis distances (D^2) were smaller than 5.99, and they were subsequently classified into 39 of the 50 pre-specified knowledge states. The classification rate was thus 90.54%. Table 9.7 shows the 50 pre-specified knowledge states (i.e., attribute mastery patterns, where "1" stands for mastery and "0" stands for non-mastery), their corresponding coordinates (θ_R, ζ_R) based on the ideal response pattern (E), and the number and percentage of participants ($N = 857$) classified into each knowledge state. In

Table 9.6 Reduced incident matrix (Q_r) based on the eight attributes

Attribute	Item type												
	i1	i2	i3	i4	i5	i6	i7	i8	i9	i10	i11	i12	i13
A1	1	1	1	1	1	1	1	1	1	1	1	1	1
A2	0	1	1	1	1	1	1	1	1	1	1	1	1
A3	0	0	0	0	0	0	0	0	0	0	0	0	0
A4	0	0	1	1	1	1	1	1	1	1	1	1	1
A5	0	0	0	1	0	0	0	1	1	1	0	0	0
A6	0	0	0	0	1	0	0	1	0	0	1	1	0
A7	0	0	0	0	0	1	0	0	1	0	1	0	1
A8	0	0	0	0	0	0	1	0	0	1	0	1	1

Attribute	Item type												
	i14	i15	i16	i17	i18	i19	i20	i21	i22	i23	i24	i25	i26
A1	1	1	1	1	1	1	1	1	1	1	1	1	1
A2	1	1	1	1	1	0	0	0	0	0	0	0	0
A3	0	0	0	0	0	1	1	1	1	1	1	1	1
A4	1	1	1	1	1	0	1	1	1	1	1	1	1
A5	1	1	0	0	1	0	0	1	0	0	0	1	1
A6	1	0	1	1	1	0	0	0	1	0	0	1	0
A7	1	1	0	1	1	0	0	0	0	1	0	0	1
A8	0	1	1	1	1	0	0	0	0	0	1	0	0

Attribute	Item type												
	i27	i28	i29	i30	i31	i32	i33	i34	i35	i36	i37	i38	i39
A1	1	1	1	1	1	1	1	1	1	1	1	1	1
A2	0	0	0	0	0	0	0	0	0	1	1	1	1
A3	1	1	1	1	1	1	1	1	1	1	1	1	1
A4	1	1	1	1	1	1	1	1	0	1	1	1	1
A5	1	0	0	0	1	1	1	0	1	0	0	1	0
A6	0	1	1	0	1	0	1	1	1	0	0	0	1
A7	0	1	0	1	1	1	0	1	1	0	0	0	0
A8	1	0	1	1	0	1	1	1	1	0	0	0	0

Attribute	Item type												
	i40	i41	i42	i43	i44	i45	i46	i47	i48	i49	i50	i51	i52
A1	1	1	1	1	1	1	1	1	1	1	1	1	1
A2	1	1	1	1	1	1	1	1	1	1	1	1	1
A3	1	1	1	1	1	1	1	1	1	1	1	1	1
A4	1	1	1	1	1	1	1	1	1	1	1	1	1
A5	0	0	1	1	1	0	0	0	1	1	1	0	1
A6	0	0	1	0	0	1	1	0	1	1	0	1	1
A7	1	0	0	1	0	1	0	1	1	0	1	1	1
A8	0	1	0	0	1	0	1	1	0	1	1	1	1

Table 9.7 Classification results based on 50 pre-specified knowledge states

Number	Attribute mastery patterns (A1, A2, … A8)	(θ_R, ζ_R)	Number of participants classified (percentage)
1	10000000	N/A*	N/A*
2	11000000	(−1.6054, 0.1621)	6 (0.7%)
3	11010000	(−1.2695, −0.3274)	2 (0.2%)
4	11011000	(−0.9928, −0.1850)	12 (1.4%)
5	11010100	(−1.0212, −0.2519)	0 (0.0%)
6	11010010	(−1.0138, −0.2341)	0 (0.0%)
7	11010001	(−1.0204, −0.2499)	0 (0.0%)
8	11011100	(−0.5535, 0.1307)	1 (0.1%)
9	11011010	(−0.5410, 0.1540)	1 (0.1%)
10	11011001	(−0.5530, 0.1320)	2 (0.2%)
11	11010110	(−0.5622, 0.1067)	2 (0.2%)
12	11010101	(−0.6530, −0.0270)	40 (4.6%)
13	11010011	(−0.5615, 0.1082)	0 (0.0%)
14	11011110	(0.0578, 0.9069)	0 (0.0%)
15	11011011	(0.0582, 0.9075)	9 (1.0%)
16	11011101	(−0.0035, 0.8112)	9 (1.0%)
17	11010111	(0.0033, 0.8277)	6 (0.7%)
18	11011111	(0.6744, 3.3664)	3 (0.3%)
19	10100000	(−1.6091, 0.1455)	2 (0.2%)
20	10110000	(−1.2758, −0.3491)	10 (1.1%)
21	10111000	(−1.0051, −0.2163)	1 (0.1%)
22	10110100	(−1.0205, −0.2528)	1 (0.1%)
23	10110010	(−1.0230, −0.2588)	0 (0.0%)
24	10110001	(−1.0245, −0.2624)	41 (4.7%)
25	10111100	(−0.5579, 0.1227)	0 (0.0%)
26	10111010	(−0.5598, 0.1185)	0 (0.0%)
27	10111001	(−0.5679, 0.1047)	2 (0.2%)
28	10110110	(−0.5642, 0.1039)	0 (0.0%)
29	10110101	(−0.5653, 0.1014)	12 (1.4%)
30	10110011	(−0.5245, 0.1764)	60 (7.0%)
31	10111110	(0.0500, 0.8957)	0 (0.0%)
32	10111011	(−0.0930, 0.6170)	82 (9.5%)
33	10111101	(0.0374, 0.8717)	4 (0.4%)
34	10110111	(0.0724, 0.9823)	42 (4.9%)
35	10111111	(0.7015, 3.4383)	1 (0.1%)
36	11100000	(−0.7387, 0.1336)	47 (5.4%)
37	11110000	(0.0268, −0.9400)	154 (17.9%)
38	11111000	(0.5322, −1.1810)	66 (7.7%)
39	11110100	(0.3088, −1.5182)	0 (0.0%)

(continued)

Table 9.7 (continued)

Number	Attribute mastery patterns (A1, A2, ... A8)	(θ_R, ζ_R)	Number of participants classified (percentage)
40	11110010	(0.3103, −1.5202)	6 (0.7%)
41	11110001	(0.3080, −1.5171)	13 (1.5%)
42	11111100	(0.9076, −1.4942)	3 (0.3%)
43	11111010	(0.9120, −1.5185)	15 (1.7%)
44	11111001	(0.9052, −1.4847)	26 (3.0%)
45	11110110	(0.7469, −1.7942)	7 (0.8%)
46	11110101	(0.8009, −1.5488)	10 (1.1%)
47	11110011	(0.7630, −1.6808)	1 (0.1%)
48	11111110	(1.5989, −0.8373)	10 (1.1%)
49	11111101	(1.5267, −0.6879)	13 (1.5%)
50	11111011	(1.6082, −0.7634)	7 (0.8%)
51	11110111	(1.4378, −0.0598)	47 (5.4%)
52	11111111	N/A*	N/A*

Note *These two knowledge states (#1, #52) were removed from final analysis, as discussed earlier

reviewing Table 9.7, it is clear that the majority of the examinees (67.1%) were found to belong to nine knowledge states, namely #37 (17.9%, mastery of A1, A2, A3, A4), #32 (9.5%, mastery of A1, A3, A4, A5, A7, A8), #38 (7.7%, mastery of A1, A2, A3, A4, A5), #30 (7.0%, mastery of A1, A3, A4, A7, A8), #36 (5.4%, mastery of A1, A2, A3), #51 (5.4%, mastery of A1, A2, A3, A4, A6, A7, A8), #34 (4.9%, mastery of A1, A3, A4, A6, A7, A8), #24 (4.7%, mastery of A1, A3, A4, A8), #12 (4.6%, mastery of A1, A2, A4, A6, A8) (refer to Table 9.5 for details of attributes A1–A8). However, there was no predominant knowledge state(s): Even though knowledge state #37 represented the profiles of the largest sub-group of examines ($n = 154$), the percentage score showed that it was still a relatively small portion of the examinee sample (i.e., 17.9%).

With a classification rate of 90.54%, it means that 9.45% (or 81) examinees were not successfully classified. As it turned out, these unclassified examinees tended to have either relatively higher or relatively lower ability: Among the 81 examinees, eighteen (or 22.22%) fell out of ±2 SDs and 57 (70.37%) fell outside ±1 SD along the ability axle. Moreover, the percentage of unclassified examinees tended to be higher among below-average-ability examinees (i.e., whose z scores were below zero) than among above-average-ability ones (i.e., whose z scores were above zero). In this study, there were 463 below-average-ability examinees, among which 54 (or 11.66%) were unclassified. In contrast, among the 394 above-average-ability examinees, 27 (or 6.85%) were unclassified. In other words, below-average-ability examinees were nearly twice as likely to be unclassified as above-average-ability examinees.

Table 9.8 further shows the mastery levels of the eight attributes for the entire examinee group. As expected, the level of mastery varied considerably across the

Table 9.8 Percentage of attribute mastery

Attribute	Percentage of mastery (%)
A1. Ability to recognize characters and words	100.0
A2. Ability to hold information in memory	60.4
A3. Ability to use given information as a basis for searching the text	79.6
A4. Ability to understand explicitly stated information	84.1
A5. Ability to understand the gist of a passage	31.1
A6. Ability to recognize relevant information	24.6
A7. Ability to understand implicit/implied meaning and/or attitude	34.8
A8. Ability to infer word meaning in context	44.6

eight attributes, with A1 (the ability to recognize characters and words) being the best mastered skills and A6 (the ability to recognize relevant information) being the least mastered skill. In general, the attributes located at the lower part of the hierarchy were better mastered than those located at the upper part of the hierarchy (refer to Fig. 9.2 for details on the hierarchy).

Because one advantage of diagnostic language assessment is to provide detailed information about individual test takers' strengths and weaknesses of targeted linguistic domain, we are able to provide individualized diagnostic reports for those successfully classified examinees. Due to space limit, we juxtaposed two such reports for two examinees in Table 9.9. It is interesting that, although the two examinees were at the same overall ability level ($\theta = 0.2029$), their knowledge patterns differed. Examinee 1 was classified into knowledge state #34, meaning that he/she had already mastered attributes A1 (ability to recognize characters and words), A3 (ability to use given information as a basis for searching the text), A4 (ability to understand explicitly stated information), A6 (ability to recognize relevant information), A7 (ability to understand implicit/implied meaning and/or attitude), and A8 (ability to infer word meaning in context) and that he/she had yet to master attributes A2 (ability to hold information in memory) and A5 (ability to understand the gist of a passage). In contrast, Examinee 2 was classified into knowledge state #37, which means that he/she had mastered attributes A1, A2, A3, and A4, but not attributes A5, A6, A7, and A8.

Finally, in reviewing our data, we also found that test takers with different ability levels belonged to the same knowledge states. For example, we found two examinees with their respective ability levels (θ) of -0.4879 and -0.1562, yet the classification results showed that they both belonged to knowledge state #37, meaning that they both mastered attributes A1, A2, A3 and A4, but not attributes A5, A6, A7, and A8.

Table 9.9 Two sample diagnostic reports of reading comprehension ability

Examinee	Examinee 1	Examinee 2
Examinee ability level	0.2029	0.2029
Attribute mastery pattern	#34 (10110111)	#37 (11110000)
Attributes already mastered	A1. Ability to recognize characters and words A3. Ability to use given information as a basis for searching the text A4. Ability to understand explicitly stated information A6. Ability to recognize relevant information A7. Ability to understand implicit/implied meaning and/or attitude A8. Ability to infer word meaning in context	A1. Ability to recognize characters and words A2. Ability to hold information in memory A3. Ability to use given information as a basis for searching the text A4. Ability to understand explicitly stated information
Attributes to be mastered	A2. Ability to hold information in memory A5. Ability to understand the gist of a passage	A5. Ability to understand the gist of a passage A6. Ability to recognize relevant information A7. Ability to understand implicit/implied meaning and/or attitude A8. Ability to infer word meaning in context

Discussion

The purpose of this study was to explore the feasibility of applying the RSM to diagnostic assessment of reading comprehension ability among learners of L2 Chinese. The results showed that 90.54% of the 857 examinees who took the test were successfully classified into the pre-specified knowledge states. This classification rate was comparable with those reported by Buck et al. (1997) and by Jang (2009a, b) and was higher than that reported by Sawaki et al. (2009). According to Tatsuoka (2009), a classification rate of 90% is an important indicator of the validity of a RSM study in showing that the proposed attributes and their relationship as illustrated in the Q matrix (Table 9.6) fit our examinees' performance well.

Nevertheless, 9.46% of our examinees were not successfully classified. A closer examination suggested that these examinees did not seem to follow a pattern of normal distribution in their overall level of reading abilities; rather, they were much more likely to have either relatively higher or relatively lower ability (i.e., outside the range of ±1 SD). Moreover, below-average-ability examinees appeared to be more likely to be unclassified than their above-average-ability counterparts. While the exact reason for these observations could not be identified based on the data we have collected, one possibility, as also expressed by Buck and Tatsuoka (1998), is that certain attribute(s) that influenced those examinees' test performance remained unidentified, which, in turn, means that certain knowledge state(s) that could explain those examinees' performance were not included in our analysis reported earlier. Lower ability or higher ability examinees might particularly utilize certain types of knowledge and/or cognitive skill(s) in responding to test items. However, without probing those examinees' online processing procedures involved in completing the test, it would be difficult to identify such knowledge and/or skill. Future research will need to employ techniques, such as a think-aloud protocol or stimulated recall, to assist with attribute identification.

Our results also showed that the examinees' knowledge states were highly diverse, covering 39 of the 50 pre-specified knowledge states. This diverse distribution of knowledge states provides a refined illustration of the individual differences in reading comprehension ability among the examinees. In this study, reading comprehension ability, as measured by 30 reading comprehension test items, was indexed through the mastery and non-mastery of eight attributes. Because each knowledge state represented a specific combination of mastered and unmastered attributes, our results showed the details of 39 types of reading comprehension ability profiles among the successfully classified examinees (see Table 9.7). In this way, a test score (or rather, a test result) becomes readily interpretable in terms of the strengths and weakness of the targeted domain of linguistic competence (i.e., reading comprehension ability).

The ease of test score (or result) interpretation, as afforded by diagnostic language assessment, can effectively facilitate the development of on-target remedial instruction and learning activities by pointing out the specific learning objectives. This point is illustrated in two scenarios extracted from this study. In the first scenario, regardless of their overall ability level, the examinees classified into the same knowledge state would benefit from the same instructional/learning package aiming at developing those yet-to-be-mastered attributes. In the second scenario, examinees with the same overall ability level might actually need different instructional/learning packages due to variations in attribute mastery patterns. The two examinee profiles illustrated in Table 9.9 are a good example here: Despite their identical overall ability level, Examinee 1 belonged to knowledge state #34 while Examinee 2 was classified into knowledge state #37. Together, these two scenarios showed the risks of relying on a single holistic ability measure in guiding the development of remedial instruction and pointed to the advantage of diagnostic language assessment in providing refined objectives for subsequent instruction and learning. Pedagogically, the implication is that, for the purpose of developing complex language skills that consist of multiple attributes, such as reading comprehension, an effective instructional program should be designed at the level of attributes in order to allow individualized remedial teaching and learning.

Finally, at the level of individual attributes, our results were consistent with previous studies (e.g., Buck et al. 1997; Jang 2009b; Kim 2015) in showing that the degree of mastery of individual attributes varied considerably, ranging from 24.6% for A6 to 100.0% for A1. In reviewing Table 9.9 along with Fig. 9.2 that illustrates the hierarchical structure of the attributes, it becomes clear that the attributes located at the lower portion of the hierarchy were better mastered than those located in the higher portion of the hierarchy. The only exception is A4, which, although located in a higher position in the hierarchy than A2 and A3, showed a better degree of mastery than the other two. This result can be explained by the structure of hierarchy, that is, there are two routes toward mastering A4, one through the mastery of A1 and A2, and the other one through the mastery of A1 and A3. In other words, in addition to the mastery of A1, mastering either A2 or A3 constitutes a necessary, but not sufficient, condition for the mastery of A4; hence, the finding that A4 exhibited a higher level of mastery than A2 and A3 is not unexpected. Overall, the mastery levels across the eight attributes as shown in Table 9.8 can lend support to the validity of the proposed attribute hierarchy—it makes good sense that more basic skills are mastered before more advanced skills.

Limitations and Issues for Future Exploration

This study explored the feasibility of applying the RSM to diagnostic assessment of reading comprehension ability in L2 Chinese. The findings suggest that the RSM can be a useful technique for providing the majority of the examinees (over 90%) with fine-grained information about their mastery and non-mastery of attributes assessed by a reading comprehension test. However, as this study represented an initial effort in diagnostic assessment for L2 Chinese, it was limited in several ways, and future studies are needed to refine this line of research.

To begin with, although the classification rate was above 90% and can thus be considered as successful from a research point of view, it is also true that nearly 10% of the examinees were not classified. If diagnostic language assessment is to be put into practice, we cannot afford to provide diagnostic information only to a subset of examinees. In fact, no previous study utilizing existing tests has achieved a classification rate of 100%. This means researchers will have to examine what factors contribute to unsuccessful classification. In this study, unsuccessful classification occurred when an examinee's test response pattern could not be categorized into any pre-specified knowledge states with an acceptable level of confidence ($p < 0.05$). As mentioned above, this was most likely due to incomplete extraction of attribute(s) (and, in turn, knowledge states) for examinees with relatively higher and relatively lower levels of ability. Conducting focused investigations into those examinees' cognition involved in reading comprehension, combined with multiple procedures for identifying and selecting attributes (as illustrated in Jang's (2009b) study), seems to be a potential solution. The problem, however, is that those post hoc procedures are inevitably influenced by the characteristics of specific test items as well as the theories and empirical findings that researchers consult with, and this is perhaps why researchers have had different sets of attributes for the same language skill assessed by similar tests. In this regard, this study was limited in that the analyses were based on an existing test (i.e., C. Test) and therefore encountered the same issues reported in previous studies (e.g., Buck et al. 1997; Jang 2009a, b).

An alternative, and probably better, solution to the above issues is to design and develop tests for the purpose of diagnostic assessment. This would involve specifying key attributes in the first place and developing test items accordingly. In this way, the influence of extraneous variables (e.g., attributes assessed by a very small number of test items) on examinee classification could be reduced. So far, little empirical effort has been made to examine the feasibility of this approach, and future research is in order.

In terms of participant sampling, the fact that our test takers were predominantly Asian tends to constrain the generalizability of the findings to all L2 Chinese learners. In this study, we made an effort to include all official test takers of a particular test administration; thus, our sample, in a realistic sense, did reflect the examinee population of the test. However, it is interesting to note that our examinees were classified into 39 of the 50 pre-specified knowledge states. While the variety of the knowledge states found among our examinees could be counted as evidence to support an argument that the findings are generalizable to a larger examinee population, whether the remaining 11 pre-specified knowledge states are more likely to be found among non-Asian learners of L2 Chinese would be an interesting question to explore in the future. Likewise, whether the overall classification rate as well as the (major) patterns of reading mastery would remain comparable for non-Asian examinees also awaits future research. Another interesting research topic is to examine whether there is any difference between heritage and non-heritage learners, given the differences in learning opportunities afforded by their respective learning environments.

Finally, because an important goal of diagnostic language assessment is to provide guidance for subsequent remedial teaching and learning, it is necessary to conduct follow-up studies to examine the usefulness of diagnostic information. With few exceptions (e.g., Jang 2009a), the field has yet to pay sufficient attention to this area.

References

Buck, G., & Tatsuoka, K. (1998). Application of the rule-space procedures to language testing: Examining attributes of a free response listening test. *Language Testing, 15*(2), 119–157.

Buck, G., Tatsuoka, K., & Kostin, I. (1997). The sub-skills of reading: Rule-space analysis of a multiple-choice test of second language reading comprehension. *Language Learning, 47*(3), 423–466.

China Educational Newspaper. (2009, September 30). International promotion of Chinese language and culture, p. 4 (中国教育报. (2009 年 9 月 30 日). 中国文化大规模走出国门。第 4 版。).

Gierl, M. J. (2007). Making diagnostic inferences about cognitive attributes using the Rule-Space Model and attribute hierarchy method. *Journal of Educational Measurement, 44*, 325–340.

Hambleton, R., Swaminathan, H., & Rogers, H. J. (1991). Fundamentals of item response theory. SAGA publications.

HSK Center. (2008). A collection of authentic C-Test administered in 2007. Beijing: Beijing Language and Culture University Press (北京语言大学汉语水平考试中心, 2008). 《C.Test 实用汉语水平认定考试 2008 年真题集》. 北京: 北京语言大学出版社).

Jang, E. E. (2009a). Cognitive diagnostic assessment of L2 reading comprehension ability: Validity arguments for Fusion Model application to LanguEdge assessment. *Language Testing, 26*(1), 31–73.

Jang, E. E. (2009b). Demystifying a Q-matrix for making diagnostic inferences about L2 reading skills. *Language Assessment Quarterly, 6,* 210–238.

Kim, A.-Y. (2015). Exploring ways to provide diagnostic feedback with an ESL placement test: Cognitive diagnostic assessment of L2 reading ability. *Language Testing, 32*(2), 227–258.

Lee, Y-W. (2015). Diagnosing diagnostic language assessment. *Language Testing, Special Issue,* 1–18.

Lee, Y.-W., & Sawaki, Y. (2009). Application of three cognitive diagnosis models to ESL reading and listening assessments. *Language Assessment Quarterly, 6,* 239–263.

Sawaki, Y., Kim, H.-J., & Gentile, C. (2009). Q-Matrix construction: Defining the link between constructs and test items in large-scale reading and listening comprehension assessments. *Language Assessment Quarterly, 6,* 190–209.

Tatsuoka, K. K. (1983). Rule space: An approach for dealing with misconceptions based on item response theory. *Journal of Educational Measurement, 20*(4), 345–354.

Tatsuoka, K. K. (1995). Architecture of knowledge structures and cognitive diagnosis: A statistical pattern recognition and classification approach. In P. D. Nichos, S. F. Chipman, & R. L. Brennan (Eds.), *Cognitively diagnostic assessment* (pp. 327–359). Hillsdale, NJ: Erlbaum.

Tatsuoka, K. K. (2009). Cognitive assessment: An introduction to the rule space method. Routledge.

Tatsuoka, K. K., & Tatsuoka, M. M. (1987). Bug distribution and pattern classification. *Psychometrika, 52*(2), 193–206.

Xu, L. (2006). It is a great good thing to accelerate the international promotion of Chinese language. Applied Linguistics, 6, 8–12 (许琳 (2006). 汉语加快走向世界是件大好事。《语言文字应用》, 2006 年6 月, 8-12 页。).

Chapter 10
Exploring the Relationship Between Raters' Personality Traits and Rating Severity in Writing Assessment of Chinese as a Second Language: A Pilot Study

Yu Zhu, Shui-Lung Fung, Shek-Kam Tse and Chi-Yi Hsieh

Abstract Subjective rating is a widely adopted practice in human assessment and measurement. Without a careful control of severity among raters in grading, both the validity and reliability of a subjective assessment will be subject to skepticism. Among many variables which may potentially impact raters' severity, raters' personality in recent years has caused concerns for many researchers. However, so far there is no study investigating such a potential relationship in the context of testing and assessing Chinese as a second language. To explore the relationship between raters' personality traits and rating severity in writing assessment of Chinese as a foreign language, master's degree students who majored in teaching of Chinese as a foreign language ($n = 28$) were asked to rate a writing test of the New HSK, a large-scale standardized test of Chinese proficiency promoted by the Chinese government. Valid data for FACETS analysis were the 28 raters' independent ratings of 77 examinees' 154 essays (2 topics) from the test. Each rater also completed NEO-PI-R, a fairly reliable personality inventory. Demographic variables such as age, gender, educational background, and rating experience, which may affect raters' severity in essay grading, were strictly controlled. The results of this pilot study showed individual differences in raters' severity and significant

Y. Zhu (✉)
Xiamen University, Xiamen, China
e-mail: zhuyu@xmu.edu.cn

S.-L. Fung
Beijing Normal University-Hong Kong Baptist University
United International College, Zhuhai, China

S.-K. Tse
The University of Hong Kong, Hong Kong, China

C.-Y. Hsieh
National Kaohsiung Normal University, Kaohsiung, Taiwan

© Springer Nature Singapore Pte Ltd. 2017
D. Zhang and C.-H. Lin (eds.), *Chinese as a Second Language Assessment*,
Chinese Language Learning Sciences, DOI 10.1007/978-981-10-4089-4_10

associations between raters' personality traits and their rating behavior in terms of severity. Findings of this study are expected to enrich our understanding of subjective rating behaviors of human assessment, especially in the field of testing and assessing Chinese as a second language.

Keywords Chinese as a second language · Writing assessment · Personality traits

Introduction

Writing is an indicator of language proficiency that keeps catching the attention of many language assessors. Although rating of compositions has long been found far more subjective than what we had thought (Gowen 1984; Jensen and DiTiberio 1989; Walter 1984), the investigation of rater effects[1] remains insufficient.

Many factors contribute to personal rater bias in the assessment of student writing. These include factors from outside sources of bias such as rater training, students' handwriting, students' personality types (Carrel 1995), as well as inner sources of raters' cognition effect such as prior experience of essay rating, teaching experience, and personality. Among these factors, raters' personality perhaps most profoundly reflects the underlying differences between human rating and machine rating of essays, and appears to be a very prominent source of variation among different raters' ratings for a particular essay from a particular writer. In the past decades, researchers have noticed and explored rater severity in relation to rater personality in many studies. These studies included those measuring the personality construct in terms of types (Branthwaite et al. 1981; Carrell 1995), as well as those examining personality as traits (Alaei et al. 2014; Bernardin et al. 2000; Bernardin et al. 2009). They, in general, confirmed a close relationship between raters' personality and rater effects (e.g., Kane et al. 1995; Tziner et al. 2002; Yun et al. 2005).

The existing literature, however, focused largely on assessment of writing in English. So far in the context of assessing writing in Chinese as a second language, no studies seemed to have investigated the influence of raters' personality, regardless the construct of personality being measured as types or traits, on rater effects. It is therefore interesting to examine whether or not the personality of raters is also correlated with rating severity in assessing writing in Chinese.

Furthermore, with regards to measurement of personality construct, Furnham et al. (2003) criticized using personality types as the indicator of personality. Their criticism included an unrealistic assumption of bimodal distribution of the measurement scores (Furnham 1996), an unreliable typological theory underlying the approach (Hicks 1984; Sticker and Ross 1964), and low construct validity of the

---

[1]Rater effects refer to a "broad category of effects [resulting in] systematic variance in performance ratings that is associated in some way with the rater and not with the actual performance of the ratee" (Scullen et al. 2000, p. 957, as cited in Myford and Wolfe 2003, p. 391).

type inventories (Saggino et al. 2001). In view of this criticism, the present study focused on personality traits rather than types when the personality construct was measured. Specifically, we adopted NEO-PI-R (Costa and McCrae 1992), the most popular personality traits inventory, to measure the personality traits of raters of Chinese essays. A more detailed comparison between trait and type approaches to the measurement of personality construct is included in the literature review section of this paper. For rater effects, we focused on rater severity as it is widely believed (Engelhard 1994) that rater severity, when more sophistically estimated under the framework of the Many-Facet Rasch modeling, is a more valid and reliable indicator of rater effects than raw score.

In summary, the current pilot study attempted to find out the relationship between raters' personality traits (as measured with NEO-PI-R) and their severity estimates (as measured with Many-Facet Rasch models) in rating essays written by foreign learners studying Chinese. It is hoped that this study will enrich our existing knowledge on rater effects, which has largely been established on the basis of research on assessment of English essay writing.

Literature Review

Rater Differences and Rating Processes

Earlier studies attributed the normally high unreliability in essay rating to such factors as marking speed, fatigue, academic competence, variations in the use of scales (Dunstan 1966), candidate characteristics (e.g., name, attractiveness, gender, handwriting, and presentation), order of marking (Wade 1978), ideological stance of the rater and that presented in the writing responses (Husbands 1976), individual approach to the task (Branthwaite et al. 1980), and differences in raters' background such as native language, training, and/or teaching experience (Lukmani 1996; Schoonen et al. 1997; Weigle 1994, 1998).

More recently, many researchers began to turn their attention to more underlying causes of variations in essay rating. For instance, some studies (Lukmani 1996; Milanovic et al. 1996; Pollitt and Murray 1996) explored rating processes so as to know how raters arrive at their ratings. Among them, the one particularly relevant to the focus of the present study is Pollitt and Murray (1996), whose study reported two contrastive approaches of essay marking they found. One was the so-called synthetic approach, which uses some aspects of the written work as a primary indicator of a writer's level, and relies heavily on a few first impressions of the essay; the other one was a more evidence-based approach, in which raters limit their comments to explicitly exhibited writing competence and weakness, and sum them up to make a final judgment of the writing quality of a particular ratee. Although Pollitt and Murray (1996) did not make it clear which factor(s) affect(s) raters' choice of the two rating approaches, it seems reasonable to consider their personality as a possible candidate.

Personality Traits and Personality Types

Personality types and personality traits are the two most popular approaches in measuring personality constructs, with the former being more widely applied in contexts of consulting and business training and the latter more frequently used for academic research purposes (Furnham et al. 2003). Table 10.1 summarizes the major distinctions between the two approaches with their representative inventories: Myers-Briggs Type Indicator (MBTI) for the type approach and Revised NEO-Personality Inventory (NEO-PI-R) for the trait approach.

It can be drawn from Table 10.1 that the NEO-PI-R seems like a more sophisticated measure of personality considering the number of items included in the inventory and the data type produced by the inventory. This strengthens our preference for using the NEO-PI-R inventory in this study as stated in the Introduction section of this paper. This preference, however, does not imply that relevant studies applying the types approach to personality do not deserve any attention in this study. As a matter of fact, researchers in recent years have found several connections between the two measurements of personality construct. For instance, McCrae and Costa (1989) re-explained personality type indicators and found that: (a) Extraversion in the NEO-PI-R was correlated positively with MBTI Extraversion-Introversion; (b) Openness was negatively correlated with sensing and

Table 10.1 Major distinctions between MBTI and NEO-PI-R

Inventory	MBTI	NEO-PI-R
Approach	Type approach	trait Approach
Year of the latest version	1985	1992
Author	Myers and McCaulley	Costa and McCrae
Underlying theory	Jung's theory of personality types	Five-Factor Model (FFM)
Dimensions	Extraversion-Introversion (E/I), Sensing-Intuition (S/N) Thinking-Feeling (T/F) Judgment-Perception (J/P).	Neuroticism Extraversion Openness Agreeableness Conscientiousness
Number of items	94	240
Output data type	Discrete data, one representative letter from each of the four dimensions, 16 possible results in total (e.g., ESTJ, ENTP.)	Continuous data (interval level), for each of the five dimensions and each of the six facets within each dimension
Data analysis	ANOVA, T-test	Regression, correlation, ANOVA, T-Test, etc.
Popular applications	Counseling, business training	Academic research

positively correlated with intuition; (c) Agreeableness was negatively correlated with thinking and positively correlated with feeling; and (d) Conscientiousness was positively correlated with judging and negatively correlated with perceiving. With 900 British participants, Furnham et al. (2003) also investigated the relationship between the NEO-PI-R and the MBTI, and the results verified the above findings in McCrae and Costa (1989). The type approach was used more frequently in earlier studies, whereas the trait approach has been more widely adopted in recent studies. Following is a brief review of empirical studies on the type and trait approaches.

Personality Types and Writing Assessment

Using the type approach to personality construct, the study conducted by Branthwaite et al. (1981) failed to find significant correlations between raters' personality, as measured by Eysenck Personality Questionnaire (Eysenck and Eysenck 1975), and the marks that they assigned for students' writings, except for the lie scale ($r = 0.70$, $p \leq 0.01$). Since the lie scale lacks a definitive interpretation because of insufficient knowledge about it (Eysenck and Eysenck 1975), Branthwaite et al. (1981) unfortunately were unable to provide a reasonable explanation for their findings.

Carrell (1995) was one of the pioneering researchers who empirically explored how raters' personality types, as well as those of students, as measured by the Myers-Briggs Type Indicator (Myers 1962, 1987; Myers and McCaulley 1985), affected 16 raters' ratings of the 90 essays written by 45 native speakers of English in a college in the USA. Consistent with his hypotheses, he found that: (a) Raters with the personality type as intuitive tend to rate essays lower than those with the personality type as sensing; (b) raters with the personality type as feeling tend to score essays higher than those with the personality types as thinking; (c) narrative essays written by introverts or the feeling types and rated by extroverts or the sensing or judging types tend to be the most highly rated; and (d) argumentative compositions rated by introverts, the sensing, feeling, or perceiving types, and written by students with the personality type as introverts tend to be rated the highest. Carrell's (1995) findings evidenced the existence of a relationship between essay ratings and personality types of both the rater and the writer.

Personality Traits and Writing Assessment

For studies examining the effects of raters' personality traits on ratings of writing samples, Agreeableness was frequently found to have a significantly positive relationship with ratings, and Conscientiousness was in general reported as a significant personality trait that negatively correlated with raters' ratings. For example, using NEO-FFI, a shortened version of NEO-PI-R developed by Costa and McCrae (1992),

Bernardin et al. (2000) found that Conscientiousness (C) scores were negatively correlated with rating leniency, and that Agreeableness (A) scores were positively correlated with rating leniency. Further, it was found that raters with low C but high A scores rated most leniently. To examine whether Agreeableness (A) and Conscientiousness (C) were correlated with rating accuracy and rating level in a low rater accountability situation, Bernardin et al. (2009) asked 126 students to give peer ratings after they took part in several group exercises.[2] The results basically confirmed Bernardin's (2000) findings in that A scores positively correlated with the average rating level[3] of the written responses and negatively correlated with measures of rating accuracy, whereas C scores had a negative correlation with rating level and a positive correlation with measures of rating accuracy.[4] More agreeable but less conscientious raters had the lowest severity and most inaccurate ratings.

Alaei et al. (2014) intended to find out whether or not genre plays a role in the relationship between raters' personality and holistic rating. They were also interested in examining the relationship between rater personality and analytic rating. Pearson's correlation analyses of the data from 31 raters and 16 essays, with four essays for each of the four genres (namely, cause/effect, descriptive, opinion [advantage/disadvantage], and argumentative), showed that raters' personality did not correlate with holistic rating regardless of the genre of the essays being rated. But for analytic rating, they did find two strong and statistically significant correlations, namely a positive relationship between Agreeableness and content score ($r = 0.787$, $p = 0.018$), as well as a positive relationship between Conscientiousness and vocabulary score ($r = 0.889$, $p = 0.003$).

Besides Agreeableness and Conscientiousness, Impulsivity was also reported as a personality trait affecting rating, though evidence supporting this was largely obtained from studies in the context of psychological measurement rather than writing assessment. One such study was conducted by Miller et al. (2011), where considerably large variance in scores of particular facets of the scale Psychopathy Checklist-Revised (henceforth PCL-R)[5] was found contributable to raters' personality traits. More specifically, relatively more agreeable raters tended to assign

---

[2]The exercises were six scenarios about human resource management. Each student was randomly assigned to a group to do a particular exercise. They had to prepare a written response before class and complete peer rating of their group members' responses during the class.

[3]The rating scale had seven levels ranging from 1 (poor) to 7 (excellent).

[4]Two measures of rating accuracy were used in the study. One was correlational accuracy which was determined by the correlations between the peer ratings and the expert ratings (i.e., ratings given by the professor and his doctoral student), and the other one was mean absolute difference which measured the difference between the peer ratings and the expert ratings. For detailed information, please refer to Bernardin et al. (2009, pp. 304–305).

[5]According to Wikipedia (Retrieved October 10, 2015, from https://en.wikipedia.org/wiki/Psychopathy_Checklist), "Psychopathy Checklist-Revised (PCL-R) is a psychological assessment tool used to assess the presence of psychopathy in individuals. It is a 20-item inventory of perceived personality traits and recorded behaviors, intended to be completed on the basis of a semi-structured interview along with a review of 'collateral information' such as official records."

lower scores on the PCL-R interpersonal facet. In addition, raters who were tender-minded showed a tendency to underestimate offenders' actual level of impulsive lifestyle on the scale, so did raters, who were classified as more excitement-seeking. On the other hand, raters who were less impulsive appeared to assign higher scores to offenders on the PCL-R impulsive life facet. Unexpectedly to some extent, raters who were more impulsive overestimated offenders' tendency of antisocial behavior.

Hypotheses

Based on the previous findings presented above, the following hypotheses for this study were proposed. Since Extraversion in NEO-PI-R positively correlates with Extraversion in MBTI (Furnham et al. 2003; McCrae and Costa 1989), and extroverts tend to rate argumentative essays lower (Carrell 1995), it would be logical to hypothesize that more extroversive raters in this study would exhibit a higher level of severity in essay rating (Hypothesis 1).

Because Agreeableness in NEO-PI-R has a positive association with feeling in MBTI, and feeling type raters have been found more lenient than those of the thinking type (Carrell 1995), it would be expected that Agreeableness would be negatively correlated with rating severity (Hypothesis 2). Although this hypothesis had been supported by previous studies in the context of assessing writing in English (Alaei et al. 2014; Bernardin et al. 2000, 2009), it is interesting to test it in the context of writing test in Chinese.

Miller et al. (2011) had reported that raters with a higher level of Impulsivity overestimated the level of impulsivity of their ratees. To be consistent, one would expect impulsive raters would be more severe in rating Chinese essays in this study (Hypothesis 3).

As Openness in NEO-PI-R has a positive relationship with intuitive in MBTI, and intuitive type raters have a tendency to assign lower scores, one would anticipate that raters with a higher level of Openness would be more severe in essay rating (Hypothesis 4).

Finally, although Conscientiousness was found to be negatively correlated with leniency in holistic ratings (Bernardin et al. 2000, 2009), it was found insignificant in holistic ratings but significant in analytic rating (i.e., positively correlated with vocabulary ratings of essays) in Alaei et al. (2014). Given the inconsistent findings in previous studies, a null hypothesis was made for Conscientiousness, which states that conscientiousness was not correlated with severity in ratings of essays written in Chinese by foreign learners (Hypothesis 5).

Method

Participants

Participants of this study were master's degree students majoring in Teaching Chinese as a Foreign Language (TCFL) at a key university in China. A study of the validity and reliability of the Chinese version of NEO-PI-R (Dai et al. 2004) suggested that for a Chinese population, the scores of NEO-PI-R were influenced significantly by demographic variables such as gender, age, and education. To reduce the complexity of research design, gender, age, and education were all controlled. In that university, there were 32 third-semester TCFL master's degree students in total. Except three foreign students and one male Chinese student, the rest of the 28 students were all female, native Chinese speakers. All of these 28 students agreed to participate in this study; their ages were between 21 and 23 years. None of the participants had any prior writing evaluation experience on any large-scale writing tests. They were randomly assigned into three groups of 10, 9, and 9 people.

Materials

Essays

The writing test of the New HSK[6] is a 40-min test consisting of three parts. The first part has eight items, each of which provides a number of jumbled words for which examinees are asked to place them in an order that makes a meaningful sentence. The total score for this part is 24, with three points for each item. The second part is essay writing based on five given keywords. The third part is essay writing based on a given picture. Both parts 2 and 3 require examinees to write an essay in Chinese with a minimum length of 80 characters. For these two parts, the full score is 21. For the purpose of the present study, a simulated writing test was specifically designed following the format and specifications of parts 2 and 3 of the New HSK Level 5 writing test.

A total of 111 foreign students studying intermediate-level Chinese at a top university in China took the simulated writing test, which consisted of two argumentative writing tasks, one on success and endeavor and the other about urban

---

[6]The New HSK (Hanyu Shuiping Kaoshi or Chinese Proficiency Test) is China's national test for non-native speakers of Chinese. It is a large-scale standardized test promulgated by Hanban (Office of Chinese Language Council International) both domestically in China and outside of China. The New HSK has six levels. The writing test under discussion here refers to that of Level 5. For detailed information about the New HSK, please refer to Teng (this volume) or the website of Hanban (http://english.hanban.org/node_8002.htm).

Table 10.2 Distribution of the 15 benchmark samples

Overall score	Number of benchmark sample(s)
0	1
1	2
2	3
3	4
4	3
5	2

traffic. All of the finished essays were first rated, using the rating scale described in detail in the next part, by four experienced full-time teachers who had been teaching Chinese as a foreign language in the university for over five years. Three of them were females and one was male. Two of them had a Ph.D. degree, one in Chinese linguistics and the other in education of Chinese as a foreign language. The other two had a master's degree in Chinese language and literature. Fifteen essays were purposefully selected as benchmark samples for the marking criteria. To be selected as a benchmark sample, an essay must have received exactly the same rating from at least three of the four experienced teachers. The distribution of the 15 samples among the 6 possible general scores is summarized in Table 10.2.

The essays of the 96 students (out of 111) which were not selected as benchmark samples were divided into three equivalent groups in term of the overall quality of the writings.[7] The groups were formed following the procedure demonstrated in Fig. 10.1.

The Essay Rating Scale

The essay rating scale for the present study was very similar to the actual one for the New HSK Level 5. According to the scale, each essay receives three scores with one for overall quality, one for grammar, and one for vocabulary.[8] The overall score contains 6 levels ranging from 0 to 5, and the score for both grammar and vocabulary has 3 levels ranging from 1 to 3. Each level has a unique description for all three rating criteria. For each essay, raters are required to first assign an overall score based on descriptions that best match the overall quality of the essay. Then, within that overall level, raters need to determine which level suits the examinee's writing performance in grammar and in vocabulary, based on the descriptions of levels for grammar and vocabulary within that overall level.

---

[7]The actual number of students included in the FACETS analyses was 77 due to missing responses from either the students or the raters.

[8]Note that although the 15 benchmark samples were selected using the overall scores only, the raters' severity discussed here was based on analyses of all the three scores for each essay by the FACET program.

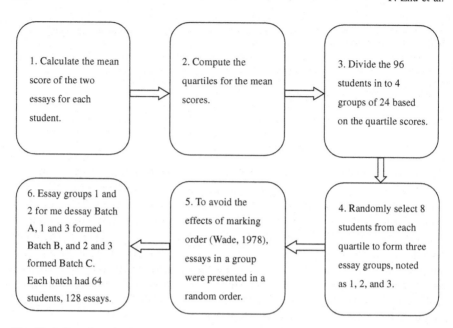

Fig. 10. 1 Procedure for forming essay groups and batches

NEO-PI-R

The NEO-PI-R is a 240-item instrument based on the Five-Factor Model of personality. It contains five domains, namely Neuroticism, Extraversion, Openness, Agreeableness, and Conscientiousness. There are 6 facets in each domain and each facet has 8 items. Each item uses a 5-point scale ranging from strongly disagrees to strongly agrees (Costa and McCrae 1992). A facet score was the total score of the eight items within a particular facet. A domain score was the total score of the 6 facets within a particular domain. The reliability of the inventory for the developmental sample was 0.86–0.95 for domain scales and 0.56–0.81 for facet scales (Costa and McCrae 1992). NEO-PI-R has been widely adopted and translated into many languages. A Chinese version of the English NEO-PI-R as used in Yang et al. (1999) was applied in this study. This Chinese version of NEO-PI-R was previously administrated to a Chinese sample of 909 normal subjects aged 21–81 years old (Dai et al. 2004). The alpha coefficients were from 0.77 (Agreeableness) to 0.92 (Neuroticism). The factor analysis also clearly verified the theoretical validity of the inventory.

Procedure

Administration of NEO-PI-R

The 28 raters were administered the NEO-PI-R (Chinese version) (Dai et al. 2004). None of them had responded to this personality inventory before, and they all had strong interests to know the result of their personality. Therefore, each of them put his/her name on the inventory. This provided convenience for later data analysis and also helped us provide feedback to the raters if there was a request from them. Although the inventory was done in a non-anonymous manner, the raters were still assured confidentiality. The administration of NEO-PI-R took about 40 min, and most of the raters finished in around 30 min.

Brief Training of Raters

None of the raters in this study ever participated in rating essays for any large-scale writing tests. To familiarize the raters with the rating scale, 15 essays were carefully chosen as benchmark samples for a training session for them (refer to essays in the materials part above for how the benchmark samples were established). The brief training lasted for two hours, including introducing the rating scale, explaining the scale as requested, first round of rating and discussion for six randomly selected benchmark essays (one essay for each possible overall score from 0 to 5), second round of rating and discussion for five randomly selected benchmark essays (one essay for an overall score from 1 to 5), and third round of rating and discussion for the four remaining benchmark essays (one essay for an overall score of 2 and 4 each, and the last two essays for a general score of 3).

Independent Rating of Student Essays

As indicated earlier, the 28 raters were divided into three groups with 10, 9, and 9 raters in Groups 1, 2, and 3, respectively. Each rater in Group 1 was assigned a copy of essay Batch A. Those in Groups 2 and 3 were each assigned a copy of Batch B and C, respectively. The raters independently finished their rating task in a central rating situation. The rating lasted for two hours.

Inter-rater Reliability

The FACETS output reported that the inter-rater reliability of the present study was 52.9%, a percentage much higher than the expected level (i.e., 35.9% as estimated by the Rasch model). This large deviation from the expectation implies that the raters in the present study agreed with each other very well, or the rater training was effective to allow more homogeneous ratings among raters.

Analyses and Findings

Many-Facet Rasch Modeling and the FACETS Program

Many-Facet Rasch modeling is an extension of simple one facet Rasch model to address the complexities in many realistic measurement contexts. Facet refers to any effects in the assessment context that may cause major concerns and/or systematic measurement error (Myford and Wolfe 2003). For example, in assessing writing, examinees, raters, writing tasks, rating items, each can become a facet in a Rasch measurement model to account for ratings of an essay.

The Rasch modeling of the present study was performed with the FACETS, which is a Windows-based software that facilitates multi-faceted Rasch model analyses, especially in the field of subjective assessments (Linacre 2014). Rater severity was estimated in the unit of logit. Ideally, these logit estimates conform to a normal distribution with a mean of 0, exactly the same as the mean of examinees' abilities. In that case, it can be concluded that raters' ratings are in general appropriate for the ability levels of the examinees. As rater facet is set with a negative sign in the model, the higher a value in the rater facet, the more severe a rater would be.

The "Table 6.0 All Facet Vertical Rulers" in the original FACETS output illustrates how rater severity is distributed in reference to examinees' writing ability. It can be drawn from the table that rater severity in general is much higher than examinees' writing severity. Meanwhile, rater severity roughly fits a normal distribution, with a mean slightly higher than positive one instead of zero.

The facets included in the Many-Facet Rasch model for the present study are examinee ability (77 elements, i.e., the 77 examinees), rater severity (28 elements, i.e., the 28 raters), session difference (3 elements),[9] essay difficulty (2 elements, i.e., the two topics), as well as item difficulty (3 elements, i.e., overall rating, rating of grammar, and rating of vocabulary). The bias examined included interactions between rater and session, rater and essay, and rater and item. The output of FACET software reports subset connection OK. The estimation was successful in general with the mean residual and the mean standardized residual to be 0.0 and 0.01, respectively, and the standard deviation of the standardized residual to be 1.02. The variance explained by the Rasch model was 46.8% (a usual amount is around 40%, according to Linacre, 2012). In summary, the data generally fit the model.

---

[9]Since each rater rated 128 essays from 64 students, it is interesting to find out whether or not raters assign ratings in different patterns across time. For this reason, session as a facet was introduced into the model. Specifically, session 1 included essays ratings for the first 21 students in each group, while session 2 included ratings for the second 21 students, and session 3 included ratings for the remaining 22 students.

Summary of Raters' Personality Traits

Each facet of the NEO-PI-R contains eight items, with each measured on a 5-point Likert scale. So each facet has a total score in the range of 8–40. In general, low scorers of a particular facet possess fewer properties of a given personality trait than high scorers. For example, low scorers of the anxiety (N1) facet tend to be calm and relaxed, while high scorers are more likely to be "shy, fearful, nervous, tensed and restless" (Costa and McCrae 2008).

The reliability of the inventory for the sample of this present study ranged from 0.726 (Agreeableness) to 0.860 (Conscientiousness) for domain scales and from 0.464 (Warmth/E1) to 0.844 (Competence/C1) for facet scales, except for the facets of Self-consciousness/N4, Feelings/O3, and Values/O6. It is clear that the reliability of the measurement of personality traits at the domain level was quite acceptable. And the majority (90%, or 27 out of 30) of the measurements of personality traits were also very reliable at the facet level. It is hard to tell, however, why the reliability of the facets of Self-consciousness/N4, Feelings/O3, and Values/O6 was unexpectedly low. Table 10.3 summarizes the reliability and the descriptive

Table 10.3 Reliability of the NEO-PI-R and descriptive statistics of personality traits

Personality traits	Mean	S.D.	Reliability
Anxiety (N1)	15.5	4.0	0.709
Angry/Hostility (N2)	11.8	3.7	0.664
Depression (N3)	13.8	5.0	0.853
Self-consciousness (N4)	16.0	2.9	0.278*
Impulsivity (N5)	14.8	3.4	0.557
Vulnerability (N6)	13.6	3.8	0.754
Neuroticism (N)	85.3	16.7	0.813
Warmth (E1)	22.9	2.7	0.464
Gregariousness (E2)	18.5	4.2	0.781
Assertiveness (E3)	15.3	3.8	0.645
Activity (E4)	15.2	4.0	0.786
Excitement-seeking (E5)	15.1	3.7	0.472
Positive emotions (E6)	21.6	4.1	0.676
Extraversion (E)	108.5	17.0	0.844
Fantasy (O1)	17.9	4.2	0.713
Aesthetics (O2)	23.3	3.7	0.735
Feelings (O3)	21.3	2.9	0.369*
Actions (O4)	16.3	3.8	0.727
Ideas (O5)	18.0	4.5	0.820
Values (O6)	23.8	2.2	0.184*
Openness (O)	120.5	14.2	0.730

(continued)

Table 10.3 (continued)

Personality traits	Mean	S.D.	Reliability
Trust (A1)	22.5	3.3	0.792
Straightforwardness (A2)	21.5	3.6	0.606
Altruism (A3)	22.0	2.4	0.357*
Compliance (A4)	18.3	4.3	0.715
Modesty (A5)	17.9	3.3	0.565
Tender-mindedness (A6)	23.2	3.1	0.490
Agreeableness (A)	125.3	13.2	0.726
Competence (C1)	19.2	4.3	0.844
Order (C2)	19.1	3.6	0.601
Dutifulness (C3)	21.8	3.2	0.601
Achievement striving (C4)	18.3	3.9	0.793
Self-discipline (C5)	19.1	3.6	0.673
Deliberation (C6)	19.1	3.7	0.729
Conscientiousness (C)	116.5	17.2	0.860

Note A symbol of * in the table indicates a reliability which is unexpectedly low

statistics of the various domains and facets of NEO-PI-R, or personality traits, based on the present sample of 28 raters.

Summary of Raters' Severity

Raters' severity was estimated in this study with FACETS (Many-Facet Rasch Measurement) version 3.71.4. The estimates of the raters' severity ranged from 0.61 to 1.56, with a mean of 1.045 and standard deviation of 0.229. Out of the 28 raters, only 10 of them had a severity lower than 1, and none of them had a severity lower than 0.

Correlation Between Raters' Personality Traits and Severity

In order to investigate whether or not a relationship existed between facets of personality and severity of the raters, a correlation analysis was conducted and the significant findings are summarized in Table 10.4. Note that the correlations without an asterisk sign were marginally significant, with a p value between 0.05 and 0.1.

In addition, at the domain level, a significant negative correlation was found between severity and Agreeableness ($r = -0.383$, $p = 0.044$), and a marginally significant positive correlation was found between severity and Extraversion ($r = 0.365$, $p = 0.056$).

Table 10.4 Statistically significant correlations between raters' severity and facets of personality traits ($n = 28$)

	Straightforwardness (A2)	Impulsivity (N5)	Gregariousness (E2)	Assertiveness (E3)	Positive emotions (E6)
Pearson correlation	−0.402*	0.393*	0.354	0.367	0.348
Significance (2-tailed)	0.034	0.038	0.064	0.054	0.07

*p value which is smaller than 0.05

Predictability of Raters' Personality Traits on Their Severity

To examine if any facets or combinations of facets of personality traits can predict severity, the best subset method[10] of automatic linear modeling, with AICC[11] as the model selection criteria and all of the 30 facets as candidate predictors of severity, was performed with IBM SPSS 20 and the results follow. Only 2 of the 30 facets were found to be significant predictors. Specifically, the coefficient of straightforwardness in the model was significant at the 0.05 level ($p = 0.026$, $n = 28$, 2-tailed significance test), and the coefficient of positive emotion was marginally significant ($p = 0.051$, $n = 28$, 2-tailed significance test). The adjusted R square for this model is 0.225.

$$\text{Severity} = -0.026 \cdot \text{A2(i.e., Straightforwardness)} + 0.02 \\ \cdot \text{E6(i.e., Positive Emotions)}$$

We also used the five domains of personality traits as candidates of predictors of severity and performed the best subset linear regression procedure with IBM SPSS 20. The linear model that best explained the data is reported as the following, with the coefficient of Extraversion significant at the 0.001 level ($p = 0.000$, $n = 26$,[12] 2-tailed significance test). The adjusted R square for this model is 0.382.

$$\text{Severity} = 0.012 \cdot \text{Extraversion}$$

---

[10]Best subset method tries to build all the possible models when given N candidate predictors/variables and then applies a particular criterion to compare and select the best model among all the possible models.

[11]AICC stands for Akaike Information Criterion with a correction for finite sample sizes. More detailed comparisons between AICC and other model selection methods can be browsed at https://en.wikipedia.org/wiki/Akaike_information_criterion#AICc. Generally speaking, AICC is at least equivalent to, if not better than the other commonly used model selection methods. More specifically, a smaller AICC value usually indicates a better linear regression model.

[12]Raters number 14 and 27 were identified as outliers and deleted from the analysis because their Cook's d were unusually large.

Discussion

For correlation analyses, this study found that facets of Gregariousness (E2), Assertiveness (E3), Positive Emotions (E6), and Impulsivity (N5) were all positively correlated with severity, while the Straightforwardness (A2) facet was found to be negatively associated with severity. In terms of domains, Extraversion and severity had a significant positive correlation, but the relationship between Agreeableness and severity was found to be significantly negative.

In regression analysis at the facet level, straightforwardness (A2) and positive emotions (E6) were found to be the only two significant predictors of severity, with the former having a negative coefficient and the latter a positive one. Extraversion was the sole significant predictor of severity among the personality traits at the domain level. It had a positive coefficient in the regression model.

Table 10.5 summarizes the hypotheses and key findings of the present study. These findings in general supported hypotheses 1 (Extraversion positively associated with severity), 2 (Agreeableness negatively correlated with severity), 3 (Impulsivity had a positive relationship with severity), and 5 (Conscientiousness

Table 10.5 Summary of the hypotheses and statistically significant findings

Hypothesis	Content	Findings in correlation analysis	Findings in regression analysis
1	Extraversion positively associated with severity.	(1) Gregariousness/E2, assertiveness/E3, and positive emotions/E6; or three out of the six facets of Extraversion, had a significantly positive correlation with severity; (2) Extraversion, as a domain, was also positively correlated with severity	(1) Positive emotions/E6 significantly and positively predicted severity; (2) Extraversion was the sole significant predictor of severity, in a positive direction and at the domain level
2	Agreeableness negatively correlated with severity	One facet of Agreeableness (i.e., straightforwardness/A2) had a significantly negative correlation with severity	Straightforwardness/A2 (with a negative coefficient) was a significant predictor of severity
3	Impulsivity has a positive relationship with severity	Confirmed	Not confirmed
4 5	Openness has a positive relationship with severity Conscientiousness has no relationship with severity	Not confirmed. Confirmed	Not confirmed. Confirmed

has no relationship with severity) in the present study. In what follows, we discuss the relationships confirmed in these hypotheses. We did not find any evidence for hypothesis 4 (Openness being positively associated with severity). The reason for the lack of evidence for a significant relationship between openness and rating severity did not seem clear to us at this moment. Instead of denying the existence of such a relationship, we would call for more studies in the future.

It has long been noticed that Extraversion as a personality type possibly affects essay rating. The exact effect of extraversion, however, seemed inconclusive. For example, Jensen and DiTiberio (1989) suggested that extraverts as raters would have a tendency to rate essays more intuitively as compared to their peers with a personality type of sensing, thus would exhibit more severity. On the other hand, Carrel (1995) reported that extraverts might not necessarily be low scorers (i.e., more severity) and the relationship between Extraversion and rating severity may depend on or be moderated by the specific situation of essay rating, such as characteristics of the essay (for example, being narrative or argumentative genre). More specifically, he noticed that when rating narrative essays, more extroversive raters tend to be relatively more lenient, but they appear to be rather severe when rating argumentative essays.

The two writing tasks in this study turned out to be more argumentative than narrative, with one discussing success and endeavor, and the other talking about urban traffic. Therefore, we would expect more extroversive raters to be more severe and more introversive raters to be more lenient in their ratings, thus the positive relationship found between severity and Extraversion does not seem surprising. Consequently, it also seems reasonable that positive emotions, being one of the strongest indexes of extraversion (Costa and McCrae 1980), positively predicted rater severity in this study. On the other hand, an interpretation of such a finding might not be so apparent given how the facet of positive emotions is defined in NEO-PI-R. According to Costa and McCrae (2008), the facet of positive emotions "assesses the tendency to experience positive emotions such as joy, happiness, love, and excitement. High scorers on the Positive Emotions scale laugh easily and often. They are cheerful and optimistic" (p. 9). It seems very natural to infer from this definition that raters with more positive emotions would rate more leniently instead of more severely. Obviously, more research is necessary for a better understanding or interpretation of how positive emotions and rating severity are related.

Besides positive emotions, the current study also found two other facets of Extraversion to be positively associated with rating severity, namely assertiveness and gregariousness. It seems relatively easy to understand why high scorers on the assertiveness scale tend to be more severe raters, because they are usually "dominant, forceful, and socially ascendant. They speak without hesitation and often become group leaders" (Costa and McCrae 2008, p. 8). More assertive raters would tend to be more self-centered and thus rate the essays lower especially when the ratees' writing performances did not meet their expectation, which is quite likely in the situation of writing in a foreign language. It does not seem hard either to imagine why the more gregarious the more severe a rater would be. More gregarious raters would not like their ratings to be outstanding when compared with ratings from other raters. Perhaps the most reliable approach to avoiding one's ratings being outliers in the group would be to rate essays strictly following the rating scale. As writing in Chinese is known to be a difficult task for most foreign learners, it would be more or less safe to rate a foreigner's essay more severely than more leniently.

Because Agreeableness in NEO-PI-R has been proven to be positively correlated with feeling in MBTI (Furnham et al. 2003; McCrae and Costa 1989), more agreeable raters in our study were thus expected to act like raters with the personality type of feeling in Carrell (1995), tending to assign higher scores or be less severe than less agreeable ones when rating student essays. Our expectation above was supported by the fact that Straightforwardness (A2) was correlated with and predicted severity in a negative direction. On the other hand, the explanation of such a finding may still remain unclear or even counter intuitive to an extent. For example, individuals with a high level of straightforwardness are frank, sincere, and ingenuous, but why these characteristics would lead to severe ratings is still hard to tell. Costa and McCrae (2008) stated that adjectives associated with low scores in this scale of "straightforwardness" include "despotic". Perhaps raters with a low level in this facet tend to consider themselves as authorities and abuse that power in an unfair manner when rating essays. Thus, the lower the level of straightforwardness the raters are the more severe their ratings tend to be.

Raters with a higher level of Impulsivity are more "irritable", "sarcastic", and "hasty" (Costa and McCrae 2008), and thus tend to assign lower scores than their peers who are less impulsive (Miller et al. 2011). In other words, persons with a higher level of Impulsivity appear to be more severe. Therefore, it seems reasonable that more impulsive raters in this study tended to assign lower scores (i.e., more severe) to essays written by learners of Chinese as a foreign language, because writings of foreigners normally are full of grammatical errors, misused words, lack of cohesion, and coherence.

Our findings also confirmed the null hypothesis about the relationship between Conscientiousness and severity. Although this finding seems to agree with Alaei et al. (2014), so far we could not offer a reasonable explanation as to why this finding does not agree with what was found about Conscientiousness by Bernardin et al. (2000, 2009).

In summary, the present study confirmed the significant relationships between (some facets/domains of) personality traits and severity as found in previous studies. To our knowledge, it confirmed for the first time that the previous findings (especially the relationships between Extraversion, Agreeableness, Impulsivity, and severity) could be generalizable to writing assessment of Chinese as a foreign language. To particularly note, the Rasch measurement applied in the study permitted a reliable examination of the relationships between raters' personality traits and rating severity, including not only their basic bivariate correlations but also regression analyses that modeled how the latter was predicted by the former. The results of the regression analyses, in particular, revealed explicitly which facet (s)/domain(s) could be a valid predictor(s) of rating severity. The findings obviously have implications for rater training or research in the future on personality traits and rating severity. For example, on the basis that straightforwardness (A2) and positive emotions (E6) were the only valid facet level predictors of severity, one might shorten the original 240-item NEO-PI-R inventory into a much shorter 16-item scale with only the items for the A2 and E6 facets, thus creating logistic convenience yet with the predictability of the NEO-PI-R maintained. In other words, this could improve the feasibility of administering NEO-PI-R for rater selection and/or training in a context of large-scale essay rating.

Limitations and Further Research

The present study was admittedly exploratory. The results were based on 28 raters' scoring of 77 students' 154 essays written in Chinese. The raters were all female native Chinese graduate students in the third semester of their study in a master program of TCFL at a Chinese university, and none of them had had any prior experience as raters for any large-scale writing assessments. Though it created an advantage in research design of this study in terms of controlling any effects of those factors that might also have an influence on rating severity (e.g., age, education, gender, prior experience), the homogeneous sampling limited the generalizability of the findings. Unless there is further supportive evidence in the future, we would be cautious about any direct application of the findings here to real writing assessment situations, especially high-stakes writing assessments. In the future, mixed methods studies could be done to investigate whether or not positive emotions are positively correlated with severity and why or why not. More diverse samples of raters that better represent those in real scoring situations should be investigated. Also, individualized training of raters based on the relationship between severity and particular personality traits could be developed and its effects on essay rating carefully examined.

The implications of this study are most relevant to the rating practice in writing assessments. In particular, it highlights the importance of assessing raters' personality before actual rating sessions begin. More specifically, it sheds lights on the importance of individualized rater training; its application in online rater training could be very promising. Nowadays, uniform rater training pervades. However, in view of the findings of the present study (and those of previous studies where rater effects were reported), it seems more desirable to conduct individualized rater training based on information about raters' personality; in other words, using the relationship between rating bias and raters' personality as the basis for individualized rater training would likely generate a better training effect in a more efficient way. For instance, if we know some raters are more subject to lenient rating due to their personality characteristics, we could individualize our training materials as well as training strategies to better suit these raters' training needs.

Acknowledgments   This study was supported by the Fundamental Research Funds for the Central Universities 0190-ZK1008.

References

Alaei, M. M., Ahmadi, M., & Zadeh, N. S. (2014). The impact of rater's personality traits on holistic and analytic scores: Does genre make any difference too? *Procedia—Social and Behavioral Sciences, 98,* 1240–1248.

Bernardin, H. J., Cooke, D. K., & Villanova, P. (2000). Conscientiousness and agreeableness as predictors of rating leniency. *The Journal of Applied Psychology, 85*(2), 6–232.

Bernardin, H. J., Tyler, C. L., & Villanova, P. (2009). Rating level and accuracy as a function of rater personality. *International Journal of Selection and Assessment, 17*(3), 300–310.

Branthwaite, A., Trueman, M., & Berrisford, T. (1981). Unreliability of marking: Further evidence and a possible explanation. *Education Review, 33,* 41–46.

Branthwaite, A., Trueman, M., & Hartley, J. (1980). Writing essays: The actions and strategies of students. In J. Hartley (Ed.), *The psychology of writing* (pp. 98–109). London: Nichols Publishing.

Carrell, P. L. (1995). The effect of writers' personalities and raters' personalities on the holistic evaluation of writing. *Assessing Writing, 2*(2), 153–190.

Costa, P. T., Jr., & McCrae, R. R. (1980). Still stable after all these years: Personality as a key to some issues in adulthood and old age. In P. B. Baltes & O. G. Brim Jr. (Eds.), *Life span development and behavior* (Vol. 3, pp. 65–102). New York: Academic Press.

Costa, P. T., Jr., & McCrae, R. R. (1992). *Revised NEO Personality Inventory (NEO-PI-R) and NEO Five-Factor Inventory (NEO-FFI) professional manual.* Odessa, FL: Psychological Assessment Resources.

Costa, P. T., Jr., & McCrae, R. R. (2008). The revised NEO personality inventory (NEO-PI-R). In G. Boyle, G. Matthews, & D. Saklofske (Eds.), *The SAGE handbook of personality theory and assessment—Personality measurement and testing* (Vol. 2, pp. 179–199). London: SAGE Publications Ltd.

Dai, X., Yao, S., Cai, T., & Yang, J. (2004). Reliability and validity of the NEO-PI R in mainland China. *Chinese Mental Health Journal, 18*(2), 171–175.

Dunstan, M. (1966). Sources of variation in examination marks. In J. Heywood & A. H. Iliffe (Eds.), *Some problems of testing academic performance, Bulletin No. 1.* Department of Higher Education, University of Lancaster.

Engelhard, G., Jr. (1994). Examining rater errors in the assessment of written composition with a many-faceted Rasch model. *Journal of Educational Measurement, 31*(2), 93–112.

Eysenck, H. J., & Eysenck, S. (1975). *Manual of the Eysenck personality questionnaire.* London: Hodder & Stoughton.

Furnham, A. (1996). The big five versus the big four: The relationship between the Myers-Briggs Type Indicator and the NEO-PI five-factor model of personality. *Personality and Individual Differences, 21,* 303–307.

Furnham, A., Moutafi, J., & Crump, J. (2003). The relationship between the revised Neo-Personality Inventory and the Myers-Briggs Type indicator. *Social Behavior and Personality, 31*(6), 577–584.

Gowen, S. (1984). Writing, rating, and personality type. Paper presented at *the Ninth Annual University System of Georgia Developmental Studies Conference,* Athens.

Hicks, L. E. (1984). Conceptual and empirical analysis of some assumptions of an explicit typological theory. *Journal of Personality and Social Psychology, 46,* 1118–1131.

Husbands, C. T. (1976). Ideological bias in the marking of examinations. *Research in Education, 15,* 17–38.

Jensen, G. H., & DiTiberio, J. K. (1989). *Personality and the teaching of composition.* Norwood, NJ: Ablex.

Kane, J. S., Bernardin, H. J., Villanova, P., & Peyrefitte, J. (1995). Stability of rater leniency: Three studies. *Academy of Management Journal, 38,* 1039–1051.

Linacre, J. M. (2012). *A user's guide to FACETS, Rasch-model computer programs.* Retrieved October, 11, 2015, from www.winsteps.com

Linacre, J. M. (2014). *Facets computer program for many-facet Rasch measurement, version 3.71.4*. Beaverton, Oregon: Winsteps.com.

Lukmani, Y. (1996). Linguistic accuracy versus coherence in academic degree programs: A report on stage 1 of the project. In M. Milanovic & N. Saville (Eds.), *Performance testing, cognition and assessment* (pp. 130–150). Cambridge: University of Cambridge Local Examinations Syndicate and Cambridge University Press.

McCrae, R. R., & Costa, P. T., Jr. (1989). Reinterpreting the Myers-Briggs Type Indicator from the perspective of the five-factor model of personality. *Journal of Personality, 57*, 17–40.

Milanovic, M., Saville, N., & Shuhong, S. (1996). A study of the decision making behaviour of composition markers. In M. Milanovic & N. Saville (Eds.), *Performance testing, cognition and assessment* (pp. 99–114). Cambridge: University of Cambridge Local Examinations Syndicate and Cambridge University Press.

Miller, A. K., Rufino, K. A., Boccaccini, M. T., Jackson, R. L., & Murrie, D. C. (2011). On individual differences in person perception: Raters' personality traits relate to their psychopathy checklist-revised scoring tendencies. *Assessment, 18*, 253–260.

Myers, L. B. (1962). *Manual: The Myers-Briggs Type Indicator*. Princeton, NJ: Educational Testing Service.

Myers, L. B. (1987). *Introduction to type* (4th ed.). Palo Alto, CA: Consulting Psychologists Press.

Myers, L. B., & McCaulley, M. H. (1985). *Manual: A guide to the development and use of the Myers-Briggs Type Indicator*. Palo Alto, CA, USA: Consulting Psychologists Press.

Myford, C. M., & Wolfe, E. W. (2003). Detecting and measuring rater effects using many-facet Rasch measurement: Part I. *Journal of Applied Measurement, 4*(4), 386–422.

Pollitt, A., & Murray, N. L. (1996). What raters really pay attention to? In M. Milanovic & N. Saville (Eds.), *Performance testing, cognition and assessment* (pp. 74–91). Cambridge: University of Cambridge Local Examinations Syndicate and Cambridge University Press.

Saggino, A., Cooper, C., & Kline, P. (2001). A confirmatory factor analysis of the Myers-Briggs Type Indicator. *Personality and Individual Differences, 30*, 3–9.

Schoonen, R., Vergeer, M., & Eiting, M. (1997). The assessment of writing ability: Expert readers versus lay readers. *Language Testing, 14*, 157–184.

Scullen, S. E., Mount, M. K., & Goff, M. (2000). Understanding the latent structure of job performance ratings. *Journal of Applied Psychology, 85*, 956–970.

Sticker, L. J., & Ross, J. (1964). An assessment of some structural properties of the Jungian personality typology. *Journal of Abnormal and Social Psychology, 68*, 62–71.

Tziner, A., Murphy, K. R., & Cleveland, J. N. (2002). Does conscientiousness moderate the relationship between attitudes and beliefs regarding performance appraisal and rating behavior? *International Journal of Selection and Assessment, 10*, 218–224.

Wade, B. (1978). Responses to written work. *Educational Review, 30*, 149–158.

Walter, K. M. (1984). *Writing in three disciplines correlated with Jungian cognitive styles*. Unpublished doctoral dissertation, University of Texas at Austin.

Weigle, S. C. (1994). *Effects of training on raters of ESL compositions: Quantitative and qualitative approaches*. Unpublished PhD dissertation, University of California, Los Angeles.

Weigle, S. C. (1998). Using FACETS to model rater training effects. *Language Testing, 15*(2), 263–267.

Yang, J., McCrae, R. R., & Costa, P. T., Jr. (1999). Cross-cultural personality assessment in psychiatric populations: The NEO-PI-R in the People's Republic of China. *Psychological Assessment, 11*(3), 359–368.

Yun, G. J., Donahue, L. M., Dudley, N. M., & McFarland, L. A. (2005). Rater personality, rating format, and social context: Implications for performance appraisal ratings. *International Journal of Selection and Assessment, 13*(2), 97–107.

Chapter 11
Computer-Mediated Corrective Feedback in Chinese as a Second Language Writing: Learners' Perspectives

Yufen Hsieh, Cha Kie Hiew and Yong Xiang Tay

Abstract Research has demonstrated the effectiveness of written corrective feedback in promoting second language (L2) learners' linguistic accuracy (Bitchener and Knoch in Language Teaching Research 12(3):409–431, 2008a, ELT Journal 63 (3):204–211, 2008b, Applied Linguistics 31(2):193–214, 2010a; Ellis et al. in System 36(3):353–371, 2008; Ferris in Journal of Second Language Writing 13 (1):49–62, 2004, Feedback in second language writing: Contexts and issues, Cambridge University Press, Cambridge, UK, pp. 81–104, 2006; Sheen in TESOL Quarterly 41:255–283, 2007; Van Beuningen et al. in Language Learning 62, 1–41, 2012). In practice, however, learners can hardly receive prompt feedback in a large class with mixed levels of language proficiency. This study explored fifth-grade students' perceptions of the benefits and challenges of using an automated essay marking system in a writing class. Chinese learners with high-intermediate and low-intermediate levels of proficiency obtained instant error feedback on Chinese characters, collocations, and grammar after submitting their essays to the system. A questionnaire and interviews were then conducted to collect the students' views. The results showed that computer-mediated corrective feedback was generally perceived as effective and helpful for improving language accuracy in writing. According to the interview results, the most commonly perceived benefits of the system included convenient and instant access to corrective feedback as well as increased awareness of L2 form. The marking system served as a supplement to teachers in the writing class. Compared to the low-intermediate group, the high-intermediate group had a more positive attitude toward metalinguistic feedback. On the other hand, negative perceptions of the system could result from

---

Y. Hsieh (✉)
National Taiwan University of Science and Technology, Taipei, Taiwan
e-mail: yfhsieh@mail.ntust.edu.tw

C.K. Hiew
The University of Hong Kong, Pok Fu Lam, Hong Kong

Y.X. Tay
Singapore Centre for Chinese Language, Singapore, Singapore

© Springer Nature Singapore Pte Ltd. 2017
D. Zhang and C.-H. Lin (eds.), *Chinese as a Second Language Assessment*,
Chinese Language Learning Sciences, DOI 10.1007/978-981-10-4089-4_11

incomprehensibility/inaccuracy of feedback, preference for handwriting over typing, as well as limitations of the system design. The findings have implications for future research and implementation of an automated marking system as a pedagogical tool in writing classes.

Keywords Corrective feedback · Computer-mediated writing · Chinese as a second language

Introduction

In the twenty-first century the use of information and communications technology (ICT) has emerged as a new trend in language education (Matsumura and Hann 2004). The latest Mother Tongue Languages Review Committee Report by Singapore Ministry of Education in 2010 has highlighted the use of ICT to facilitate self-directed learning as students with diverse Chinese language proficiency levels could initiate learning activities at their own level and develop personal knowledge and skills in a technology-enhanced instructional environment (Benson 2007; Sinclair 2000; Smeets and Mooij 2001; Warschauer 2000). Learners who enjoy a high degree of autonomy are more likely than otherwise to put efforts in learning and exploiting language knowledge, which then contribute to language development (Little 2002).

The need for promoting self-directed learning according to different learners' needs and characteristics is clear in the Singaporean context. Over the past decades, the proportion of primary students from predominantly English-speaking homes has risen from 36% in 1994 to 59% in 2010 (Mother Tongue Languages Review Committee Report 2010). This trend has led to the situation that an increasing number of Singaporean students learn Chinese as a second language (L2), and they enter the classroom with diverse proficiency levels. These students need individualized instruction and support in language use during the writing process, which is, however, not feasible in a class of more than 20 students.

While students need individualized feedback, responding to student papers can be a challenge for teachers. Particularly, if they have a large number of students or if they assign frequent writing assignments, providing individual feedback to student essays might be time consuming. As teachers in Singapore typically teach several classes of about 30 students each, the amount of work to be graded often limits the number of writing assignments teachers can offer to students. Moreover, providing accurate and informative feedback on the language use of student writing requires a certain degree of linguistic proficiency and knowledge that are conceived or possessed differently by teachers as some of them developed their expertise without being explicitly taught grammar (Johnson 2009; Johnston and Goettsch 2000). Furthermore, although instant corrective feedback on linguistic errors has been found beneficial to L2 learners (Ellis 2001; Ellis et al. 2006; Lyster 2004;

Russell and Spada 2006), it is often not feasible to supply individualized feedback in class because students have different levels of language proficiency.

To support the teaching and learning of Chinese writing for students of different levels of language proficiency, Singapore Centre for Chinese Language[1] has developed a prototype of an automated essay marking system. This system aims to detect linguistic errors in Chinese writing and provides corrective feedback on language use, including Chinese characters, lexical collocations, and grammar. The target users are higher primary Chinese language learners in Singapore. The prototype system integrates a user interface and a linguistic analysis module to perform the automated essay marking process. An essay can be submitted through the user interface for marking by the linguistic analysis module and then returned to users instantly with error marking and corrective feedback in terms of language use. The system has great potential to enhance the teaching and learning of Chinese writing by providing students with individualized feedback and reducing teachers' workload in marking and correcting linguistic errors. This system will also be scaffolding students' writing process by providing prompt feedback at the linguistic level to encourage autonomous revision.

The system relies on information from a training corpus plus three databases, i.e., lexicon, grammar, and lexical collocation, to achieve automated detection and correction of linguistic errors. For Chinese characters, the system can circle out incorrect characters and display the correct ones. For lexical collocation, the system flags incorrect collocations and lists out the common collocates that a particular word has based on the corpus so that users could have a better understanding of the usage of a particular word. At the sentence level, the system underlines an ungrammatical sentence and provides metalinguistic feedback,[2] namely a simple, short explanation of a rule along with an example sentence.

The marking accuracy and speed of the prototype system has been evaluated using randomly selected, authentic narrative essays from Primary 3 to Primary 6 students from various schools in Singapore. According to the results, the system has achieved an accuracy rate of around 80% in detecting linguistic errors in intermediate-level essays on common topics while the accuracy rate for high- and low-level essays is around 70%. Error deduction includes misses (errors not recognized by the system) and false positives (correct usages identified as errors) with the former higher than the latter. As for the processing speed, it generally takes less than 1 min. to process a Chinese essay of 500 characters. Time increases with the length of the sentences in the text.

The present study aimed to investigate students' perceptions of the automated essay marking system developed by Singapore Centre for Chinese Language. Students' feedback was collected as part of the efforts to evaluate the prototype

---

[1]Singapore Centre for Chinese Language aims to enhance the effectiveness of teaching Chinese as a second language and to meet the learning needs of students in a bilingual environment.

[2]According to Ellis (2009), "Metalinguistic [corrective feedback] involves providing learners with some form of explicit comment about the nature of the errors they have made" (p. 100).

system and to further improve it in order to ensure that the intent of the system was fulfilled and that all the features laid out in the development phase could be successfully implemented in Singapore's primary schools. A questionnaire and focus group survey were conducted to identify the specific factors that might influence the perceived effectiveness of and satisfaction with the system. This would help the researchers identify the strengths and weaknesses of the system from the perspectives of target users. Students' feedback was integrated into the continuous improvement of the system.

The following literature review first summarizes the most common automated writing evaluation (AWE) programs, which are developed for English learners, and then examines studies on learners' perceptions regarding the effectiveness of AWE software.

Literature Review

Writing ability is directly related to language proficiency as good writing must conform to the conventions of grammar and usage of the target language (Frodesen and Holten 2003). For L2 learners, especially those with low language proficiency, writing often appears as a daunting task as they lack vocabulary and grammar to produce the required work. The process approach to writing instruction views writing as a process rather than a product and emphasizes revision and feedback as essential aspects of the process (Weigle 2002; Flower and Hayes 1981).

A major challenge to learners with low Chinese proficiency is that their limited knowledge of vocabulary and grammar hinders the development of writing skills (Cumming and Riazi 2000). In addition, these learners need substantial support to improve their linguistic accuracy in writing as they often make errors in language use and yet have difficulties in recognizing and correcting the errors (Bitchener et al. 2005; Ferris 2002, 2006). The best way to prevent error fossilization is to receive feedback from an instructor, revise based on the feedback, and then repeat the whole process as often as possible (Hyland 2003). Students need to consciously pay attention to the errors they have made in order to recognize the gaps between the correct form and their own usage (Schmidt 1990, 1993; Sheen 2010).

Automated Writing Evaluation

The needs for students to receive writing practice and feedback at their own level and for teachers to increase effectiveness have raised the importance of computer-assisted AWE. Research has revealed that computers have the capacity to function as an effective cognitive tool (Attali 2004). AWE is a computer technology that aims not only to evaluate written work but also to offer essay feedback (Shermis and Barrera 2002; Shermis and Burstein 2003). AWE systems are developed to assist teachers in low-stakes classroom assessment as well as graders in large-scale, high-stakes assessment. Moreover, the systems could help students to review, redraft, and improve their text easily on a word processor before the work is submitted to the teacher or published online for peers. While students can work autonomously, teachers can focus on reviewing students' final drafts and providing instructor feedback (Warschauer and Grimes 2008). In other words, AWE tools are designed to support student learning and to supplement teachers and graders rather than to replace them.

The most widely used AWE programs are mainly developed for the English language, including Project Essay Grader (PEG), Intelligent Essay Assessor (IEA), E-rater, and Criterion, as well as IntelliMetric and My Access! Table 11.1 summarizes the four AWE programs.

These AWE programs are typically able to provide holistic scoring and diagnostic feedback, which require topic-specific training as the systems evaluate a new essay by comparing its linguistic features to the benchmark set in the training corpus. It is worth mentioning that the use of AWE programs has moved from a summative to a more formative assessment (Shermis and Burstein 2003). Criterion and MY Access! are two instructional-based AWE programs that support process writing and formative assessment by allowing students to save and revise drafts based on the feedback and scoring received from the computer and/or the teacher. This leads to a paradigmatic shift from a teacher-centered assessment toward a learner-centered evaluation. While the product approach views writing assessment as a summative practice, the process approach views it as a formative practice (Weigle 2002). The process-oriented AWE applications guide students through essay drafting and revision before submitting the final version, which could not otherwise take place inside a classroom.

Research has demonstrated that AWE could facilitate essay revision and that revision based on corrective feedback is beneficial to L2 learning. Attali (2004) found that the use of Criterion led to significant improvement in student writing during the five revisions in terms of the total holistic score (from 3.7 to 4.2 on a six-point scale) as well as the scores in organization, style, grammar, and mechanics. Students were able to significantly reduce the error rates by improving ungrammatical sentences, incorrect words, and mechanical errors that had been identified by the system. Organization and coherence of the revised essays were

Table 11.1 Summary of widely used AWE programs

AWE program	Developer (year)	Main focus	Instructional application
PEG	Page (1966)	Language	N/A
IEA	Landauer et al. (1997)	Content	N/A
E-rater	ETS (Burstein et al. 1998)	Language and content	Criterion
IntelliMetric	Vantage learning (Elliot et al. 1998)	Language and content	My Access!

also enhanced by adding discourse elements. Sheen (2007) found that corrective feedback on language use resulted in improved accuracy in immediate writing tests compared to no correction. Furthermore, compared to direct correction, metalinguistic feedback had a greater positive effect on intermediate learners' performance in delayed writing tests. This suggests that supply of comments or information related to the well-formedness of sentences without explicit correction could be beneficial to L2 acquisition as the indirect approach engages learners in a deeper cognitive processing (Lyster and Ranta 1997). The results in Sheen (2007) also revealed a significantly positive correlation between students' improvement in writing accuracy and their language analytic ability.

Overall, L2 studies have shown that students need immediate feedback to support their writing processes (Hyland and Hyland 2006). Also, corrective feedback facilitates the acquisition of linguistic features and helps to improve the overall quality of essays (Bitchener et al. 2005; Ellis et al. 2008; Ferris 2003, 2004, 2006; Lyster and Ranta 1997). AWE programs have great potential to enhance learning and teaching processes by pointing out the weak aspects of student writing as early as possible. In light of the previous research, the marking system focused on detecting linguistic errors and providing instant corrective feedback to help improve students' linguistic accuracy in writing based on the individualized feedback. The system served as an aid, rather than a replacement, for human evaluation as it took care of the language part and allowed the teacher to focus on other important aspects of an essay, such as content, organization, and style.

Learners' Perceptions of Automated Writing Evaluation

While many studies have reported the effectiveness of AWE software in improving L2 learners' essay quality and L2 accuracy (e.g., Bitchener et al. 2005; Ellis et al. 2008; Ferris 2003, 2004, 2006; Lyster and Ranta 1997), few have focused on learners' perceptions of AWE use. Learners' perceptions could affect their use of the AWE software and eventually their learning outcomes (Dörnyei 2001; Gardner 1972; Wigfield and Wentzel 2007). If learners are not motivated to use the tools, very little learning will take place in the long run. It has been suggested that learners' perceptions of the possible benefits of technological tools, such as accessibility and enhancement of learning, could increase their motivation (Beauvois and Eledge 1996; Gilbert 2001; Warschauer 1996a, b). Furthermore, successful implementation of AWE in classroom settings depends on factors beyond high reliability or agreement between system and human evaluation. Technology can only be effective if learners' needs are met in various learning contexts. This highlights the importance to investigate the AWE effectiveness from learners' perspectives.

Grimes and Warschauer (2010) investigated learners' use of the AWE program My Access! in middle schools through interviews, surveys, and classroom observations. Immediate feedback was generally perceived as the most valuable benefit of the AWE software and was of greatest use in correcting errors in mechanics (spelling, punctuation, and grammar). Learners corrected errors in response to automated feedback but made little revision on content and organization, probably because they were unable to view their own writing critically. Furthermore, the usefulness of AWE was perceived differently by learners at various proficiency levels. Intermediate-level learners benefited most from the AWE software as they were still trying to master the mechanisms of writing and yet had sufficient knowledge to understand system feedback. In contrast, learners who lacked the necessary language and computer skills could not make effective use of the AWE software. Importantly, whether AWE encourages revision is affected by complex factors. Students revised more when writing for authentic audiences, when having the awareness of both meaning and surface revisions, and when giving ample time for revision.

Chen and Cheng (2008) explored students' perceptions using My Access! as a pedagogical tool in three college writing classes. The AWE program was perceived as only slightly, or even not, helpful to writing improvement, largely due to the limitations of software design and the way it was implemented in class. Most students did not trust computer-generated scores due to discrepancies between automated scores and instructor/peer assessment results. The AWE program favored lengthiness and formulaic writing styles, thus failing to assess the content and coherence of the writing and also restricting the expression of ideas. Similar to the findings in Grimes and Warschauer (2010), automated feedback was perceived helpful in reducing language use problems as it allowed immediate identification of errors in L2 writing. However, My Access! was not helpful in improving essay content and organization because it was unable to provide concrete and specific comments on the global aspects of writing.

In addition to the limitations in software design, the ways of implementing AWE significantly influenced the perceived effectiveness. Students' perceptions were more positive if the program was utilized as a self-evaluation tool followed by teacher assessment. In this case, automated feedback was used to assist students in improving their writing at the drafting stage rather than to assess them. This might promote students' self-confidence and encourage reflection on writing before final submission to the teacher. Moreover, teacher support was essential for effective implementation of AWE. Teacher feedback could complement automated feedback, and sufficient guidance was necessary as students learned to use the program. The implementation of AWE must also take students' proficiency level into consideration. Chen and Cheng (2008) noted that automated feedback seemed most helpful to learners who needed assistance on the formal aspects of writing.

Although research on students' perceptions of AWE is limited, it has been shown that the effectiveness of AWE depends upon the interactions among multiple factors, including learner characteristics as well as program design and implementation. Also, there has been a shift of focus from the assessment function of AWE to the assistance function, particularly when the program was used in classroom settings. AWE is not intended to replace teachers but to support them. As Grimes and Warschauer (2010) state,

[The] benefits [of AWE] require sensible teachers who integrate AWE into a broader writing program emphasizing authentic communication, and who can help students recognize and compensate for the limitations of software that appears more intelligent at first than on deeper inspection. (p. 34)

As a relatively new approach to writing instruction, the effectiveness of AWE is inconclusive and needs to be evaluated from the perspective of different learner groups in different contexts. As revealed in the literature review, the studies on AWE programs have mostly focused on English learners at the college and middle school levels. Clearly, further studies that investigate the use of AWE programs by younger and other language learners are warranted. The present study attempted to contribute to the literature on learners' perceptions of AWE by examining L2 Chinese in the Singapore primary school context as an under-investigated area.

Method

Participants

Participants were two classes of fifth-grade students (mean age = 11 years) at two primary schools in Singapore. All the students in these schools followed the regular stream of Chinese language education, where Chinese was taught as a single subject from the first grade, while all the other subjects were instructed in English. The two classes differed in the level of Chinese language proficiency. Class A was at the low-intermediate level and took the normal Chinese lessons. Class B was at the high-intermediate level and took the higher Chinese lessons.[3] There were 28 students in Class A and 25 in Class B. According to the teachers' reports, these students mainly spoke English at school, and they used either English or a combination of English and their mother tongue at home.[4] All the students in Class B were ethnic Chinese, whereas Class A had 5 non-ethnic Chinese students who had little exposure to the Chinese language outside the class.

---

[3]According to the primary Chinese Language syllabus (MOE 2007), pupils are allowed to take the Chinese subject at the higher standard or foundation level depending on their aptitudes and abilities. The content of higher Chinese language is at an advanced level and is more in depth so as to help students achieve a higher language proficiency and cultural knowledge.

[4]The home language background of Singaporean students is complicated as they typically command several codes and frequently code-switch depending on the interlocutor and the topic of conversation (Bolton and Ng 2014; Siemund et al. 2014).

The Automated Essay Marking System

Given the benefits of AWE software in facilitating essay revision as reviewed above, the present study implemented an automated essay marking system that targeted L2 Chinese learners. The automated essay marking system used in the study is composed of a linguistic analysis module and a user interface. The development and implementation of the system involved forefront school teachers to ensure the practical applicability of the system.

Linguistic Analysis Module

The system architecture comprises two major components: a user interface and a linguistic analysis module. The linguistic analysis module adopts a corpus-driven approach to error detection and requires training on an annotated corpus of Chinese texts. The analyzer uses machine learning to exploit information from three databases— i.e., lexicon, collocation, and grammar—in order to achieve error detection and correction. The lexicon database contains the Chinese lexical items drawn from the training corpus. The grammar database includes syntactic rules as well as grammatical and ungrammatical sentence patterns, which enable the system to detect grammar errors. Language use problems are identified based on the corpus-induced grammars plus probabilistic parsing. Unlike a system that employs a broad-coverage grammar aiming to describe any well-formed structures in Chinese (Baldwin et al. 2004), the linguistic analyzer is trained with a corpus containing written Chinese data commonly engaged by higher primary students in Singapore and thus aims to capture common correct and incorrect usage in Singapore students' writing. The collocation database supports error detection in three common types of collocations: verb-noun (V-N), adjective-noun (A-N), and classifier-noun (CL-N). In addition to the information from the three databases, lexical co-occurrence frequencies extracted from the training corpus are incorporated into system processing.

The training corpus is specialized to cover language use of the target users rather than to exhaust linguistic rules in the Chinese language. The annotated corpus has 3,000,000 Chinese character tokens, including authentic student essays as well as texts from Chinese textbooks, student newspapers, and storybooks. The student essays represent various levels of language proficiency and cover common writing topics in order to maximize the coverage of language use in different text types. Textbook material, student newspapers, and storybooks are included as part of the training data because these are main sources of Singapore students' linguistic knowledge, and they are common sources of training data for error detection and correction systems (De Felice and Pulman 2008). The corpus is dynamic as it can be further expanded and continuously updated with new data.

User Interface

The marking system provides a student interface and a teacher interface with functions to facilitate an array of user tasks.

Through the student interface, users can submit an essay by typing, uploading, or copying and pasting it. For automated marking, the essay will be returned to the user with error markings and corrective feedback on language use. Alternatively, the user can submit the essay to the teacher for commenting after revising it according to system feedback. While a marked essay is displayed as the original version, the user can select the markup option to view the error markings and corrections in Chinese characters, lexical collocation, and grammar together or separately. Also, the user can place the cursor on the text to view teacher comments, which appear as pop-ups. For revision, the user can edit the original essay in one window while viewing the marked version in another window, which provides a convenient way of referring to system and/or teacher feedback.

The student interface facilitates data storage, tracking, and retrieval. Users can search and access all the comments and feedback on their own writing. They can also view linguistic errors they have made in order of frequency and retrieve a cumulative listing of all the instances where these errors appear in their essays. The annotated and searchable database of linguistic errors provides an opportunity for users to notice patterns of their own errors that might persist across several essays spanning a long period of time. In other words, the configuration supports a systematic display of student errors that makes it easier to see what specific error types occur frequently, which is usually not feasible under traditional pen and paper corrections with red marks representing simply a raw accumulation of errors.

The teacher interface supports single or batch upload of text files. Teachers are allowed to manually change system feedback before the texts are sent to students. Teachers can also mark a portion of a text with a comment by simply typing or choosing a comment that has been stored in a comment database from a drop-down menu. The feedback can be either displayed or hidden when the texts are returned to students. In the teacher interface, a variety of reports can be generated, including a consolidation of student errors as well as tracked records of individual students and/or a whole class. Teachers are able to access student data any time for formative assessment and to easily monitor student progress online. The error compilation feature allows the teacher to generate a list of linguistic errors made by students in order of frequency or error types for further instruction. This feature informs the teacher about students' learning difficulties and provides a holistic view of student' performance.

Procedure

Prior to the commencement of the study, the teachers of the participating classes attended a one-hour training session with the researchers, which explained the functions as well as the capabilities and limitations of the essay marking system. They were prepared to implement the system in class and solve problems for students. Afterward, the students received training on how to use the marking system, including typing, submitting, and revising/editing their essays on the system. During the training process, the students were encouraged to try the system as much as possible and to ask questions, which were immediately answered by the teacher or researchers. The training continued till the students were able to use the system independently. Meanwhile, the students were informed that the main purpose of the marking system was to assist them to improve language accuracy in their draft and that a score and comments on the content would be given by the teacher after the final version was submitted.

After the training, the students were required to write a 500-word essay within 50 min. and submit it to the system for marking. The writing requirements were the same as those for their regular assignments. Once the essay was submitted, the students received feedback within a few minutes, including markings of language errors and correction suggestions. The essay was submitted to the teacher once the revisions were completed. Throughout the process, the teacher responded to student inquiries and provided individual assistance regarding the use of the system if necessary. After the writing activity, a questionnaire survey was administered, followed by individual interviews that focused on students' perceptions of the effectiveness and design of the marking system as well as their attitudes toward using the system to complete a writing assignment.

Data Collection and Analysis

The data were obtained through a questionnaire with a 4-point Likert scale ranging from 1 ("strongly disagree") to 4 ("strongly agree"), followed by individual interviews by the researchers. The questionnaire and interviews were administered in both Chinese and English depending on the student's preference. The questionnaire contained ten Likert scale questions (as shown in Tables 11.2, 11.3, 11.4 and 11.5) and one open-ended question requesting free comments on the marking system (i.e., "What do you think about the essay marking system? Please provide any comments you have about the system."). The Likert scale questions asked about the perceived effectiveness, overall satisfaction, attitude toward using the system, as well as reactions toward system feedback. In total, 53 students (28 at the low-intermediate level of Chinese proficiency and 25 at the high-intermediate level) responded to the questionnaire.

To gather more in-depth insights on the questionnaire survey results, face-to-face interviews were conducted with eight of the students from each class. The students participating in interviews were randomly selected and were all volunteers. Each interview lasted approximately 20 min. The interviewees were asked to talk about

Table 11.2 Perceived effectiveness of using the essay marking system

	Strongly agree	Agree	Disagree	Strongly disagree
The error correction suggestions provided by the system can help me improve my writing				
Class A (low-intermediate proficiency level) (N = 28) (%)	21	64	14	0
Class B (high-intermediate proficiency level) (N = 25) (%)	48	44	8	0
Using the system can help me learn Chinese words and sentences				
Class A (low-intermediate proficiency level) (N = 28) (%)	36	57	7	0
Class B (high-intermediate proficiency level) (N = 25) (%)	64	28	8	0

Table 11.3 Attitude toward using the essay marking system

	Strongly agree	Agree	Disagree	Strongly disagree
I like to correct errors in my writing according to the system's correction suggestions				
Class A (low-intermediate proficiency level) (N = 28) (%)	25	50	25	0
Class B (high-intermediate proficiency level) (N = 25) (%)	64	28	8	0
I am willing to use the system to write a Chinese composition in class				
Class A (low-intermediate proficiency level) (N = 28) (%)	25	61	14	0
Class B (high-intermediate proficiency level) (N = 25) (%)	68	16	16	0
I am willing to use the system to practice Chinese writing after school				
Class A (low-intermediate proficiency level) (N = 28) (%)	7	54	39	0
Class B (high-intermediate proficiency level) (N = 25) (%)	44	40	16	0

Table 11.4 Reactions toward system feedback

	Strongly agree	Agree	Disagree	Strongly disagree
The error markings can help me notice language errors in my own writing				
Class A (low-intermediate proficiency level) (N = 28) (%)	21	61	18	0
Class B (high-intermediate proficiency level) (N = 25) (%)	48	40	12	0
The error correction suggestions provided by the system are easy to understand				
Class A (low-intermediate proficiency level) (N = 28) (%)	11	57	32	0
Class B (high-intermediate proficiency level) (N = 25) (%)	52	40	8	0

Table 11.5 Overall satisfaction with the essay marking system

	Strongly agree	Agree	Disagree	Strongly disagree
The system is easy to use				
Class A (low-intermediate proficiency level) (N = 28) (%)	43	54	4	0
Class B (high-intermediate proficiency level) (N = 25) (%)	56	44	0	0
The system runs smoothly				
Class A (low-intermediate proficiency level) (N = 28) (%)	36	64	0	0
Class B (high-intermediate proficiency level) (N = 25) (%)	52	48	0	0
The system has complete functions				
Class A (low-intermediate proficiency level) (N = 28) (%)	7	54	39	0
Class B (high-intermediate proficiency level) (N = 25) (%)	36	36	28	0

their experience with the essay marking system, their opinions regarding the benefits and limitations of the system, as well as their willingness of using the system. The interviews were structured around the following questions: Overall, how do you feel about the essay marking system? How do you think the system can help you with your writing? What do you think are the strengths of the system? What do you think are the drawbacks of the system? Are you willing to use the system at school and at home? Why or why not? The interview results were used to further illustrate the questionnaire findings.

Results and Discussion

Perceived Effectiveness of Using the Essay Marking System

According to the questionnaire survey, the essay marking system was generally perceived as an effective tool. As shown in Table 11.2, more than 80% of the students from Class A (low-intermediate proficiency level/LI level henceforth) and Class B (high-intermediate proficiency level/HI level henceforth) agreed that the system was helpful for their writing improvement and for Chinese learning. Around 10% of the students from the two classes had negative reactions to the marking system. Some of these students only wrote a few sentences due to their slow typing speed and/or low motivation for writing and thus had little experience with system feedback. Some of them had difficulty understanding the metalinguistic feedback at the sentence level, namely a short explanation of a rule along with an example (as illustrated below[5]) and were unable to correct the errors marked by the system.

> *Rule*:
> 地点放在动作前面。 'Location is placed before the action.'
> *Example*:
> 他在客厅看电视。 'He watched TV in the living room.'

Moreover, since the students only had the opportunity to make a single round of revisions before submitting their work to the teacher, some noted that the lack of immediate feedback on their hypothesized corrections was a barrier to learning. The implementation of the automated marking system needed to take into consideration the trial and error nature of L2 learning. In short, the perceived effectiveness of technology use depended on learner readiness, including typing skills and language proficiency, as well as the way the program was implemented in class.

Attitude Toward Using the Essay Marking System

As shown in Table 11.3, the majority of students liked to use the system to improve their language use in writing. They thought the system was convenient, fast, and easy to use, allowing them to receive timely feedback. A few students mentioned that they became less worried about the language aspect of writing as they had a chance to correct errors before submitting their work to the teacher. Furthermore, Class B (HI level) had a more positive attitude toward using the marking system compared to Class A (LI level). About 25% of the students from Class A disliked automated feedback, which was probably due to two reasons. For one thing, the metalinguistic feedback (i.e., an explanation of a rule plus an example) might not be comprehensible to the students who did not reach a certain level of Chinese language proficiency. Several students from Class A (LI level) indicated in the interview that direct correction would be more useful as they had difficulty correcting errors based on the metalinguistic suggestions. For the other, the students' attitude might be negatively affected by the limitation of the marking system itself. When a sentence contained errors, the system underlined the whole sentence and provided the relevant structure(s)/rule(s). It was, however, unable to specify the exact location of errors in an ungrammatical sentence. Thus, the students had to first understand the rule(s) and then apply the knowledge to identify errors and rewrite the sentence. The error correction task became more demanding when a sentence involved multiple grammatical errors, which was common in the writing of lower-proficiency students. The delay in access to the target form might have a negative impact on students' learning attitude and might cancel out the potential cognitive benefit of metalinguistic feedback (Chandler 2003).

---

[5]Rules and examples were provided in Chinese on the marking system.

As for the incentive to use the marking system in class and after school, more than 80% of the students from Class B (HI level) responded positively (see Table 11.3). The reasons were probably that the system was easy to use and that prompt feedback was perceived helpful in enhancing the language accuracy, as discussed above. Unlike Class B (HI level), only 60% of the students from Class A (LI level) were willing to use the system after school. The interview data revealed three factors that might affect students' motivation to use the system. First, students might prefer handwriting over typing because they were not used to typing Chinese on a computer and sometimes typing interfered with their writing. Second, students might consider the system as a support tool to complete writing assignments in class but not as a tool for self-learning outside the class, which might, in part, be due to the fact that the system was only used for in-class writing in this study. In addition, students might prefer to have assistance from the teacher and be relatively less motivated to engage in Chinese learning activities outside the class.

Reactions Toward System Feedback

As indicated in Table 11.4, more than 80% of the students from both classes agreed that error markings could help them notice language errors in their writing. As the students might lack the ability to identify their own errors, an overt and clear indication of errors could draw their attention to new features of the L2 (Schmidt 1990, 1993). The students became aware of the gap between their usage and the target form. However, it was found that sometimes system detection was inaccurate and thus might lead to confusion. Solving the problem would require an increase in the detection accuracy of the prototype system.

The students from Class A (LI level) and B (HI level) had different opinions regarding the ease of understanding system feedback. There was an overall positive response from Class B (HI level), where 92% of the students thought the feedback was comprehensible and could help them correct language errors immediately. In contrast, 32% of the students from Class A (LI level) did not think that the feedback was easy to understand. As discussed above, students might need to reach a certain level of Chinese proficiency in order to benefit from the metalinguistic feedback, as the error correction process required awareness of grammatical rules as well as the ability to apply the rules to construct new sentences. Some students indicated that the system suggestions might be easier to understand if presented with English translation and/or more explanations. This suggested that the automated feedback might be insufficient or incomprehensible to them.

Overall Satisfaction with the Essay Marking System

The questionnaire survey showed high satisfaction with the ease of use and smooth operation of the marking system (see Table 11.5). As confirmed by the interview, the students generally agreed that they could submit their work and receive feedback in just a few steps and that the system interface was intuitive with clear buttons. According to Davis (1989), the ease of use of a technology will influence learners' intention in using it and hence their learning effectiveness. When learners perceive a technology as easy to use, they will be more likely to accept it and find it useful with respect to improving their performance, especially for those with weak learning motivation (Huang et al. 2011; Liu et al. 2010). Smooth operation is also important for a computational system as bugs or defects will decrease its effectiveness (Holland et al. 1995).

While the system was perceived as easy to use and smooth, the students had much lower satisfaction with its functions, as indicated in Table 11.5. About 39 and 28% of the students from Class A (LI level) and B (HI level), respectively, disagreed that the system had complete functions. They pointed out the need for additional learning aids, including access to an online dictionary, model essays, written comments on essay content, and even games. In addition, the interface design was not sufficiently attractive and motivative to them. The findings raised important issues for the development and implementation of an essay marking system. For one thing, students must be aware of the specific purpose of using technology in learning. In this case, the marking system was designed to address language errors, and thus giving comments on essay content would be beyond the scope of the system. Students should have a clear understanding of what the technology was capable of doing before using it. For another, the development of the marking system should be based on the basic nature of learning. It has been suggested that computational aids for language learning should be not only easy to use but also intrinsically motivating and enhancing the user experience (Nokelainen 2006; Norman 2002). From this point of view, the marking system needed to be further improved in order to create an enjoyable, supportive, and aesthetically pleasing environment for writers.

General Discussion

This study investigated fifth-grade students' perceptions of the automated essay marking system developed by Singapore Centre for Chinese Language. The purpose was to gather user feedback for further improvement of the system. The study added to the limited literature on the use of an automated system as a tool for formative feedback on the language aspect of writing. The questionnaire survey and interview results indicated that the marking system was generally perceived as effective and helpful in improving language accuracy, with the advantages of being easy to use and prompt in providing feedback. The timely feedback could promote noticing of L2 form and reduce the anxiety about making errors during the writing process.

Some may argue that error correction does not necessarily lead to proper use of the target form in future and that it may result in a negative attitude toward writing (e.g., Truscott 1996). For one thing, L2 development is a gradual process of trial and error, and corrective feedback provides opportunities for learners to notice the target form and to test linguistic hypotheses. As demonstrated in Ferris and Roberts (2001), error marking helped learners self-edit their text compared to no feedback. For the other, corrective feedback would not discourage or demotivate learners if used as a formative tool. Similar to Chen and Cheng (2008) and Grimes and Warschauer (2010), the present study showed evidence that immediate feedback was considered valuable, especially if utilized as an assistant tool that helped learners improve their work at the drafting stage of writing. The provision of automated feedback was based on a non-judgmental and process-oriented approach that could reduce writing anxiety caused by the fear of teachers' negative feedback and the lack of linguistic knowledge (Leki 1999).

While there was a generally positive perception of the automated marking system, the students' attitude might be affected by several factors, including their Chinese proficiency level, cognitive ability, as well as the presentation of metalinguistic feedback. First of all, it is important to note that the study only included non-advanced, young learners of Chinese. Thus, the findings might not be generalizable to other proficiency and/or age groups. In fact, those who have mastered the formal system of the target language might benefit more from content-focused feedback than from form-focused feedback in an AWE learning environment (Chen and Cheng 2008). Moreover, metalinguistic feedback was perceived less useful among the low-intermediate students compared to the high-intermediate students. The finding is in line with the argument that direct correction could best work with elementary learners as it offers immediate access to the target form (Ferris 2006). The lack of sufficient and comprehensible information to resolve errors might lead to confusion (Ferris and Roberts 2001; Leki 1991). In contrast, metalinguistic feedback has been found effective mostly for improving L2 accuracy of advanced or post-intermediate learners with high language analytic ability (e.g., Bitchener and Knoch 2010b; Bitchener et al. 2005; Sheen 2007). Given that most of the previous studies were conducted with adult university learners, it is possible that metalinguistic feedback imposes different cognitive demands on primary-level learners whose cognitive abilities are still in process of development. Further research is thus required to understand how cognitive factors impact the effects of corrective feedback. In addition, while the metalinguistic feedback was provided in Chinese on the automated marking system, some students might prefer English translation as evidenced in the interview data.

The students' perceptions of the marking system might also be influenced by the implementation and the limitations of the system. The necessity of providing different types of support to suit learners' needs raises critical issues in the implementation of such a system. First, the use of the technology needs to take into account learner characteristics and learning goals. The students in this study were fifth-graders who had learned to compose essays since the third grade. Most of them still needed assistance in the formal aspects of writing. Also, they were aware that reducing language errors in their writing could help them achieve a better score on school tests. Before the essay marking system was employed in class, the students were informed that the major purpose of using the system was to facilitate their revising process and that the teacher would give comments and assign a score after the final version had been submitted. In this case, the students understood that they were not to be assessed by a machine, and the use of the marking system met their learning goals to some extent. The system might have been perceived differently if implemented with other learner groups or in other learning contexts.

Furthermore, teacher support could compensate for the limitations of the automated marking system and thus increase its effectiveness. While the students worked individually with the system, the teacher was available to answer questions from the students. This might be particularly important for lower-proficiency students who had difficulty understanding the automated feedback. As the marking system was only able to underline an ungrammatical sentence and provide metalinguistic explanations of rules, the teacher could help to pinpoint errors and clarify a grammar point that could not be explained clearly in generic feedback. Also, the automated responses might not be at the students' level and were not targeted at specific ideas to be conveyed. Therefore, teacher input was necessary to address individual writing problems and to alleviate confusion. In other words, the marking system served as a supplement to teachers rather than as a replacement of them (Ware 2005; Warschauer and Ware 2006).

Another limitation of the marking system was its inability to give specific and individualized comments on essays, as some students pointed out in this study. While the system took care of language accuracy, the teacher could attend to the content and offer focused advice regarding the strengths and weaknesses of each student's essays. According to the teachers participating in this study, before using the marking system, they used to spend a great deal of time and effort providing corrective feedback on students' errors, and it was impossible to do so in class due to time constraints and classroom management concerns. Thus, the students did not receive feedback until a few days after submitting their work. The delayed feedback in fact might not be of much use as the students had already lost the motivation to reflect on and improve their writing (c.f. Evans et al. 2011; Hartshorn et al. 2010). The integration of machine and human feedback allowed for the delivery of timely feedback on linguistic form during the writing process and facilitated teacher response to meaning construction and individual learning needs of students.

Conclusion

This study explored fifth-grade students' perceptions of utilizing an automated essay marking system that provided corrective feedback on lexical and grammatical errors in Chinese. The system was not aimed to eliminate human elements during the essay marking process but to allow teachers to place more attention on the content and other important aspects of student writing by reducing their time and effort investments in error marking and correction. While this study is the first that investigates the implementation of an automated Chinese writing system in Singapore's primary schools, it has limitations that can be addressed in future research.

First, the system design was preliminary, and further improvement in the accuracy of error detection and the use of metalanguage was necessary. Any changes in system features or processes might lead to different user perceptions. Second, the effectiveness of the marking system was investigated only through students' perceptions after a single writing session. Further research could examine the short-term and long-term impact of automated feedback on student's writing improvement by comparing their essays before and after revision. It is also valuable to conduct longitudinal studies that track changes in students' awareness of and attitude toward self-editing through automated feedback. In addition, it was unclear how the system effectiveness would be influenced by different pedagogical designs, learning contexts, as well as individual teacher and student factors. A complete understanding of these variables and their interactions will help to guide the implementation and maximize the benefits of similar technologies.

References

Attali, Y. (2004). *Exploring the feedback and revision features of criterion*. Paper presented at the National Council on Measurement in Education (NCME), San Diego, CA.

Baldwin, T., Beavers, J., Bender, E., Flickinger, D., Kim, A., & Oepen, S. (2004). Beauty and the beast: What running a broad-coverage precision grammar over the BNC taught us about the grammar—and the corpus. In *Proceedings of the International Conference on Linguistic Evidence: Empirical, Theoretical, and Computational Perspectives*, Tübingen, Germany.

Beauvois, M. H., & Eledge, J. (1996). Personality types and megabytes: Student attitudes toward computer mediated communication (CMC) in the language classroom. *CALICO Journal, 13* (2/3), 27–46.

Benson, P. (2007). Autonomy in language teaching and learning. *Language Teaching, 40*(1), 21–40.

Bitchener, J., & Knoch, U. (2008a). The value of written corrective feedback for migrant and international students. *Language Teaching Research, 12*(3), 409–431.

Bitchener, J., & Knoch, U. (2008b). The value of a focused approach to written corrective feedback. *ELT Journal, 63*(3), 204–211.

Bitchener, J., & Knoch, U. (2010a). The contribution of written corrective feedback to language development: A ten month investigation. *Applied Linguistics, 31*(2), 193–214.

Bitchener, J., & Knoch, U. (2010b). Raising the linguistic accuracy level of advanced L2 writers with written corrective feedback. *Journal of Second Language Writing, 19*(4), 207–217.

Bitchener, J., Young, S., & Cameron, D. (2005). The effect of different types of corrective feedback on ESL student writing. *Journal of Second Language Writing, 14*, 191–205.

Bolton, K., & Ng, B. C. (2014). The dynamics of multilingualism in contemporary Singapore. *World Englishes, 33*(3), 307–318.

Chandler, J. (2003). The efficacy of various kinds of error feedback for improvement in the accuracy and fluency of L2 student writing. *Journal of Second Language Writing, 12*, 267–296.

Chen, C. F., & Cheng, W. Y. (2008). Beyond the design of automated writing evaluation: Pedagogical practices and perceived learning effectiveness in EFL writing classes. *Language Learning & Technology, 12*(2), 94–112.

Cumming, A., & Riazi, A. M. (2000). Building models of adult L2 writing instruction. *Learning and Instruction, 10*, 55–71.

Davis, F. D. (1989). Perceived usefulness, perceived ease of use, and user acceptance of information technology. *MIS Quarterly, 13*(3), 319–339.

De Felice, R., & Pulman, S. (2008). A classifier-based approach to preposition and determiner error correction in L2 English. In *Proceedings of COLING* (pp. 169–176).

Dörnyei, Z. (2001). *Motivational strategies in the language classroom*. Cambridge: Cambridge University Press.

Ellis, R. (2001). Introduction: Investigating form-focused instruction. In R. Ellis (Ed.), *Form-focused instruction and L2 learning* (pp. 1–46). Oxford: Blackwell.

Ellis, R. (2009). A typology of written corrective feedback types. *ELT Journal, 63*(2), 97–107.

Ellis, R., Loewen, S., & Erlam, R. (2006). Implicit and explicit corrective feedback and the acquisition of L2 grammar. *Studies in Second Language Acquisition, 28*(2), 339–368.

Ellis, R., Sheen, Y., Murakami, M., & Takashima, H. (2008). The effects of focused and unfocused written corrective feedback in an English as a foreign language context. *System, 36*(3), 353–371.

Evans, N. W., Hartshorn, K. J., & Strong-Krause, D. (2011). The efficacy of dynamic written corrective feedback for university-matriculated ESL learners. *System, 39*(2), 229–239.

Ferris, D. (2002). *Treatment of error in L2 student writing*. Ann Arbor, MI: University of Michigan Press.

Ferris, D. (2003). Responding to writing. In B. Kroll (Ed.), *Exploring the dynamics of second language writing* (pp. 119–140). NY: Cambridge University Press.

Ferris, D. (2004). The "grammar correction" debate in L2 writing: Where are we, and where do we go from here? (and what do we do in the meantime…?). *Journal of Second Language Writing, 13*(1), 49–62.

Ferris, D. R. (2006). Does error feedback help student writers? New evidence on the short- and long-term effects of written error correction. In K. Hyland & F. Hyland (Eds.), *Feedback in second language writing: Contexts and issues* (pp. 81–104). Cambridge, UK: Cambridge University Press.

Ferris, D. R., & Roberts, B. J. (2001). Error feedback in L2 writing classes: How explicit does it need to be? *Journal of Second Language Writing, 10*, 161–184.

Flower, L., & Hayes, J. R. (1981). Plans that guide the composing process. In C. H. Frederiksen & J. F. Dominic (Eds.), *Writing: The nature, development and teaching of written communication* (Vol. 2, pp. 39–58). Hillsdale, NJ: Lawrence Erlbaum Associates.

Frodesen, J., & Holten, C. (2003). Grammar and the ESL writing class. In B. Kroll (Ed.), *Exploring the dynamics of second language writing* (pp. 141–161). Cambridge: Cambridge University Press.

Gardner, R. C. (1972). Attitudes and motivation in L2 learning. In A. G. Reynolds (Ed.), *Bilingualism, multiculturalism, and second language learning* (pp. 43–64). Hillsdale, NJ: Lawrence Erlbaum Associates Inc.

Gilbert, S. D. (2001). *How to be a successful online student*. New York: McGraw-Hill.

Grimes, D., & Warschauer, M. (2010). Utility in a fallible tool: A multi-site case study of automated writing evaluation. *Journal of Technology, Learning, and Assessment, 8*, 4–43.

Hartshorn, K. J., Evans, N. W., Merrill, P. F., Sudweeks, R. R., Strong-Krause, D., & Anderson, N. J. (2010). Effects of dynamic corrective feedback on ESL writing accuracy. *TESOL Quarterly, 44*(1), 84–109.

Holland, V. M., Kaplan, J., & Sams, M. (Eds.). (1995). *Intelligent language tutors: Theory shaping technology*. NY: Lawrence Erlbaum Associates.

Huang, Y. M., Chiu, P. S., Liu, T. C., & Chen, T. S. (2011). The design and implementation of a meaningful learning-based evaluation method for ubiquitous learning. *Computers & Education, 57*(4), 2291–2302.

Hyland, K. (2003). *Second language writing*. NY: Cambridge University Press.

Hyland, K., & Hyland, F. (2006). *Feedback in second language writing: Contexts and issues*. New York: Cambridge University Press.

Johnson, K. E. (2009). Trends in second language teacher education. In A. Burns & J. C. Richards (Eds.), *The Cambridge guide to second language teacher education* (pp. 20–29). New York: Cambridge University Press.

Johnston, B., & Goettsch, K. (2000). In search of the knowledge base of language teaching: Explanations by experienced teachers. *Canadian Modern Language Review, 56*, 437–468.

Leki, I. (1991). The preferences of ESL students for error correction in college level writing classes. *Foreign Language Annals, 24*, 203–218.

Leki, I. (1999). Techniques for reducing L2 writing anxiety. In D. J. Young (Ed.), *Affect in foreign language and second language learning: A practical guide to creating a low-anxiety classroom atmosphere* (pp. 64–88). Boston: McGraw-Hill College.

Little, D. (2002). Learner autonomy and second/foreign language learning. In *The guide to good practice for learning and teaching in languages, linguistics and area studies*. LTSN Subject Centre for Languages, Linguistics and Area Studies, University of Southampton.

Liu, I. F., Chen, M. C., Sun, Y. S., Wible, D., & Kuo, C. H. (2010). Extending the TAM model to explore the factors that affect intention to use an online learning community. *Computers & Education, 54*(2), 600–610.

Lyster, R. (2004). Differential effects of prompts and recasts in form-focused instruction. *Studies in Second Language Acquisition, 26*(3), 399–432.

Lyster, R., & Ranta, L. (1997). Corrective feedback and learner uptake: Negotiation of form in communicative classrooms. *Studies in Second Language Acquisition, 19*(1), 37–66.

Matsumura, S., & Hann, G. (2004). Computer anxiety and students' preferred feedback methods in EFL writing. *The Modern Language Journal, 88*(3), 403–415.

Ministry of Education (MOE). (2007). *2007 syllabus: Chinese language primary*. Singapore: Ministry of Education.

Mother Tongue Languages Review Committee. (2010). *Mother tongue languages review committee report*. Singapore: Ministry of Education.

Nokelainen, P. (2006). An empirical assessment of pedagogical usability criteria for digital learning material with elementary school students. *Educational Technology & Society, 9*(2), 178–197.

Norman, D. A. (2002). *The design of everyday things*. NY: Basic Books.

Russell, J., & Spada, N. (2006). The effectiveness of corrective feedback for acquisition of L2 grammar: A meta-analysis of the research. In J. Norris & L. Ortega (Eds.), *Synthesizing research on language learning and teaching* (pp. 133–164). Amsterdam: John Benjamins.

Schmidt, R. (1990). The role of consciousness in second language learning. *Applied Linguistics, 11*(2), 129–158.

Schmidt, R. (1993). Awareness and second language acquisition. *Annual Review of Applied Linguistics, 13*, 206–226.

Sheen, Y. (2007). The effect of focused written corrective feedback and language aptitude on ESL learners' acquisition of articles. *TESOL Quarterly, 41*, 255–283.

Sheen, Y. (2010). Differential effects of oral and written correct feedback in the ESL classroom. *Studies in Second Language Acquisition, 32*(2), 203–234.

Shermis, M., & Barrera, F. (2002). *Exit assessments: Evaluating writing ability through automated essay scoring* (ERIC document reproduction service no ED 464 950).

Shermis, M., & Burstein, J. (2003). *Automated essay scoring: A cross disciplinary perspective.* Mahwah, NJ: Lawrence Erlbaum Associates.

Siemund, P., Schulz, M. E., & Schweinberger, M. (2014). Studying the linguistic ecology of Singapore: A comparison of college and university students. *World Englishes, 33*(3), 340–362.

Sinclair, B. (2000). Learner autonomy: The next phase? In B. Sinclair, I. McGrath, & T. Lamb (Eds.), *Learner autonomy, teacher autonomy: Future directions* (pp. 4–14). London: Longman.

Smeets, E., & Mooij, T. (2001). Pupil-centred learning, ICT, and teacher behaviour: Observations in educational practice. *British Journal of Educational Technology, 32*(4), 403–417.

Truscott, J. (1996). The case against grammar correction in L2 writing classes. *Language Learning, 46,* 327–369.

Van Beuningen, C. G., De Jong, N. H., & Kuiken, F. (2012). Evidence on the effectiveness of comprehensive error correction in second language writing. *Language Learning, 62,* 1–41.

Ware, P. (2005). Missed communication in online communication: Tensions in a German-American telecollaboration. *Language Learning & Technology, 9*(2), 64–89.

Warschauer, M. (1996a). Comparing face-to-face and electronic discussion in the second language classroom. *CALICO Journal, 13,* 7–25.

Warschauer, M. (1996b). Computer-assisted language learning: An introduction. In S. Fotos (Ed.), *Multimedia language teaching* (pp. 3–10). Tokyo: Logos International.

Warschauer, M. (2000). On-line learning in second language classrooms: An ethnographic study. In M. Warschauer & R. Kern (Eds.), *Network-based language teaching: Concepts and practice* (pp. 41–58). Cambridge: Cambridge University Press.

Warschauer, M., & Grimes, D. (2008). Automated writing assessment in the classroom. *Pedagogies: An International Journal, 3*(1), 52–67.

Warschauer, M., & Ware, P. (2006). Automated writing evaluation: Defining the classroom research agenda. *Language Teaching Research, 10*(2), 1–24.

Weigle, S. C. (2002). *Assessing writing.* Cambridge: Cambridge University Press.

Wigfield, A., & Wentzel, K. R. (2007). Introduction to motivation at school: Interventions that work. *Educational Psychologist, 42*(4), 191–196.

Part IV
Assessment, Teaching, and Learning

Chapter 12
Developing a Speaking Diagnostic Tool for Teachers to Differentiate Instruction for Young Learners of Chinese

Xiaoxi Sun, Jinghua Fan and Chee-Kuen Chin

Abstract Chinese language (CL) education in Singapore is encountering increasing challenges as a possible result of the familial language shift from Chinese toward English in the last few decades. One such challenge is the diversity of students' level of Chinese proficiency. To address this challenge, the Singapore Ministry of Education recommended that CL teachers make instructional differentiation based on good knowledge about students' Chinese proficiency levels and different developmental trajectories. It was against such a background that the package of Chinese language Oral Proficiency Diagnostic Tool (OPDT) was developed by the Singapore Centre for Chinese Language for Primary 1 (Grade 1) CL teachers in Singapore. The OPDT was comprised of the Chinese Oral Proficiency Diagnostic Rubrics, the Diagnostic Activity Package, and the Differentiated Instruction Activity Package that aimed to assist CL teachers to diagnose the strengths and weaknesses of Primary 1 students' Chinese oral proficiency, to engage students in using Chinese so that teachers could have adequate student output for diagnosis purposes, and to enable teachers to differentiate their instruction with reference to the result of their diagnosis. This chapter reports on our development of the OPDT, its key features, and our effort to validate it as a useful tool for CL teachers. We hope the Singapore experience would shed light on Chinese as a second language education in other contexts and informs classroom-based formative assessment, instruction, as well as professional learning of CL teachers.

Keywords Chinese language education · Chinese language oral proficiency diagnostic tool · Language assessment · Classroom assessment · Assessment for learning

X. Sun (✉) · J. Fan · C.-K. Chin
Singapore Centre for Chinese Language, Singapore, Singapore
e-mail: sunxiaoxi1234@gmail.com

© Springer Nature Singapore Pte Ltd. 2017
D. Zhang and C.-H. Lin (eds.), *Chinese as a Second Language Assessment*,
Chinese Language Learning Sciences, DOI 10.1007/978-981-10-4089-4_12

Introduction

Singapore is a multilingual society with a population comprised of three major ethnic groups, including Chinese, Malay, and Indian. The ethnic languages of the three groups (i.e., Chinese, Malay, and Tamil) as well as English (i.e., the medium of school instruction) are the four official languages of the country. Under the bilingual education system in Singapore, all school students are required to study English as well as their respective mother tongue or ethnic language (Pakir 2008; Shepherd 2005). For example, ethnic Chinese Singaporeans are required to be competent in both English and Chinese. However, becoming bilingual (and biliterate) in the country is becoming an increasingly challenging task. A recent survey revealed that 59% of Chinese children spoke English as their dominant home language as a possible result of the importance ascribed to English as the medium of instruction in schools (Ministry of Education 2011). The familial language shift from Chinese toward English in the last few decades has brought about great changes to the sociolinguistic milieu in Singapore, and more importantly, it has created a lot of challenges for school education in the country, one being the diversity of students' level of oral proficiency in Chinese (Zhao and Liu 2010; Zhao et al. 2007). While some children have developed some level of oral competence, albeit not always satisfactorily, in Chinese at the commencement of primary schooling, others have to learn Chinese as a completely new language in primary school.

To address the aforementioned challenges, policies concerning mother tongue education, including Chinese language education, have been constantly reviewed and curriculum refined in Singapore. A notable, recent policy, as recommended in the 2010 report of the Mother Tongue Language (MTL) Review Committee (Ministry of Education 2011), is that MTL teaching should "first build the oracy foundation before learning reading and writing" (p. 15) and "recognise different starting points and apply appropriate methods for different learners" (p. 13). With this policy recommendation, an important focus of Chinese education in early primary grades, especially Primary 1 (P1) (Grade 1), is on the development of children's oral competence in Chinese. Teachers are thus advised to adapt their instruction to meet the learning needs of students from different home language backgrounds and with diverse levels of oral proficiency in Chinese.

However, instructional adaptation or differentiation is arguably not easy for Chinese language (CL) teachers as it is conditional upon their clear awareness of individual differences among children and good knowledge about their proficiency levels and different developmental trajectories. In other words, CL teachers first need to be able to appropriately assess students and diagnose their specific needs so as to inform their instructional planning and differentiation. There are, however, several challenges in practice. Firstly, current assessments commonly administered in early primary grades in Singapore do not align with the curricular focus on oral proficiency. For example, school examinations largely focus on vocabulary, grammar, and reading with speaking only taking up 10–20% of students' grades.

Consequently, test results provide very limited information for CL teachers to implement effective practice in oracy-focused instruction in their classrooms. Secondly, students' oral competence is commonly tested by means of out-loud-reading and picture-describing. Such ways of testing measures students' prepared "performance" rather than their abilities to use Chinese interactively in authentic or real communicative contexts. Thirdly, and most importantly, the assessments commonly adopted in schools are summative in nature (e.g., end-of-semester examination). As a result, CL teachers know little about their students' specific strengths and weaknesses in oral language development. Such a lack of knowledge about students' learning needs apparently hinders teachers' practice of differentiated teaching. Thus, it is very important that teachers know how to appropriately and effectively use performance-based, formative assessments in their everyday classroom instruction to diagnose the performance of their students so that differentiated instruction could be possible. Yet, most CL teachers in Singapore have not been prepared or supported to conduct such assessments.

It was against such a backdrop that, in 2010, the Singapore Ministry of Education (MOE) commissioned the Singapore Centre for Chinese Language (SCCL) to undertake a two-year project to develop a scientific, effective, and user-friendly assessment tool to support CL teachers' use of formative assessment and differentiated instruction to promote students' oral proficiency development. Specifically, the objectives of the project were threefold: (1) to develop a scale that would allow Singapore CL teachers to diagnose the strengths and weaknesses of P1 students' Chinese oral proficiency; (2) to develop a set of diagnostic oral activities that could engage students in using Chinese so that teachers could have adequate student output for diagnosis purposes; and (3) to develop a set of exemplar classroom activities that would enable teachers to differentiate their instruction with reference to the result of their diagnosis. The end product of the project was the P1 Chinese language Oral Proficiency Diagnostic Tool (hereafter, the OPDT), which is a package comprised of three components that serve different purposes, including the P1 Chinese Oral Proficiency Diagnostic Rubrics (hereafter, the Diagnostic Rubrics); the Diagnostic Activity Package (DAP); and the Differentiated Instruction Activity Package (DIAP).

In the following sections of this chapter, we report on the process of developing the OPDT and the different purposes of its three components. To show the effectiveness of the OPDT for enhancing students' oral proficiency development, we also report an intervention study in which P1 teachers were trained to use the package for in-class assessment and differentiated teaching. Although this project was conducted with young learners in Singapore, it sheds light on Chinese language education in other contexts with respect to using assessment to inform instruction and enhance students' CL learning.

The Diagnostic Rubrics

As a crucial component of the OPDT, the Diagnostic Rubrics are a formative assessment tool designed by the project team for CL teachers to diagnostically assess P1 students' oral performance in Chinese when they are participating in classroom oral activities. Teachers use the Diagnostic Rubrics to assess students' oral competence in Chinese with both a holistic score that represents the students' overall level and a set of analytic scores to demonstrate their strengths and weaknesses in different areas. The Diagnostic Rubrics cover four levels defined as four developmental stages, and include indicators of vocabulary, grammar and sentence structure, pronunciation and intonation, and interpersonal interaction and expression. Within each level and for each indicator, there are specific descriptors that represent how strong or weak a student's performance is.

Construction of the Diagnostic Rubrics

The development of the Diagnostic Rubrics began with developing a prototype, which was then validated and calibrated with some iterative processes. The prototype of the Diagnostic Rubrics took its form on the basis of empirical data of one-to-one interviews with 184 P1 students sampled from different modules (i.e., Bridging, Core, and Enrichment) in four primary schools.[1] The final composition of students from the three modules was 59, 70, and 55, respectively. Each interview lasted for 25–30 min, with three main topics on food, toys, and festivals. The children were first asked to describe or compare pictures shown to them with guiding questions like "What do you see in these pictures?" and "Do you see any difference between the two pictures?" They were then engaged in interactions about the pictures with the interviewer, who asked open questions according to a child's previous descriptions of the pictures. The interviews were both audio- and video-taped.

The audio-taped data were transcribed and coded on four categories, namely, lexical, sentential, pronunciation and intonation, and discourse. With the coded speech data as the baseline, four levels were created to represent the participating students' Chinese oral proficiency. In addition, key characteristics of the speeches

---

[1]All of the participating schools in the project were selected with recommendation from CPDD (Curriculum Planning and Development Division), MOE, and they consisted of an equal number of mission and neighborhood schools, with comparable student composition ratios. Students attending mission schools in Singapore generally come from English-speaking homes, whereas those in neighborhood schools show a variety of home language use patterns, but typically with a significant proportion using Chinese as the major home language. It is beyond the scope of this paper to provide details of the three different modules. The modular approach is an essential characteristic of the (differentiated) Chinese curriculum in Singapore. Interested readers can refer to Li et al. (2012) for an introduction to the modular curriculum.

of those students within each of the four proficiency levels were constructed into four indicators that belonged to two main aspects of oral language proficiency, including linguistic (i.e., lexical, sentential, and pronunciation and intonation) and communicative competence (i.e., discourse).

The prototype Diagnostic Rubrics were first used by some members of the research team as well as master teachers affiliated with SCCL for trial assessment of some P1 students with the speech data previously collected. In addition, we also consulted a panel of experts of Chinese language education and assessment to solicit their feedback and professional input. The panel was comprised of a former member of the Singapore Examinations and Assessment Board, an assessment expert from National Institute of Education (a teacher training college in Singapore), and a visiting professor of Chinese language education at SCCL.

After incorporating the experiences from trial use and the experts' input, a full version of the Diagnostic Rubrics (with a user's manual and speech samples) was prepared. In the Diagnostic Rubrics, there were four distinguishing levels, which were metaphorically named as emerging stage (萌芽期), developing stage (展叶期), blooming stage (开花期), and accomplishing stage (幼果期) to symbolize the developmental levels of students' Chinese oral competence at the beginning of primary schooling. Across all four levels, the Diagnostic Rubrics described two main areas of oral proficiency, namely, linguistic competence and communicative competence. Linguistic competence was presented with indicators of vocabulary, grammar and sentence structure, and pronunciation and intonation. Communicative competence was indicated as interaction and expression, which looked into actual language use in interpersonal interaction. Each indicator included qualitative descriptors drawing on ascending quantifiers that represented degrees to which students demonstrate evidence of linguistic and communicative abilities across the four stages. For example, vocabulary at the emerging stage is described as "very poor or limited vocabulary; vocabulary restricted to simple responses and incomplete meaning expressions;" and communicative competence at the accomplishing stage is described as "sufficient responses that often include details; natural pausing and smooth turn-taking; frequent initiations through questioning; chunks of coherent discourse on a given topic." Finally, in addition to these four indicators for analytic rating, the Diagnostic Rubrics also included a holistic rating option to assign an overall performance level/stage of students.

Validation of the Diagnostic Rubrics

Unlike speaking scales used primarily in a high-stakes testing context, our Diagnostic Rubrics were designed to be used in classrooms by CL teachers as a formative assessment tool that could guide instructional planning for differentiation. To examine whether the Diagnostic Rubrics could be effectively used by teachers to diagnose their students' oral Chinese proficiency, a validation study with iterative processes was conducted.

A group of 20 P1 teachers participated in the study. They came from four different schools that did not participate in the study described earlier, where some P1 students were sampled and interviewed to provide the baseline data for developing the prototype Diagnostic Rubrics. After training through a workshop, those teachers independently used the Diagnostic Rubrics for three weeks, and focus group discussions were also conducted with them at this time. The tool was then calibrated based on the feedback from the teachers. Afterward, members of the research team were assigned to visit the classes of the 20 teachers for two weeks, during which time, the teachers and members of the research team (or co-raters) referred to the calibrated Diagnostic Rubrics independently and assessed the same group of students identified for this study in each teacher's class.[2] A total number of 196 students across 20 P1 classes were diagnosed. Table 12.1 shows the distributions of different ranges of intra-class correlation coefficients between the ratings of a teacher and his/her co-rater. The degree of rating consistency indicates the inter-rater reliability of the Diagnostic Rubrics.

Table 12.1 shows that the correlations between the ratings given by most teacher-and-co-rater pairs were significant, which means that the teachers used the Diagnostic Rubrics in a fairly consistent way as did the members of the research team who developed the tool. The proportions of significant correlation coefficients in vocabulary, grammar, pronunciation, communication, and overall score were, respectively, 65, 70, 70, 80, and 80%. Take communication as an example; the ratings of most of the teachers ($N = 12$ or 60%) were strongly correlated with those given by the research team (with intra-class correlation coefficients being 0.800 or higher); and there were only four teachers (20%) whose ratings did not show significant correlations with those of the research team. The inter-rater reliability for overall performance was particularly high, as all of the 16 significant cases displayed significant correlations greater than 0.700. The high agreement between teacher-and-researcher pairs indicates that the Diagnostic Rubrics are a fairly reliable tool for CL teachers to use to diagnose the speaking ability of P1 students in the classroom context.

On the other hand, as shown in Table 12.1, there were still a small number of teacher-and-co-rater pairs that did not seem to have given consistent ratings. The major disagreement seemed to pertain to vocabulary and pronunciation, as there were, respectively, 7 (35%) and 6 (30%) cases in which the inter-rater reliability was not significant. Even within the significant cases, the inter-rater reliability of two teacher-and-co-rater pairs was below 0.600 for vocabulary. Taken together, the findings suggested that the indicators related to linguistic form, unlike communication and overall performance, would require further calibration to ensure consistent understanding. At the completion of this first round of the validation study,

---

[2]Because the limited size of the research team, each member of the team visited multiple teachers' classes and rated multiple groups of students. Previously, during the process of developing the Diagnostic Rubrics, the inter-reliability among project team members was 0.849 (vocabulary), 0.862 (grammar), 0.820 (pronunciation), 0.868 (communication), and 0.882 (overall). All were intra-class correlation coefficients.

Table 12.1 Distribution of ranges of intra-class correlation coefficients

	Non-sig. cases no. (%)	Sig. cases no. (%)					Total no. (%)
		<0.600	0.600–0.699	0.700–0.799	0.800–0.899	0.900–1	
Vocabulary	7 (35%)	2 (10%)	0 (0%)	4 (20%)	2 (10%)	5 (25%)	20 (100%)
Grammar	6 (30%)	0 (0%)	3 (15%)	1 (5%)	4 (20%)	6 (30%)	20 (100%)
Pronunciation	6 (30%)	2 (10%)	0 (0%)	5 (25%)	4 (20%)	3 (15%)	20 (100%)
Communication	4 (20%)	1 (5%)	1 (5%)	2 (10%)	7 (35%)	5 (25%)	20 (100%)
Overall	4 (20%)	0 (0%)	0 (0%)	2 (10%)	9 (45%)	5 (25%)	20 (100%)

an in-depth discussion was conducted between the participating teachers and the research team to find out possible reasons behind the disagreement (especially for vocabulary and grammar). Based on the feedback during the discussion, the descriptors for each indicator or diagnosing category at each level were further refined and finalized.

Diagnostic Activity Package (DAP)

Teachers' appropriate and effective use of the Diagnostic Rubrics arguably depends on students' classroom discursive participation. In other words, only when students make full use of their knowledge and skills in actual communication can their oral performance reflect their true level of oral proficiency and can this oral proficiency be reliably assessed by their teacher. To maximize students' classroom oral output and support teachers' classroom use of the Diagnostic Rubrics, we also developed the DAP with 33 curriculum-aligned interactive activities. Of the 33 oral diagnostic activities, the first three are about self-introduction, toys, and food, which P1 students should feel most comfortable talking about at the beginning of their first school year and CL teachers are supposed to focus their instruction on *Hanyu Pinyin*. The remaining 30 activities were designed to align with the topics of the 15 units of the P1 Chinese textbook (two activities for each topic/unit). All of the DAP activities were initially used by the 20 teachers who participated in the aforementioned validation study; their feedback was solicited to refine the activities.

Activity Outline

Table 12.2 shows the outline or major components of a DAP activity. It is the first of the two activities designed to be aligned with Unit 1 (*Going to School*) of the children's P1 Chinese textbook. As Table 12.2 shows, in addition to *Topic*, a DAP activity outline is comprised of *Activity Type, Content, Objective, Prerequisite Knowledge, Suggested Class Period, Length of Activity, Organization and Procedure, Resources*, and *Assessment*.

Table 12.2 Example of outline of a DAP activity

1.	Unit/topic 课文	Unit 1 going to school (diagnostic activity 1) 第一课《上学校》(口语诊断活动一)
2.	Activity type 活动类型	Elaboration and group interaction 话题展开、小组对话
3.	Content 活动内容	Locations in school that you like and do not like 喜欢和不喜欢的学校地点
4.	Objective 活动目的	Diagnose students' knowledge of the following words, sentence structures, and expressions, and their ability to use them for communication Location nouns: campus, canteen, library, etc. Verbs: eat, play, watch/see, etc. Adjectives: beautiful, yummy, sweet, good (in smell), interesting, etc. Sentence structures: clauses that begin with *because*; coordination sentences Expressions/speech acts: explaining, questioning, and giving opinions Pronunciations and tones 诊断学生使用下列词语、句型、表达方式及进行沟通的交流能力。 处所名词: 校园、食堂、图书馆等 动词: 吃、玩、看等 形容词: 美丽、好吃、甜、香、好玩等 语法句型: "因为"起头单句、并列句 交际表达: 解释、提问、表达意见 语音语调
5.	Prerequisite knowledge 活动所需先备知识	Nouns for different locations of the school 学校各个地点的名词
6.	Suggested class period 建议活动进行时间	As part of the aural/oral class period 配合听听说说课进行
7.	Length of activity 活动时间	30 min 30分钟
8.	Organization/procedures 活动安排/组织	Suggested grouping: three students per group [a]Procedures: sharing and questioning-answering in group; group presentation 建议人数:每组三名学生 [a]流程:小组分享与问答、呈现
9.	Recourses 活动资源	PowerPoint, question cards, checklist, pictures of different school locations 简报、提问卡、检查表、学校不同地点的图片
10.	Assessment 活动评价	Diagnostic rubrics 口语诊断量表

Note [a]Procedures are further specified in the DAP (see Activity Procedures below). All three components of the OPDT, including the DAP, are in Chinese for teachers. The examples here and below are presented in both Chinese and English for non-Chinese speaking readers of this paper

Activity Type informs teachers about what their students are supposed to do for an activity. There are altogether seven activity types in DAP. In addition to elaboration (话题展开) and group interaction (小组对话) shown in Table 12.2, there are situational interaction (情境会话), picture-based interaction/talk (看图对话/说话), decision making (决策活动), game (游戏), and role play (角色扮演). They are all student-centered and communication-oriented activities to involve students in interactional use of the Chinese language. In the present example, students are expected to elaborate on a topic based on group interaction. They may express ideas, ask questions, give clarifications, etc. *Objective* provides guidance to teachers on what to focus on in the process of diagnosing based on their students' Chinese oral output. In this example, teachers are encouraged to focus on how competent their students are at interacting with each other by use of specific words and sentence structures; whether they are capable of performing particular speech acts; and how good their pronunciation and intonation are. *Prerequisite Knowledge* helps teachers figure out how much the activity fits their students' Chinese proficiency level, and what their students need to be warmed up for. Other information like *Activity Length, Suggested Class Period* to use the activity, and group size helps teachers evaluate the feasibility of the activity for a particular class, and if needed, make reasonable adjustments to the organization of the activity. To provide teachers with clear guidance on activity organization, the procedure of each activity is carefully designed and specified in the DAP with step-by-step directions (see Activity Procedures below for details). Activity resources including PPTs, pictures, worksheets, checklists, etc. are also prepared and attached to each activity. All these efforts are to make it possible for teachers to use the Diagnostic Rubrics effectively to diagnose students' performance while they are participating in the activity.

Activity Procedures

As indicated above, specific procedures with step-by-step directions are provided for each activity. Table 12.3 shows an example of how the DAP supports teachers to conduct an activity procedurally. It is the second of the two activities designed to align with Unit 2 (*Schoolbag Says...*) of the children's textbook. It shows how procedurally a decision-making activity is to be conducted on what stationery students would like to bring to school and why. As this example shows, each diagnostic activity typically begins with a warm-up session, in which students are exposed to a set of pictures to get prepared for participating in the group activity, such as words and basic sentence structures to be used. The class is then divided into groups; and tasks are then assigned to each group with clear task instructions prepared in the DAP for the teacher. The warm-up session is followed by teacher and/or student demonstration, so that students can get deeper insight into the nature of the activity, what they are supposed to do, and how to apply the required knowledge they have learned in the warm-up session.

Students then participate in the group activity during which they interact with each other in Chinese, and the teacher diagnoses target students' Chinese abilities against the Diagnostic Rubrics. In this example, students as a group need to make a decision on ranking the popularity of different stationeries through discussion.

Table 12.3 Example of DAP activity procedures

1.	Teacher presenting pictures and asking a few students to say the names and utilities of the stationeries in the pictures 教师展示图片并请几个学生轮流说出文具的名称和用途。
2.	Teacher distributing to each group a set of picture cards, a table for ranking stationaries, and a checklist 教师给每组学生一套图卡、文具排行榜表格和检查表。
3.	Teacher giving detailed task instructions Form groups of four with members numbered 1, 2, 3, and 4, respectively Each member to share for 2 min with reference to the following questions: If you are allowed to bring only one stationery to school, which one would you choose? Why? (Note: if a student does not like the stationaries on the picture cards, s/he is allowed to choose any other stationaries that s/he likes.) Why would you not choose other stationeries (choose one to give your explanation)? (Note: more capable students can be asked to additionally explain what they could possibly do if these unchosen stationaries turn out to be needed later in school.) Group discussion to decide which stationery is the best and the most useful, and then rank all the stationeries based on their levels of usefulness When one student is sharing, another student takes note on the checklist of the presenting student's choice and the number of reasons s/he explained 教师交付任务: 你们四人一组,一个是1号,一个是2号,一个是3号,另一个是4号。 每个人有2分钟的时间分享: 如果你只能带一样文具来学校,你选哪一样?为什么?(注:如果学生不喜欢这些文具,可以选自己喜欢的其他文具来代替。) 为什么不选其他文具呢?选一个文具来说(注:程度较好的学生,要求他们解释不选其他文具的原因,还有需要用到它们的时候怎么办。) 过后小组讨论哪一样文具最好、最有用,并给文具排名。 说的同学请另一个同学在检查表写明自己的选择、说了几个原因。
4.	Teacher demonstration: I would choose a pencil, because I can use it to do classwork I would not choose a ruler, because my pencil can be used as a ruler to help me draw a line I think a pencil is the best choice, because I can use it to both write and draw 教师示范如下: 我选择带铅笔。因为要做功课的时候,我可以用铅笔做功课。 我不选尺,因为我会用铅笔画直线。 我觉得铅笔最好,因为我可以用铅笔写字和画画。
5.	Teacher asking a student to demonstrate 教师请一个学生出来示范。
6.	Teacher diagnosing a group of students or circulating around the classroom 教师诊断一组学生或即处巡视。

(continued)

Table 12.3 (continued)

7.	Group presentation
	Each group member first tells his/her choice, and then provides reasons for the choice and describes the chosen stationery
	Group explains how the stationeries that their members chose were ranked
	Teacher invites other students to ask questions or comment on the presenting group's ranking result
	Teacher collects the checklist
	Teacher gives remarks on students' performance in this activity
	教师请小组出出来呈现。
	各组员先说出自己的选择,并说明理由、形容所选择的文具的样子。
	小组解释自己怎样为这些文具排名。
	过后,教师请其他学生提问或评论该组的排名。
	教师回收检查表。
	教师总结活动。

To complete the task, they need to hold an argument, express opinions, and give explanations, which provide output for the teacher to diagnose their linguistic and communication competence in Chinese. It is notable that notes are also embedded in procedural descriptions to guide the teacher in adapting the difficulty level of one or more steps of the tasks to cater to the needs of individual students. As shown in this example, if a student is perceived to have demonstrated a stronger performance than others or be learning faster than others, the teacher can ask the student to explain why other stationeries were not chosen (over and beyond explaining why one was chosen, which is expected of every student) and how the student would handle the situation when those stationeries turn out to be needed in school.

Teaching Resources

In addition to specifying procedures for teachers to organize a DAP activity, teaching resources related to that activity are also provided. They include pictures, cards, worksheets, PowerPoints, checklists, etc. that can be directly used by teachers to generate student output for diagnostic purposes. Figure 12.1 shows an example of teaching resources provided for a DAP activity. This picture shows the typical schedule of a student; each section includes a clock face with the time indicated. Students are expected to work in pairs or small groups to ask and answer questions about the picture using appropriate words (e.g., 踢足球 play soccer; 做功课 do homework) and sentence structures (e.g., …每天几点… /when does … [do

Fig. 12.1 Picture as a DAP teaching resource for teachers

something] every day?) to describe when the student does what every day. While this picture-based activity was designed for diagnostic purposes, it could also be used by the teacher as a pedagogical task to scaffold students to work on subsequent communicative activities in which students may ask each other authentic questions about what they themselves typically do at what time every day.

To sum up, with clear instructional procedures and resources, the DAP enables teachers to conduct in-class diagnosis of their students' oral performance as a natural or normal component of their everyday classroom teaching. As these activities are curriculum-aligned, they can easily fit in the classroom without interfering normal teaching practice. Teachers do not need to pull their students out for individual assessments, which would be very time-consuming and is often logistically challenging for CL teachers in Singapore.

Differentiated Instruction Activity Package (DIAP)

The OPDT project did not stop at helping teachers diagnose their students' CL performance. An important objective of the project was to help teachers make use of the diagnostic results of individual students so that they could benefit from differentiated learning opportunities for enhanced development of Chinese oral proficiency. To help CL teachers address students' weaknesses as informed by the diagnostic information, the DIAP, which includes a set of exemplar oral interactive activities, was developed with joint collaboration among the project team, experienced CL teachers, as well as master teachers affiliated with SCCL. A key characteristic of the DIAP is thus that all the activities are diagnosis-informed. More specifically, when we developed the DIAP, we referred carefully to the indicators (e.g., vocabulary and communication) and performance levels or developmental stages in the Diagnostic Rubrics. We then used our expert knowledge to develop exemplar activities that could address the challenges that were expected to be faced by some students during their learning of the 15 curricular units.

There were altogether 30 DIAP activities, with two for each of the curricular units. These DIAP activities fall into two types, with one more form-focused to highlight linguistic knowledge (hereafter, Type-I) and the other more oriented for interactive competence in communicative contexts (hereafter, Type-II). A rationale behind such a design is the enhancement of input (Wong 2005), which seeks to integrate traditional form-focused exercises into communicative contexts. For each of the 15 units from the P1 Chinese textbook, activities of the two types are paired, with Type-I allowing for essential practice of language forms and getting students ready for communicative use of them in Type-II activities.

Table 12.4 shows the two types of ability focus and their corresponding indicators in the Diagnostic Rubrics for the 30 DIAP activities across 15 curricular units. As the table shows, all the DIAP activities not only cover all key indicators but also consider the four developmental stages of competence as reflected in the Diagnostic Rubrics. In addition, when we designed the 30 activities, we also

Table 12.4 Ability focus of DIAP activities and corresponding indicators in the diagnostic rubrics

Unit	Type-I activity ability focus	Corresponding indicators in diagnostic rubrics	Type-II activity ability focus	Corresponding indicators in diagnostic rubrics
1.	Simple sentence	Grammar and sentence	Turning-taking and the turn of roles in a dialogue	Response and initiation
2.	Statement and simple question conversion	Sentence pattern	Enhancing the ability to initiate by asking questions	Initiation and sustaining a dialogue
3.	Continuous questioning and information supplement	Response	Situational question and answer	Sustaining a dialogue
4.	Comparative sentence	Sentence and function	Sustained output based on comparison	Sentence function and continuous utterance
5.	Using different question sentence structure to ask for one questions	Sentence functions	Questions and description	Sustaining a conversation with continuous utterance
6.	Asking questions	Sentence functions	Situational conversation with sentence pattern changes	Sentence function and sustained conversation
7.	Word order and sentence expansion	Grammar	Description with a chunk of meaning unit	Extended output
8.	Sentence expansion and word order	Vocabulary and grammar	Explaining with a chunk of meaning unit	Extended output
9.	Word order and sentence pattern change	Grammar and sentence	Report and quoting others	Extended output
10.	Different sentence structures for the same function	Sentence function	Appropriateness in communication	Naturalness and fluency
11.	Word order and compound sentence	Grammar and sentence function	Question, ask for clarification and sustained conversation	Topic expansion and extended output
12.	Choice of sentence structure	Sentence function	Group discussion	Negotiation of meaning and expansion of topic
13.	Word order and collocation	Vocabulary and grammar	Asking for clarification and questioning	Turning-taking and negotiation of meaning
14.	Word class and collocation	Vocabulary	Descriptive chunk	Order of meaning units
15.	Variety of sentence pattern	Sentence function	Group discussion and coherency	Quality and quantity in an extended output

consulted the curricular objectives of the 15 units. This means that all of the activities for linguistic forms and functions or communication are aligned with the objective designations in the P1 CL curriculum in Singapore. Naturally, the complexity of language forms and use in these DIAP activities increases across the 15 units. In other words, the DAP activities can be regarded as representing a general progression of growing competence (e.g., linguistic sophistication and complexity of language functions) across the 15 units in an academic year.

Because they are closely curriculum-aligned, the DIAP activities can be easily integrated into daily classroom teaching while highlighting particular language points or skills that students may be diagnosed to be underdeveloped. On the other hand, it is noted that intended to be exemplars, the two activities in each unit necessarily could not address the differential learning needs of all students, and thus could and should not be used for all students without any adaptations. When we developed the DIAP, we were clearly aware that there was no way that we could capture all (unique) needs of students across all P1 classrooms in Singapore. Consequently, while each exemplar activity provides some space for adaptation (e.g., different degrees of intensity and various forms of practice with the targeted learning points) by teachers, they are expected to develop their own interventional activities to expand the capacity of the DIAP for differentiated teaching and meet the unique situation or set of diagnosis results among their students.

Table 12.5 shows an exemplar DIAP activity that addresses Type-I ability (i.e., language forms). It illustrates how an activity targets a specific diagnosed error in students' use of place adverbials in Chinese. In English, place adverbials typically follow a verb, such as in the sentence *I study in the library*. In Chinese, however, a place adverbial usually appears between the subject and a verb, such as 我 (*I*) 在 (preposition *in/at*) 食堂 (*canteen*) 吃饭 (*eat*). Likely due to negative transfer from English, Singaporean students who come from an English-speaking family often make an error of putting the prepositional phrase "在 (in/at)...," which indicates where an action happens, after a verb or a verbal phrase.

To address this predicted challenge in Chinese learning, we designed this form-focused language game as a DIAP activity. As shown in Table 12.5, the game is separated into several steps. The whole class is first divided into groups of three students. Then, a set of flash cards with words of a different category are given to each group member. As shown in the table, Student 1 would have words of animated nouns such as people or animals; the cards taken by Student 2 would show words of actions such as *read*, *sing*, and *eat*; and Student 3 would receive a number of words indicating places such as *canteen* and *library*. Finally, the three group members interact with each other in the modeled format with the help of the keywords on the cards in their hands. This game, through constructing funny sentences, thus facilitates students' learning of the correct order of the subject (animated nouns; e.g., *the schoolmaster*), place adverbials (e.g., *in the toilet*), and the action verb or verbal phrase (e.g., *made a handstand*).

Table 12.5 Exemplar DIAP activity

Grouping and activity instructions 分组与活动说明	Teacher forms groups of three students, and informs the class that they are going to play a game called "*Our Sentence is the Funniest.*" Each group member gets a set of cards with words of a particular category (i.e., *something/somebody, somewhere, and doing something*), and asks questions following the format below Student 1 (word in hand about *something/somebody* indicated by X): Where is X? Student 2 (word about *somewhere* indicated by Y): X is at/in Y Student 1 (to Student 3): What is X doing? Student 3 (word in hand about *doing something* indicated by Z): X is doing Z at/in Y After everyone makes at least one full sentence with words of all three types (like what Student 3 gives), the group discusses which sentence is the funniest 学生分三人一组,安排为1、2、3.说明要玩一个游戏:"我们的句子最有趣"。每人分得一组手中词卡上的词汇[某人物、(在)某处、(做)某事]进行提问.形式如下: 学生1(手中的是主语X):X在哪里? 学生2(地点词):X在Y(地点)。 学生1(对学生3): X在做什么? 学生3:X在Y做Z(事)。 每人都至少造一个句子后,就讨论决定哪个句子最有趣。
Demonstration 示范	Teacher invites a group to demonstrate the game with three rounds in which the three sets of word cards rotate among the three members. In each round, each member works with a word of a different category. After three rounds, the group decides which of the three sentences is the funniest 教师请一组学生出来示范,确定学生1、2、3。在三轮示范中,他们轮流抽取不同范畴的词卡。问答示范结束后,请学生讨论并决定哪个句子最有趣。
Tips 小贴士	1. Design of word cards In order for students to construct funny sentences, the words for *somebody/something* can initially be from the textbook and then include other things or people that students are familiar with. The words for *somewhere* and *doing something* can be new words annotated with *pinyin*, such as canteen, bus station, change clothes, swim, etc. 2. Differentiation A slip of paper with the sentence frame (i.e., [who] in/at [where] [do what]) can be provided for students with low oral proficiency; they can produce a sentence by filling in the slots with appropriate words. Students with strong oral proficiency can follow the procedure of the game and give their sentences, and then be encouraged to construct additional sentences on paper with different but reasonable words using either characters or *pinyin*. They are encouraged to add modifiers to construct expanded or more complex sentences, such as *a beautiful fairy, beside a quiet pond, eating yummy chicken rice*, etc. 1. 词卡的设计 为了让学生设计出有趣的句子,开始时的"某人/某物"词卡可以是书上的人物,过后可以用身边的人物;"某处"和"某事"的词可以是注上汉语拼音的学生词,例如食堂、车站、换衣服、游泳等。 2. 学习的差异性 如果是口语能力较弱的学生,可以提供让他们填好句型的纸条[什么人/在哪里/做什么],让他们跟着读者句子来填入词语后说话。如果是口语能力较强的学生,他们可以按游戏步骤的要求说几个句子,然后鼓励他们自己白纸上填入不同的、合理的词语(或汉语拼音),还加入修饰词来进行造句游戏.例如加入"美丽的仙女""安静的水池边""吃香喷喷的鸡饭"等。

It is noted that while students of all ability levels could engage in a DIAP activity, we also considered the capacity of an activity for differentiation for students with different levels of proficiency. In the game presented in Table 12.5, for example, students with stronger oral competence could be encouraged to discuss and decide on one or two sentences that they agree to be the funniest, while less capable students could just focus on practicing the basic sentence structure targeting the order of place adverbials. This activity also has a capacity to allow more capable students to practice expanded or more complex sentences on the target structure. For example, an adverb(s) could be added to modify a target verb, and an adjective (s) could be included to modify a target animated noun. There is also a possibility to get students to use conjunctives (e.g., 可是 but/however) to connect different parts of a compound sentence. If writing Chinese characters is a learning objective, students could also be asked to write out the sentences they and their peers produced while playing the game. In addition, the design of the flash cards also allows teachers to make adaptations. For example, different sets of cards can be prepared for the same set of words, with diverse combinations of Chinese characters, *pinyin*, and pictures, and then be given to different students with varied levels of word recognition ability.

Effect of Using the OPDT on Students' Oral Proficiency Development

To examine if using the OPDT, including the DIAP, could achieve its expected positive effect on enhancing students' oral proficiency development, an intervention study with an interval of about three months was conducted subsequently in four primary schools with 16 P1 teachers who had not participated in any previous stages of the OPDT project. Sixteen teachers and their P1 classes from four other schools served as the control group in which no one had been exposed to the OPDT. In both the intervention and the control groups, two of the four schools were mission schools where, in the Singapore context, students tend to largely come from an English-speaking home; whereas, the other two schools were neighborhood schools where typically a significant proportion of students use Chinese as their major home language. Given the centralized education system in Singapore, all schools followed the same curriculum developed by the MOE. The teachers participating in the intervention were first trained to use the Diagnostic Rubrics, and their ratings were analyzed for inter-rater reliability. They were then trained to use the DAP for in-class diagnosis of students' oral Chinese competence against the levels and indicators in the Diagnostic Rubrics; and the DIAP to differentiate classroom instruction based on the assessment results. The teachers in the control group followed their regular instructional arrangement (i.e., business-as-usual group).

Table 12.6 Distribution of ranges of intra-class correlation coefficients

	Sig. cases no. (%)					Total no. (%)
	<0.600	0.600–0.699	0.700–0.799	0.800–0.899	0.900–1	
Vocabulary	0 (0%)	4 (25%)	4 (25%)	6 (37.5%)	2 (12.5%)	16 (100%)
Grammar	2 (12.5%)	2 (12.5%)	4 (25%)	8 (50%)	0 (0%)	16 (100%)
Pronunciation	4 (25%)	6 (37.5%)	3 (18.8%)	3 (18.8%)	0 (0%)	16 (100%)
Communication	0 (0%)	1 (6.3%)	5 (31.3%)	8 (50%)	2 (12.5%)	16 (100%)
Overall	0 (0%)	2 (12.5%)	3 (18.8%)	8 (50%)	3 (18.8%)	16 (100%)

Teacher Training in Using the Diagnostic Rubrics

After being trained in a workshop, the 16 P1 teachers participating in the intervention were asked to use the Diagnostic Rubrics to assess 14 randomly selected student speech samples from the pool of interviews collected at the initial stage of developing this tool. The coefficients of intra-class correlations among the 16 teachers were all statistically significant with a range of 0.705–0.752 across the diagnosing indicators. It means the teachers were able to assign highly consistent ratings among themselves for different indicators in the Diagnostic Rubrics. In addition, their ratings were also compared with those of the research team who developed the Diagnostic Rubrics for further inter-rater reliability analysis, following the same procedure that we used to calibrate the tool.

Like Table 12.1, Table 12.6 presents the distribution of different ranges of intra-class correlation coefficients for each diagnosis category. All of the correlation coefficients were significant. Specifically, the correlation coefficients varied from 0.600 to 0.931 for vocabulary, from 0.542 to 0.876 for grammar, from 0.479 to 0.819 for pronunciation, from 0.640 to 0.957 for communication, and from 0.669 to 0.942 for overall performance. The inter-rater reliability of all sixteen teachers' ratings was above 0.600 for vocabulary, and among them, inter-rater reliability of eight teachers' ratings was above 0.800. A similar pattern was also found for communication and overall performance. On the other hand, a few teachers seemed to have had difficulty in rating for grammar and pronunciation, especially the latter. The intra-class correlation coefficients of two teachers' ratings were as low as 0.580 and 0.542 for grammar. Similarly, in the case of pronunciation, the inter-rater reliability of four teachers' ratings was below 0.600. This result seemed to echo the findings of some previous studies, albeit on languages other than Chinese and in different contexts. For example, Hendricks and colleagues (1980; cf. Fulcher 2003) found in their study that the inter-rater reliability for pronunciation was as low as 0.43. In the Singapore context, teachers' relatively less prevalent agreement with the research team on grammar and pronunciation did not seem to be a big surprise, given that people may have different understandings about what constitutes correct grammar and pronunciation, and thus may have different levels of tolerance (and ratings) of grammatical use and pronunciation that seemed to "deviate" from the standard of the research team (Shang and Zhao, this volume). To reconcile any

Table 12.7 ANCOVA comparing post-assessment ratings between the control and the intervention groups with pre-assessment ratings as the covariate

	Control ($N = 133$)	Intervention ($N = 139$)	F
Vocabulary	8.93	8.96	122.66***
Grammar	8.72	8.80	118.64***
Pronunciation	10.08	9.85	115.37***
Communication	8.94	9.06	135.26***
Overall	8.94	9.06	152.85***

***$p < 0.001$

discrepancy that the intervention teachers appeared to have with the research team, a group discussion session was organized before the teachers were trained to use the DAP to elicit student output for classroom diagnosis purposes and the DIAP for differentiating instruction.

Pre- and Post-assessments

Experienced research assistants from the project team observed all 32 classes in the intervention and the control groups, and use the Diagnosis Rubrics to assess the oral language proficiency of a selected sample of students in each class. Altogether 139 students were sampled from the 16 classes in the intervention group with an average of about 8.7 students from each class; about 133 students were sampled from the 16 classes in the control group with an average of about 8.3 students from each class. For each diagnosis indicator (i.e., vocabulary, grammar, pronunciation, communication, and overall performance), the score ranged from 1 to 12.[3] Two rounds of assessments were conducted, one prior to the intervention and the other after the intervention, with an interval of about three months. In between these two assessments, the research assistants continued to observe all of the classes and record focal students' oral language output for subsequent qualitative analyses. Due to the limited space of this chapter, we only report the result of the quantitative analyses that compared the two groups. Table 12.7 shows the two groups' post-assessment ratings and the ANCOVA results with the pre-assessment ratings as the covariate. As shown in the table, after adjusting for the difference between the two groups prior to the intervention, the post-assessment ratings of the intervention group were significantly greater than those of the control group (all ps < 0.001).

---

[3]Within each level or stage (i.e., emerging, developing, blooming, and accomplishing), we further distinguished three sub-levels, including lower, middle, and upper. Thus, a score of 1 indicates lower emerging; that of 12 indicates upper accomplishing.

Conclusions

In this chapter, we reported a project conducted to address the challenges posed to CL teachers in Singapore where an increasing number of students come from English-speaking families and learn Chinese as a second language in school. In response to this change in the language background of CL learners, the Mother Tongue Languages Review Committee (Ministry of Education 2011) recommended that more pedagogical emphasis be put on oral proficiency development in early primary grades and that teachers adopt differentiated strategies to support oral language development of all students. Again this backdrop, the OPDT project was conducted to develop a set of tools that P1 teachers could use to conduct formative assessments of students' oral proficiency, diagnose individual students' learning needs in different areas, and then implement differentiated teaching. Specifically, the Diagnostic Rubrics allow teachers to conduct in-class diagnostic assessments of their students in regard to both linguistic and communicative competence at four levels. The DAP provides student-centered activities for teachers to engage students in communicative use of Chinese to generate output for reliable and effective diagnosis. Finally, the DIAP provides exemplar activities that teachers can directly adopt to enhance students' linguistic knowledge as well as communicative competence, or they can use these activities as references and their diagnostic assessment results as the basis to develop their own classroom activities for differentiated teaching. A subsequent intervention study with P1 teachers also confirmed that the OPDT was a useful and effective tool for CL teachers to use to inform instructional differentiation for Chinese learners with different learning needs.

While the project was conducted in Singapore with a focus on young learners, the implications for Chinese as a second language assessment and instruction are far beyond that particular learning context. As a matter of fact, the increasing diversity among learners of Chinese does not pertain to Singapore alone. Historically, the teaching and learning of Chinese in non-Chinese-speaking countries happened largely in tertiary institutions, and learners were primarily adult learners studying in a university-based Chinese program. However, with the increasing popularity of Chinese language and culture, particularly recently under the Chinese government's promotion of the Confucius Institutes and Confucius Classrooms (Zhao and Huang 2012; see also Teng, this volume), people from diverse backgrounds are learning Chinese globally. One notable characteristic of recent changes is the fast growth of Chinese programs in K-12 schools and an increasing number of young learners (Asia Society and The College Board 2008). Along with this increase of popularity of Chinese, however, are challenges for teachers like those faced by teachers in Singapore.

In the United States, for example, there is typically no centralized regulation on Chinese offerings at different grade levels across schools in a school district, not to mention across districts. Although ACTFL proficiency guidelines (ACTFL 2012) provide a framework for curriculum development, assessment, and instructional planning (in many states, there are state World Language standards, which can also be a framework of reference), in practice, articulations on what should be learned at which stage are rare (Asia Society and The College Board 2008). Teachers usually develop their own curriculum and teach in their own way to meet the needs of a particular class of students. While this flexibility in curriculum and instruction is not contested, it often results in a conundrum when students move up the ladder in their Chinese learning in that a high-grade CL class could be comprised of students with very different learning histories and consequently different learning needs. The challenge for teachers is often doubled up with students from different ethnic or cultural backgrounds. It is not uncommon to see heritage language learners of Chinese, English Language Learners learning Chinese as their third language, as well as English-speaking students learning Chinese in the same classroom. To address these challenges, differentiation is arguably the key; and to make differentiation appropriate and effective, it is essential, as is evidenced in the OPDT project, that teachers know how to diagnose the strengths and weaknesses of individual learners and subsequently use assessment information to inform their pedagogical adaption or differentiation (Blaz 2006; Reese 2011). In this respect, the Singapore experience reported in this chapter certainly sheds light on Chinese as a second language education in other contexts and informs classroom-based formative assessment, instruction, as well as professional learning of CL teachers.

Acknowledgements The authors would like to thank the Singapore Centre for Chinese Language for granting the permission to reproduce in this chapter example activities from its copyrighted book entitled *Primary 1 Chinese Language Oral Proficiency Diagnostic Tool: Diagnositic Activity Package* (小学一年级华文口语能力诊断工具—诊断活动).

References

ACTFL. (2012). *ACTFL proficiency guidelines 2012*. Alexandria, VA: American Council on the Teaching of Foreign Languages.

Asia Society and The College Board. (2008). *Chinese in 2008: An expanding field*. Retrieved on April 2, 2016 from http://asiasociety.org/files/Chinesein2008.pdf

Blaz, D. (2006). *Differentiated instruction: A guide for foreign language teachers*. New York: Routledge.

Fulcher, G. (2003). *Testing second language speaking*. London: Pearson Education.

Li, L., Zhao, S., & Yeung, A. S. (2012). Chinese language reform in Singapore: Teacher perceptions of instructional approaches and curriculum implementation. *International Journal of Bilingual Education and Bilingualism, 15*, 533–548.

Ministry of Education. (2011). *Nurturing active learners and proficiency users: 2010 mother tongue languages review committee report*. Singapore: Ministry of Education.

Pakir, A. (2008). Bilingual education in Singapore. In J. Cummins & N. H. Hornberger (Eds.), *Encyclopedia of language and education Volume 5: Bilingual education* (2nd ed., pp. 91–203). New York: Springer.

Reese, S. (2011, August). Differentiation in the language classroom. *The Language Educator*, 40–46.

Shepherd, J. (2005). *Striking a balance: The management of language in Singapore*. Frankfurt: Peter Lang.

Wong, W. (2005). *Input enhancement: From theory and research to the classroom*. New York: McGraw-Hill.

Zhao, H., & Huang, J. (2012). China's policy of Chinese as a foreign language and the use of overseas Confucius Institutes. *Educational Research for Policy and Practice, 9*, 127–142.

Zhao, S., & Liu, Y. (2010). Chinese education in Singapore: Constraints of bilingual policy from the perspectives of status and prestige planning. *Language Policy and Language Planning, 34*, 236–258.

Zhao, S. H., Liu, Y. B., & Hong, H. Q. (2007). Singaporean preschoolers' oral competence in Mandarin. *Language Policy, 6*, 73–94.

Chapter 13
Self- and Peer Assessment of Oral Presentation in Advanced Chinese Classrooms: An Exploratory Study

Dan Wang

Abstract Self- and peer assessment allows students to play a greater role in the assessment process. Twenty-one non-heritage undergraduate students who took the *Advanced Chinese* course at Duke University were involved in a project on self- and peer assessment of oral presentations. The project included rubric designing, training, practice, observation, evaluation, discussion, survey, and feedback. The assessment components were designed by the instructor and the students collaboratively during the first week of the course. They included content and organization of presentation, vocabulary and grammar, fluency and voice, accuracy of pronunciation, posture, and support. In addition to scoring for each of these components, the students were also asked to provide written comments on their own presentation and those of their peers. Self-, peer, and instructor assessments were analyzed and compared quantitatively and qualitatively. The results showed that the practice and discussion in the training session had a positive effect on the accuracy of students' self- and peer assessment. Over 90% of the students liked participating in the assessment process and thought the self- and peer assessment conducive to their Chinese language learning. This study highlights the potential pedagogical benefits of involving students in assessment at both the cognitive and affective levels.

Keywords Self-assessment · Peer assessment · Advanced Chinese · Oral presentation · Assessment feedback · Learning outcome

Introduction

In an advanced Chinese language class, developing students' oral presentation skills is one of the most challenging tasks. Students usually have varied levels of oral abilities because of different learning experiences and different learning goals. At Duke University, we also noticed this challenge in the third-year Chinese course.

D. Wang (✉)
University of Tennessee, Knoxville, USA
e-mail: dwang46@utk.edu

© Springer Nature Singapore Pte Ltd. 2017
D. Zhang and C.-H. Lin (eds.), *Chinese as a Second Language Assessment*,
Chinese Language Learning Sciences, DOI 10.1007/978-981-10-4089-4_13

Students enrolled in *Chinese 305* (Chn305) usually have a range of experiences and proficiency levels in Chinese. Typically, about 30% of them are very fluent in Chinese because they have studied abroad in China or Taiwan in the summer. Other students, however, are less fluent in Chinese because they have never been exposed to the Chinese language in a Chinese-speaking environment. As a result, many students are reluctant to participate in oral activities since they worry that their speaking ability is not as proficient as others.

Self-assessment (SA) and peer assessment (PA) were thus introduced to address this situation. It was hoped that SA and PA could encourage all students to participate actively in classroom activities. Traditionally, assessment was the job of the teacher, and students were rarely, if at all, directly involved in the assessment process. Students only provided materials (e.g., spoken or written outputs) for teachers to evaluate their knowledge and performance. Teacher-controlled assessment, however, does not fit such learning goals as reflective thinking, problem solving, and lifelong learning (Dochy and Moerkerke 1997). In the recent two decades, SA and PA have received increasing attention (Birenbaum and Dochy 1996) as their pedagogical value was gradually recognized. It is argued that SA and PA can promote independent leaning, raise students' learning autonomy, and develop a sense of responsibility among students for their own learning (Sambell and McDowell 1998). In other words, SA and PA can transfer some of the learning responsibilities from the teacher to students, which increase students' learning motivation and autonomy. In an autonomy supportive environment, students are less likely to feel anxious in the learning process (Kwan and Leung 1996; Noels et al. 2000). SA and PA seem to be a dynamic tool that can help students develop learning goals and reflect on the past, present, and even possible future (Cotteral 2002; Noels et al. 1999).

One concern about using SA and PA is their reliability and validity, which have been examined in the literature with contradictory findings. Bachman and Palmer (1989), for example, reported excellent correlations between SAs and instructor assessments and concluded that "self-ratings can be reliable and valid measures of communicative language abilities" (p. 14). Similar results on PA were observed in other studies, such as Hughes and Large (1993), Miller and Ng (1994) and Freeman (1995), where the authors reported a high agreement between PAs and instructor assessments. Other studies on PA, however, failed to produce a similar result (e.g., Kwan and Leung 1996; Mowl and Pain 1995; Stefani 1994). They found that students tended to over- or under-evaluate their own or peers' language proficiency, and consequently, the reliability of PA and SA was jeopardized.

Researchers also investigated the role of students' psychological and personality traits in the validity of SA and PA. The traits include anxiety, self-esteem, motivation types, and motivational intensity (Gregersen and Horwitz 2002; Kitano 2001; Lindholm-Leary and Borsato 2002; Morton et al. 1999). AlFallay (2004) reported that "learners possessing the positive side of a trait are more accurate than those who have its negative side, with the exception of students with high classroom anxiety" and "students with low self-esteem are the most accurate in assessing their performance, whereas learners with instrumental motivation are the least accurate" (p. 407).

In the field of second language assessment, a number of studies have been conducted on SA and PA over the last two decades (Chen 2006; Hansen and Liu 2005; Patri 2002; Rollinson 2005). However, those studies focused primarily on English as a second language (ESL); studies on SA and PA in learning Chinese as a second language are sparse. While there are clearly similarities in assessment principles across target languages in second language education, essential differences can also exist due to different learning experiences and/or cultural backgrounds of instructors and students. For instance, due to his/her different personal assessment experiences, a native Chinese instructor may have different opinions from a native English instructor on how different aspects of language proficiency should be assessed. Thus, a study focusing on Chinese language can enrich our understanding about SA and PA in language assessment. In addition, from the perspective of practice, many teachers in Chinese language classrooms hesitate to apply SA and PA because they believe students' assessments are not reliable. As a result, the potential benefits of incorporating SA and PA into regular classroom assessments of Chinese language are given up. It is certainly not a smart idea to "throw out the baby with the bathwater." Instead, one should have a balanced consideration of the advantages of SA and PA, such as those discussed earlier in this section and the influence of possible factors on their reliability and validity. If used appropriately, SA and PA can supplement other classroom assessments with great benefits to student learning in Chinese language classrooms.

This Study

This study aimed to explore the reliability and potential benefits of using SA and PA over a 15-week period in an advanced course in a university-based Chinese as a foreign language (CFL) program. The following questions were investigated:

1. What assessment criteria did the students set for themselves?
2. How could the reliability of SA and PA be increased?
3. What were the attitudes of the students toward SA and PA?

Method

This study was conducted in the third-year advanced Chinese course (Chn305) at Duke University. This course is designed for students who have studied two years of Chinese language at the college level or have a level of proficiency in Chinese language equivalent to that learning experience. After taking this course, students are expected to perform all informal and some formal language tasks with ease, confidence, and competence. Students should be able to comfortably discuss a variety of topics beyond day-to-day survival. In addition, they should also be able to discuss certain topics abstractly, especially those relating to their particular interests. This course was taught over one semester (15 weeks) and consisted of 4.5 h per week. There were two parallel sessions/classes for this course. Class size varied from 9 to 12. Two experienced instructors taught this course almost entirely in Chinese. The author was a lead teacher teaching the lecture session and in charge of the assessment process. The other teacher was not involved in this project. All assessments were completed during the lecture session.

As a requirement of this course, each student was to give an oral presentation on a topic related to Chinese traditions, culture, or society. Oral presentations are used widely in language courses because the ability to present information orally is a valuable skill. The oral presentation was worth 10% of the final grade. Self- and peer assessment methods were involved in this oral task.

Participants

Twenty-one students participated in this study, including 11 females and 10 males. Eighteen of the students were native speakers of English, two native speakers of Korean, and one native speaker of Japanese. Their majors were diverse, including public policy studies, computer science, economics, and some undeclared ones. Before taking this course (i.e., Chn305), 11 students had studied Chinese for two years domestically without any study abroad experience; and the other 10 students participated in a two-month intensive study abroad program in China after their first year Chinese study at Duke University. When asked to rate their oral and aural abilities in Chinese on a 5-point scale (5 = very strong, 4 = strong, 3 = medium, 2 = not strong, 1 = weak), 4% of the students rated at strong, 66% at medium, 18% at not strong, and 12% at weak. None of the participants had any prior experience of assessing or grading their own or peers' oral performances. In other words, this course was their first exposure to and practice of SA and PA.

Data Collection

Three tools were used to collect data, including a self-assessment form and a peer assessment form distributed to all students throughout the semester, and an anonymous SA and PA project evaluation questionnaire completed by all students at the end of the semester.

The design of the self- and peer assessment forms was based on the course objectives. For oral presentation, the learning objectives were that the students are able to: (a) demonstrate content preparation and organization skills for oral presentations, (b) show confidence and clarity in public speaking projects, and

(c) articulate and enunciate words and sentences clearly and efficiently. The assessment components were developed by the instructor and students collaboratively. In the first week, the SA and PA project was introduced to the students. They were told the purpose of implementing SA and PA is to help with their language study. More specifically, they would internalize the characteristics of quality work by evaluating the work of themselves and their peers. To offer effective feedback for their peers, students must have a clear understanding of what is to be assessed. To this end, assessment categories or criteria were discussed by the students and the instructor together. Following the suggestions in Nitko and Brookhart (2007), the students were informed that several principles needed to be followed for designing the assessment criteria: (a) Students should be clear about the learning targets they want to assess; (b) the assessment criteria they design should match each learning target; (c) the selected assessment criteria should serve students' needs; and (d) students should be sure to use multiple indicators of achievement for each learning target.

The nine students in Session 1 of the course were divided into three groups, and the 12 students in Session 2 were divided into four groups. The instructor first discussed with the students and identified what was being assessed. Each group was then given 20 min to design assessment criteria according to the aforementioned principles. During the process, the students put forward reasonable suggestions, which not only focused on content and delivery of presentation but also put emphasis on accuracy of grammar, vocabulary, and pronunciation. After the students' discussion, the instructor and the students went over the assessment categories collected from all groups, discarded similar assessment criteria, and summarized the criteria and standards based on the course objectives. Finally, the students and the instructor worked together to develop a rating scale with the levels of mastery to complete the development of the SA and PA forms described below.

SA Form

The SA form included six scoring elements or criteria with a total of 100 points for the oral presentation: organization and content (30 points), vocabulary and grammar (30 points), fluency and voice (15 points), accuracy of pronunciation (15 points), posture (5 points), and support (5 points). For each criterion, the scoring scale included four levels: excellent (90% and above), good (80–89%), fair (60–79%), and poor (below 60%). Each element also had a space that allowed a student to provide open-ended comments on his/her specific strengths and weaknesses. The instructor's grade and comments are listed at the end of the SA form.

PA Form

The PA form was a simplified version of the SA form with the scoring criteria being essentially the same. It was designed to be easier for the students to assess their peers given the limited class time. It included nine items as follows: (1) Presentation was interesting; (2) gave an interesting introduction; (3) pronunciation was understandable; (4) presented information in acceptable order; (5) offered a concluding summary; (6) spoke clearly, correctly, distinctly, and confidently; (7) maintained eye contact; (8) maintained acceptable posture; and (9) handled questions and comments from the class very well. Each item was to be rated on a four-point scale including "excellent," "good," "fair," and "poor" as well. One-fourth of the form was provided as a space for a student to write down his/her specific comments on a peer's presentation.

Project Evaluation

A project evaluation questionnaire was completed at the end of the semester. This questionnaire was designed by the instructor to find the students' perspective on the SA/PA project. The questions ranged from the students' feeling about the project, the necessity and appropriateness of the SA/PA process, to a variety of effectiveness criteria. They were simple and direct in wording so as to elicit direct responses from the students. The questions can be found in Tables 13.3 and 13.4 in the Data Analysis section below, for SA and PA, respectively. The students were required to answer all of the questions.

The SA and PA forms and the project evaluation questionnaire items were stated in English rather than Chinese to avoid ambiguity and misunderstanding. However, the students could write their open-ended comments either in English or in Chinese.

Training Session

Quite a few researchers believe that students should be trained and have some experiences to do SA and PA accurately (e.g., Davidson and Henning 1985; Miller and Ng 1994; Patri 2002; Rolfe 1990). Patri (2002), for example, mentioned that learners could assess their peers' performances effectively only if assessment rubrics are firmly set after training. Davidson and Henning (1985) also pointed out that as far as the reliability of SA and PA is concerned, learners should be trained in the effective use of SA and PA instruments.

In view of the importance of SA and PA training, in the first two weeks of the course after the development of the aforementioned forms was completed, the participants received training in SA and PA so as to help them gain a deeper understanding of the SA and PA process and criteria. The training was comprised of two cycles and lasted for about 1.5 h of class time. At the first class meeting of the training session, the students practiced assessing a video-recorded oral presentation given by a former student of the same course. Each student first assessed the same oral presentation with the SA and PA forms and gave scoring and comments individually. Then, the students were divided into groups and discussed their observations and shared the results with their group members. During this process, the instructor walked around the classroom, discussing with those students who she believed rated too low or too high and providing advising comments. After the discussion was over, the instructor demonstrated her scoring and comments on the presentation to the whole class and gave the students feedback on their assessments. In the second meeting of the training session, the students were required to do the same practice again following the same procedure but with the video recording of another presentation. Throughout the training session, the instructor gave comments as both encouragement and instructions for the students to improve on SA and PA assessment. Besides the assessment skills, the students also learned about basic presentation skills in the training session. These skills included speech speed, volume and pitch of voice, use of body language and eye contact, and standing in a posture of confidence.

Implementation of SA and PA

After the training session, the students took turns to give presentations on the topics of their choice. This process lasted until the end of the semester, with 2 students per week. Each presentation lasted for about 10 min, followed by a question and answer session of five minutes. The students were required to prepare a PowerPoint and vocabulary list for the presentation to facilitate their peers' understanding of their presentations. Images, title, subtitles, and key words could all be shown on the PowerPoint, but sentences and paragraphs were not allowed. Almost all students used graphs or illustrations from the Internet as visuals. Before the presentation, the students could schedule an appointment with the instructor to discuss the content and organization of the presentation. The instructor provided feedback and corrected typos on the PowerPoint at the meeting. A few students also prepared a script of their presentations and asked for suggestions from the instructor. The instructor only corrected the grammatical errors without tampering with the original meaning of sentences. Neither scripts nor hand-notes were allowed during the presentation.

The presentations were video-recorded by a flip camcorder. The procedure of conducting the PA and SA is shown in Fig. 13.1. Specifically, after each individual's presentation, the student audience had five minutes to assess the performance using the PA form. Peers also gave comments verbally on the strengths and weaknesses of the presentation as immediate feedback to the presenter in class. The instructor collected all the PA forms after the in-class assessment. After the class, the presentation recording was uploaded on Sakai, a web-based course management system. The presenter then viewed his/her recorded presentation and used the SA form to complete a self-assessment and write down the reflections on his/her own performance, such as strengths and problems. He/she then handed in the SA form to the instructor at the next class meeting. Shortly afterward in the semester, the instructor returned to the presenter all of his/her peers' PA forms and the presenter's own SA form together with the instructor's score and comments. Thus, each student

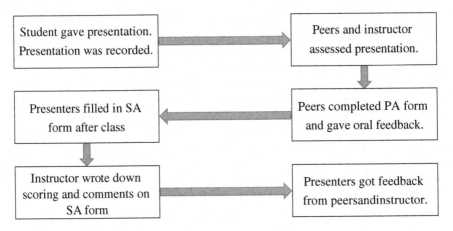

Fig. 13.1 Procedure of SA and PA implementation

had his/her own reflections on the presentation as well as received feedback from his/her peers and the instructor.

Data Analysis and Findings

The data collected included scorings from the students' and the instructor's assessment in the training session; PA and SA forms with scorings and comments from the presenters, their peers, as well as the instructor; and the end-of-semester SA and PA project questionnaire. The scores obtained from the two cycles of the training session and all official assessment cycles were analyzed statistically. In particular, means and standard deviations were drawn upon to examine any difference between the students' SA ratings and those of the instructor. A t-test was then conducted to compare PA ratings and instructor ratings. Qualitative analyses were conducted on the written comments the students marked on the PA and SA forms. Positive comments were identified as the strengths of a presentation, whereas negative comments were identified as problems, which also included a student's self-reflection on his/her SA form and the suggestions for improvement marked by his/her peers on their PA forms.

Comparison of Scores of the Students and the Instructor

To examine if there was any difference between the scores of the students and the instructor, the mean scores of the students and the instructor's scores as well as the standard deviation of their score difference were calculated. They included the

Table 13.1 Comparison of student and instructor scores in training and official assessment

Training		Number of presentations	Mean	Standard deviation[a]
First cycle	Students	1	80.6	6.7
	Teacher	1	85.0	
Second cycle	Students	1	92.5	5.5
	Teacher	1	94.0	
Assessment		*N*	*Mean*	*Standard deviation[a]*
Students		21	88.8	4.1
Teacher		21	90.5	

[a]The standard deviations pertain to the difference between student and instructor scores

scores the students and the instructor assigned to the two presentations in the training videos (i.e., training assessment) as well the scores of the students' SAs of their own presentations and the instructor's assessment scores (i.e., official assessment). The results are summarized in Table 13.1.

In the training session, the teacher had only one score. So, the standard deviation of the difference scores between the students and the teacher was the same as that of the scores of the students. In the first training cycle, the mean score of the students was 4.4 less than the instructor's score, and the standard deviation of score difference was 6.7. This indicates a big difference between the instructor and the students and a heavy dispersion among the students. In the second training circle, the score difference dropped to 1.5 and the standard deviation of score difference was also reduced. Thus, the first training cycle helped bring the students' assessment closer to that of the instructor. However, note that the standard deviation of the students' scores was still as high as 5.5. This indicates that the difference among students was still notable. In the official assessment cycle, the mean difference between the students' SA scores and the instructor's scores was further narrowed to 1.7; the standard deviation of the rater differences also became further smaller and was reduced to 4.1.

Comparison of PA Scores and Instructor Scores

For each of the 21 oral presentations, there were 20 peer assessment scores and one teacher score. The average of the 20 peer scores was considered as the final score of the peer assessment for each student. Table 13.2 shows the mean and variance of the scores of peer assessment and the teacher's assessment. A between-group t-test was conducted to analyze the difference between peer and instructor ratings. The result is also presented in Table 13.2. The following findings are noted: (1) There was only a small difference (about 2.7 points) between the mean scores of the peer assessment and the instructor's assessment, although this difference was statistically significant ($p < 0.001$). (2) The correlation between the peer assessment and the teacher's assessment was 0.9, indicating that the peer assessment of the oral presentations was highly consistent with the assessment of the teacher. In other words,

Table 13.2 Comparison of peer and instructor scoring in the assessment cycle

	PA scores	Instructor scores
Mean	93.2	90.5
Variance	4.4	12.3
Observations	21	21
t-statistics	6.73***	
Pearson correlation	0.90***	

***$p < 0.001$

if the teacher thought an oral presentation was excellent, most students tended to rate the oral presentation as excellent, and vice versa. (3) The variance of the peer assessment was much smaller than that of the instructor's assessment. This means the peer assessment scores were more concentrated, whereas the scores of the instructor's assessment were more dispersive. A possible explanation for this phenomenon might be that the instructor had a better ability to differentiate the students' performance.

Comparison of the Students' and the Instructor's Written Comments

In the training cycle, the students' comments mainly focused on content and delivery. Almost all students mentioned the interesting topics of the presentations as a strength and the presenters' lack of confidence as a weakness. In the assessment cycles, however, student's SA comments expanded to presentation organization, language (vocabulary and grammar), pronunciation, and manner. These can be seen in the following remarks in the students' self-reflections: "*Clearly organized. Logical order with example*"; "*Incorporated new words and previous words*"; "*Need to use more transition words besides the basics 'danshi, keshi, etc.'*"; "*Some tones are lost/incorrect, some second and third tones mixed together*"; and "*Maintained eye contact with different member of the audience.*" The majority of the students' PA comments also identified content and manners as strengths or weaknesses. Other criteria, such as vocabulary, pronunciation, and audio/visual support, were also mentioned in PA comments. For example, "*Topic works well with the recent Chinese New year. Great Job*"; "*Good presentation and easy to follow vocabulary, smooth transitions and confidence could tell you practices a lot. Speaking tones are always clear*"; "*Your tone of your voice is a bit low and hard to hear from a distance*"; and "*You could have more pertinent questions.*" Interestingly, very few students commented on grammatical errors. Compared to the students, the instructor made comments on all aspects of presentation that appeared on the SA and PA forms, especially language (vocabulary, grammar, and pronunciation) and presentation skills. These comments highlighted the students' strengths as well as problems and also offered suggestions for improvement.

SA and PA Project Evaluation

At the end of the semester, the SA and PA project questionnaires were completed anonymously by all participating students. The purpose was to explore the students' perception of the project. Tables 13.3 and 13.4 summarized the SA and PA questionnaire results, respectively. The students' responses indicated the majority of them were satisfied with the practice of SA and PA.

For self-assessment, as shown in Table 13.3, over 90% of the students liked the idea of involving students in assessment, agreed with its ability in identifying their strengths and weaknesses, and recognized the helpful feedback and comments from the instructor. More than 80% of the students were comfortable with the SA process and thought the SA helped with their learning and encouraged greater effort and participation. Over 70% agreed that the instructor and students should develop the assessment criteria together. Over 60% reported that SA was fair. Overall, 90% would like to recommend the use of self-assessment in the future.

As for peer assessment, as Table 13.4 shows, 80–85% of the students thought they should take part in assessing their peers and felt comfortable with the PA process. They also reported they made fair and responsible assessments and felt the peer feedback was helpful. Concerning the benefits of PA, 57–76% agreed that the PA helped them improve their Chinese-speaking ability in content, organization, and pronunciation. On the other hand, the students' opinions on PA helping with speaking ability in grammar were diverse. The numbers of students agreeing and disagreeing with it were comparable. A majority of the students reported PA increased the motivation to practice more before giving presentation and made presentation more interesting. In general, 85% of the students regarded PA as a good tool for learning and would like to recommend the use of PA in the future.

Table 13.3 SA evaluation questionnaire

Items	Agree (%)	Not sure (%)	Disagree (%)
I feel comfortable with the self-assessment process	85.7	9.5	4.8
Students should be involved in assessment	90.5	9.5	0
The assessment criteria should be developed by the instructors and students collaboratively	76.2	9.5	14.3
Self-assessment helps with my learning	81	9.5	9.5
Self-assessment encourages greater effort and participation	81	9.5	9.5
Self-assessment helps me recognize my strengths and weaknesses	90.5	9.5	0
Self-assessment is fair	66.7	23.8	9.5
The comments or feedbacks from the instructor are helpful	95.2	4.8	0
I would recommend the use of self-assessment in Chn305 in the future	90.5	4.8	4.8

Table 13.4 PA evaluation questionnaire

Items	Yes (%)	No (%)	Not sure (%)
Do you think students should take part in assessing their peers?	80	15	5
Did you feel comfortable when you assess your peers' performance?	85	10	5
Do you think you have made a fair and responsible assessment of your peers?	80	5	15
Do you feel peer evaluation provides helpful feedback?	80	10	10
Do you think peer evaluation helps you improve your Chinese-speaking ability?	67	14	19
Do you believe peer evaluation helps you improve your Chinese-speaking ability in content and organization?	76	10	14
Do you feel peer evaluation helps you improve your Chinese-speaking ability in pronunciation?	57	28	15
Do you think peer evaluation helps you improve your Chinese-speaking ability in grammar?	43	23	34
Do you think peer evaluation increases your motivation to practice more before your oral presentation?	70	10	20
Do you feel oral presentation becomes more interesting through peer evaluation?	65	15	20
Would you like to recommend this type of activity be continued with your juniors?	85	5	10

Discussion

This study investigated self-assessment and peer assessment in American college students' CFL learning. By implementing SA and PA in an oral presentation activity, both the instructor and the students perceived the benefits of SA and PA. However, SA and PA cannot be used as an isolated activity. All students should be fully engaged in the whole process of assessment. In this study, all students were involved in the following procedures: developing assessment components, training, observation, peer assessment, self-assessment, discussion, and reflection.

As far as the first research question "What assessment criteria did the students set for themselves?" is concerned, we found the answer in the stage of developing assessment components for the SA and PA forms. Students not only paid attention to content, organization and linguistic features (vocabulary and grammar), but also put a lot of emphasis on delivery (posture and eye contact) and accuracy. As a language course, language components are presumably more important than presentation skills. Therefore, it was not a surprise that the students and the instructor both agreed that content, organization, and linguistic features should be given more weight than others. During the process of constructing the assessment rubric and scoring standards, the students showed high cognitive ability and analytical and critical thinking skills. It seemed that developing the assessment components had achieved its purpose of encouraging the students to take greater responsibilities for their own learning. As assessment criteria designers, the students got a clear understanding of what should be assessed and how to better prepare their oral presentation, which in turn increased their confidence and participation. The instructor's retrospective reflections on the implementation of the project also indicated that the SA and PA improved the students' oral presentation skills.

Regarding the second research question on the reliability of SA and PA, we found that after two circles of training, the students gained significant progress in assessment accuracy, and the difference of their scorings from those of the instructor was significantly narrowed. Later in the official assessment cycle, their SA and PA scores demonstrated a high level of agreement with those of the instructor. As previous studies indicated, training enabled students to perform SA and PA tasks effectively (Adams and King 1995; Freeman 1995; Pond et al. 1995). Freeman (1995), for example, reported that students need more training in order to minimize potential inconsistencies associated with subjective rating. In this project, a training session with two cycles was conducted to provide the students with information about what to assess and how to assess. During the training session, the students practiced and received feedback on how to assess peers and themselves and gradually developed a strong sense of and skills in assessment. The training also provided the students with details on effective use of the PA and SA instruments. In addition to demonstrating increasing approximation to the instructor's scores, we also found the students' comments became more specific and constructive in the assessment cycles than in the training cycles. Therefore, it was obvious that the training was effective in preparing the students for the SA and PA procedure.

On the other hand, it is noted that there was still a gap between the students' PA scores and the instructor's scores. The students' PA scoring data seemed to show over-rating in which the average score of peer assessment was significantly higher than that of the instructor's assessment (see the t-test result in Table 13.2). Pond et al. (1995) named over-rating by peers as "friendship marking" or "decibel marking." Falchikov (1995) claimed that this could be because peers find it difficult to criticize their friends. We speculate that part of the over-rating in PA observed in this study might be caused by friendships as well. Because of the unreliability of PA, many instructors hesitate to adopt it into curriculum. Nevertheless, the benefits of PA are obvious. For example, PA can give students an opportunity to provide each other with useful feedback. Furthermore, discussions among peers as part of PA can also lead to closer agreements between instructor assessment and students' SA. In this regard, PA also serves to inform SA during the assessment process.

To answer the third research question, the students had very positive attitudes toward the SA and PA project, which can be seen from their responses to the project evaluation questionnaires at the end of the semester. Overall, the project helped the students develop two types of skills: assessment skills and learning skills. The students expressed that they had a better understanding of what they were supposed to do for the oral presentation task. More importantly, the project helped them recognize their strengths and weaknesses and facilitated their reflections on how to improve their oral performance and establish learning goals in the future. Undoubtedly, the project achieved its purpose to encourage students to be self-regulated learners, who could "monitor their own performance and evaluate their own progress and accomplishments" (O'Malley and Pierce 1996, p. 5).

Conclusion

This paper reported a study on SA and PA in university CFL context. Through self-assessing their own oral presentation and the oral presentations of their classmates, advanced CFL learners had the learning objectives clarified, improved their oral language performance, and increased their motivation and classroom participation. The comparisons between the students' SA and PA ratings and those of the instructor suggested that CFL learners, with necessary training, can conduct SA and PA effectively to facilitate their Chinese language learning.

Despite the positive project outcomes, some issues also seem to warrant attention in future research on and classroom applications of SA and PA. For example, some students might have over-rated their peers because of "friendship." Such a possibility might be attributed to a number of reasons, such as students' personality traits, cultural background, and the type of training provided to them. Because the number of student participants was very limited, and this study was exploratory in nature, questions like how various factors may impact students' peer assessment (and self-assessment) were not addressed and certainly deserve attention in future research. In addition, in this study, we only compared the scoring consistency between the students and the instructor on the total scores of the oral presentation. Comparisons between students' and instructor's assessment on each specific criterion (e.g., vocabulary, grammar, and organization) would help generate a more nuanced understanding about classroom implementation of SA and PA and provide implications on how to have different scoring components prioritized during student training. Finally, in this study, all students participated in the training on SA and PA. In other words, there was not a control group where training was not provided. Consequently, it was unknown whether student training would be causally related to scoring consistency between the students and the teacher and the students' oral presentation performance. This issue certainly deserves attention in the future.

Acknowledgements The research described in this paper was conducted when I worked at Department of Asian and Middle East Studies, Duke University.

References

Adams, C., & King, K. (1995). Towards a framework for student self-assessment. *Innovation in Education and Training International, 32,* 336–343.

AlFallay, I. (2004). The role of some selected psychological and personality traits of the rater in the accuracy of self- and peer-assessment. *System, 32,* 407–425.

Bachman, L., & Palmer, A. (1989). The construct validation of self-ratings of communicative language ability. *Language Testing, 6,* 14–25.

Birenbaum, M., & Dochy, F. (Eds.). (1996). *Alternatives in assessment of achievement, learning processes and prior knowledge.* Boston, MA: Kluwer.

Chen, Y. M. (2006). Peer and self-assessment for English oral performance: A study of reliability and learning benefits. *English Teaching and Learning, 30*(4), 1–22.

Cotteral, S. (2002). Promoting learner autonomy through the curriculum: Principles for designing language courses. *ELT Journal, 54*(2), 109–117.

Davidson, F., & Henning, G. (1985). A self-rating scale of English difficulty. *Language Testing, 2,* 164–178.

Dochy, F., & Moerkerke, G. (1997). The present, the past and the future of achievement testing and performance assessment. *International Journal of Educational Research, 27,* 415–432.

Falchikov, N. (1995). Peer feedback marking: Developing peer assessment. *Innovation in Education and Training International, 32,* 175–187.

Freeman, M. (1995). Peer assessment by groups of group work. *Assessment & Evaluation in Higher Education, 20*(3), 289–300.

Gregersen, T., & Horwitz, E. (2002). Language learning and perfectionism: Anxious and non-anxious language learners' reactions to their own oral performance. *Modern Language Journal, 86,* 562–570.

Hansen, J. G., & Liu, J. (2005). Guiding principles for effective peer response. *ELT Journal, 59*(1), 31–39.

Hughes, I. E., & Large, B. (1993). Assessment of students' oral communication skills by staff and peer groups. *New Academic, 2*(3), 10–12.

Kitano, K. (2001). Anxiety in the college Japanese language classroom. *Modern Language Journal, 85,* 549–566.

Kwan, K., & Leung, R. (1996). Tutor versus peer group assessment of student performance in a simulation training exercise. *Assessment and Evaluation in Higher Education, 21,* 205–214.

Lindholm-Leary, K., & Borsato, G. (2002). Impact of two-way immersion on students' attitudes toward school and college. *Eric Digest.* EDO-FL-02-01.

Miller, L., & Ng, R. (1994). Peer assessment of oral language proficiency. In *Perspectives: Working papers of the department of English, City Polytechnic of Hong Kong* (Vol. 6, pp. 41–56).

Morton, L., Lemieux, C., Diffey, N., & Awender, M. (1999). Determinants of withdrawal from the bilingual career track when entering high school. *Guidance and Counseling, 14,* 1–14.

Mowl, G., & Pain, R. (1995). Using self and peer assessment to improve students' essay writing: A case study from geography. *Innovations in Education and Training International, 32*(4), 324–335.

Nitko, A. J., & Brookhart, S. M. (2007). *Educational assessment of students* (5th ed.). Upper Saddle River, NJ: Pearson Education.

Noels, K. A., Clément, R., & Pelletier, L. G. (1999). Perceptions of teachers' communicative style and students' intrinsic and extrinsic motivation. *Modern Language Journal, 83,* 23–34.

Noels, K. A., Pelletier, L. G., Clément, R., & Vallerand, R. J. (2000). Why are you leaning a second language? Motivational orientation and self-determination theory. *Language Learning, 50*(1), 57–85.

O'Malley, J. M., & Pierce, L. V. (1996). *Authentic assessment for English language learners: Practical approaches for teachers.* New York: Addison-Wesley Publishing Company.

Patri, M. (2002). The influence of peer feedback on self and peer-assessment of oral skills. *Language Testing, 19*(2), 109–131.

Pond, K., Ul-Haq, R., & Wade, W. (1995). Peer review: A precursor to peer assessment. *Innovation in Education and Training International, 32,* 314–323.

Rolfe, T. (1990). Self- and peer-assessment in the ESL curriculum. In G. Brindley (Ed.), *The second language curriculum in action.* Research series 6. NCETR. Sydney: University of Macquarie.

Rollinson, P. (2005). Using peer feedback in the ESL writing class. *ELT Journal, 59*(1), 23–30.

Sambell, K., & McDowell, L. (1998). The value of self and peer assessment to the developing lifelong learner. In C. Rust (Ed.), *Improving student learning—Improving students as learners* (pp. 56–66). Oxford, UK: Oxford Centre for Staff and Learning Development.
Stefani, L. A. J. (1994). Peer, self and tutor assessment: Relative reliabilities. *Studies in Higher Education, 19*(1), 69–75.

Index

© Springer Nature Singapore Pte Ltd. 2017
D. Zhang and C.-H. Lin (eds.), *Chinese as a Second Language Assessment*,
Chinese Language Learning Sciences, DOI 10.1007/978-981-10-4089-4

CPSIA information can be obtained
at www.ICGtesting.com
Printed in the USA
BVOW06*0831150517
484166BV00001B/1/P